BALANCED SCORECARD STEP-BY-STEP FOR GOVERNMENT AND NONPROFIT AGENCIES

Second Edition

BALANCED SCORECARD STEP-BY-STEP FOR GOVERNMENT AND NONPROFIT AGENCIES

Second Edition

Paul R. Niven

WILEY

John Wiley & Sons, Inc.

Copyright © 2008 by John Wiley & Sons, Inc. All rights reserved.
Published by John Wiley & Sons, Inc., Hoboken, New Jersey.
Published simultaneously in Canada.

For general information on our other products and services, or technical support, please contact our Customer Care Department within the United States at 800-762-2974, outside the United States at 317-572-3993 or fax 317-572-4002.

Wiley also publishes its books in a variety of electronic formats. Some content that appears in print may not be available in electronic books.

For more information about Wiley products, visit our Web site at http://www.wiley.com.

Library of Congress Cataloging-in-Publication Data:

Niven, Paul R.
    Balanced scorecard step-by-step for government and nonprofit agencies / Paul R. Niven.—2nd ed.
        p.   cm.
    Includes index.
    ISBN 978-0-470-18002-0 (cloth)
        1. Total quality management in government.   2. Administrative agencies—Management—Evaluation.   3. Nonprofit organizations—Management—Evaluation.   4. Benchmarking (Management)   5. Performance standards.   6. Organizational effectiveness—Measurement.   I. Title.
    JF1525.T67N58   2008
    352.3'57—dc22
                                                            2007051409

Printed in the United States of America

10   9   8   7   6   5   4   3   2   1

For my wife Lois, with much love and many thanks

Contents

Preface

Although it was almost six years ago, it seems like last week. A retired client asked me to join him for coffee, and during our wide-ranging and, as usual, very enjoyable chat, asked if I had considered writing a "Balanced Scorecard Step-by-Step" book for the public and nonprofit sectors. My first book, written with the private sector as the target audience, had recently been released and, coincidentally, I had begun to receive correspondence from public sector and nonprofit leaders posing the same question. Many had purchased my first book, and while the overall guidance offered was relevant, they craved a text customized to fit the unique challenges they faced when implementing a performance measurement system. Intrigued, I engaged in some additional study and research, and found overwhelming evidence of the need for such a book. Many months of research, interviews, and writing later, in early 2003, *Balanced Scorecard Step-by-Step for Government and Nonprofit Agencies* was released. I have been amazed and very humbled at the success of the *First Edition*, which has been translated widely and used by organizations around the globe committed to improving their performance by focusing on the execution of strategy.

This *Second Edition* contains the same core implementation guidance offered in the first volume, but has been significantly updated and enhanced to ensure it reflects the latest theory and practice of performance management for the nonprofit and public sectors. Every single word covering the pages of the *First Edition* was put to the tests of relevancy, accuracy, and importance during the alteration process. In addition to modifying topics appearing in the earlier edition, this text contains expanded coverage of subjects that have matured significantly since its first printing in 2002. My coverage of Strategy Maps—powerful communication tools signaling to everyone, within the organization and beyond, the drivers of organizational success—has been completely revamped with entirely new sections on how to facilitate a Strategy Map session as well as increased coverage of developing objectives for each perspective. The book also features a robust examination of strategy-centered review meetings. I have provided my latest thinking, based on years of field experience, on how to conduct productive meetings that put strategy at the heart of the agenda. Finally, the book will introduce you to a new, and vitally important topic—the Office of Strategy Management (OSM). You'll learn how this promising function seamlessly marries the worlds of strategy formation and execution.

THE BALANCED SCORECARD

In the early 1990s, Robert Kaplan and David Norton sought to solve a measurement problem plaguing corporations around the globe. The dynamics of business were changing rapidly; globalization, customer knowledge, and the rise of intangible assets were all converging to forever change the way business was conducted. Strategy was considered a potent defense for succeeding in this changing landscape. However, the facts suggested that about 90% of organizations were unable to execute their strategies.

Kaplan and Norton made the startling discovery that performance measurement systems utilized by most firms were incapable of providing the information needed to compete in this new knowledge economy. Most were unchanged from those developed by the early industrial giants at the turn of the twentieth century. Characterized by an almost exclusive reliance on financial measures of performance, these systems were ill-prepared for the challenges faced by modern organizations. Kaplan and Norton believed that organizations should attempt the introduction of balance to their measurement systems. Specifically, the historical accuracy and integrity of financial measures must be balanced with the drivers of future financial performance in an attempt to view a wider spectrum of performance and execute strategy. Their radical, yet profoundly simple, approach was labeled a "Balanced Scorecard" and featured measurement in four distinct, yet related areas: customer, internal processes, employee learning and growth, and financial.

Since its introduction in 1990, the Balanced Scorecard has been embraced by corporations around the world. Recent estimates suggest that at least 60% of Fortune 1000 organizations use a Balanced Scorecard system. For-profit companies have used the system to generate improved financial results, foster accountability, align employees with corporate goals, enhance resource allocation decisions, improve collaboration, and most critically, execute their strategies.

USING THE BALANCED SCORECARD IN THE PUBLIC AND NONPROFIT SECTORS

Public and nonprofit organizations today face unprecedented challenges in carrying out their vital mission-oriented tasks. Increased public scrutiny, demands for accountability, cries of enhanced transparency, and donations linked to stipulations of success, are but a few of the piercing calls you must answer in meeting stakeholder expectations. And of course, you're required to achieve all of this and more in an environment marked by shrinking budgets, strict regulations, and changing workforce demographics.

Speaking of demographics, the retirement of 76 million baby boomers in the United States will push the ranks of the elderly to more than 20% of the country's population during the next 20 years. In Japan and Europe during the same period, the legions of elderly will account for almost 30% of the population.[i] Balancing the needs of retirees (all of whom will require increasing levels of government services) with younger citizens, while still holding taxes to politically sustainable levels, leads to one undeniable conclusion: It's imperative we get the most from every government dollar.

In the years to come, enhanced productivity, performance improvements, and strategy execution will be transformed from private sector topics that drive bestseller lists to survival imperatives for every public sector agency.

Nonprofit organizations are certainly not immune to the tempest of change swirling about our modern world. Whether it's a small local arts organization or a national charity, virtually all of the demands faced by public and private sector firms are shared by nonprofits. The laser of scrutiny is being applied with unprecedented vigor everywhere in the nonprofit world; even charitable foundations established by professional athletes have come under the glare of public inquiry. The *Wall Street Journal* recently dedicated a two-page feature story to an examination of philanthropy in the sports world.[ii] Given the "gotcha" mentality so popular in our watchdog culture, it's absolutely essential that nonprofits demonstrate results while simultaneously exhibiting prudent financial stewardship.

Take another look at the list of achievements private sector firms have seen from their investment in the Balanced Scorecard: accountability, collaboration, alignment, resource allocation improvement, enhanced financial results, and strategy execution. Each and every one of those benefits is equally available to government and nonprofit agencies willing to implement the Balanced Scorecard system with rigor and discipline. The City of Charlotte, North Carolina, profiled in Chapter 12, embraced the Scorecard framework over a decade ago and has reaped many of the benefits noted above. So too have countless other public sector and nonprofit agencies around the globe. They've discovered that with minor modifications, and

---

[i] Thomas Dohrmann and Lenny T. Mendonca, "Boosting Government Productivity," *The McKinsey Quarterly*, 2004, Number 4, pp. 89–103.
[ii] G. Bruce Knecht, "Big Players in Charity," *Wall Street Journal*, Saturday/Sunday, April 28–29, 2007, p. P1.

rendered with care and precision, the tool can be customized to benefit any organizational setting or structure.

Making the transition to this new world of measurement, management, and strategy execution is not without its share of potential pitfalls. This book has been written to help you navigate this sea of change, and capitalize on the many benefits of the Balanced Scorecard, while concurrently avoiding costly implementation errors. Let's look at what you'll find in the chapters ahead.

HOW THE BOOK IS ORGANIZED

This *Second Edition* of *Balanced Scorecard Step-by-Step for Government and Nonprofit Agencies* is comprised of 13 chapters and an appendix, spanning the entire spectrum of a Balanced Scorecard implementation. The opening chapter introduces the Balanced Scorecard tool, providing an historical perspective and discussing the many facets of this tool. Adapting the Balanced Scorecard to the public and nonprofit sectors is the subject of Chapter 2. You'll learn that with only minor "geographical" modifications, the Balanced Scorecard is well-suited to meet your measurement and strategy execution challenges.

Upon embarking on a Balanced Scorecard implementation, you'll quickly discover it is more than a "measurement" initiative. In fact, the Scorecard will touch many disparate elements of your organization. The next four chapters outline the many and varied elements that must be in place to ensure your Scorecard outcomes are successful. Chapter 3 is entitled "Before You Begin" and discusses a number of items that must be considered prior to building a Scorecard, including: your rationale for engaging in this effort, gaining executive sponsorship for the initiative, and building an effective team. Many organizations rush into the Scorecard building process without the aid of training on the subject. Poorly designed Scorecards, and little if no alignment throughout the organization, frequently result from this decision. Chapter 4 provides a training curriculum for your Balanced Scorecard initiative and also discusses the importance of communication planning. In Chapter 5, we begin our transition to the core elements of the Balanced Scorecard beginning with mission, values, and vision. The Scorecard will ultimately act as a translation of these critical enablers of organizational success. In this chapter we'll explore the nature of these building blocks and offer tools for developing or refining your current statements. Strategy is at the core of every Balanced Scorecard, and Chapter 6 examines this widely discussed, but often poorly understood subject. A straightforward approach for developing strategy is offered.

The next block of chapters will provide you with a guided tour through the development of a Strategy Map of objectives and Balanced Scorecard of performance measures. Chapter 7, which has been extensively updated for this edition, outlines the Strategy Map concept of graphically displaying the key objectives that serve as the translation of your strategy. You'll find advice on everything from how to interview executives to customizing your Map. Chapter 8 ushers in an examination of how to populate your Balanced Scorecard by examining measures, targets, and initiatives. You'll learn how to develop measures in each of the four perspectives, why targets are critical, and how initiatives can mean the difference between success and failure on performance.

The final five chapters of the text are dedicated to helping you get the most out of your Balanced Scorecard system. We begin in Chapter 9 which probes the concept of cascading the Balanced Scorecard. This term refers to the process of generating goal alignment throughout the organization by the development of Strategy Maps and Balanced Scorecards at each and every level of the agency. In an era of shrinking budgets, we're constantly reminded of the importance of aligning spending with results. Chapter 10 provides a method of linking the Balanced Scorecard to your budgeting process, and in so doing aligning spending with strategy. Chapter 11 canvasses the many reporting options available to Scorecard-adopting organizations. Whether you choose to buy an automated software package or develop your own tool, you'll find the information you need to make an informed decision. This chapter also includes a robust dialog on the concept of strategy-centered management meetings. Like you, I've sat through my fair share of boring and unproductive meetings. With the advice offered in this chapter I'm throwing down the gauntlet—no more bad meetings! In Chapter 12, we're treated to an insider's view of the Balanced Scorecard at the City of Charlotte, North Carolina. These Scorecard pioneers share their secrets for success, and offer pitfalls that must be avoided on the road to strategy execution. The final chapter provides you with a glimpse into what is necessary to sustain your Scorecard success. A highlight of the chapter is an introduction to the Office of Strategy Management (OSM) concept. You'll also learn how one organization utilized the concept to tremendous advantage. The book concludes with an appendix outlining the critical nature of terminology to your implementation and a glossary of key Scorecard-related terms.

It's a pleasure to serve as your guide through the rewarding territory that is the Balanced Scorecard. My goal is to steer you through the terrain that follows by offering a text that is exhaustive in scope without being excessively complex or unduly simplistic. Let's get started!

February 2008   PAUL R. NIVEN
                                                            San Diego, California

Acknowledgments

Isaac Newton once remarked that "If I have seen farther than others, it is because I was standing on the shoulders of giants." And so it is that I am able to deliver this book to you. The individuals mentioned below, and countless others, are largely responsible for giving me the opportunity to share the ideas in this book with you. In many ways, I am merely a vessel through which their ideas, inspiration, and wisdom pass to you, and hopefully from you to many others.

This being a second edition, rigorous scrutiny was applied to every page, with an eye towards updating, clarifying, and enhancing each subject covered. Upon reading the previous paragraph, however, I was unable to change a single word. It rings as true today as it did over five years ago when I completed the first manuscript for this text. Without the kindness, knowledge, and spirit of learning I received from those listed below, this book would never have reached your hands.

NEW ACKNOWLEDGMENTS FOR THE SECOND EDITION

Interest in, and enthusiasm for, applying the Balanced Scorecard to public and nonprofit environments has grown substantially since the *First Edition* of this book appeared. I've been extremely fortunate during that time to work with several organizations from both sectors that have provided immense assistance in advancing my knowledge and expanding the horizons of the Scorecard framework.

From the Corporation for Enterprise Development (CFED) in Washington DC, my thanks go out to Andrea Levere, Genevieve Melford, and Kim Pate for their honesty, sincerity, and earnest commitment to this tool. At the Regulatory Affairs Professionals Society (RAPS), also in DC, I am deeply indebted to Sherry Keramidas for her enthusiastic support of the Balanced Scorecard. Food for the Hungry U.S. (FHUS) provided perhaps the most inspirational environment I've ever had the pleasure of working in. My sincerest thanks to the entire senior management team, but in particular: Ben Homan, Loren Kutsko, Matt Panos, and Peter Mawditt. At the Coordinating Office for Terrorism Prevention and Emergency Response (COTPER) of the CDC in Atlanta, thank you to Rich Besser and Galen Carver for your tireless work in support of the principles of performance management. Merl Waschler and Katherine Cecala of the Valley of the Sun United Way in Phoenix have been ardent supporters of the Balanced Scorecard and I thank them for their vision and inspiration. At the Rural Health Resource Center, an outstanding organization demonstrating passionate commitment to the ideals of performance improvement, my thanks to Terry Hill and his enormously talented staff. Finally, to David Hay, Sharon MacFarlane, Christian Richard, and Karin Row of New Brunswick (NB) Power in Fredericton New Brunswick, thank you for your support, generosity of time and spirit, and dedication—I enjoyed every minute we spent together. Christian Richard receives the "above and beyond the call of duty" award. In the midst of guiding the organization's new Office of Strategy Management with passion and poise, and adjusting to life at home with a new baby girl, Chris, in a request from me, wrote over 20 pages of notes on NB Power's Scorecard implementation that proved immensely helpful.

In addition to clients, I have benefited from the insights and kindness of many others, including my consulting partner Dennis Barnhart. Thank you for your wise counsel and boundless capacity for learning. To Tor Inge Vasshus and Eric Peterson of Corporater, thank you for embracing the true spirit of partnership as we work together to expand the frontiers of the Scorecard. Oh, and by the way, you've built an incredible software product! And finally, to Gerardo Pustelnik and Claudio Nassar of Strategy Execution Consulting in Mexico City (my Latin American partners), thank you for your energy, commitment, and dedication to strategy execution.

ACKNOWLEDGMENTS FROM THE FIRST EDITION

There is a charming story about George Bernard Shaw perusing the shelves of a used bookstore one day and coming across one of his own volumes. Upon turning the cover he found the inscription: "*To_____, with esteem, George Bernard Shaw*." He promptly bought the book and returned it to_____, adding the line: "*With renewed esteem, George Bernard Shaw*." So it is with this *Second Edition*, I would like to offer renewed thanks to the following people.

My deepest gratitude is extended to the many individuals kind enough to share their time and information with me. Special thanks to Bobbi Bilnoski at the Concitti Network, Colleen Tobin formerly of Women's World Finance, Rhonda Pherigo from the Center for Nonprofit Management, Bruce Harber of the Vancouver Coastal Health Authority, Dr. Howard Borgstrom from the Department of Energy, Nancy Foltz at the State of

Michigan, Rick Pagsibigan from the Red Cross of Southeastern Pennsylvania, Abbi Stone and Katy Rees from the San Marcos campus of the California State University, consultant Donald Golob, author and consultant William P. Ryan, Jake Barkdoll and the Balanced Scorecard Interest Group, Betty Cabrera at the Dallas Family Access Network, Diane Williams of the Safer Foundation, Dennis Feit from the Minnesota Department of Transportation, Philippe Poinsot from the United Nations Development Programme, and Jeff Celentano from the City of North Bay, Ontario.

An innumerable number of other individuals have an imprint on this book. Let me conclude by mentioning just a few: Lisa Schumacher, Kim Eagle, Tiffany Capers, and Matt Bronson from the City of Charlotte, North Carolina. They were gracious enough to submit to interviews for both editions of this book. Joe and Catherine Stenzel have been wonderful friends and great supporters for many years; my thanks to both of you. Steve Mann provided invaluable assistance with early interviews and research for the *First Edition* of this book, despite recently retiring! Andra Gumbus of Sacred Heart University offered insight and assistance that is greatly appreciated. Finally, I would like to thank Teri Anderson. Teri gave me my start in the performance measurement field many years ago, and has been a supporter and great friend ever since.

1

Introduction to the Balanced Scorecard

Roadmap for Chapter 1 Before you can begin developing a Balanced Scorecard for your organization, we must ensure that you have a solid foundation of Scorecard knowledge and understanding from which to build. This chapter will provide that base.

We'll begin by considering just why measurement is so important to the modern public and nonprofit organization. We'll then look at three factors that have led to the rising prominence of the Balanced Scorecard since its inception over seventeen years ago. You'll learn that our changing economy, which places a premium on intangible assets, demands more from our measurement systems. Financial measurements and their significant limitations will then be examined. The final factor escalating the growth of the Balanced Scorecard is the inability of most organizations to effectively execute their strategies. We'll review a number of barriers to strategy implementation.

The Balanced Scorecard has emerged as a proven tool in meeting the many challenges faced by the modern organization. The remainder of the chapter introduces you to this dynamic tool. Specifically, we'll examine the origins of the Scorecard, define it, and look at the system from three different points of view: as a communication tool, measurement system, and strategic management system.

WHY MEASUREMENT IS SO IMPORTANT

One of the themes of this book is that regardless of what sector your organization represents, there is a role for measurement to improve your performance. So it is in the vein of connecting measurement to virtually any field of endeavor that I offer this historical account to begin our expedition together. In the dense fog of a dark night in October 1707, Great Britain lost nearly an entire fleet of ships. There was no pitched battle at sea; the admiral, Clowdisley Shovell, simply miscalculated his position in the Atlantic and his flagship smashed into the rocks of the Scilly Isles, a tail of islands off the southwest coast of England. The rest of the fleet, following blindly, went aground and piled onto the rocks, one after another. Four warships and 2,000 lives were lost.

For such a proud nation of seafarers, this tragic loss was distinctly embarrassing. But to be fair to the memory of Clowdisley Shovell, it was not altogether surprising. Although the concept of latitude and longitude had been around since the first century B.C., still, in 1700, no one had devised an accurate way to measure longitude, meaning that nobody ever knew for sure how far east or west they had traveled. Professional seamen like Clowdisley Shovell estimated their progress either by guessing their average speed or by dropping a log over the side of the boat and timing how long it took to float from bow to stern. Forced to rely on such crude measurements, the admiral can be forgiven his massive misjudgment. What caused the disaster was not the admiral's ignorance, but his inability to measure something that he already knew to be critically important—in this case longitude.[1]

We've come a long way since Clowdisley Shovell patrolled the seas for his native Great Britain. If you're a sailor, today's instrumentation ensures that any failure of navigation may be pinned squarely on your own shoulders. But for those of you who spend your days leading public and non-profit organizations, how far have you come in meeting the measurement challenge? Can you measure all those things you know to be critically important? Today's constituents and donors are better informed than at any time in history. That knowledge leads to a demand of accountability on your part to show results from the financial and human resources entrusted to you. To do that, you must demonstrate tangible results which are best captured in performance measures.

Over 150 years ago the Irish mathematician and physicist Lord Kelvin reminded us that "When you can measure what you are speaking about, and express it in numbers, you know something about it; but when you cannot measure it, when you cannot express it in numbers, your knowledge is of a meager and unsatisfactory kind . . ." The goal of this book is to help you do just that: to measure all those things that you know to be important. Those areas that truly define your success and allow you to clearly demonstrate the difference you're making in the lives of everyone you touch. Welcome to your Balanced Scorecard journey!

WHY THE BALANCED SCORECARD?

In the span of the Balanced Scorecard's lifetime—some 17 years—hundreds, if not thousands, of business ideas, fads, and fetishes have been paraded in front of a beleaguered, change-weary organizational world searching for the secret that will elevate them above the rest. Promising near instant success in a hyper-competitive world, most of these panaceas have come and gone with barely a whisper and yet the Scorecard drumbeat marches on, gaining momentum with each successive beat. The question is, why?

Before we explore the Balanced Scorecard in detail, it's important to examine some of the factors that have given rise to this proven framework for tracking organizational performance and executing strategy. Understanding these pillars of the Balanced Scorecard's success will not only enhance your appreciation of the tool, but the insights gained will also assist you as you begin implementing the system within your own organization. In the pages ahead, we'll examine these three factors that are fundamental to the success of any organization, whether public sector, nonprofit, or private: the increasing role of intangible assets in creating value in today's economy, our long-standing over-reliance on financial measures of performance to gauge success, and most importantly, the challenge of executing strategy. Let's look at each of these and discover how they've contributed to the need for a Balanced Scorecard system. We'll then return to an overview of the Balanced Scorecard and learn how this deceptively simple tool has revolutionized the management of performance (see Exhibit 1.1).

THE RISE OF INTANGIBLE ASSETS IN VALUE CREATION

As you read the heading for this section, what images flashed through your mind? An assembled throng of twenty-first century pocket-protector-wearing geeks at Google creating the next killer app of the Internet perhaps? Or maybe you wondered what the Red Bull–driven minds at Apple or Microsoft might dream up next? I can almost guarantee you didn't think about unloading timber ships at the London docks in 1970. But as much of a revolution occurred there as we're seeing in the halls of Silicon Valley today. In 1970, when a timber ship dropped anchor at the dock in London, it took 108 men about five days to unload it, equating to 540 man days. Today, that same ship would be stripped of its cargo in one, yes one, day. That's eight man days, meaning that over the past 37 years, workers have registered a whopping 98.5% improvement in the time to unload a ship. What could possibly account for this extraordinary enhancement? Steroid-popping ste-vedores? Hardly. The diminishing time requirement is a function of three things: containerization, modern processes for swift unloading, and ena-bling technology. Two out of those three of are quintessential examples of

Exhibit 1.1   The Balanced Scorecard Solves Fundamental Business Issues

the power of intangible assets: processes and technology. They both emanate from and harness the only power we'll never run out of: brain power![2]
   From barnacle-laden docks to computer-controlled manufacturing
facilities to meeting rooms around the world, this scenario is transforming the
way work is done in today's organizations. While this switch is probably evident
to anyone working in today's frenzied times, it is also borne out of research
findings by the Brookings Institute. Take a look at Exhibit 1.2 that illustrates
the transition in value from tangible to intangible assets. Speaking on National
Public Radio's *Morning Edition*, Ms. Margaret Blair of the Brookings Institute
suggests that tangible assets have continued to tumble in value:

> If you just look at the physical assets of the companies, the things that you
> can measure with ordinary accounting techniques, these things now account
> for less than one-fourth of the value of the corporate sector. Another way of
> putting this is that something like 75% of the sources of value inside corpora-
> tions is not being measured or reported on their books.[3]

Exhibit 1.2   The Increasing Value of Intangible Assets in Organizations

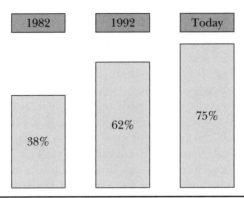

Adapted from *Balanced Scorecard Step-by-Step: Maximizing Performance and Maintaining Results, 2nd Edition,* Paul R.Niven (John Wiley & Sons, 2006).

Being keen-eyed denizens of the public and nonprofit sectors, I'm sure you noticed Ms. Blair's use of the term "corporations." Believe me, your organizations are being affected every bit as much as your corporate counterparts. The challenges represented by this switch are not going unnoticed in Washington, DC. David M. Walker, Comptroller General of the United States, said in a February 2001 testimony to the U.S. Senate that "human capital management is a pervasive challenge in the federal government. At many agencies, human capital shortfalls have contributed to serious problems and risks."[4] President George W. Bush, in his President's Management Agenda, echoes Walker's comments and adds that: "We must have a Government that thinks differently, so we need to recruit talented and imaginative people to public service."[5] Talented people, armed with the tools necessary to succeed and operating in an environment conducive to growth and change is the recipe for twenty-first century success.

Unfortunately, our measurement systems have failed to keep pace with the rate of change occurring in the workplace. As we'll see in the next section of the chapter, our performance measurement systems have focused almost exclusively on financial measures, and more specifically, they've relied on counting tangible things—inventory, monetary exchanges, and so on. However, the new economy, with its premium on intangible value creating mechanisms, demands more from our performance measurement systems. Today's system must have the capabilities to identify, describe, monitor, and fully harness the intangible assets driving organizational success. As we will see throughout this book, particularly in our discussion of the Employee Learning and Growth perspective, the Balanced Scorecard provides a voice of strength and clarity to intangible assets, allowing organizations to benefit fully from their astronomical potential.[6]

Financial Measurement and Its Limitations

Despite the changes in how value is created today, estimates suggest that 60% of metrics used for decision-making, resource allocation, and performance management in the typical organization are still financial in nature.[7] It seems that for all we've learned, we remain stuck in the quagmire of financial measurement. Perhaps tradition—where the measurement of all organizations has been financial—is serving as a guide unwilling to yield to the present realities. Bookkeeping records used to facilitate financial transactions can literally be traced back thousands of years. At the turn of the twentieth century, financial measurement innovations were critical to the success of the early industrial giants like General Motors. The financial measures created at that time were the perfect complement to the machine-like nature of the corporate entities and management philosophy of the day. Competition was ruled by scope and economies of scale with financial measures providing the yardsticks of success.

Over the last one hundred years, we've come a long way in our measurement of financial success, and the work of financial professionals is to be commended. Innovations such as Activity-Based Costing (ABC) and Economic Value Added (EVA) have helped many organizations make more informed decisions. However, as we begin the twenty-first century, many are questioning our almost exclusive reliance on financial measures of performance, suggesting that these measures may be better served to report on the stewardship of money entrusted to management's care rather than a means to chart the organization's future. Here are some of the criticisms levied against the over-abundant use of financial measures:

- *Not consistent with today's business realities.* Tangible assets no longer serve as the primary driver of enterprise value. It is employee knowledge (the assets that ride up and down the elevators), customer relationships, and cultures of innovation and change that create the bulk of value provided by any organization—in other words, intangible assets. If you buy a share of Microsoft's stock, are you buying buildings and machines? No, you're buying a promise of value to be delivered by innovative people striving to continually discover new computing pathways. Traditional financial measures were designed to compare previous periods based on internal standards of performance. These metrics are of little assistance in providing early indications of customer, quality, or employee problems or opportunities.

- *Driving by rear view mirror.* This is perhaps the classic criticism of financial metrics. You may be highly efficient in your operations one month, quarter, or even year. But does that signal ongoing financial success? As you know, anything can, and does, happen. A history of strong financial results is not indicative of future performance. As an illustration of this rear view mirror principle, look no further than the storied *Forbes* lists, regaling spellbound executives since 1917 with drool-inducing tales of heroic capitalism. *Forbes* published a 70th anniversary issue in 1987, and of the 100 companies that graced the inaugural roll, 61 were dead and gone, with only memories of their former fiscal glory remaining. Of the 39 companies that existed, many were on life support, with only 18 still named on the list. Similar statistics can be trotted out for the Standard and Poor's 500 list of top companies. Forty years after it began in 1957, only 74 of the initial 500 companies existed. More than 80% failed to survive.[8]

- *Tendency to reinforce functional silos.* Working in mission-based organizations, you know the importance of collaboration in achieving your goals. Whether it's improving literacy, decreasing HIV rates, or increasing public safety, you depend on a number of teams working seamlessly to accomplish your tasks. Financial statements don't capture this cross-functional dependency. Typically, financial reports are compiled by functional area. They are then "rolled-up" in ever-higher levels of detail and ultimately reflected in an organizational financial report. This does little to help you in meeting your noble causes.

- *Sacrifice long-term thinking.* If you face a funding cut, what are the first things to go in your attempt to right the ship? Many organizations reach for the easiest levers in times of crisis: employee training and development, or even employees themselves! The short-term impact is positive, but what about the long-term impact? Ultimately, organizations that pursue this tactic may be sacrificing their most valuable sources of long-term advantage and often to no avail. Recent research suggests that tools such as downsizing not only damages workers who are laid off, but destroy value in the long-term. One study found that downsizing in the corporate world never improved profits or stock market returns.[9]

- *Financial measures are not relevant to many levels of the organization.* Financial reports by their very nature are abstractions. Abstraction in this context is defined as moving to another level leaving certain characteristics out. When we roll-up financial statements throughout the organization, that is exactly what we are doing: compiling information at a higher and higher level until it is almost unrecognizable and useless in the decision making of most managers and employees. Employees at all levels of the organization need performance data they can act on. This information must be imbued with relevance for their day-to-day activities.

Thus far, I've taken a hard line on financial measures of performance. We just reviewed their many limitations, and with only a modicum of exaggeration, it could be suggested that a single-minded focus on financial success may be among the causes for the epidemic of scandals currently plaguing the corporate world. So, do financial metrics deserve a place on your Balanced Scorecard? Absolutely. Despite their many shortcomings, financial yardsticks are an entirely necessary evil. This is especially the case in the public and nonprofit sectors. In an era of limited, often decreasing, funding you must consistently tread the delicate balance between effectiveness and efficiency. Results must be achieved, but in a fiscally responsible manner.

Your stakeholders will be looking to you to achieve your missions, and thus, nonfinancial measures of performance become critical in your efforts. However, pursuing your goals with no regard to the financial ramifications of your decisions will ultimately damage everyone: You'll be the victim of decreased funding as it becomes clear that you're unable to prudently manage your resources. Your funders will be discredited, and potentially, unwilling to support you in the future. Most importantly, your target audiences will not receive the services they need as a result of your inability to reach them in both an effective and efficient way.

Strategy: Execution is Everything

When I was conducting research for my book on private-sector Balanced Scorecard development, I knew I would come across many references to strategy. After all, strategy is probably among the most discussed and debated topics in the world of organizations. Of course, it's not just organizations that wrestle with strategy—the concept is one that has truly entered the mainstream of our society. Professional sports teams all have a strategy to beat their opponents (and their owners have a strategy to separate us fans from our money!). I have a strategy for writing this book, and I'm sure you all employ strategies in achieving your daily tasks both at home and at work. The interesting thing about strategy in the business sense of the word is that nobody seems to agree on what it is specifically. There are as many definitions as there are academics, writers, and consultants to muse on the topic. In fact, a favorite book of mine on the subject nicely summarizes both the confusion and the ultimate quest of those pursuing the strategy development challenge: *Strategy Safari*.[10] I enjoy conjuring up that image of strategy—picturing myself cutting through the dense forest of research, attempting to find my quarry: the holy grail of strategy.

One thing strategy gurus seem to agree on is this: despite the challenges of creating a strategy, ultimately it is more important and valuable to demonstrate the ability to execute the strategy. It's one thing to sit down and craft what is seemingly a winning strategy, but successfully implementing it is another thing entirely. For those who can execute, the rewards are significant. In the for-profit world, a 35% improvement in the quality of strategy implementation, for the average firm, is associated with a 30% improvement in shareholder value.[11] While shareholder value is not the end game of your organization, you too will benefit greatly from an ability to carry out your strategies. Unfortunately, the vast majority of organizations fail miserably when attempting to execute their strategies. A 1999 *Fortune* magazine story suggested that 70% of CEO failures were not a result of poor strategy, but rather of poor execution.[12] More recently, The Center for Creative Leadership has reported that 40% of CEOs fail in their first 18 months.[13] Why is strategy so difficult for even the best organizations to effectively implement? Research and experience in the area have suggested a number of barriers to strategy execution, and they are displayed in Exhibit 1.3. Let's take a look at these in turn.

The Vision Barrier   Employee empowerment, two-way communication, and information sharing are terms whose benefits executives and managers alike frequently espouse. Talk is cheap. The fact of the matter is that the vast majority of organizations have a long way to go when it comes to communicating their most important messages—vision and strategy—to their most important constituents: employees.

An earlier section discussed the fact that many financial measures were developed at the turn of the twentieth century. Transport yourself back there for a moment and put yourself inside one of those fortresses of industry, complete with towering walls and smokestacks billowing who-knows-what into the atmosphere. Chances are you'd be told what to do, when to do it, where to do it, and how to do it. Would knowledge of the organization's

Exhibit 1.3   Barriers to Implementing Strategy

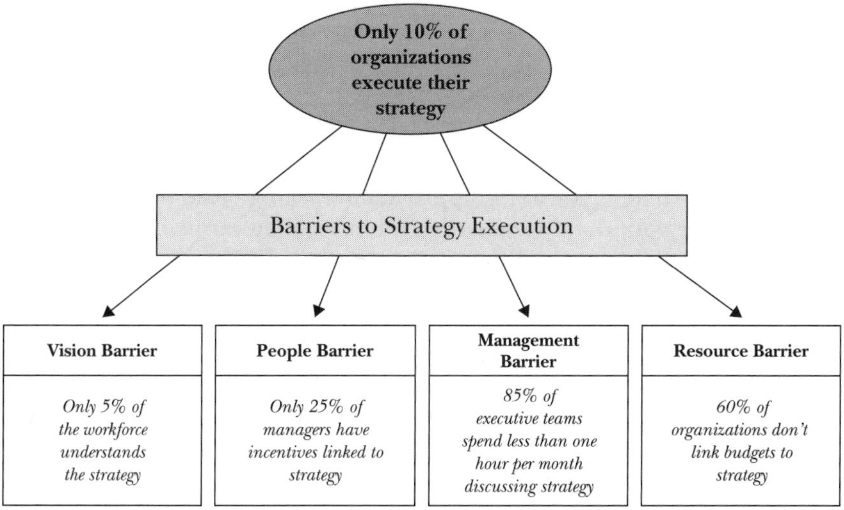

Vision Barrier	People Barrier	Management Barrier	Resource Barrier
Only 5% of the workforce understands the strategy	*Only 25% of managers have incentives linked to strategy*	*85% of executive teams spend less than one hour per month discussing strategy*	*60% of organizations don't link budgets to strategy*

Adapted from material developed by Robert S. Kaplan and David P. Norton.

vision and strategy have been the least bit relevant or helpful in your task? Probably not. But today the world is an entirely different place. Value is created largely from intangible assets such as customer knowledge and information-rich networks. If you're going to contribute in a meaningful way you must know where the organization is headed and what the strategy is to get there. Only then can you combine your talents with others from across your agency to create value for your stakeholders and ultimately achieve your mission.

The People Barrier   For decades, debate has raged on whether incentive compensation plans really do lead to improved performance. We may never know the answer, but it is probably safe to suggest that an incentive of any kind tends to increase focus—at least temporarily. The danger with incentive plans is the possibility that managers will sacrifice long-term value-creating activities and initiatives in order to reach a short-term financial target and receive a monetary award. Strategy cannot be executed if the focus is continually on the short term. By its very nature, strategy demands a longer-range view of an organization's landscape. Financial incentives can distort or entirely block an organization's strategic view.

The Resource Barrier   60% of organizations don't link budgets to strategy. If that's the case, then what are they linking their budgets to? For many organizations, it's as simple as looking at last year's budget and adding or subtracting a few percentage points as appropriate. This is a particularly damaging blow to the hopes of executing strategy. What is a budget if not a detailed articulation of the priorities of the enterprise for the next fiscal year? If the budget is not linked to some form of strategic plan and goals, then what does that say about the organization's priorities? Do they even possess any, or are they simply spinning their wheels and wasting precious resources in the process. We'll return to the important topic of budgets in Chapter 10.

The Management Barrier   Have you ever heard the phrase "management by walking around?" It suggests an approach of staying close to your employees by speaking with them frequently and informally, ensuring communication is two-way and beneficial to all. By contrast, I believe most of us live in the age of "management by firefighting!" We move from one crisis to the next, never taking the time to pause and reflect on our larger objectives, strategies, and mission. A client of mine uses the analogy of "working *in* the business," that is, fighting fires, versus "working *on* the business," that is taking the necessary break to examine things from a larger perspective.

Many would argue there is literally no time to slow down, not even for a minute. Undoubtedly, we live in an era of brutally fast-paced organizations, but virtually all of us attend regular management meetings. In order to have any chance of executing strategy, these meetings must be transformed.

No longer should we sit around and examine what we deem as "defects" when results do not meet budget expectations. Instead, these meetings must be used to discuss, learn about, and debate our strategy.

THE BALANCED SCORECARD

When sharing Balanced Scorecard concepts with audiences for the first time, it's at this point in my presentation that I show a slide depicting a poor soul standing defenseless under three black clouds pelting him with rain. The clouds are labeled "the rise of intangible assets," "our over-reliance on financial measures," and "the difficulty of executing strategy." Just as my clip art friend is being doused with no defense against the elements, organizations too are vulnerable to the storm clouds of twenty-first century commerce. But their umbrellas, the traditional methods of monitoring and managing performance, are ill-equipped to navigate us through the changes we face on a seemingly daily basis. As the title of my slide says, "Clearly a Change is Needed!"

A change has come, one that has literally revolutionized the way organizations around the globe measure performance, monitor operations, and ultimately execute their unique strategies. The powerful transformation to which I'm referring comes in the form of the Balanced Scorecard: a tool that balances the historical accuracy and integrity of financial numbers with the drivers of future fiscal success; a tool that provides both visibility and insight into intangible assets; and finally, a tool that has been proven to help organizations successfully combat and overcome the barriers of executing strategy.

In the remainder of this chapter, we will begin our exploration of the Balanced Scorecard by discussing its origins, reviewing the conceptual model of the Scorecard, and considering what separates the Balanced Scorecard from other systems. The model is presented graphically in Exhibit 1.4.

Origins of the Balanced Scorecard

The Balanced Scorecard was developed by Robert Kaplan, an accounting professor at Harvard University, and David Norton, a consultant also from the Boston area. In 1990, Kaplan and Norton led a research study of a dozen companies exploring new methods of performance measurement. The impetus for the study was a growing belief that financial measures of performance were ineffective for the modern business enterprise. The study companies, along with Kaplan and Norton, were convinced that a reliance on financial measures of performance was affecting their ability to create value. The group discussed a number of possible alternatives but settled on the idea of a Scorecard featuring performance measures capturing activities from throughout the organization—customer issues, internal business

Exhibit 1.4   The Balanced Scorecard

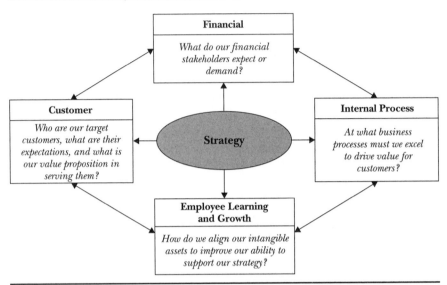

Adapted from material created by Robert S. Kaplan and David P. Norton.

processes, employee activities, and of course shareholder concerns. Kaplan and Norton labeled the new tool the Balanced Scorecard and later summarized the concept in the first of several *Harvard Business Review* articles, "The Balanced Scorecard—Measures that Drive Performance."[14]

Over the next four years, a number of organizations adopted the Balanced Scorecard and achieved immediate results. Kaplan and Norton discovered these organizations were not only using the Scorecard to complement financial measures with the drivers of future performance, but were also communicating their strategies through the measures they selected for their Balanced Scorecard. As the Scorecard gained prominence with organizations around the globe as a key tool in the implementation of strategy, Kaplan and Norton summarized the concept and the learning to that point in their 1996 book, *The Balanced Scorecard*.[15] Since that time, the Balanced Scorecard has been adopted by more than half of the Fortune 1000 organizations, and the momentum continues unabated. So widely accepted and effective has the Scorecard become that the *Harvard Business Review* recently hailed it as one of the 75 most influential ideas of the twentieth century.

Once considered the exclusive domain of the for-profit world, the Balanced Scorecard has been translated and effectively implemented in both the nonprofit and public sectors. Success stories are accumulating from all corners of the globe as eager public and nonprofit sector leaders apply the Balanced Scorecard, enhancing their capacity, strengthening their core processes, and better serving their constituents. While empirical evidence of

Scorecard use and efficacy outside the private sector remains relatively scarce, in one public sector study funded by the Sloan Foundation, 70% of respondents agreed that their governmental entity was better off since implementing performance measures.[16]

What Is A Balanced Scorecard?

We can describe the Balanced Scorecard as a carefully selected set of measures derived from an organization's strategy. The measures selected for the Scorecard represent a tool for leaders to use in communicating to employees and external stakeholders the outcomes and performance drivers by which the organization will achieve its mission and strategic objectives.

A simple definition, however, cannot reveal everything about the Balanced Scorecard. In my work with many organizations, and in conducting Scorecard best-practices research, I see this tool as three things: a communication tool, a measurement system, and a strategic management system. In the following sections, we'll examine each of these Scorecard uses, but first let's consider the four perspectives of performance, perhaps the most fundamental aspects of the Balanced Scorecard (see Exhibit 1.5).

Balanced Scorecard Perspectives

The etymology of the word perspective is from the Latin perspectus "to look through" or "see clearly," which is precisely what we aim to do with a Balanced Scorecard—examine the strategy, making it clearer through the lens of different viewpoints. For any strategy to be effective, it must contain descriptions of financial aspirations, markets served, processes to be conquered, and of course the people who will steadily and skillfully guide the ship to success. Thus, when measuring our progress, it would make little sense to focus on just one aspect of the strategy when in fact, as Leonardo da Vinci reminds us "Everything is connected to everything else."[17] To compose

Exhibit 1.5   What is the Balanced Scorecard?

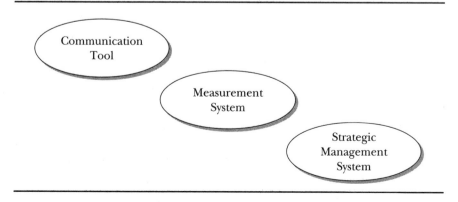

an accurate picture of strategy execution, it must be painted in the full palette of perspectives that comprise it. Therefore, when developing a Balanced Scorecard we use the following four: Customer, Internal Processes, Employee Learning and Growth, and Financial.

When building your Balanced Scorecard, or later when it is up and running, you may slip and casually remark on the four "quadrants" or four "areas," but as colloquial and seemingly inconsequential as this slip appears, I believe it has serious ramifications. Take for example the word quadrant. The Oxford dictionary begins its definition by describing it as a quarter of a circle's circumference. The word reflects the number four and in that sense is almost limiting to the flexible approach inherent in the Scorecard. You may wish to have five perspectives or only three. With its focus on viewing performance from another point, perspective is far more representative of the spirit of the Balanced Scorecard and I encourage you to be disciplined in the use of this term.[18]

The Balanced Scorecard as a Communication Tool: Strategy Maps

When Kaplan and Norton originally developed the Balanced Scorecard, their creation was a direct response to what some might realistically describe as the tyranny of financial measures. These dollar-based metrics seemed to wield unlimited power yet were utterly incapable of gauging value in what has become known as the "new economy"—one in which intangibles rule and execution of strategy is everything. The Balanced Scorecard posited a simple yet revolutionary idea: complement the financial numbers (which will always be required of any enterprise) with the drivers of future financial success represented by such disparate but critical elements as innovation, customer satisfaction, and employee engagement.

The Balanced Scorecard represented a profound and simple idea, but as with many such notions, it was not always easily implemented. Pioneers of the system, while anxious to develop the breakthrough metrics that would ensure strategy execution, often struggled when it came to actually articulating what they would track in each of the perspectives. For many, the challenge lay in translating vague and obtuse strategy dictums such as "quality service" or "product development" into meaningful measures, since the nebulous nature of such terms could lead to any number of suitable metrics based on one's individual interpretation. Early Balanced Scorecard adopters faced this challenge and found themselves instinctively spanning the strategy/measures chasm with a discussion of *objectives*, or what needed to be done well, in order to implement the essence of the strategy. So, rather than beginning the Scorecard process with the sometimes futile effort of creating measures, they first asked themselves, "What do we need to do well in order to execute?" Splitting the chore in this way added a level of granularity to the strategy thereby rendering the task of creating associated performance measures that much simpler. For example, if the strategy devoted a section to new service development, stressing the need to bring new services to customers at a faster rate, this narrative was translated into the simple objective of "accelerate new service development," which may be accurately measured by the new service development life cycle.

As with any business tool, the Balanced Scorecard has a vocabulary of its own, and earlier, I distinguished between two of the most important terms you'll find in the Scorecard lexicon: objective and measure. Understanding the definitions of these terms is critical should you hope to derive the maximum benefit from your efforts. An objective is a succinct statement, normally beginning with a verb, describing what we must do well in each of the four perspectives in order to implement our strategy. Examples vary widely but could include: "Improve service delivery time," "Leverage partnerships," and "Close our skills gap." Strategy Maps are comprised entirely of objectives. Tracking our success in achieving the objective is the domain of the measure, a (typically) quantitative device used to monitor progress.

If you've already started your own Balanced Scorecard glossary of terms, something I strongly recommend, here's what I would offer for Strategy Maps: *a one-page graphical representation of what you must do well in each of the four perspectives in order to successfully execute your strategy.* Let's break that definition down. First, why do we use the term map, and not "Strategy Sheet" or "Must-Do List?" A map serves the function of getting us from point A to point B, outlining the pathways of our journey that ultimately lead to our chosen destination. So it is with the Strategy Map, we're defining the pathways (objectives) that will lead us to the execution of our strategy. When charting your course on a map, you move sequentially from one location to the next and the Strategy Map serves a similar function. The objectives appearing on the Map should not be viewed as isolated elements but should be woven together, taking you on a journey that leads to the execution of your strategy.

Why just one page for the Map? One page is critical; many strategic plans suffer from severe information overload for readers—dozens if not hundreds of pages of dizzying graphs, numbing narratives, and 8-point Excel financial tables. This isn't the strategy binder, it's the map—one simple page telling your strategic story. Finally, "graphical representation," means the Map is drawn as a picture, not a list of bulleted points that would cause even the most earnest student of your strategy to glaze over at first glance. As you'll see when we explore Strategy Maps in detail in Chapter 7, your creativity will be tapped to the fullest when creating this document, bringing the strategy to life and creating a powerful communication tool signaling to everyone in the organization what you must do well in order to execute your unique strategy. A sample Strategy Map, representing a fictitious performing arts organization is shown in Exhibit 1.6.

Exhibit 1.6 Example Strategy Map for a Fictitious Performing Arts Organization

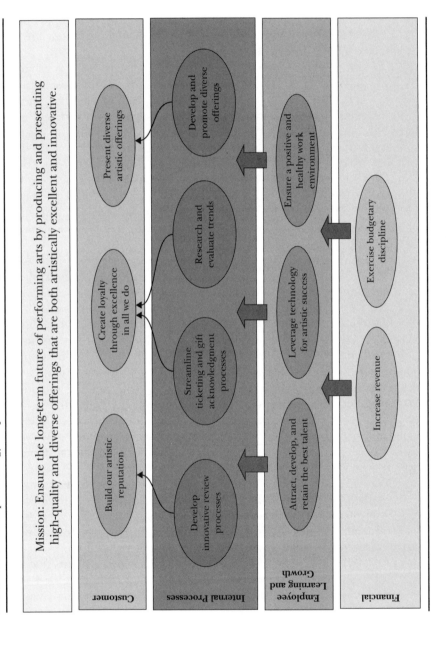

Mission: Ensure the long-term future of performing arts by producing and presenting high-quality and diverse offerings that are both artistically excellent and innovative.

Customer

Build our artistic reputation

Create loyalty through excellence in all we do

Present diverse artistic offerings

Internal Processes

Develop innovative review processes

Streamline ticketing and gift acknowledgment processes

Research and evaluate trends

Develop and promote diverse offerings

Employee Learning and Growth

Attract, develop, and retain the best talent

Leverage technology for artistic success

Ensure a positive and healthy work environment

Financial

Increase revenue

Exercise budgetary discipline

Creating Objectives for the Four Perspectives of a Strategy Map

As a preview of what's to come later in the book, let's take a glimpse of what you might consider when populating each of the four perspectives of your Strategy Map with objectives.

Customer Perspective   When choosing objectives for the Customer Perspective of the Strategy Map, organizations must answer three critical questions: "Who are our customers?" "What do our customers expect or demand from us?" and finally, "What is our value proposition in serving them?" Sounds simple enough, but each of these questions offers many challenges. Most organizations state that they do in fact have a target customer audience, yet their actions reveal an "all things to all customers" strategy. Strategy guru Michael Porter says that this lack of focus will prevent an organization from differentiating itself from competitors.[19] Understanding what customers truly value can pose no less of a challenge. Without near constant feedback and communication, we're often left gazing hopefully into a crystal ball to determine customers' wishes. Finally, choosing an appropriate value proposition also represents a formidable test to most organizations. What is a value proposition? It simply represents how you propose to add value for your customers, what makes you stand out from others. When considering this important point many will choose one of three "disciplines" articulated by Treacy and Wiersema in their bestselling book, *The Discipline of Market Leaders*.[20] They are:

- *Operational excellence.* Organizations pursuing an operational excellence discipline focus on low price, convenience, and often "no frills." Wal-Mart provides a great representation of an operationally excellent company.

- *Product leadership.* Product leaders push the envelope of their firm's products. Constantly innovating, they strive to offer simply the best product in the market. 3M is an example of a product leader in the private sector, a company long known for breakthrough products that frequently solve needs we didn't even know we had. Who could now live without Post It Notes, for example?

- *Customer intimacy.* Doing whatever it takes to provide solutions for unique customer's needs help define the customer intimate company. These organizations don't look for one-time transactions but instead focus on long-term relationship building through their deep knowledge of customer needs. In the retail industry, Nordstrom epitomizes the customer intimate organization.

As organizations have developed, and experimented with, value propositions, many have suggested it is difficult, if not impossible, to focus exclusively on just one. A more practical approach is to choose one discipline in which you possess particularly strong attributes, and maintain at least threshold standards of performance in the other disciplines. McDonald's, for example, is a truly operational excellent organization, but that doesn't stop them from continually introducing new menu items. In Chapter 7, we will take a closer look at the Customer Perspective, and identify what specific steps your organization should take to develop customer objectives. Included in our discussion will be ideas you can use to apply the "value proposition" concept to your organization.

Internal Process Perspective   In the Internal Process Perspective of the Strategy Map, we identify the key processes at which the organization must excel in order to continue adding value for customers. Each of the customer disciplines outlined above will entail the efficient operation of specific internal processes in order to serve our customers and fulfill our value proposition. Our task in this perspective is to identify those processes and develop the best possible objectives with which to execute our strategy. To satisfy customers, you may have to identify entirely new internal processes rather than focusing your efforts on the incremental improvement of existing activities. Service development and delivery, partnering with the community, and reporting are examples of items that may be represented in this perspective. We will examine the development of performance objectives for Internal Processes in greater depth in Chapter 7.

Financial Perspective   Financial objectives are an important component of the Strategy Map, in the for-profit, public, and nonprofit worlds. In the for-profit domain, the objectives in this perspective represent the end in mind of our strategic story, typically culminating in objectives such as "Increase shareholder value," "Grow revenues," and "Lower costs." In the nonprofit and public sectors, financial objectives ensure we're achieving our results, but doing so in an efficient manner that minimizes cost. Typical examples include: "Expand revenue sources," "Contain costs," and "Utilize assets effectively." We will return to have another look at financial objectives during Chapter 7.

Employee Learning and Growth Perspective   If you want to achieve ambitious results for internal processes and customers, where are these gains found? The objectives appearing in the Employee Learning and Growth Perspective of the Strategy Map are really the enablers of the other perspectives. In essence, they are the foundation upon which this entire house of a Strategy Map is built. Once you identify objectives in your Customer and Internal Process Perspectives, you can be certain of discovering some gaps between your current organizational infrastructure of employee skills, information systems, and organizational climate (e.g., culture) and the level necessary to achieve the results you desire. The objectives you design in this perspective will help you close that gap and ensure sustainable performance for the future.

Many organizations I've worked with struggle in the development of Employee Learning and Growth objectives. It is often the last perspective developed and it's likely that the teams are intellectually drained from their earlier efforts of developing new strategic objectives, or they simply consider this perspective "soft stuff" best left to the human resources group. No matter how valid the rationale seems, this perspective cannot be overlooked in the development process. As I mentioned earlier, the objectives you develop in the Employee Learning and Growth perspective are really the enablers of all other measures on your Map. As with the other three perspectives, we will re-examine this important topic in Chapter 7.

The Balanced Scorecard as a Measurement System

Many organizations have inspiring visions and compelling strategies, but are often unable to use those beautifully crafted words to align employee actions with the firm's strategic direction. In his book, *The Fifth Discipline*, Peter Senge describes this dilemma when he notes, "Many leaders have personal visions that never get translated into shared visions that galvanize an organization."[21] The Balanced Scorecard system allows an organization to translate its vision and strategies by providing a new framework—one that tells the story of the organization's strategy through the objectives of the Strategy Map and measures chosen to represent those objectives on the Balanced Scorecard. Rather than focusing on financial control devices that provide little in the way of guidance for long-term employee decision-making, the Scorecard system uses measurement as a new language to describe the key elements in the achievement of the strategy.

Measures for the Balanced Scorecard are derived from the objectives appearing on the Strategy Map, which itself serves as a direct and clarifying translation of the organization's strategy. These two links in the chain of success remind me of the old song "Love and Marriage"—you can't have one without the other. A Strategy Map may prove to be the most inspirational document you've ever produced but without the accountability and focus afforded by accompanying performance measures, its value is specious to say the least. Conversely, performance measures serve as powerful monitoring devices, but without the benefit of a clear and compelling Strategy Map, much of their contextual value is lost. It would not be an exaggeration to suggest that measurement is at the very heart of the Balanced Scorecard system, it's in the tool's very DNA, and has been from its inception in 1990. Strategy Maps communicate the strategic destination, while performance measures housed within the Balanced Scorecard monitor the course allowing us to ensure we remain on track. We'll return to the vital concept of measurement in Chapter 8.[22]

Before we move on, a quick check. Are you confused over the difference between a Strategy Map and a Balanced Scorecard? If so, this is the time to clear things up because it's a crucial distinction that you must understand should you hope to use this tool effectively. Step number one in the overall process is creating a Strategy Map that tells the story of your strategy (on one page, remember) through the use of objectives—concise statements of what must be done well in each of the four perspectives. Once you've developed a clear and compelling Map, you will create performance measures for each of the objectives. You'll use the measures to hold yourself accountable for achieving the objectives and ultimately executing your strategy. The measures are housed in a Balanced Scorecard since they are the ultimate arbiters of success, providing the actual score for us to tally and analyze.

The confusing part, to me at least, is that we call the entire system a "Balanced Scorecard" when in fact it is composed of both Strategy Maps of objectives and Balanced Scorecards of measures. Chronology should shoulder the blame for this perplexing situation. As previously discussed, when Kaplan and Norton developed this system, the notion of Strategy Maps wasn't even a glint in their eye. They were focused entirely on solving a measurement issue and through their efforts, and those of the pioneering firms with which they worked, the Balanced Scorecard was born. Several years later, the concept of Strategy Maps emerged primarily from the struggles of early Scorecard adopters. The two have been working harmoniously together ever since, and while we may call the entire framework the "Balanced Scorecard," and I will do so throughout the book, you need to keep in mind that it contains both objectives on the Strategy Map and measures in the Scorecard. And guess what? There's even more to the system: targets and initiatives. But don't worry about them yet, we'll have plenty of time to explore both in the following chapters, and you'll discover how they blend seamlessly into the overall fabric of the system.

The Balanced Scorecard as a Strategic Management System

For many organizations, the Balanced Scorecard has evolved from a communication and measurement tool to what Kaplan and Norton have described as a "Strategic Management System."[23] While the original intent of the Scorecard system was to balance historical financial numbers with the drivers of future value for the firm, more and more organizations experimented with the concept and found it to be a critical tool in aligning short-term actions with their strategy. Used in this way, the Scorecard alleviates many of the issues of effective strategy implementation we discussed earlier in the chapter. Let's revisit those barriers and examine how the Balanced Scorecard may in fact remove them.

Overcoming the Vision Barrier through the Translation of Strategy   The Balanced Scorecard is ideally created through a shared understanding and translation of the organization's strategy into objectives (on the Strategy Map), measures, targets, and initiatives in each of the four Scorecard perspectives. The translation of vision and strategy forces the executive team to specifically determine what is meant by often vague and nebulous terms contained in vision and strategy statements, for example: "superior service" or "targeted customers." Through the process of developing the Strategy Map and Scorecard, an executive group may determine that "superior service" translates to the objective "provide fast turnaround." That may then be translated into the measure of "response time to inquiries." All employees can now focus their energies and day-to-day activities toward the crystal clear goal of response times rather than wondering and debating about the cliché "superior service." Using the Balanced Scorecard system as a framework for translating the strategy, these organizations create a new language of measurement that serves to guide all employees' actions toward the achievement of the stated direction.

Cascading the Scorecard Overcomes the People Barrier   To successfully implement any strategy, it must be understood and acted upon at every level of the firm. Cascading the Scorecard means driving it down into the organization, giving all employees the opportunity to demonstrate how their day-to-day activities contribute to the company's strategy. In this way, organizational "ranks" distinguish their value-creating activities by developing Scorecards that link to the highest-level organizational objectives.

Through cascading, you create a line of sight from the employee on the front line to the director's office. Some organizations have taken cascading all the way down to the individual level with employees developing personal Balanced Scorecards that define the contribution they will make to their team in helping it achieve overall objectives. In Chapter 9, we will take a closer look at the topic of cascading and discuss how you can develop aligned Scorecards throughout your organization.

Rather than linking incentives and rewards to the achievement of short-term financial targets, managers now have the opportunity to tie their team, department or agency's rewards directly to the areas in which they exert influence. All employees can now focus on the performance drivers of future value, and what decisions and actions are necessary to achieve those outcomes.

Strategic Resource Allocation Overcomes the Resource Barrier   Developing your Balanced Scorecard provides an excellent opportunity to tie resource allocation and strategy. When we create a Balanced Scorecard, we not only think in terms of objectives, measures, and targets for each of our four perspectives, but just as critically, we must consider the initiatives or action plans we will put in place to meet our Scorecard targets. If we create long-term stretch targets for our measures we can then consider the incremental steps along the path to their achievement.

The human and financial resources necessary to achieve Scorecard targets should form the basis for the development of the annual budgeting process. No longer will departments submit budget requests that simply take last year's numbers and add or subtract an arbitrary 5%. Instead, the necessary costs (and profits) associated with Balanced Scorecard targets are clearly articulated in their submission documents. This enhances executive learning about the strategy, as the group is now forced (unless they have unlimited means) to make tough choices and trade-offs regarding which initiatives to fund and which to defer.

The building of a Balanced Scorecard also affords you a tremendous opportunity to critically examine the current myriad initiatives taking place in your organization. As a consultant, when I begin working with a new client, one of the laments I hear repeatedly from front-line employees is, "Oh no, another new initiative!" Many executives have pet projects and agendas they hope to advance, often with little thought to the strategic significance of such endeavors. Initiatives at every level of the organization and from every area must share one common trait: a linkage to the organization's overall strategic goals. The Balanced Scorecard provides the lens for making this examination. Once you've developed your Map and Scorecard, you should review all the initiatives currently underway in your organization to determine which are truly critical in the fulfillment of your strategy, and which are merely consuming valuable and scarce resources. Obviously, the resource savings are beneficial, but more importantly, you signal to everyone in the organization the critical factors for success, and the steps you are taking to achieve them. Chapter 10 is devoted to a greater review of this topic and provides guidance on how you can link your budgets to strategy.

Strategic Learning Overcomes the Management Barrier   In today's rapidly changing environment, we need more than an analysis of actual versus budget variances to make strategic decisions. Unfortunately, many management teams spend their precious time together discussing variances and looking for ways to correct these "defects." The Balanced Scorecard provides us with the necessary elements to move away from this paradigm to a new model in which Scorecard results become a starting point for reviewing, questioning, and learning about our strategy.

Much has been written in recent years about knowledge management strategies within organizations, and many schools of thought exist. One common trait of all such systems is the desire to make the implicit knowledge held within the minds of your workforce explicit and open for discussion and learning. We live in the era of the knowledge worker, the employee who—unlike his organizational predecessors who relied on the company's physical assets—now owns the means of production: knowledge. There may be no greater challenge facing your organization today than codifying and acting on that knowledge. In fact, Peter Drucker, widely considered the father of modern management, has called managing knowledge worker productivity one of the great management challenges of the twenty-first century.[24] Sharing Scorecard results throughout the organization provides employees with the opportunity to discuss the assumptions underlying the strategy, learn from any unexpected results, and dialogue on future modifications as necessary. Simply understanding the firm's strategies can unlock many hidden organizational capacities as employees, perhaps for the first time, know where the organization is headed and how they can contribute during the journey. One organization I worked with conducted employee surveys before and after the development of the Balanced Scorecard. Prior to implementation, less than 50% said they were aware of, and understood, the strategy. One year following a full Balanced Scorecard implementation, that number had risen to 87%! If you believe in openly disseminating information to your employees, practicing what some would call "open-book management," then I can think of no better tool than the Balanced Scorecard to serve as your open book.

In my work with the Balanced Scorecard over the last 12 years, I have come to believe that its greatest power and potential lies in the opportunity to improve management learning and discussion through an improved meeting structure and process. We will examine this critical topic in greater detail in Chapter 11.

NOTES

1. Marcus Buckingham and Curt Coffman, *First Break All The Rules,* (New York: Simon & Schuster, 1999), p. 21.

2. Tom Peters, *Re-Imagine* (London, Dorling Kindersley, 2003), p. 50.

3. Interview on National Public Radio's Morning Edition, October 27, 2000.

4. Testimony by David M. Walker, Comptroller General of the United States, before the Subcommittee on Oversight of Government, Management, Restructuring, and the District of Columbia Committee on Governmental Affairs, U.S. Senate.

5. Found at: www.whitehouse.gov/omb/budget/fy2002/mgmt.pdf

6. Paul R. Niven, *Balanced Scorecard Step by Step: Maximizing Performance and Maintaining Results, 2nd Edition* (Hoboken, NJ: John Wiley & Sons, 2006), p. 8.

7. Institute of Management and Administration Controllers' Report, "20 Best Practice Insights: How Controllers Promote Faster, Better Decisions," Institute of Management and Administration, 2001.

8. Tom Peters, *Re-Imagine* (London, Dorling Kindersley, 2003), p. 33.

9. Lauri Bassi and Daniel McMurrer, "Are Skills a Cost or an Asset?," *Business Ethics*, Fall 2004.

10. Henry Mintzberg, Bruce Ahlstrand, and Joseph Lampel, *Strategy Safari* (New York: The Free Press, 1998).

11. Brian E. Becker, Mark A. Huselid, and Dave Ulrich, *The HR Scorecard* (Boston: Harvard Business School Press, 2001), p. 213.

12. R. Charan and G. Colvin, "Why CEOs Fail,"*Fortune*, June 21, 1999.

13. Dan Ciampa, "How Leaders Move Up,"*Harvard Business Review,* January 2005, pp. 46–53.

14. Robert S. Kaplan and David P. Norton, "The Balanced Scorecard–Measures That Drive Performance,"*Harvard Business Review*, January–February 1992: pp. 71–79.

15. Robert S. Kaplan and David P. Norton, *The Balanced Scorecard* (Boston: Harvard Business School Press, 1996).

16. Governmental Accounting Standards Board, "Performance Measurement at the State and Local Levels." 2001.

17. Michael J. Gelb, *How to Think Like Leonardo da Vinci* (New York: Random House, 2004).

18. Paul R. Niven, *Balanced Scorecard Step by Step: Maximizing Performance and Maintaining Results, 2nd Edition* (Hoboken, NJ: John Wiley & Sons, 2006), pp. 13–14.

19. Michael E. Porter, "Strategy and the Internet,"*Harvard Business Review*, March 2001, pp. 62–78.

20. Michael Treacy and Fred Wiersema, *The Discipline of Market Leaders* (Reading, MA: Perseus Books, 1995).

21. P. Senge, *The Fifth Discipline: The Art and Practice of the Learning Organization* (New York: Currency Doubleday, 1990).

22. Paul R. Niven, *Balanced Scorecard Step by Step: Maximizing Performance and Maintaining Results, 2nd Edition* (Hoboken, NJ: John Wiley & Sons, 2006), p. 20.

23. Robert S. Kaplan and David P. Norton, "Using the Balanced Scorecard as a Strategic Management System,"*Harvard Business Review*, January–February, 1996, pp. 75–85.

24. Peter F. Drucker, *Management Challenges for the 21st Century* (New York: HarperCollins, 1999).

2

Adapting the Balanced Scorecard to Fit the Public and Nonprofit Sectors

---

Roadmap for Chapter 2   "Adapt or perish, now as ever, is nature's inexorable imperative." So said English author and historian H.G. Wells many years ago. Applied to the Balanced Scorecard, this colorful language suggests that if you expect to achieve success with this tool, you must adapt it to fit your organization. Detailing that process is the subject of this chapter.

Chapter 1 focused on the Balanced Scorecard as it was originally conceived with the for-profit world in mind. As private-sector firms around the world began to harness the power of the Balanced Scorecard, public and nonprofit agencies, in their own quest to improve results, turned to the Scorecard with intrigue. Curiosity soon led to actual use as early adopters discovered that with some modifications, the Balanced Scorecard readily adapted to their circumstances and provided swift and tangible benefits. In this chapter, we explore the nature and history of public and nonprofit performance measurement, and discover how the Balanced Scorecard can fill voids in their measurement efforts.

We'll begin by looking back at performance measurement initiatives in both the public and nonprofit sectors. You'll discover that both sectors have a long history of measuring performance using a variety of techniques. We'll also look at some of the struggles that have been encountered in the pursuit of meaningful performance measurement.

Adapting the "geography" of the Scorecard to fit nonprofit and public sector enterprises will be our next topic. I'll dissect the model and detail both the subtle and not-so-subtle changes in application. As you'll see, one factor that separates the Balanced Scorecard from other performance measurement systems is the notion of cause and effect—how the measures link together to tell a strategic story. We'll explain this concept and look at an example to illustrate how it may be utilized in practice. We'll conclude this chapter by reviewing a sample of the many benefits you can derive from employing a Balanced Scorecard system.

PERFORMANCE MEASUREMENT IN THE PUBLIC AND NONPROFIT SECTORS

Assessing the Landscape of Public-Sector Performance Measurement

Attempts to monitor government performance are not without precedent. In 1960, Robert McNamara was appointed Secretary of Defense by newly elected President John F. Kennedy. Among McNamara's first undertakings was to centralize decision-making control within the Department of Defense. To do this, he turned to the so-called Planning, Programming, and Budgeting System (PPBS), a budgeting system and suite of analytical techniques developed by the RAND Corporation.[1]

Zero-Based Budgeting and Management by Objectives (MBO) replaced PPBS as the programs *du jour* of the 1970s; and the 1980s saw the rise of productivity improvement and quality management. In 1988, a President's Quality Award was established. The new program was closely aligned with the Malcolm Baldrige National Quality Award, and focused on customer-driven quality, continuous improvement and learning, and employee participation and development, among a host of criteria. As you will see later in this chapter, things changed again in the early 1990s.

Government Performance and Results Act (GPRA)   Time certainly does fly. It's been over a decade since former President Bill Clinton signed into law the Government Performance and Results Act (GPRA) on August 3, 1993. You talk about a noble cause, the GPRA sought to affect a fundamental transformation in the way government was managed by placing increased emphasis on what was being accomplished as opposed to what was being spent. The act required that federally-funded agencies develop and implement an accountability system based on performance measurement, including setting goals and objectives and measuring progress toward achieving them.

Once President Clinton assumed control of the Oval Office in 1993, he was eager to leverage the new focus on quality with the performance improvement ethic he championed during his tenure as Arkansas governor in the 1980s. In March 1993, he appointed Vice President Al Gore to head a six-month study on what had to be done to further improve government performance. "Creating a Government that Works Better and Costs Less" was the resulting report that eventually led to the development of the National Partnership for Reinventing Government.

This leads us to August 1993 and the signing of the GPRA. Under the act, all federal agencies are required to develop mission statements, overall outcome-related goals, internal performance goals and objectives, and measures to be used to evaluate progress toward those goals and objectives.[2]

The GPRA was not the only performance-related legislation passed during the early- and mid-nineties. There was the Government Reform Act of 1994 as well as the Information Technology Management Reform Act of 1996. They required federal agencies to strategically plan how they would deliver high-quality goods and services to their customers, and specifically measure their programs' performance in meeting those commitments.

GPRA has received mixed reviews since its enactment, and it is difficult to assess whether the goals originally espoused in the Act are being consistently achieved. However, some findings have suggested very positive outcomes resulting from GPRA, including: the development of consistent mission statements, communication of strong departmental commitment, clearly stated performance objectives and accountability, and the placement of high value on customer service.[3]

The President's Management Agenda (PMA)   In 2002, President George W. Bush introduced the President's Management Agenda (PMA). This inspirational, yet practical, document is consistent with the aims found in the GPRA and benefits from the highest-level support of the Oval Office. In his introduction to the text, President Bush notes, ". . . what matters most is performance and results. In the long-term, there are few items more urgent than ensuring that the federal government is well-run and results-oriented."[4]

The PMA suggests that government reform should be guided by three principles: a citizen-centered rather than bureaucracy-centered focus, an orientation towards results, and a move towards becoming market-based, actively promoting rather than stifling innovation through competition. These principles would be brought to life through five government-wide strategic initiatives: Strategic Management of Human Capital, Competitive Sourcing, Improved Financial Performance, Expanded Electronic Government, and Budget and Performance Integration.

Many Balanced Scorecard adopting organizations will utilize the easy to grasp traffic light metaphor: green equals good, yellow equates to caution, and red signals that improvement is necessary. The PMA also uses this method of scoring for each department of the federal government. If you're interested in following along from home, you can find the most current results posted at www.results.gov.

State and Local Government Performance Measurement Efforts   Results-based management certainly isn't limited to the federal sector. With increasing momentum, this movement is finding its way into state and local government as well. Studies suggest that 34% of counties with populations of over 50,000 and 38% of cities with populations of over 25,000 use some type of performance measurement system.[5] State and local governments that voluntarily embark on performance measurement systems are probably just staying slightly ahead of the curve. Many experts believe that the Government Accounting Standards Board (GASB) will soon require these jurisdictions to provide "service efforts and accomplishments" that are tantamount to performance measures.

Perhaps the best-known example of Balanced Scorecard use in the public sector comes from a local government organization. The City of Charlotte, North Carolina, was an early adopter of the Balanced Scorecard system and has been using the tool for well over a decade. Its inspiring success story was featured in the *First Edition* of this book, and I'm very pleased to include an update on their progress in Chapter 12 of this edition.

Measuring Performance in Nonprofit Organizations

There are over 1.5 million nonprofit organizations registered with the Internal Revenue Service here in the United States, and they are growing! Revenues have soared from $1.4 trillion to over $2.1 trillion during the past five years, and during the same period, nonprofit assets have risen from just over $2 trillion to $4.1 trillion, a 95% increase.[6] In 2004, nonprofits—including public charities, private foundations, and all others—represented 8.3% of the wages and salaries paid in the United States. Approximately 29% of Americans over the age of 16 volunteered through or for an organization in 2005.[7] Upon reading these statistics, perhaps you will be, as I was, quite surprised. However, when you pause to reflect on this sector for a moment, you realize just how immense and broad it is. Nonprofit organizations touch every aspect of our modern societies, although typically, "charity" organizations come to mind first. In fact, so-called charity organizations are but one of a host of diverse players in the nonprofit space. Also included under the moniker "nonprofit" are religious organizations, social service agencies, some healthcare organizations, membership-based associations, educational establishments, arts and culture enterprises, and many others. While each serves a different constituency, what they do have in common is the trait of being mission-based.

Summing up the vital work performed by organizations in this sector is difficult to do in a few sentences. Fortunately, in their book *High Performance Nonprofit Organizations,* Christine Letts, William Ryan, and Allen Grossman provide this very compelling synthesis: "The nonprofit sector is filled with great ideas and thoughtful, caring people. In many ways, it represents our collective best inclinations: generosity, inclusivity, and determined optimism. The nonprofit sector attempts to bridge the many gaps in our society by bringing people together, proposing alternatives, advocating for change, and implementing remedies . . . As one of the underpinnings of American Society, the nonprofit sector has built an enduring legacy of community and service."[8] Well said indeed!

Nonprofit agencies have been measuring their performance for many years. Here is a summary of areas typically addressed by performance measurement:[9]

- *Financial accountability.* The original focus of nonprofit measurement was on documenting how funds were spent. "Standards of Accounting and Financial Reporting for Voluntary Health and Welfare Organizations" provided early guidelines. Demonstrating fiscal stewardship remains a principle tenet of nonprofit measurement efforts to this day.

- *Program products or outputs.* This category represents the classic measurement efforts of most nonprofit and government organizations— counting the number of products or services delivered and the number of people served.

- *Adherence to standards of quality in service delivery.* Concerns with service delivery practices led to the development of regional and national certification and accreditation groups. These agencies ensured consistent and quality delivery of products and services.

- *Participant-related measures.* The seeds of this measurement movement can be traced back to the 1980s when funders began requiring assurances that those most in need were indeed being served. Nonprofits responded by measuring client demographics and status prior to service.

- *Key performance indicators.* Often referred to in abbreviated terms as "KPIs," this category can serve as a repository for all areas of measurement. Originally, key performance indicators were mainly comprised of ratios among various categories of performance.

- *Client satisfaction.* Measuring the satisfaction of clients served began to gain prominence in the late 1980s. Among the determinants of satisfaction that have been measured are: timeliness of the service, accessibility, and overall satisfaction.

The increasing interest in measurement among nonprofits is very encouraging, particularly the adoption of these techniques by organizations historically allergic to such interventions. For example, many academic institutions have long been reluctant to measure and report performance. Fortunately, the rising tide that is performance measurement is capturing this group in its wake as evidenced by a recent announcement from The National Association of State Universities and Land-Grant Colleges and the American Association of Colleges and Universities. They are designing a template for college Web sites that, for those who choose to use it, show in standard format: details about admission rates; costs and graduation rates to make comparisons simple; results from surveys of students designed to measure satisfaction and engagement; and results of tests given to a representative sample of students to gauge not how smart they were when they arrived, but how much they learned about writing, analysis, and problem-solving between freshman and senior years.[10]

Former classics professor Robert Connor, now head of the Teagle Foundation that is helping finance the effort, says: "A year ago, or even six months ago, the idea of greater accountability had little traction in higher education. The status quo was just fine. Now a consensus seems to be emerging that colleges and universities need to provide more information about the outcomes."[11] Lawrence Summers, Harvard University's former President, is also an enthusiast of the movement. He believes these measures are crucial to self-improvement: "Unless you have some way of noticing when you are doing a better job of educating, you're not likely to do a better job of educating."[12]

The measurement efforts of higher education, and the historical methods chronicled above are noble in cause, and reflect a sincere desire to improve performance. However, most nonprofits would agree that measurement is not an area of real competence, and frankly, is not done frequently enough to demonstrate real results. In the next section, we'll contemplate why this may be the case.

Nonprofits Struggle to Invest in Organizational Capacity   In their annual reports, many nonprofits feature pie charts depicting the allocation of funds received during the previous year. From which slice of that pie do you suppose most nonprofit executives derive the bulk of their satisfaction? Usually, it's the tiny sliver that displays what proportion of their funds went to "administration" or "overhead." Those categories are anathema to any self-respecting nonprofit executive director. At least that's the standard thinking. It's little wonder they feel this way when you consider the tremendous pressure exerted by influential donors who proclaim they won't tolerate any of their largess going to fund overhead. Rhonda Pherigo is the Director of Consulting Services at the Center for Nonprofit Management in Dallas, Texas. The Center's mission is to improve the management effectiveness of the nonprofit sector as it seeks to enhance the quality of life of its community. Rhonda explains the struggle for building capacity: "There is a tendency for private foundations to fund the heartstring stories, and we don't have a case like that. We help organizations improve their ability to do good."[13]

Interestingly, in the for-profit world, organizational capacity is a prominent driving force in the race for competitive success. It's not the products and services corporations sell that ultimately determine their achievements, but their ability to constantly innovate, cleverly market, and continuously improve their offerings. In other words, it's their commitment to investing in capacity. Nonprofits appear to view this investment choice as a zero-sum game in which anything invested in capacity is considered lost to direct service.[14] Ironically, that thinking may lead to decreased service delivery and, ultimately, reduced funding. Jeffrey Bradach, a consultant to nonprofits sums it up nicely: "Generally, they (nonprofits) are vastly undercapitalized, understaffed, and poorly managed. Most nonprofits use their limited resources to market themselves to the same donors and foundations year after year. There's little if any investment in organizational infrastructure or staff development. Compared to the for-profit sector, the nonprofit world is back in the late 1970s and early 1980s, when Japan was beating up on American businesses . . . It's only beginning to understand that if you want good outcomes, you have to invest in building strong organizations."[15]

In defense of nonprofits, what has been absent is a framework that possesses the capability of demonstrating that investments in capacity have a direct and positive impact on service delivery and, ultimately, the ability of the agency to achieve its vision. The Balanced Scorecard is just such a framework. Its four perspectives allow any organization to cogently display how their outlay in capacity, in the form of employee training or research and development of best practices for example, yield tangible benefits for customers and stakeholders.

ADAPTING THE BALANCED SCORECARD

The chapter thus far has given you a look through the window of performance measurement in both the public and nonprofit sectors. Clearly, both sectors have experienced the benefit of measurement and, with varying levels of effort and success, have embarked on measurement initiatives. What has been lacking, however, is the answer to this seemingly simple question: "Is what we're doing (both in the public and nonprofit sectors) making a difference? Is anyone better off as a result of our efforts?" To answer this question, executives, managers, and employees alike need to view performance from a broader perspective. They require a system that not only counts the inputs and outputs of the system, but one that provides an opportunity to assess progress in reaching the organization's true mission.

The Balanced Scorecard has risen to the performance measurement challenge of the private sector and is equally well-equipped to facilitate a rapid and dramatic transition of twenty-first-century nonprofit and public organizations. Exhibit 2.1 displays the Balanced Scorecard model that is applicable to public and nonprofit enterprises. We can use this diagram to differentiate between private and public and nonprofit sector use of the Scorecard.

Mission Moves to the Top of the Balanced Scorecard

In the for-profit Balanced Scorecard model, all the measures appearing on the Scorecard should lead to improved bottom-line performance. Improving shareholder value is the endgame for profit-seeking enterprises and they

Exhibit 2.1   Balanced Scorecard for the Public and Nonprofit Sectors

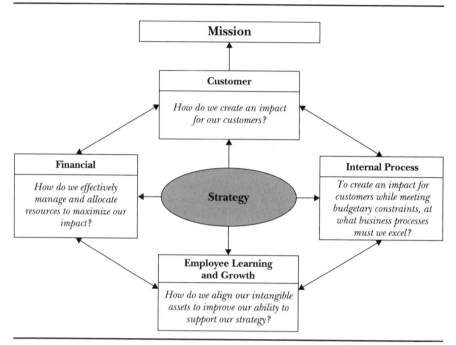

are accountable to their financial stakeholders to do just that. Not so in either the public or nonprofit organization.

While you are accountable for the efficient allocation of funds (a topic we'll examine more closely in the financial perspective), that is not your ultimate aspiration. You exist to serve a higher purpose (e.g., to reduce the incidence of HIV, to bring classical music to your community, or to increase public safety). You may be hesitant to include such lofty objectives on your Balanced Scorecard claiming, "We don't have total control over our mission," or "we can't influence the outcomes." However, it is only through measurement that you are able to claim any real difference in the lives or circumstances of your constituents.

Consider the case of the American Heart Association whose mission is "building healthier lives, free of cardiovascular diseases and stroke." Historically, this Dallas-based organization with over $650 million in annual revenue measured items such as fundraising efforts or the number of people reached. Incremental improvements were registered but CEO M. Cass Wheeler opted to take a bolder stance. They put in place one grand "impact" or mission goal: "To reduce coronary heart disease, stroke, and key risk factors by 25% by 2010." What makes this goal all the more remarkable is that it encompasses the entire U.S. population, not a subset over which the association can exert particular influence. They can't control what you or I drink, what we eat, or how often we exercise. But that hasn't stopped them from putting a number on their mission and aligning all of their people and efforts towards it.[16]

Of course, The American Heart Association won't achieve their mission overnight, nor will you—only periodic progress may be noticed. This is precisely why the other perspectives of the Balanced Scorecard are so vital. Monitoring performance, and learning from the results, in the Customer, Internal Process, Employee Learning and Growth, and Financial perspectives will provide you with the short- to medium-term information you require to guide you ever closer to achievement of the mission.[17] Oh, and by the way, as of 2005, death rates of coronary heart disease declined by 12.7% and those of stroke were down by 9.1%. Could it be the power of measurement at work?

Strategy Remains at the Core of the Balanced Scorecard

Strategy remains at the core of the Scorecard system, regardless of whether it's a local theater company, city government, Fortune 500 company, or a mom-and-pop store. It's the game plan for success, the blueprint that must inform your measurement efforts. Nonprofit and government organizations often have a difficult time cultivating a clear and concise strategy. While many attempt to develop statements of strategy, they amount to little more than detailed lists of programs and initiatives used to secure dollars from funding bodies. Many so-called strategy documents are upwards of 50 pages.

We'll break down the topic of strategy and strategic planning in Chapter 6. For now, suffice to say that strategy is about those broad priorities you plan to pursue in order to achieve your mission. The priorities must be consistent with your unique situation and fit one another in an effort to respond effectively to your challenges and opportunities. Once you've developed your strategy, the Balanced Scorecard serves as the device for effective translation and implementation.

Customer Perspective is Elevated

A clear distinction between private versus nonprofit and public sector Balanced Scorecards is drawn as a result of placing mission at the top of the framework. Flowing from the mission is a view of the organization's customers, not financial stakeholders. Achieving a mission does not equate to fiscal responsibility and stewardship, instead, the organization must determine whom it aims to serve and how their requirements can best be met. Rick Pagsibigan is the Chief Strategy Officer at the Red Cross of Philadelphia. When developing their Balanced Scorecard, placing the Customer Perspective at the top of the model was a logical choice. Pagsibigan explains, "We put the Customer Perspective at the top. The message is that anything and everything we do (financials, revenues, etc.) is there to support our customers."[18]

In the profit-seeking world, companies are accountable to their capital providers (shareholders) for results, and they monitor this accountability through the results attained in the Financial Perspective of the Scorecard. Again, this is not the case in the nonprofit and public sectors. Here, the focus is on customers and serving their needs in order to accomplish the mission. But the question "Who is the customer?" is one of the most perplexing issues that nonprofit and government Scorecard adopters face. In these sectors, different groups design the service, pay for the service, and ultimately benefit from the service. This web of relationships makes determining the customer a formidable challenge. Establishing the real customer in many ways depends on your perspective. In the public sector, the legislative body that provides funding is a logical choice as is the group you serve. However, think about that group you "serve." Would law enforcement agencies consider the criminals they arrest their customers? You could probably make a case for that. Conversely, many would argue that constituents are the ultimate beneficiaries of policing activities and are therefore the real customers.

Grappling with and answering this vexing question may represent one of the most significant benefits you'll derive from implementing the Balanced Scorecard. Many public sector and nonprofit agencies have failed to invest the intellectual rigor and discipline necessary to tackle this issue head-on and as a result, despite their dedicated effort and hard work, have created workplaces in which they attempt to serve several masters simultaneously, thereby satisfying no one and leaving a trail of frustrated and confused employees in their wake. Once you make *a* choice, entirely new worlds of possibilities open up to you: resource allocation decisions become clearer, human capital quandaries gain new focus, and the entire organization can rally around a united voice of serving *the* customer. We'll return to this provocative question in Chapter 7 and I'll offer two questions that will help you begin your deliberations.

No Balanced Scorecard Is Complete without a Financial Perspective

No organization, regardless of its status, can successfully operate and meet customer requirements without financial resources. Financial measures in the public and nonprofit sector Scorecard model can best be seen as either enablers of customer success or constraints within which the group must operate. Many will argue, with merit, that it's difficult to put a financial price on the work they perform. Consider a nonprofit agency that provides prenatal care to disadvantaged expectant mothers. Its prized outcome is the birth of a healthy baby, which is as far from the world of dollars and cents as you can stray. Nonetheless, the agency must persuade occasionally reluctant managers that financial measures aren't inconsistent with quality service delivery and achieving the mission. In fact, when services are performed at least cost, or with great efficiency, the program will likely attract more attention and warrant even greater investment from funders. A win for everyone.

Identifying Internal Processes That Drive Value for Customers

When developing objectives and measures for this perspective, we ask our-selves, "at what business processes must we excel to create an impact for customers while meeting budgetary constraints?" Every organization from the smallest local service agency to the largest departments of the federal government will have documented processes for establishing their goals. Small organizations may have dozens, while larger entities may have proc-esses numbering in the hundreds.

The key to Balanced Scorecard success lies in selecting and measuring just those processes that lead to improved outcomes for customers, and ultimately allow you to work towards your mission. The processes you choose to focus on will flow directly from the objectives and measures chosen in the Customer Perspective, and in fact signal a major transition in the model from "what" to "how." The job of the Customer Perspective is to determine what customers expect or demand and what it is we'll do to create a positive impact for them. In the Internal Process Perspective, our empha-sis shifts to how we as an organization can create that impact. It's not uncommon for the Internal Processes Perspective to house the greatest number of objectives and measures on the Balanced Scorecard.

Employee Learning and Growth Perspective Provides the Foundation for a Well-Constructed Balanced Scorecard

Operating as mission-based organizations, nonprofit and public-sector agen-cies rely heavily on the skills, dedication, and alignment of their staff to achieve their socially important goals. Employees and organizational infra-structure represent the thread that weaves through the rest of the Balanced Scorecard. Success in driving process improvements, operating in a fiscally responsible way, and meeting the needs of your customers depends largely on the ability of employees and the tools they use in support of your mission.

As crucial as the objectives and measures of the Employee Learning and Growth Perspective are, they're often overlooked. Considered "soft stuff" or "pure overhead," many organizations ignore these base ingredients to building a successful Balanced Scorecard at their own peril. Motivated employees with the right mix of skills and tools operating in an organiza-tional climate designed for sustaining improvements are the key ingredients in driving process improvements, working within financial limitations, and ultimately driving customer and mission success.

Three distinct areas of "capital," representing vital intangible assets, must be captured in this perspective. The first is human capital, which chal-lenges you to consider your current inventory of skills in the context of your mission and strategy. Do your employees have the skills they require to execute your strategy? The second area of capital is the flow of information or what is termed "information capital." Do employees have the tools and information they require to make effective decisions that impact customer outcomes? Finally, the organizational climate should be addressed under the label organizational capital. Culture and climate are frequently included in Balanced Scorecards under this heading.

IMPORTANCE OF CAUSE AND EFFECT

Which would you find easier to remember, a passage from the novel you're currently reading or a paragraph from this book? I'm pretty sure I can guess how you answered that question—and don't worry, you didn't hurt my feelings. Fortunately for my ego, I know why the novel is easier to remember, and I'm sure you do as well: It's a story. There is nothing like a good story, whether it's the latest bestselling novel or blockbuster movie, to draw us in and capture our full attention. Now a second question for you: Can an organizational model accomplish the same results? I believe the answer is yes. A good organizational model is really just a story that explains how the organization works. The best-told stories help every employee see what the organization is trying to accomplish and how they fit into that context.[19] But how do you tell your strategic story? Through the objectives on the Strategy Map and, later, the measures on the Balanced Scorecard.

A powerful story is composed of a number of elements: an intriguing plot, interesting characters, and stimulating dialog, to name but a few. If any of these elements is missing from the story, the whole suffers. Now think for a moment about your organization and how you describe success. You could, for example, focus on customer satisfaction, adherence to budget, and quality, but what is missing? What ultimately drives success in any enterprise? Employees. If you don't include employees in your story, a hole develops. And it isn't just employees. You could focus on skills, training, and dozens of other employee-related attributes, but if you then choose to ignore how these effect outcomes for your customer, you've again failed to tell a coherent story. All of your organization's constituents must be present in your system if you hope to create a captivating story that draws in all of your stakeholders.

A well-constructed Strategy Map and Balanced Scorecard should describe how our organization works and what is critical to your success through a series of interconnected objectives (on the Map) and measures (on the Scorecard) running through the four perspectives. Rather than focusing exclusively on any one element of success, you're painting a full canvas of what is necessary to succeed. Your story should include outcomes for customers, the processes at which you must excel, the enabling infrastructure required, and the financial resources necessary to sustain your service delivery. Each element represents a vital link in the powerful chain of cause-and-effect relationships that run through the Strategy Map and Scorecard.

Exhibit 2.2 provides an excerpt of the performing arts organization's Strategy Map from Chapter 1. We can use it to demonstrate the cause and effect linkages that help bring strategy to life. Beginning at the top, in the

Exhibit 2.2   Telling Your Strategic Story through Cause-and-Effect Linkages

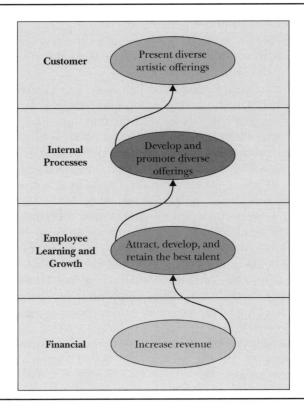

Customer Perspective, we see the objective "Present diverse artistic offerings." But how do you present diverse artistic offerings sure to wow your patrons and ensuring their return again and again? At what processes must you excel? You hypothesize that presenting diverse artistic offerings is a function of the number of new and diverse performances you stage. As a result, you decide to add the objective, "Develop and promote diverse offerings" in your Internal Process Perspective. After all, before the audience can enjoy these performances, they must be developed and promoted. Now we move to the Employee Learning and Growth Perspective. What—from an employee perspective—will allow you to stage diverse performances? You believe that in order to develop and stage world-class performances, you need the very best talent, and therefore you add the objective, "Attract, develop, and retain the best talent." Finally, you realize that you live in a world of budgetary constraints and won't be able to achieve any of your objectives unless you run a tight financial ship. More donations would be tremendously helpful, so you add "Increase revenue" as an objective in the Financial Perspective. You've now created a series of linked objectives that run through the Map, telling your strategic story.

The linkage of measures throughout the Strategy Map is constructed with a series of "if-then" statements: *If* we increase our revenue, *then* we'll have the resources to acquire the very best talent available. *If* we attract the best talent, *then* we'll have the means necessary to develop and promote diverse offerings. *If* we develop and promote more diverse offerings, *then* we'll be able to present them to the public.

Developing tight cause-and-effect linkages is a challenge for any organization. Going through the mental gymnastics required to build a seamless integration of objectives is hard and draining work. The degree of difficulty is compounded in the nonprofit and public sectors by the myriad influences surrounding your work. Nevertheless, I encourage you to attempt this task when developing your Strategy Map. Once you've made an initial set of hypotheses about your performance, you're in a great position to begin learning which levers really drive your success.

For many Scorecard-adopting organizations, the greatest benefit has not been a ready supply of answers to all that ails their agencies but rather, the provocative questions that arise from the review of results. Questions lead to discussion, discussions lead to spirited debate, debate contributes to insight, and insights often lead to knowledge and breakthroughs. So while creating a Balanced Scorecard may not supply all the answers, I can guarantee you'll be generating better questions. And as the great management guru Peter Drucker reminds us, "The most common source of mistakes in management decisions is the emphasis on finding the right answer rather than the right question."[20]

BENEFITS OF USING A BALANCED SCORECARD

Many organizations struggle with performance measurement and management. In fact, 80% of respondents in one study reported making changes in their performance management system during the last three years. The same study reported that for 33% of those organizations, the change was described as a "major overhaul."[21] The Balanced Scorecard has emerged as a proven tool in the battle to provide meaningful performance information. Organizations around the globe are taking notice and turning to the Balanced Scorecard. In the United States, about 60% of the Fortune 1000 are using the Balanced Scorecard.[22]

Of course, the Scorecard isn't just for large corporations. Small and medium-sized enterprises have embraced the concept as well. All cite the Scorecard's elegant simplicity, focus on strategy, and the ability to drive alignment as key benefits of the framework. What about nonprofit and government agencies? What benefits might they expect from investing in the Scorecard? In the sections which follow are some of the most commonly mentioned benefits users from your sectors have received.

Demonstrate Accountability and Generate Results

President George W. Bush has said that "Government likes to begin things—to declare grand new programs and causes. But good beginnings are not the measure of success. What matters in the end is completion. Performance. Results. Not just making promises, but making good on promises."[23]

The stakes, both in the public and nonprofit arenas, are high. For example, charitable donations by individuals grew by 50%, from $110 billion in 1990 to $164 billion in 2001. This new philanthropy demands results. The new philanthropists attach a lot of strings. Recipients are often required to meet milestone goals, to invite foundation members onto their boards, and to produce measurable results—or risk losing their funding.[24] Never before have results mattered so much to government and nonprofit organizations.

In tandem with the cry for results is the demand for accountability which has become a near slogan in all three sectors of the economy: private, public, and nonprofit. The accountability alarm was sounded at the turn of the twenty-first century with the collapse of Enron and a number of other high-profile corporate collapses all triggered by jaw-dropping accounts of executive malfeasance. Sadly, government and nonprofit organizations have not been immune to the spate of headline-grabbing scandals plaguing the economy. In 2002, the former Chief Executive Officer (CEO) of the United Way of the National Capital Area (UWNCA), Oral Suer, was charged with defrauding the charity out of almost $500,000 in the form of unreimbursed advances, questionable vacation and sick-leave payments, and excess deferred pay. In May 2004 he was sentenced to 27 months in prison.[25]

The task of monitoring results and accountability has created a virtual industry of its own, with many organizations and Web sites setup to track your local government's or favorite nonprofit's performance.[26] Rick Pagsibigan of the Philadelphia Red Cross sums up the current environment very nicely: "It used to be that people gave because it felt good, now they give to feel good, and look at their return on investment. To show them the outcomes we first have to measure."[27] That's where the Balanced Scorecard comes in. To be accountable and demonstrate results, you need to accurately measure the true performance of your organization. Simply counting people served or dollars spent won't cut it in today's environment. You need to demonstrate advancement on the high-level, mission-based objectives that your constituents are requiring you to provide. The Balanced Scorecard with its focus on mission and strategy and broad view of performance allows you to do just that. Former New York City Mayor Rudy Giuliani understands the bond between measurement and accountability. He writes in his book *Leadership* that "objective, measurable indicators of success allow governments to be accountable, and I relentlessly pursued that idea."[28] The time has clearly passed when constituents, donors, and funders took for granted the best intentions of government and nonprofits. To keep the checkbooks from slamming shut and the citizens from storming your gates, you must demonstrate results and accountability.

Improving Performance Against Your Mission

Effective and efficient execution of an agency's mission is what taxpayers pay for and why donors and funders continue to support nonprofits. To continue generating the goodwill of citizens and volunteers alike, the first priority for any public sector or nonprofit organization must be to improve performance against the stated mission. Performance measurement has proven to be a powerfully effective tool in doing just that, as the story of the Occupational Safety and Health Administration (OSHA) illustrates.

OSHA's principal aim is to ensure employee safety and health in the United States by working with employers and employees to create better working environments. The administration has over 2,000 employees and a budget of approximately $500 million. The OSHA agency Joseph Dear inherited in 1993 measured success primarily through counting the number of inspections conducted and fines imposed. In some circumstances, inspections and fines were an appropriate response but they were not the only, and sometimes not the most effective, way of advancing OSHA's mission. Their performance management transition began with a renewed commitment to their mission—to reduce the number of injuries, illnesses, and deaths in the workplace—and then continued with a grand leap beyond. Under Dear's leadership, OSHA called for the elimination of all preventable workplace ills in 10 years. Achieving this audacious objective was quite literally impossible but it sent a powerful signal that change was in the air and innovative thinking was required by every person at OSHA.

OSHA convened a change team to lead the transition and introduced a number of improvement efforts, including process redesign workshops in which new models of high-performance were created for field enforcement officers. This and a host of other initiatives yielded tangible benefits, and perhaps more importantly, those benefits were derived relatively quickly. For example, at every one of OSHA's field offices, compliance officers were given a menu of improvement opportunities and tasked with choosing the one they felt was most urgently needed in their vicinity. Once they made a choice, they committed themselves to achieving performance goals within only eight weeks. At OSHA's Parsippany, New Jersey office, response time to employee complaints of serious hazards was cut in half after only eight weeks. Rollout of the entire improvement effort at OSHA took almost three years during which there was a leadership change. Because the program had gained employee support, sustained momentum, and was demonstrating results, OSHA was able to overcome this often turbulent event and achieve its goals.[29]

Attract Scarce Resources (Funding and Employees)

Imagine the unenviable task faced by former California Governor Gray Davis in 2002. He had to inform an already fuming populace of the state's budget deficit for the upcoming fiscal year. The final tally? A whopping $34.8 billion dollars![30] It's hard to fathom a number of that magnitude, but for the thousands of agencies counting on money from Sacramento, the pain was all too real. Davis was soon swept unceremoniously out of office in favor of "The Terminator" Arnold Schwarzenegger.

Competition for money and talent has never been more demanding. In the nonprofit sector, the race for donor dollars is increasingly intense, with competition coming from some very unconventional places. The next time you're online, try typing "e-panhandling" into the search box on Google. You'll find that it has its own category and there are scads of Web sites exclusively dedicated to soliciting personal handouts. My favorite is "Make me richer than Bill Gates." At a buck a pop, this person is going to be waiting a while!

While the Balanced Scorecard may not make your organization richer than Bill Gates, it can help you attract scarce resources. By developing a Balanced Scorecard, reporting progress on achieving your strategic objectives, and proving your efficiency and effectiveness, you can ensure the migration of scarce resources to your organization, department, or agency. As an example, The Broad Foundation of Los Angeles, California awarded a $195,000 grant to Detroit Public Schools District. Part of the rationale for the behest was the fact that Detroit Public Schools will be using the Balanced Scorecard. "The Detroit Public Schools are among the first K-12 districts to adopt the Balanced Scorecard process," said Geri Markley, Executive Director, Office of Continuous Improvement. "The Scorecard provides a balanced view of district-wide performance from four perspectives: students, funders, internal systems, and employees."[31]

Create a Focus on Strategy

Translating your strategy into action is the true purpose of the Balanced Scorecard. While many organizations measure, they frequently lose sight of the fact that measurement should be about achieving strategy, not "counting widgets." Bill Ryan, a consultant to nonprofit organizations and coauthor of *High Performance Nonprofit Organizations* offers this regarding this "measurement gap": "People are measuring performance, financial performance, programmatic performance, certain narrow indicators of organizational performance—maybe board diversity or composition for instance—they're measuring lots of different aspects of performance at the behest of lots of different stakeholders—usually multiple funders. And yet none of those performance measurement systems actually correspond to their own values, their own objectives, their own really fundamental goals and social missions . . . So something like a Balanced Scorecard can help people integrate all those fragmented performance measurement systems into something coherent, that's aligned with their real fundamental purpose."[32]

Simply put, the Balanced Scorecard allows you to focus on what really matters, the few critical drivers of success that power your strategy and lead to the achievement of your mission. The Safer Foundation is a Chicago-based organization that assists ex-offenders in becoming productive, law-abiding members of the community. Executive Director Diane Williams says using the Balanced Scorecard "allows us to focus on our strategy."[33] To achieve demonstrated results, attract resources, and prove your accountability, you absolutely must keep your eyes on your strategy at all times.

Produce Information, Not Data

Have you ever noticed that there are unintended consequences by every so-called innovation? Consider the great boon of technology. In the 1950s, pundits suggested that the proliferation of labor-saving devices would mean shorter work weeks and more time for leisure. Well, technology has definitely improved productivity but we're working longer and harder than ever.

Technology has also produced a Grand Canyon-sized gap between data and information. We're awash in data these days. Every office I go into features binder-filled walls that seem to be creeping ever closer to the inhabitants. Those same binders are chock full of data, but they tend to be lacking in a supply of real information. Healthcare consultant James Lifton has seen the problem first hand: "What we're really talking about is information . . . Voluntary trustees can get a lot of data and not understand what they mean or not have time to review them all. I've seen boards get a three-ring binder or a large packet, and sometimes they don't know what to make of it, or they're unwilling or unable to take the time to go through it."[34] The Balanced Scorecard resides exclusively in the information domain. It does so by measuring only the critical few drivers of organizational success. A Balanced Scorecard that contains 50 or 60 measures probably has abundant data, but I'll take a Scorecard that has 10 or 12 measures for real information value.

Self-Preservation

Did you know that nearly half of all federal employees perform tasks that are readily available in the commercial marketplace?[35] It's true—they perform activities such as data collection, administrative support, and payroll services. Having your function outsourced to a third-party (private sector) provider is definitely an option these days, as taxpayers and funders continue to scrutinize how their dollars are being spent and what results are coming of those investments. For those of you in the public sector, there is even scrutiny from within! In 2002, the Office of Management and Budget (OMB) bid out the process of printing the federal budget for the first time. Since the 1860s, Congress had mandated that all executive branch agencies give their printing business to the Government Printing Office (GPO). OMB director Mitch Daniels felt a monopoly of over 140 years was enough. In the end, the GPO won the work, but their fee was reduced from $505,000 to $387,000.[36] Amazing what a little competition will do.

The Balanced Scorecard allows you to demonstrate quality results at efficient prices. That is, if you're not afraid to cast a bright light on your current processes. The Scorecard also helps you do that by pinpointing the vital few processes that really drive customer outcomes.

Drive Change

Charles Darwin once noted that "the survivors of any species are not necessarily the strongest. And they are not necessarily the most intelligent. They are those who are most responsive to change." This quote can be aptly applied to any modern organization as well. Only the change-ready survive! Measurements from a Balanced Scorecard can help drive the change you need to meet your desired outcomes. Shelley Metzenbaum, the Director of the Performance Management Project at the Kennedy School of Government at Harvard University, tells the story of the Charles River in Massachusetts. The goal of the "Clean Charles 2005" initiative was to make the Charles River swimmable in 10 years. In just five years, the river went from being swimmable a mere 19% of the time to 65% of the time. And in April 2006, the lower Charles River, for the second consecutive year, achieved its highest-ever grade from the EPA—a B+, as efforts to restore the river to health continue to progress.[37] Metzenbaum notes it was a monthly measurement system, establishing water quality every few miles along the river, that provided the information needed to drive the change.[38]

Inspire Trust

I've already discussed how the Balanced Scorecard can help you demonstrate accountability and attract scarce resources to your organization. The driver of both outcomes is enhanced trust. Trust from the community, from your funders, and from your employees. The benefits of increased levels of trust are by no means limited to the intangible. Research has demonstrated that "those who have high confidence in charities as well as believe in their honesty and ethics give an average annual contribution of about $1,800. This is about 50% greater than the amount given by those sharing neither opinion, who average just over $1,200 in annual household contributions to charity, once again underscoring the strong connection between public trust and giving."[39]

These are just a sampling of the many benefits conferred by the application of a Balanced Scorecard. You'll also see that creative links from the Scorecard to your key management processes such as budgeting and planning will make your entire organization even stronger. And using the Balanced Scorecard to drive the agenda of your management meetings will ignite learning in a way you've never experienced. However, as with most things we encounter in life, the more effort and focus you put into the Balanced Scorecard the more you'll get out of it.

NOTES

1. Andrea Gabor, *The Capitalist Philosophers* (New York: Times Business, 2000), p. 143.

2. Carl G. Thor, "The Evolution of Performance Measurement in Government," *Journal of Cost Management,* May/June 2000.

3. Ron Carlson, "A Look at GPRA Practices: How Far Have We Traveled?" *The Public Manager,* Fall 2000, pp. 25–29.

4. George W. Bush, "The President's Management Agenda," www .whitehouse.gov/omb/budget/fy2002/mgmt.pdf

5. Evan Berman and Xiao Hu Wang, "Performance Measurement in U.S. Counties: Capacity for Reform," *Public Administration Review*, September/October 2000.

6. Bill Birchard, "Nonprofits by the Numbers," *CFO Magazine*, July 2005. Article referenced at www.cfo.com

7. From the National Center for Charitable Statistics, www.nccs .urban.org

8. Christine W. Letts, William P. Ryan, and Allen Grossman, *High Performance Nonprofit Organizations* (New York: John Wiley & Sons, 1999), p. 1.

9. Margaret C. Plantz, Martha Taylor Greenway, and Michael Hendricks, "Outcome Measurement: Showing Results in the Nonprofit Sector," *New Directions for Evaluation*, Fall 1997.

10. David Wessel, "Accountability 101: State Colleges Prepare to Measure Their Own Performance," *Wall Street Journal*, August 9, 2007, p. A2.

11. Ibid.

12. Ibid.

13. Interview with Rhonda Pherigo, July 23, 2002.

14. Christine W. Letts, William P. Ryan, and Allen Grossman, *High Performance Nonprofit Organizations* (New York: John Wiley & Sons, 1999), p. 32.

15. John A. Byrne, "The New Face of Philanthropy," *Business Week*, December 2, 2002, pp 82–94.

16. Bill Birchard, "Nonprofits by the Numbers," *CFO Magazine*, July 2005. Article referenced at www.cfo.com

17. Robert S. Kaplan, "The Balanced Scorecard and Nonprofit Organizations," *Balanced Scorecard Report*, November-December, 2002, pp. 1–4.

18. Interview with Rick Pagsibigan, September 19, 2002.

19. Joan Magretta, "Why Business Models Matter," *Harvard Business Review*, May 2002, pp. 86–92.

20. Bob Frost, *Crafting Strategy*, (Dallas, TX: Measurement International, 2000), p. 12.

21. Mark L. Frigo, "The State of Strategic Performance Measurement: The IMA 2001 Survey," *Balanced Scorecard Report*, November-December 2001, pp. 13–14.

22. Robert S. Kaplan and David P. Norton, "On Balance," *CFO Magazine*, February 2001, p. 74.

23. George W. Bush, "The President's Management Agenda," www.whitehouse.gov/omb/budget/fy2002/mgmt.pdf

24. John A. Byrne, "The New Face of Philanthropy," *Business Week*, December 2, 2002, pp 82–94.

25. Bill Birchard, "Nonprofits by the Numbers," *CFO Magazine*, July 2005. Article referenced at www.cfo.com

26. See for example www.guidestar.org or www.charitynavigator.com

27. Interview with Rick Pagsibigan, September 19, 2002.

28. Rudolph W. Giuliani, *Leadership* (New York: Hyperion, 2002).

29. Frank Ostroff, "Change Management in Government," *Harvard Business Review*, May 2006, pp. 141–147.

30. The *Wall Street Journal* online, "California's Gray Hole," December 20, 2002.

31. U.S. Newswire, "Detroit Public Schools Awarded Grant by The Broad Foundation," December 10, 2002.

32. Interview with Bill Ryan, September 17, 2002.

33. Interview with Diane Williams, October 3, 2002.

34. Michelle Bitoun, "Show Them the Data," *Trustee*, September, 2002, p. 18.

35. From "The President's Management Agenda" at www.whitehouse.gov/omb/budget/fy2002/mgmt.pdf. p. 17

36. George Will, "Why Privatization Will Work," *Washington Post*, December 22, 2002.

37. Clean Charles River Initiative—2006 Report, www.epa.gov/region1/charlesriver/2006.html

38. Presentation by Shelley Metzenbaum to the San Diego County Leadership Team, October 26, 2001.

39. Independent Sector, "Keeping the Faith: Confidence in Charitable Organizations in an Age of Security," 2002.

3

Before You Begin

Roadmap for Chapter 3   It was Christian Bovee who observed that "The method of the enterprising is to plan with audacity and execute with vigor." This chapter is devoted to the first half of Bovee's inspirational wisdom. Planning is crucial in virtually every initiative we undertake, whether it's building a house, writing a report, or developing a Balanced Scorecard. There are a number of elements of a task that must be considered long before any nails can be driven, pens lifted, or metrics debated and decided upon. In this chapter, we'll take a careful look at each of the building blocks of a successful Balanced Scorecard implementation.

The chapter begins by posing the question, "Why do we need the Balanced Scorecard?" It then challenges you to develop specific reasons for using the Scorecard in your organization. It'll then transition to the human element of the Balanced Scorecard, beginning with a review of the vital nature of executive sponsorship. Next, we'll take a close look at your Balanced Scorecard team, considering the size of the team, skills necessary, and roles and responsibilities of all members. Once you've determined your rationale and have gained support and established a team, you must decide where to build your first Scorecard. We'll consider this question and I'll provide a number of criteria to help you make this important decision. No initiative of this magnitude can be completed without the allocation of human and financial resources. We'll review each of these elements. The chapter concludes with a development plan for your Balanced Scorecard implementation.

DO YOU KNOW WHY YOU'RE DEVELOPING A BALANCED SCORECARD?

I'd like to begin this chapter with a cautionary tale illustrating the importance of clearly outlining to all stakeholders, especially staff, why you've decided to invest the resources necessary to develop a Balanced Scorecard. As you read it, I urge you to think about your own budding implementation and any other change initiatives you've launched in the past.

A couple of years back, I began a Scorecard implementation with a government organization under the sponsorship of their senior executive. To my absolute delight, he was downright inspirational in our initial meetings and training sessions with employees. He frequently repeated such refrains as, "the Balanced Scorecard is the single greatest priority of this organization this year," "my number one priority is the successful implementation of the Balanced Scorecard,," "I'm committing all the resources necessary to develop the Balanced Scorecard." Wonderful statements: inspirational, direct, and indicative of true sponsorship. But have you noticed what is missing? Not once did he address why the organization had determined the Balanced Scorecard was an appropriate tool at this moment. I suggested he insert the "why" message in all future correspondence but he hesitated for some reason.

Despite our best efforts, over time the implementation began to struggle and we rapidly began losing momentum. Eventually, I turned to that most reliable of corporate news sources—the grapevine—to find out what people were saying about the Balanced Scorecard. It turned out most employees were convinced that in the absence of a stated reason for the Balanced Scorecard, their boss was planning to use it as a tool for generating layoffs within the group. As a result, they were refusing to provide any support for the implementation. "Why lead ourselves to the chopping block?" was the defining sentiment among the rank and file. The executive sponsor was shocked by this news since he sincerely saw the Balanced Scorecard as a tool that could eventually lead to the attraction of new resources for the group. He attempted to re-engage, but the damage was done and we literally spent weeks thereafter communicating the true message of why the Balanced Scorecard was being implemented. It's a sad but true fact of the business world—in the absence of a motive for change, employees will generate one, and chances are it won't be the message you had in mind![1]

Understanding and Communicating the "Why" of the Balanced Scorecard

There are two fundamental issues at play here, both of which were ignored by the agency discussed in the preceding section. Number one is senior leadership's determination of why the Balanced Scorecard is the right tool for the organization at that juncture; what we'll refer to as the guiding rationale for developing a Scorecard system. Number two is clearly communicating that guiding rationale to employees, ensuring they understand it and will support it. Let's discuss each.

The Balanced Scorecard has proven to be remarkably effective since its inception over 17 years ago. It has been used by thousands of organizations to generate focus, alignment, and to execute their unique strategies. The question is, will it work for you? To answer that question you must first diagnose your organization and determine whether you have a specific issue the Scorecard can help you combat, one that is evident to everyone in the organization and the importance of which is universally acknowledged. Absent this "burning platform," the Balanced Scorecard is likely to be seen as yet another panacea grasped at by management in the vain hopes of altering the organization's veering course.

Exhibit 3.1 provides a number of possible reasons for launching a Balanced Scorecard program. While all these reasons are valid, you should not consider this a "pick and choose" exercise of selecting a rationale that sounds good to you. In order to realize real benefits from the Balanced

Exhibit 3.1   Rationale for the Balanced Scorecard

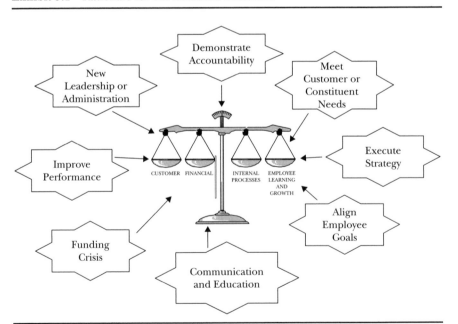

Adapted from *Balanced Scorecard Step-by-Step: Maximizing Performance and Maintaining Results,* by Paul R. Niven (John Wiley & Sons, 2002).

Scorecard, you must determine your specific justification for launching this implementation. The Michigan Department of Transportation described their motivation for using the Balanced Scorecard: "The Balanced Scorecard was selected as a tool to identify the commonalities of strategy, expand our focus and understanding of customer needs, and align systems and structures to meet customer needs."[2] All excellent reasons for launching a Scorecard effort. The City of North Bay, Ontario also felt the Scorecard would assist them in meeting the many challenges facing their organization. They described their principal objective in building a Scorecard this way: "There was an increased desire both politically and administratively for improved accountability."[3] This is an objective that will most likely motivate many public and nonprofit organizations.

Of course I can't dictate why your specific agency or organization should develop a Balanced Scorecard; there could be any number of possible motivations. However, I can provide you with reasons that you definitely should not use to support an implementation. For example, if you find yourself answering the "why the Balanced Scorecard?" query with a response such as "we're going for excellence," or "we need a full-court press this year," or my personal favorite, "we want to go from good to great!" hit the stop button immediately. These are slogans that are most likely devoid of any real meaning to the average worker. In fact, the typical executive may not be able to penetrate the shiny veneer of these platitudes. I'm all for going from "good to great." In fact, Jim Collins's book by the same name is among the best business books I've ever read. But unless you possess a deep knowledge of what it specifically entails and how the Scorecard will help you traverse the rocky path from good to great, you're better off investing your Scorecard budget in mouse pads and coffee cups emblazoned with the phrase.

The problem with cliché-driven rationales such as those outlined earlier is their nebulous and fuzzy nature that makes them difficult to implement on a day-to-day basis. When well-meaning CEOs and executive directors trot out such phrases, even very senior managers tend to nod in polite agreement, punctuated by the occasional "YES," or "AMEN!" But deep within they may feel confused, wondering whether they truly understand the essence of the vision presented so enthusiastically. Rather than asking for clarification and risk looking stupid in front of their peers, these managers will demur and proceed to pass on watered-down interpretations of these vague marching orders to their own teams, all of whom subsequently develop meanings at least three times removed from the original intent of the leader. The result of this mess is often misalignment, sloppy behavior, and lots of wasted time.[4]

You've Got the "Why," Now Spread the Word!

Once you've developed your guiding rationale for the Balanced Scorecard—the well-conceived justification that solves a pressing issue or issues endemic to your particular situation—you need to clearly communicate it to all of your employees. While it may seem obvious to you, that insight was most likely the result of hours of deliberation and debate, a full commitment of intellectual resources. Not so for your employees. Chances are they didn't have the opportunity to sit in on the lively and spirited discussions and witness the crammed whiteboards that produced your guiding rationale for the Balanced Scorecard. So tell them. Do it simply, loudly, and often! In a study straight out of the "Duh" file, researchers last year discovered employees are—get this—more likely to support decisions when they are told about the rationale.[5] What will they uncover next, employees like recognition? People will only support what they understand, thus the importance of communicating your justification for investing in a Balanced Scorecard. Share the rationale with employees, engage them in discussions, listen to their feedback good and bad, and whenever possible, incorporate it. Only by doing this will you avoid the fate of the organization chronicled at the outset of the chapter.

A well-articulated, widely understood, and ceaselessly communicated rationale for the Balanced Scorecard will prove to be a huge asset in your efforts. The simple act of developing your objectives will force the establishment of consensus among all team members. Building that consensus will greatly assist your communication and education efforts as everyone will truly be on the same page. Objectives are also critical at those inevitable moments when your project loses some momentum. The focal point of your guiding objectives can serve as a rallying cry to re-energize and refocus your team's efforts, reminding everyone of exactly why you chose to develop a Scorecard. Author and consultant to nonprofits Bill Ryan sums it up nicely: "Organizations must really understand their motivation in doing this (Balanced Scorecard) work. Because with these systems there will come daunting stretches, there will come times when people are wondering, why are we doing this? What will get organizations over those humps is understanding the relevance of these tools to the social vision they have. More attention to the rationale is really useful and important."[6]

EXECUTIVE SUPPORT: A CRITICAL ELEMENT OF YOUR BALANCED SCORECARD

Would you sky dive without a parachute? Would you go for a mid-winter skate on a lake without first knowing the depth of the ice? Would you agree to fly in a small airplane across the Atlantic at night, in a storm, with a pilot boasting of his two hours of solo flight time? Of course not. So why are you paying so much for car insurance? Oops, sorry, this isn't a car insurance commercial, it's something far more important should you hope to achieve results from your Balanced Scorecard implementation. You wouldn't engage in any of the endeavors outlined above because they're all fraught with a significant degree of risk, and in fact the risk outweighs the reward substantially in each scenario. But many organizations will embark on the Balanced Scorecard trail accompanied by the most risky behavior of all— no executive support for the effort.

More than a measures effort, the Balanced Scorecard represents a change initiative. A change in how you measure, in the way you manage, and in the way you demonstrate accountability and show results. To facilitate this dramatic transformation, you absolutely must have the support of your senior executive.

Senior managers and executives set the tone for any organization. If these leaders provide only shallow and casual support for the Balanced Scorecard, this demonstration will be rapidly translated by all employees as a sign the implementation probably isn't worth their time and effort. Employees "watch what the boss watches"[7] and know what initiatives are likely to merit their attention. We've all seen the train wrecks of abandoned initiatives and have witnessed the impact theses debacles have on employees coping to keep their heads above the waters of change that really does matter. In their provocatively titled book *Confronting Reality*, authors Charan and Bossidy provide this very compelling description of the syndrome:

> The usual reason for the failure of an initiative is that it was launched half-heartedly, or was beyond the ability of the organization to master. Here's what tends to happen: the leaders announce a bold new program and then walk away from it, leaving the job to others. With no clear impetus from the top, the program will wander and drift. An initiative, after all, is add-on work, and people already have full plates. Few of them can take it seriously if the boss doesn't. Eventually the effort bogs down and dies . . . Real results do not come from making bold announcements about how the organization will change. They come from thoughtful, committed leaders who understand the details of an initiative, anticipate its consequences for the organization, make sure their people can achieve, it, put their personal weight behind it, and communicate its urgency to everyone.[8]

The only thing potentially worse than a lack of support from the executive is "lip service." This "behavioral integrity" has been proven in the for-profit world to have a significant impact on profits. In one study of 6,500 hotel workers, researchers discovered that a 12% improvement in a hotel's score on leadership integrity (following through on promises and demonstrating values they preached) resulted in increased profits of $250,000 per year.[9] That's a strong statistic but I don't think any of us need empirical evidence to be convinced of the doom that awaits any program launched with a splash of fanfare, only to be abandoned by a senior executive and leadership team swimming with the prevailing current for the next "new greatest thing."

Scorecard architects Kaplan and Norton believe senior management commitment to the Balanced Scorecard is necessary for a number of reasons:[10]

- *Understanding of strategy.* Most middle managers lack an in-depth knowledge of the organization's strategy. Only the senior management team is able to effectively articulate an ongoing strategy.

- *Decision rights.* Strategy involves trade-offs between alternative courses of action, determining which opportunities to pursue, and more importantly, which not to pursue. Middle management does not possess the decision making power to determine strategic priorities such as customer value propositions and related operating processes that are critical to the development of any Balanced Scorecard.

- *Commitment.* While knowledge of the enterprise's strategy is necessary, the emotional commitment of executives to the Scorecard program is the true differentiating feature of successful programs. Kaplan and Norton summarize this well: "More important is the time spent in actual meetings where the senior executives debate and argue among themselves. . . . These meetings build an emotional commitment to the strategy, to the scorecard as a communications device, and to the management processes that build a Strategy-Focused Organization."

You're probably saying, "Okay, I get it, tell me something I don't know! But how do I get a reluctant or skeptical executive on board?" Well, read on.

Securing Sponsorship for Your Balanced Scorecard

Some organizations are extremely fortunate to enjoy executive sponsorship and have noted the tremendous benefit it confers. Bridgeport Hospital and Healthcare Services of Bridgeport, Connecticut is one such organization. "Though the Scorecard is continually being refined and changed, one thing that hasn't changed over the three years is top management's commitment. From the start, senior management endorsed and has driven the card with support from all relevant stakeholders plus buy-in from the Board of Directors. Its enthusiasm for the Balanced Scorecard has spread to its parent organization. The Yale New Haven Health System now uses a Balanced Scorecard of performance metrics."[11]

I'm sure you've witnessed the power and importance of executive sponsorship for change initiatives during your career. I'm equally convinced that many of you know the maddening frustration that results from seeing a potentially beneficial change vanish almost instantly because your leaders could not be convinced of its importance, relevance, or worth. Assuming you don't want the Balanced Scorecard to suffer this ignominious fate, let's examine a number of techniques you can use to convince even the most skeptical senior executive of the Balanced Scorecard's worth:

- *Demonstrate results.* Former Mayor of New York City Rudy Giuliani noted that "in government . . . the temptation to cover shortfalls by increasing taxes can make political leaders lazy. Worse, the 'customers' of government—the citizens—can and will eventually do just what any dissatisfied customer does—go elsewhere, and eventually vote elsewhere too."[12] In the public sector, your senior leaders are accountable to elected officials. Those elected to public office normally wish to remain in office, and thus need to demonstrate results lest they be voted out. Advise your executives that a Balanced Scorecard system can be used to demonstrate accountability and show real results signaling your progress on important issues.

- *Job security.* Elected officials want to stay in office and executives want to keep their jobs, however, both are difficult to do if you prove unable to execute a strategy as we discussed in Chapter 1. What are the repercussions of not making a difference while you're at the helm? In one recent study, analyzing more than 450 CEO successions at large publicly traded companies between 1988 and 1992, the authors discovered that only 35% of dismissed CEOs returned to an active executive role within two years of departure, but for 43%, the ouster effectively ended their careers. This evidence seems to support the observation of F. Scott Fitzgerald who once opined: "There are no second acts in American lives."[13]

- *Attract resources.* Nonprofit agencies rely heavily on funders to provide the financial resources they require to serve targeted constituents. If agencies do not effectively measure performance, funders receive meaningless data or must acknowledge that they are supporting ineffective programs.[14] Using the Balanced Scorecard demonstrates to funders a willingness on the part of the nonprofit to provide meaningful information that can be used in future resource decisions.

- *Show progress.* Administrations and boards of directors change, but that doesn't mean you have to shift your priorities with every deck reshuffling. As the OSHA story in Chapter 2 illustrates, with demonstrated progress and sustained momentum, a Balanced Scorecard can survive a regime change, perhaps even lubricating a smooth transition.

- *Look for a good fit.* You need to identify senior executives who believe in the value, and indeed necessity, of balanced performance measurement and management. Senior managers who have gone through a strategic planning process designed to help them focus their efforts and define their objectives will also be more amenable to the Balanced Scorecard approach. Find a senior manager who fits this profile and make sure their door is the first stop on your sponsorship tour.

- *The power of peer pressure.* Outline the many achievements of other organizations pursuing a Balanced Scorecard approach. Success stories of Balanced Scorecard implementations abound in the business literature and at conference venues around the world. Testimonials from other senior executives are also very convincing, like this one from Charlotte Mayor Pat McCrory: "The Balanced Scorecard has helped me to communicate a strategic vision for the city to my constituents, the citizens, and to prospective businesses that are considering locating here. It helps the City Manager focus on things that will have the biggest impact on the city."[15]

- *Read what the "survey says."* We all want to feel needed, and you can make your senior management feel very needed in the Balanced Scorecard by sharing a couple of key statistics on the implementations of other organizations. A Best Practices LLC study found that half of benchmark participants' CEOs took part in the process.[16] In a study conducted for the Balanced Scorecard Report, respondents reported that CEOs, more than any other individual, were the sponsors of the Balanced Scorecard. 31% of the organizations stated the CEO was their sponsor.[17] The upshot of this bullet is this—get them involved, and the sooner the better! For true sponsorship to emerge, the senior executive of the organization must see their fingerprints all over the product you're creating, their intellectual sweat must stain the document if you hope to see them walking this talk.

- *Educate.* In order to engage employees you must first provide training. Before you train your employees, however, you must ensure your senior leaders understand this tool and the value it presents. Exhibit 3.2 outlines a potential agenda for such a training session.

- *Link the Balanced Scorecard to something the executive is passionate about.* Any executive is more inclined to lend vocal and active support to an initiative appealing to a core belief or value, thus it is incumbent upon you to find that linchpin and discuss how the Balanced Scorecard can transform it from rhetoric to reality. For example, perhaps the executive is acutely aware of the power of intangible assets such as culture and customer relationships in transforming your business. Discuss the proven ability of the Balanced Scorecard to translate intangibles into real business value. If fundraising is their

---

Exhibit 3.2   A Balanced Scorecard Education Session for Senior Executives

---

Paul Niven Leads a Balanced
Scorecard training session

Prior to the session, you should consider distributing Balanced Scorecard literature to your executive team. Copies of books (like this one!), or good articles on the subject will help your audience prepare for the presentation to come. Regarding the session itself, if possible I would suggest holding it at an off-site location. Keeping distractions to a minimum will prove beneficial for all involved. To have an administrative assistant knock on the door and shuttle an engaged executive out of the room at a pivotal moment can be disastrous to your momentum.

Consider using an outside consultant to deliver the actual material or at least participate in the event. There are a number of reasons I take this position. First, a well-trained consultant will have delivered countless presentations of this nature and used time tested material. Second, and unfortunately, many times an outside voice will carry more weight with, and be assumed to have more credibility by, executives than will an internal one. This is a sad but true reality of modern organizational life. Finally, and perhaps most importantly, you're holding this event because you want to win the support of your executive team. An experienced consultant will have faced similar crowds many times and be well-prepared to answer all queries and objections raised by the audience. And believe me, cogent and articulate responses here can translate to real support down the road.

Regarding the actual agenda, I suggest a two- to three-hour event structured as follows: 30 minutes on your organization and why a change is necessary (defining your "burning platform"), and 90 minutes on performance management and the Balanced Scorecard. Topics covered should include background information, a detailed review of the methodology, case studies, and success stories. Spend the final 30 to 60 minutes answering questions, and soliciting support for the implementation. Oh, and one final thing, don't forget to feed them. I say that only half jokingly. If your culture is one in which food is present at all meetings, don't leave those sandwiches and cookies out of this session!

---

first love, demonstrate the idea of cause and effect, outlining the fact that fundraising effectiveness is a result of unique organizational elements such as training and innovative processes; and fundraising drives financial growth that will allow you to focus on customer outcomes, all key dimensions of the Scorecard framework.[18]

Always remember that we're dealing with human beings, and human behavior can be shaped, as this story of Andrew Carnegie, the Scottish-born industrialist and philanthropist humorously illustrates. Carnegie's sister-in-law was worried sick over her two boys. They were so busy at Yale with their own affairs that they neglected to write home and paid no attention whatsoever to their mother's frantic letters. Carnegie offered to wager $100 that if he wrote them a letter he would get an answer from the boys by return mail, without even asking for it. Someone called his bet so he wrote his nephews a chatty letter, mentioning casually in a postscript that he was sending each one a five-dollar bill (this was in the very early 1900s remember). He neglected, however, to enclose the money. Back came replies by return mail thanking "Dear Uncle Andrew" for the kind note and . . .—you can finish the sentence yourself.[19]

Two Types of Leadership Skill

Some of you may be reading this and thinking, "but I don't have the power to make these changes—to drive any initiatives forward on my own. I've got to work through a board, or an array of regional bodies . . ." There is still hope! *Good to Great* author Jim Collins suggests there are two types of leadership skill: executive and legislative. When the senior executive of an organization has the concentrated power to make isolated decisions, they are exercising executive power. Collins hypothesizes that this is an uncommon commodity in the social sectors and suggests most leaders of public and nonprofit organizations must rely at least equally on legislative power. This branch of influence surfaces when the chief executive lacks the structural power to make the most important decisions and must utilize persuasion, political currency, and shared interests to create the environment for the right decisions to emerge.

You don't require pure executive power to make a tremendous difference in your organization. Take the case of Frances Hesselbein, who led the Girl Scouts of America through a period of rapid and significant transition from 1976 to 1990. She was once asked by a columnist what it felt like to be at the top of such a large organization. Rather than parading a stock answer, the type commonly employed by most luminaries when faced with a microphone, Hesselbein began rearranging items on a lunch table in front of her. She formed a set of concentric circles consisting of plates, cups, and saucers, connected by various pieces of cutlery. The finishing touch of this innovative organizational chart was the placement of a glass directly in the middle. Pointing to the center of this constellation she quietly declared, "I'm here." The message being, I may be the CEO but I'm really not on top of anything.

The Girl Scouts of America during Hesselbein's tenure relied on a volunteer workforce of 650,000 to carry out the work of hundreds of local Girl Scout councils all operating under a complex governance structure. In such an environment, she couldn't simply reign imperiously (not that she ever would), waving a magic wand of change and expecting the masses to obsequiously comply. Instead, she moved people to understand and confront the facts facing girls in America, such as teen pregnancy and alcohol use. She created materials on the issues, spoke about them ceaselessly, and simply gave the independent councils the opportunity to make changes of their own volition. Most did.[20] Hesselbein, who lacked pure executive power, excelled in the art of yielding legislative power and her results speak for themselves.

EXECUTIVE SPONSORSHIP IN ACTION[21]

If you are a senior executive sponsoring the Balanced Scorecard program within your organization, how do you know you're "walking the talk?" Try this test: When you feel that you are talking up a change initiative at least three times more than you need to, your managers will feel that you are backing the transformation.[22] It takes that much, probably more, to get the message across to a change-weary employee base that is looking to you to set the course your ship is going to sail.

Every opportunity to reinforce the importance of the exercise must be utilized. One of my favorite examples of this stems from a common lament I hear during Balanced Scorecard workshops: the woe is me "what time is this session going to end? I have real work to do" complaint often lobbed from a disengaged participant slumping wearily in their chair. I was once in a Strategy Mapping workshop with a large organization when a vice president tossed just such a verbal grenade into the late afternoon air. I was poised to answer his query in my most restrained manner when I was rescued by the CEO himself. It was as if he were literally riding in on a white horse ready to save the day when he said to the unsuspecting culprit: "What could possibly be more important than what we are doing right here and now? We're shaping the tool that we'll use to execute our strategy over the next three years, and frankly if you don't understand the importance of this exercise then maybe you don't belong at this table." The silence that followed was, as they say, deafening. In the intervening moments before he went on to further articulate his feelings, everyone sitting around that table had to dig deep and critically evaluate their commitment knowing full well the views of their boss. Not surprisingly as the implementation unfolded it was among the most successful I've ever had the privilege to engage in. I pin that success not to my consulting acumen but to that single incident that clearly demonstrated the passion this executive felt for the Balanced Scorecard.

As a consultant and writer, I have the unique opportunity to learn from organizations around the world. Over the past several years I've consulted with scores of organizations, have spoken at and attended conferences around the world, and have read stacks of case studies on organizational change. The theme of executive sponsorship is the one unifying element running through every encounter I've had. One statistic in particular dramatically demonstrates the importance of sponsorship. In "Driving Corporate Culture for Business Success," the researchers found that a massive 98.7% of respondents stated senior executives' role modeling of new behaviors and changes is key to enabling change.[23] As the iconoclastic physicist Albert Einstein, a man who produced as many memorable and poignant quotes during his life as he did mathematical equations, once said: "Setting an example is not the main means of influencing others; it is the only means."[24]

YOUR BALANCED SCORECARD TEAM

Teams have become a very popular concept in today's organizational world, and for good reason. Enterprises around the globe are realizing that in an economy dominated largely by intangible assets, it's collaboration among employees spanning the entire organization that drives results. The Balanced Scorecard is very well suited to a team approach. No one person in your organization possesses the singular knowledge requisite to build a Strategy Map and Balanced Scorecard that tells your strategic story. The best Maps and Scorecards represent the collective know-how and experience of people from across the enterprise. In the following sections of the chapter, we'll consider the key aspects of your Balanced Scorecard team, and look at the roles and responsibilities of team members.

How Many People Should Be On Your Balanced Scorecard Team?

We have a love affair with the "bigger is better" concept in the modern world—cars with bigger engines, big box retail stores that span city blocks, and of course big serving sizes at our favorite restaurants that are rapidly contributing to our big waists. We could debate the merits of bigger equating with better for days, maybe while sucking down a 32-ounce Coke at Costco before we load our Hummer with the 44 packages of paper towels we just bought, but let's isolate the discussion to the notion of Balanced Scorecard team size.

In the *First Edition* of this book, I quoted a study that suggested that a majority of Balanced Scorecard implementations utilized teams consisting of ten or more people.[25] Ahh, the beauty of a second edition—while I didn't endorse that number back then, I didn't reject it either. Let me be very clear in this edition, based on my experience having facilitated thousands of workshops. Ten people on a team is way too many if you expect to have meaningful discussions that result in decisions being made. Come to think of it, if you hope to have meetings in general, ten people is far too large a crowd. Think about it. Start with one person, that's one calendar to manage.

Add a second and the task of finding a mutually convenient time to meet has doubled in complexity. A third person makes it three times as difficult, but when you get to about the fifth person, the challenge expands exponentially. By the time you add the tenth person, it might actually be simpler to convene the leaders of the G-7 nations. I worked with a large nonprofit client a few years back that insisted on having a hefty team to develop their Balanced Scorecard. I knew that simply scheduling meetings would be a challenge with this not-so-intimate group of 12, but when I learned almost half the group was on the East Coast and half were stationed on the West Coast, I knew we were headed for trouble. Sure enough, the development of the Map and measures took almost twice as long as we had originally estimated because of the difficulties of balancing calendars. And the final product didn't benefit from the sizable grey matter that occupied the meeting room either. In fact, coming to consensus was almost impossible for this mammoth group and ultimately nobody was truly satisfied with what was developed.

The U.S. Navy SEALs, who know a thing or two about complex missions, suggest that six is the ideal number of participants on any high intensity team.[26] I can't say with certainty that six is the exact right number for your Scorecard team, however, I like the five to seven notion very much. This size, while still presenting logistical challenges, is a relatively small number that allows for cognitive space to emerge where meaningful discussions occur. A group of this size can find its own identity and members can take the necessary time in their discussions to truly understand the point of views of their colleagues without feeling the necessity to get something out before losing the floor to a host of other people craving the momentary spotlight.

If you're not comfortable designating a certain number, use this approach. Base the team size on the precept of representing all the areas of your organization that you expect to be using the Scorecard. If, for example, you're creating a high-level Balanced Scorecard, you should strive for representation from each of your departments or groups. Should you have more than five or six departments, you may require a larger Balanced Scorecard team than I normally advise. If your Scorecard effort is beginning at the department level, then key representatives within the unit should have a presence on the team. Remember our earlier admonition—no one person has all the knowledge of strategy, stakeholder needs, and competencies to build an effective Scorecard. The knowledge you need to build an effective Balanced Scorecard resides in the minds of your colleagues spanning the entire organization.

What Skill Sets Should Team Members Possess?

"Mix it up" could be our tag line for this discussion. Any team will thrive on a mix of complementary skills. As a prerequisite, all members of the team should be experts in their individual areas while also possessing a solid understanding of the entire organization. Beyond functional skills, you should attempt to fill the team with a mix of *visionaries* (people who see what the organization can be and can rally people around that vision) and *action-aries* (people who will ensure the goals and tasks of the project are realistic and are accomplished).[27] Expect heated debates and exchanges as the visionaries passionately depict a bold future while the actionaries attempt to articulate current realities.

Depending on the size of your organization, there is a chance that at least some team members will not have previously met. This was the case with a client team I worked with recently. At first, I saw this as a disadvantage, fearing it would take extra time for the team to "gel." While there was definitely a period of growing pains for the team, in the end, the lack of personal relationships strengthened the level of debate around the Scorecard. There were no preconceived notions among the members, and everyone felt comfortable defending their positions. This team formed its own identity and found a place of mutual respect and collaboration that resulted in tremendous end products.

Team Member Roles and Responsibilities

Many academics and consultants suggest a Balanced Scorecard should be the exclusive domain of the executive team. In other words, for the Scorecard to prove successful, it must be crafted solely by your senior leaders. There are exceptions to every rule, and I have witnessed successful Scorecard implementations led by teams comprised of mid-level staffers. However, their path to success was about as smooth as landing a Cessna in a snowstorm. To prove beneficial, your Balanced Scorecard must ultimately be owned by the senior leadership of your organization, and it is therefore vital to ensure, whenever possible, your Scorecard development team is comprised of senior-level people possessing the knowledge, credibility, and decision-making rights to build a tool that will be accepted, and more importantly, utilized by the ruling body. Let's look specifically at typical roles and responsibilities that should be present on your Balanced Scorecard team.

Executive Sponsor   In *The Heart of Change*, authors Dan Cohen and John Kotter observe that "many change initiatives flounder because they're headed up by people who lack the time or the clout to accomplish what's necessary."[28] The Balanced Scorecard can easily suffer this fate without a strong executive sponsor skillfully orchestrating the process. Using the knowledge they've accumulated, the sponsor will provide invaluable insights into mission and strategy. They will also be relied upon to maintain constant communication with key stakeholder groups such as boards of directors and elected officials. As the senior member of the Balanced Scorecard team, the sponsor should also ensure the team receives the human and financial resources necessary for a successful implementation, something we'll discuss towards the end of the chapter.

Perhaps most important, the sponsor must prove to be a tireless advocate and enthusiastic ambassador of the Balanced Scorecard. As we previously discussed, people watch what the boss watches and will be carefully evaluating both the words and actions of your executive sponsor. To accomplish this and still have time for a day job, the sponsor must possess ample credibility within the organization. In an article for the *Harvard Management Update*, Nick Wreden writes that "credibility derives from organizational achievements, trust, and the visible support of other top executives. Every time he's been asked to perform, he has always delivered."[29] The executive sponsor is not expected to provide full-time support to the Scorecard effort. However, attendance at Scorecard meetings and an "open door policy" for the Scorecard team should be considered mandatory.

Balanced Scorecard Champion (or Team Leader)   Balanced Scorecard co-developer David Norton believes many Scorecard success stories share a common trait. Virtually every senior executive sponsor had a partner, "a change agent who played the lead role in introducing the Balanced Scorecard."[30] I'll call this change agent the Balanced Scorecard *champion*, and suggest this role is the most vital ingredient of Scorecard success. If the executive sponsor paves the way for success, it's the champion who ensures the smooth flow of traffic on the Scorecard freeway. This individual will guide the Scorecard process, both philosophically (providing thought leadership and best practices) and logistically (scheduling meetings, ensuring tasks are completed, etc.).

The role is a challenging one and demands a skilled communicator and facilitator. While the champion is fully expected to contribute to Scorecard development, he or she also has the challenging tasks of team building and conflict resolution. As with the executive sponsor, the champion should enjoy widespread credibility throughout the organization. However, the source of credibility does not necessarily need to emanate from a long history within the organization. Some very skilled champions are recruited from outside the ranks of current employees based on their Scorecard knowledge and expertise. This confers credibility of another sort: expert credibility, which is often in short supply at the outset of a Scorecard implementation. I recently completed work with a client that recruited a person from outside their industry to run the Balanced Scorecard program. This individual's track record of Scorecard success and deep reservoir of tools and techniques has helped the organization reap swift benefits from their implementation.

The Balanced Scorecard champion should transition into the leadership of your Office of Strategy Management, which will be examined in Chapter 13. While the role is permanent, you can expect some variations in the key tasks over time. At various times the champion will act as missionary, consultant, point person to fighting resistance, and chief of staff or general manger.[31]

Balanced Scorecard Team Members   Your executive sponsor and Balanced Scorecard champion will provide background, context for the Scorecard implementation, and subject matter expertise. The job of the Scorecard team members is to translate that material into a working Strategy Map and Scorecard that effectively tells the story of your strategy. You'll rely on your team members to bring specialized knowledge of their functional area, and if they are not senior leadership team members themselves, to liaise closely with their own senior leaders. Building support and momentum is a never-ending task of any Scorecard implementation. Team members must constantly communicate with their leaders; building support, sniffing out any possible resistance, and providing feedback to the larger Scorecard team. They should also identify resources within the organization that will prove valuable as the Scorecard development continues. For example, noting who controls key performance data.

During the implementation phase of the initiative, expect your team members to devote approximately 25% of their time to this effort. Any potential team member who can offer only 5 to 10% of their time must be viewed with caution. While they may carry valuable knowledge of their particular area, this must be weighed against the very negative lack of participation in the effort.

Some teams inaugurate the process by making the formation of a "team charter" their first order of business. The charter may include key milestones, group values, and important resources. I'm all for a team charter, but with this caveat: Don't let this ostensibly helpful step turn into a debilitating headache. One nonprofit I worked with spent about two weeks deliberating feverishly over the team's name! That is not a valuable use of anyone's time. Exhibit 3.3 summarizes the roles and responsibilities of your Balanced Scorecard team.

In the Spirit of "Learning by Doing"[32]   I would suggest your team develop a Strategy Map and set of Balanced Scorecard measures specifically for the implementation. The purpose of this exercise is two-fold. First, a pragmatic reason: The Strategy Map will act as a powerful communication tool for the implementation's stakeholders, and performance measures serve to keep the team focused on the critical tasks at hand. Your team will require yardsticks to gauge their implementation progress, and the Balanced Scorecard provides a powerful means for accomplishing this task. Secondly, developing the objectives and measures for their Scorecard gives team members a unique opportunity to engage in the mental gymnastics required to create an effective Scorecard. Who are our customers? What are their requirements? At what processes must we excel? What competencies do we require? These are all questions your team will be posing to others in your organization very soon, so isn't it perfectly appropriate that they go through the process

Exhibit 3.3   Balanced Scorecard Team Roles and Responsibilities

Role	Responsibilities
Executive Sponsor	• Assumes ownership for the Balanced Scorecard implementation • Provides background information to the team on mission, strategy, and methodology • Maintains communication with internal and external stakeholders • Commits resources (both human and financial) to the team • Provides support and enthusiasm for the Balanced Scorecard throughout the organization
Balanced Scorecard Champion	• Coordinates meetings; plans, tracks, and reports team results to all audiences • Provides thought leadership on the Balanced Scorecard methodology to the team • Ensures all relevant background material is available to the team • Provides feedback to the executive sponsor and senior management • Facilitates the development of an effective team through coaching and support
Team members	• Provide expert knowledge • Inform and influence their respective senior leaders • Act as Balanced Scorecard ambassadors within their unit or department • Act in the best interests of the organization as a whole

Adapted from *Balanced Scorecard Step-by-Step: Maximizing Performance and Maintaining Results, 2nd Edition,* Paul R. Niven (John Wiley & Sons, 2006).

themselves? Exhibit 3.4 presents a sample Team Strategy Map and set of Balanced Scorecard measures.

WHERE SHOULD WE BUILD THE BALANCED SCORECARD?

This chapter opened with a discussion of the guiding rationale for your Balanced Scorecard program. I emphasized the importance of developing a solid foundation for the Scorecard before embarking on the actual work of building performance objectives on the Strategy Map and measures on the Scorecard. Determining where to build your first Balanced Scorecard is another important step in the momentum building phase.

The size of your organization will, to a great degree, dictate where your first Scorecard is developed. Those of you working in larger organizations will be faced with the most choices. You could decide to develop a high-level

Exhibit 3.4 A Sample Strategy Map and Set of Balanced Scorecard Measures for Your Implementation Team

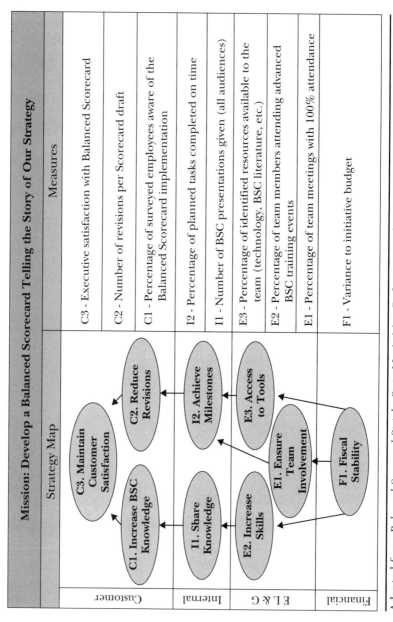

Mission: Develop a Balanced Scorecard Telling the Story of Our Strategy

	Strategy Map	Measures
Customer	C3. Maintain Customer Satisfaction / C2. Reduce Revisions / C1. Increase BSC Knowledge	C3 - Executive satisfaction with Balanced Scorecard C2 - Number of revisions per Scorecard draft C1 - Percentage of surveyed employees aware of the Balanced Scorecard implementation
Internal	I2. Achieve Milestones / I1. Share Knowledge	I2 - Percentage of planned tasks completed on time I1 - Number of BSC presentations given (all audiences)
EL&G	E3. Access to Tools / E1. Ensure Team Involvement / E2. Increase Skills	E3 - Percentage of identified resources available to the team (technology, BSC literature, etc.) E2 - Percentage of team members attending advanced BSC training events E1 - Percentage of team meetings with 100% attendance
Financial	F1. Fiscal Stability	F1 - Variance to initiative budget

Adapted from *Balanced Scorecard Step-by-Step: Maximizing Performance and Maintaining Results, 2nd Edition,* Paul R. Niven (John Wiley & Sons, 2006).

organizational Scorecard, or choose a "pilot" location for your first development efforts. Departments within the organization, or even support groups such as Finance or Human Resources, could launch the Balanced Scorecard.

For many organizations, starting at the top and building a high-level Balanced Scorecard that represents the entire enterprise is often the best choice for a number of reasons. First, the Strategy Map and measures can be widely communicated to all employees, ensuring everyone is aware of the critical drivers of success for your organization. Second, this Map and set of measures will provide focus for all groups and promote collaboration among departments in an effort to implement the strategy and work towards the mission. Finally, starting at the top greatly assists your cascading efforts. "Cascading" the Balanced Scorecard represents the process of driving the Scorecard to lower levels of the organization, giving all employees the opportunity to demonstrate how their day-to-day actions contribute to long-term goals. The high-level Strategy Map and Balanced Scorecard will then serve as the logical starting point for cascaded Balanced Scorecards.

Starting at the top is clearly not for everyone, and in some cases a pilot Scorecard effort is the best course of action. The most common reason for choosing a pilot approach is a lack of enthusiasm for the Balanced Scorecard at the highest echelons of the organization. Senior leadership may not be convinced of the efficacy of the tool or may lack passion on the idea of performance measurement, or they may feel they have too much on their plates already to invest in another program. Despite reluctance at the top, it's not uncommon for a departmental leader to recognize the model's merits and understand how the initiative could pay instant rewards in the form of increased focus, alignment, and accountability.

Should you choose to pilot the Balanced Scorecard at a department or team level, a critical consideration is ensuring your work is consistent with the overall strategic direction of the organization. Kaplan and Norton recommend sending representatives from the pilot location to the organization's headquarters in order to solicit feedback from the top level executives on how your unit "fits in" with the organization-level strategy. What priorities must you consider and what organization-level themes should be incorporated?[33] Making this pilgrimage not only fosters alignment with "corporate" priorities, but also promotes the Balanced Scorecard to the executive team, which may enhance the likelihood of adoption at a higher-level.

CRITERIA FOR CHOOSING AN APPROPRIATE ORGANIZATIONAL UNIT

To help you make the important decision of where to develop your first Balanced Scorecard, I've developed a number of criteria you should consider. They are presented in Exhibit 3.5. Let's review these and determine how they might impact your Scorecard development decision.

Exhibit 3.5   Seven Criteria for Choosing Where to Begin Your Balanced Scorecard

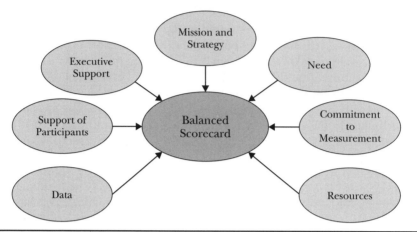

Adapted from *Balanced Scorecard Step-by-Step: Maximizing Performance and Maintaining Results, 2nd Edition,* Paul R. Niven (John Wiley & Sons, 2006).

Mission and Strategy

Chapter 2 reviewed the new "geography" of the nonprofit and public sector Balanced Scorecard. You learned that mission is elevated to the top of the Scorecard since you do not have a profit or shareholder imperative. Your organizations are chartered with the obligation of serving customers to fulfill a social, business, or societal need. Therefore, any group you select for your first Scorecard should possess a mission for their existence.

A strategy is also critical since at its core the Balanced Scorecard is a tool designed to assist you in translating strategy into action. Without a strategic stake in the ground, you're very likely to end up with an ad-hoc collection of financial and nonfinancial objectives and measures that do not link together to tell the story of your strategy.

Executive Support

The topic of executive support for a Balanced Scorecard implementation was covered in detail earlier in the chapter. Based on what we covered, you should recognize that no Scorecard initiative, at any level of the organization, will survive without the active and sincere sponsorship of the lead executive.

Need for a Balanced Scorecard

Any unit you choose, including the overall organization, should have a clear and compelling need to adopt a Balanced Scorecard system—its own "burning platform" for change. Exhibit 3.6 provides an assessment guide you can

Exhibit 3.6 Assessing the Need for a Balanced Scorecard

1 2 3 4 5	1. Our organization has invested in Total Quality Management (TQM) and other improvement initiatives but we have not seen a corresponding increase in customer results.
1 2 3 4 5	2. If we did not produce our current Performance Reports for a month, nobody would notice.
1 2 3 4 5	3. We create significant value from intangible assets such as employee knowledge and innovation, customer relationships, and a strong culture.
1 2 3 4 5	4. We have a strategy (or have had strategies in the past) but have a hard time successfully implementing.
1 2 3 4 5	5. We rarely review our performance measures and make suggestions for new and innovative indicators.
1 2 3 4 5	6. Our senior management team spends the majority of their time together discussing variances from plan and other operational issues.
1 2 3 4 5	7. Budgeting at our organization is very political and based largely on historical trends.
1 2 3 4 5	8. Our employees *do not* have a solid understanding of our mission, vision, and strategy.
1 2 3 4 5	9. Our employees *do not* know how their day-to-day actions contribute to the organization's success.
1 2 3 4 5	10. Nobody owns the performance measurement process at our organization.
1 2 3 4 5	11. We have numerous initiatives taking place at our organization, and it's possible that not all are truly strategic in nature.
1 2 3 4 5	12. There is little accountability in our organization for the things we agree as a group to do.
1 2 3 4 5	13. People tend to stay within their "silos," and as a result we have little collaboration among departments.
1 2 3 4 5	14. Our employees have difficulty accessing the critical information they need to serve customers.
1 2 3 4 5	15. Priorities at our organization are often dictated by current necessity or "firefighting."
1 2 3 4 5	16. The environment in which we operate is changing, and in order to succeed we too must change.
1 2 3 4 5	17. We face increased pressure from stakeholders to demonstrate results.
1 2 3 4 5	18. We *do not* have clearly defined performance targets for both financial and nonfinancial indicators.
1 2 3 4 5	19. We cannot clearly articulate our strategy in a one-page document or "map."
1 2 3 4 5	20. We sometimes make decisions that are beneficial in the short-term, but may harm long-term value creation.

(continued)

Exhibit 3.6   Assessing the Need for a Balanced Scorecard *(continued)*

Scoring Key:

20–30: If your score fell in this range you most likely have a strong performance measurement discipline in place. The program has been cascaded throughout your organization, to ensure all employees are contributing to your success, and is linked to key management processes.

31–60: You may have a performance measurement system in place but are not experiencing the benefits you anticipated or need to succeed. Using the Balanced Scorecard as a Strategic Management System would be of benefit to you.

61–100: Scores in this range suggest difficulty in successfully executing your strategy and meeting the needs of your customers and other stakeholders. A Balanced Scorecard system is strongly recommended to help you focus on the implementation of strategy and align your organization with overall goals.

---

review with potential groups to determine need for a Balanced Scorecard effort. To complete this exercise, read each statement and consider how much you agree with what is stated. The more you agree, the higher the score you assign. For example, if you fully agree, assign a score of 5 points.

Support of Participants

There is no doubt that executive support is critical for a Balanced Scorecard implementation to succeed. However, while executives may use Scorecard information to make strategic decisions, you will also depend heavily on managers and first-line supervisors using the tool in their jobs. When the Scorecard is driven down to all levels through a process of cascading, the alignment and focus derived across the organization can lead to real breakthroughs in performance.

Managers and supervisors make this happen with their understanding, acceptance, support of, and usage of the Balanced Scorecard. Not all members of these groups will demonstrate such a willingness to participate, however. While open criticism of new senior management initiatives is fairly rare, these managers and supervisors will often remain silent or demonstrate only mild enthusiasm, which workers quickly interpret as a questionable show of support for the program.[34] When choosing your organizational unit for the Balanced Scorecard, make an honest evaluation of the management team and supervisors you'll be relying on for participation and support.

Commitment to Measurement

The Balanced Scorecard represents a new way of assessing performance, one that introduces significant accountability for results. Making the transition to this new environment is as much a philosophical and cultural transformation as it is a business adaptation. Therefore, you must ensure that any group you choose is committed to using this new system to clearly demonstrate its results.

Data

This criterion raises two questions: Firstly, does this unit support a culture of measurement—that is, would they be amenable to managing by a balanced set of performance measures? While every group within a modern organization should rely on performance measures, for your first attempt, you may wish to choose a unit with a history of reliance on performance measures. Second, will the unit be able to supply data for the chosen performance measures? This may be difficult to assess initially, since at least some of the measures on your Balanced Scorecard may be new, with data sources as yet unidentified. However, if the unit has difficulty gathering data for current performance measures, they may be reluctant or unable to source the data you'll ultimately require for your Balanced Scorecard.

Resources

The group you choose must be willing and able to ante up appropriate resources of both the human and financial variety. We'll be exploring each of these investments in the next section of the chapter.

In Exhibit 3.7, I have created a sample worksheet you can use to determine the right organizational unit for your initial Balanced Scorecard effort. In this example, the Finance department is being considered for a Scorecard implementation. Let's walk through the example.

Plotted along the left-hand side of the table are the seven criteria I discussed above. In the next column, I have assigned a score out of ten for this unit against each of the criteria. The third column represents weights for each of the seven dimensions based on my judgment and experience. You may feel more comfortable assigning equal weights to the seven items, but clearly some areas, such as mission and strategy and executive support are imperative to success and should be weighted accordingly. The fourth column contains the score for the unit within each criteria. Under "mission and strategy," they were assigned a score of ten, which when multiplied by the weight for that category yields three total points. In the final column, I've provided a rationale for the scores assigned based on an assessment of the unit in the context of that specific criteria. It's important to document your decision-making process in order to validate it with others responsible for choosing the Balanced Scorecard organizational unit. Finally, a total score is calculated and an overall assessment provided.

Exhibit 3.7 Sample Worksheet for Choosing Your Organizational Unit

BALANCED SCORECARD PROJECT
ORGANIZATIONAL UNIT ASSESSMENT
Finance Department

Criteria	Score (Out of 10)	Weight	Total Points	Rationale
Mission and Strategy	10	30%	3	The Finance team recently completed a retreat, during which they developed a new mission and strategy.
Executive Support	9	30%	2.7	The Finance director has experience with performance measurement and is very enthusiastic about this change.
Need	10	15%	1.5	Finance has been plagued with errors and as a result has poor customer satisfaction.
Support of Participants	7	10%	0.7	This young, energetic management group is willing to experiment with new approaches.
Commitment	8	5%	0.4	The team realize they must change in order to improve and are ready to embrace the accountability of the BSC
Data	10	5%	0.5	Finance has ready access to anticipated Scorecard data requirements.
Resources	4	5%	0.2	The unit is understaffed and will have difficulty finding resources for this project.
Total		100%	9.0	

Overall Assessment

The Finance department seems to be an excellent candidate for the development of a Balanced Scorecard. They score 9 out of a possible 10 points. The staffing issue, while significant, should be mitigated by the fact that the group is motivated to use the Scorecard system and is clearly in need of a new performance measurement system.

Adapted from *Balanced Scorecard Step-by-Step: Maximizing Performance and Maintaining Results*, Paul R. Niven (John Wiley & Sons, 2002).

This assessment tool provides participants with the opportunity to discuss potential strengths and weaknesses of the unit, mitigate significant risks, and offer opinions on the viability of this group for a Balanced Scorecard implementation.[35]

HUMAN AND FINANCIAL RESOURCES NECESSARY FOR THE BALANCED SCORECARD

Earlier in the chapter, we examined the critical role of executive sponsorship in a successful Scorecard initiative. Even if you're fortunate enough to enjoy complete support from your senior leaders, you can be sure that at some point, someone will ask, "what is this going to cost?" You should be prepared to answer that question, and in this section we'll look at both the human and financial resources required when developing and using a Balanced Scorecard system.

A caveat at the outset: You won't find an exact Scorecard budget in this section or at any point in this book. I've already touted the Balanced Scorecard's wide applicability as a strong attribute of the system. Given the fact that virtually any organization can enjoy the benefits offered by the Scorecard, and there are thousands of organization types and sizes out there, it's difficult to pin down exact resource requirements. Every organization will have differing levels of comfort expending both human and financial resources, and each will have diverse limitations. Therefore, the purpose of this section is to provide a guide to the general classifications of resources required.

No Balanced Scorecard system can be built in isolation. The best Strategy Maps and Scorecards represent the collective inspiration and knowledge from a team of organizational experts. This means, as we discussed earlier, you'll need a group of people devoted to your Scorecard initiative. The Scorecard also comes with a financial price tag. The good news is you don't have to break the bank in order to develop a highly successful and sustainable Balanced Scorecard program. Here are a number of items you may wish to consider when building a budget for your Balanced Scorecard:

- *Employee time.* There is a salary cost associated with the time committed to the Balanced Scorecard. This cost will be skewed toward the front end of the implementation as your team works together building the components of the Balanced Scorecard.

- *Consulting.* A highly qualified and skilled consultant can mean the difference between a well-developed Scorecard tool embraced by all employees and one that languishes in a binder on your office shelf.

- *Software.* When I began working with the Balanced Scorecard many years ago, Microsoft Excel charts were considered the vanguard of Scorecard reporting. Since that time, Scorecard reporting systems have proliferated exponentially. Today there are over a hundred choices available, with price tags ranging from a few hundred to several hundred thousand dollars. Chapter 11 provides an in-depth look at Balanced Scorecard reporting options.

- *Educational materials.* I consider training and education a key differentiator in successful Balanced Scorecard implementations. There is absolutely no substitute for learning. Your investment in education can range from a few copies of a book to sending your entire team to one of the many Scorecard conferences held around the world. We'll revisit the topic of training and education in Chapter 4.

- *Logistical expenses.* Many organizations will do much of their initial Scorecard development off-site. I strongly advocate this approach. Concentration on the task at hand is definitely enhanced when participants aren't lured by ringing phones, assistants passing urgent notes, and a screen full of attention-demanding e-mail emanating from your BlackBerry. Your costs here may include rental fees, supplies, and meals.

- *The Office of Strategy Management.* Like any other change-related initiative, the Balanced Scorecard requires ongoing care and feeding to flourish. One of the biggest mistakes I see client organizations making is not thinking about who will run the Scorecard program on a day-to-day basis when my work with them is completed. It's always one of the first questions I ask, but the quizzical looks I receive in return may indicate that when the sun is shining brightly on the implementation, it's difficult for them to look that far into the future and realize what is necessary to fully ingrain this system into the fabric of the organization. In Chapter 13, we'll explore the role of the Office of Strategy Management and you will learn much more about the specific roles and responsibilities of this critical group. For now, please do yourself a favor and begin thinking carefully about whether, and how many, resources you'll be willing to commit to the Balanced Scorecard on a continuing basis.

The part of my job as a consultant I like the least is the inevitable fee negotiation that takes place with most of my clients. "Do more with less," "be financially responsible," "ensure proper stewardship of funds," are battle cries I hear every single day, whether at client locations or in the business press. I recognize that a never-ending tap of funds is not flowing from your offices, but if dollars and cents is your overarching and primary concern when considering a Balanced Scorecard, perhaps you should think again. A more suitable mental model may be that of an investment, perhaps the most important you will ever make, in executing strategy. What would it be worth to your organization if you could successfully demonstrate your progress in meeting the needs of your customers and working towards your mission? That is the promise of the Balanced Scorecard and as the ads say, it's priceless.

YOUR BALANCED SCORECARD DEVELOPMENT PLAN

In many ways, this entire book is your Balanced Scorecard development plan. Each chapter lays out in detail the steps necessary to develop a powerful Balanced Scorecard system. This section will serve as a primer of what's to come, as well as providing you with input you can use right now to develop your own Scorecard plan.

The word "plan" could conjure up as many different meanings as the word "strategy." I remember one client several years ago. I had barely completed the introductory hand shakes when into my hands was thrust a Scorecard plan as thick as a phone book. Other organizations have chosen to keep it simple, focusing on the big chunks necessary to produce an effective work product. Ultimately, the plan you develop will be dictated by your culture, history of planning, and amount of expertise you possess in the subject. One thing is certain, however, regardless of the plan you adopt you will be spending lots of time in meetings while developing your Balanced Scorecard. For some suggestions on maximizing this time see the box entitled "Meetings, Meetings, Meetings."[36]

Meetings, Meetings, Meetings

It seems we spend more time than ever in meetings, but is the time well spent? There's a tale about the humorist Will Rogers being invited to sit in on a committee meeting of an organization that ordinarily didn't permit the presence of outsiders. When the meeting was over Will remarked, "I agreed to repeat nothing and I'll keep my promise. But I gotta admit, I heard nothing worth repeating." You can't afford to have your Scorecard team members thinking, or worse yet, saying something similar after your meetings. And you will have meetings—recent studies suggest over 65% of Scorecard implementing organizations used work meetings to accomplish their tasks. Here are a few things you can do to maximize the effectiveness of your Balanced Scorecard meetings:

- *Determine your purpose.* Are you holding the meeting to share information, generate ideas, etc.?

- *Determine desired outcomes.* What do you want to accomplish during the session? Ensure everyone is aware of the desired outcomes when the meeting begins.

(continued)

Meetings, Meetings, Meetings (continued)

- *Evaluate attendance.* Nobody likes being invited to a meeting in which they have little to contribute. Determine who you need in attendance and simply distribute minutes to those who are not essential to achieving your outcomes.

- *Assign roles.* Determine in advance who will facilitate the meeting, who will act as the scribe, and who will fulfill the vital role of timekeeper.

- *Provide structured pre-work.* Provide attendees with relevant materials well in advance of the meeting and emphasize the importance of completing the pre-work.

- *Stay on time.* Get in the habit of starting and ending all meetings on time. Don't reward late comers by reviewing what they've missed.

Several excellent articles and books have been written on the topic of effective meeting management. For a simple and pragmatic look at the subject I recommend Thomas Kayser's 1990 book, *Mining Group Gold*.

THE PLANNING PHASE OF BUILDING A BALANCED SCORECARD

This chapter has provided you with everything you need to place a solid Scorecard stake in the ground as you begin your efforts. Chapter 4 will build on this foundation and provide two additionally essential elements; training and communication. To summarize, the tasks you may consider part of your "planning phase" of Scorecard development are:

- Developing your guiding rationale for using the Balanced Scorecard

- Gaining senior leadership support and sponsorship

- Forming your Balanced Scorecard team

- Deciding where to build your first Scorecard

- Determining resource requirements and availability

- Developing a Training and Communication plan for your Balanced Scorecard implementation (the subject of Chapter 4)

It's often tempting to dive right in to the Scorecard waters and begin developing Strategy Map objectives and translating them into measures without laying the foundation described above. Trust me, you'll find the water very chilly if you do. Without a guiding rationale for your Scorecard, you'll have a difficult time determining whether you should develop 10, 20, or

50 objectives and measures. A lack of sponsorship will see your Scorecard fade away at the first sign of crisis and conflicting demands. Without Scorecard training, you'll likely develop a jumbled mix of financial and nonfinancial measures that add little value above and beyond your current measurement solution. Take the necessary time to complete each of the steps above. When your Scorecard journey faces challenges, as it inevitably will, these steps will ensure you have a steady compass by which to steer the tool's future development.

THE DEVELOPMENT PHASE

Outlined below are the steps typically undertaken during the development phase of a Balanced Scorecard implementation. In addition to the "hard scaffolding," items such as developing a Strategy Map and measures, I've included a number of executive workshops throughout the process. Gaining executive consensus as you build this tool absolutely cannot be overemphasized, and these checkpoints allow you to ensure the entire team is reading from the same sheet of music as you build your Scorecard. Logistical challenges may not permit you to have as many executive sessions as I've listed below, and if that's the case, ensure your team members are consistently checking in with their "home" executives, providing progress updates, soliciting feedback, and gaining approval for the direction in which the Scorecard train is headed.

Step One: Gather and Distribute Background Material

The Balanced Scorecard is really a tool of translation: subjecting sometimes vague and nebulous concepts such as mission, values, vision, and strategy to the glare of analysis through the transformative power of objectives and measures. To fulfill this promise, your team must be supplied with ample background on the organization, including but not limited to: organizational charter, mission, values, vision statement, strategic plan, past consulting studies, performance reports, and third-party ratings or assessments.

Step Two: Provide Balanced Scorecard Education

Before the first flip chart is dragged into a conference room, before the coffee and donuts arrive for your first workshop, you must educate as many people as you can on what the Balanced Scorecard is, and how it will be used at your organization to solve a specific issue (or issues) you face. With a name like "Balanced Scorecard," most people can guess with some accuracy what the tool is all about, but this model has many, many subtleties and attributes that must be fully comprehended should you hope to wring the most from its potential. You need to win the hearts and minds of every employee; thus, informing them of what this tool is all about represents a vital first step on that journey.

Step Three: Develop or Confirm Mission, Values, Vision, and Strategy

As discussed in step one, the purpose of the Balanced Scorecard is to chisel your strategic story from these blocks of organizational clay. If any, or—gasp—all, of these raw materials are missing, you have a decision to make. Do you stop the Scorecard process and create what's missing, or forge ahead and simply go with what you have? Upon intense inspection what you're most likely to be lacking is a true strategy, a game plan for your success that will distinguish you from other like organizations. This is a vital ingredient to any organization's success and its absence should be treated accordingly.

Step Four: Conduct Executive Interviews

This is a great chance to get the fingerprints of your executive team all over the Balanced Scorecard by simply asking them their opinions at the outset. How do they view the organization's strategy? What are the compelling issues that must be solved? What objectives are most critical to them from the Customer's Perspective? Your Strategy Map and Scorecard should clearly reflect what you hear in these exchanges.

Step Five: Develop Your Strategy Map

We've now been cleared for takeoff! You've engrossed yourself in the Balanced Scorecard, your team has pored over every crinkled archive it could dig up, you've checked the validity of your Scorecard building blocks, and your executive team has given their two-cents worth. It's time to use all of that in crafting the one-page graphical representation of your strategy in the form of a Strategy Map. This simple (hopefully—but much more on that later) will describe and powerfully communicate to everyone in the organization the objectives that are absolutely critical to your success in each of the Balanced Scorecard perspectives. We'll immerse ourselves deeply in the development of Strategy Maps in Chapter 7.

Step Five (a): Executive Workshop

The purpose of this sub-step is to gain senior management consensus on the Strategy Map developed by the team. You should capture and incorporate any recommendations from the executive group.

Step Five (b): Gather Employee Feedback

This is optional, but recommended. The Strategy Map should be more than a pretty poster thumb-tacked to a wall across from elevator. It should be a dynamic document capable of inspiring people to live your mission. Give those who will be doing the living the opportunity to dissect the Map given their proximity to the real world in which your work gets done.

Step Six: Develop Performance Measures

Returning to the ancestral homeland of the Balanced Scorecard that was created many years ago as a measurement system, your team will translate each of the objectives on the Strategy Map into metrics you can track to provide insight into the execution of your strategy and establish accountability throughout the company. Chapter 8 is devoted to the topic of performance measures.

Step Six (a): Executive Workshop

These will be the ultimate arbiters of your success and therefore it's critical your executives commit themselves fully to the measures that have been developed.

Step Six (b): Gather Employee Feedback

This is another optional step. If you're building a Balanced Scorecard for the entire organization then it's more important that executives buy into the measures than it is to have employees support them. Please don't misunderstand, I'm not suggesting you don't want employee commitment to the metrics you choose, I'm simply noting that if yours is a high-level organizational Scorecard, it's the executives who must manage and own those measures. However, this would be a great opportunity to explain to your staff precisely why the particular measures you plan to use were chosen.

Step Seven: Establish Targets and Prioritize Initiatives

Without a target at which to aim, you're just practicing. Targets bring context to performance measures by detailing improvements required and sparking the creativity necessary to excel. Additionally, all measures should be accompanied by initiatives designed to bring the targets to fruition. Chapter 8 explores these topics in greater depth, providing advice on setting targets and methods to prioritize competing initiatives.

Step Eight: Gather Data for Your First Balanced Scorecard Report

Speaking of targets, why not take the bold step of proclaiming that within 60 days of developing your Strategy Map and measures, you will be holding your first meeting to discuss results? Are you chuckling? I know, you probably won't have all the data, in fact, if experience is any guide, you'll likely be missing upwards of 30% of the data for your measures at the outset of the implementation. But of course that leaves a sizable chunk of wisdom to be derived from the 70% that remain.

Step Nine: Hold Your First Balanced Scorecard Meeting

My wife loves horses—they're her passion and she spends as much time as she can grooming, exercising, and of course, riding our boys Thunder and Storm (we don't have a weather fetish—they came with those names). Her vision, one I share, is for us to spend lazy afternoons riding the winding trails near our house, talking, laughing, simply treasuring the moment. Sounds idyllic, doesn't it? But it's probably never going to happen until I find the time to take some riding lessons! At my current skill level, one sudden side step from the horse and, let's just say I wouldn't be treasuring the moment. It's pretty hard to do that with your butt in the dirt. Some organizations that implement the Balanced Scorecard entertain a similar fallacy of hoping for something without exerting the requisite effort. They expect to derive all the benefits promised from the tool—alignment, focus, and accountability among them, but they refuse to place the Scorecard at the center of their management meeting and reporting agenda. To execute strategy you must analyze it, discuss it, and learn about it. All of which is easily accomplished if you simply use the Scorecard to drive your management meeting agenda. We'll discuss the new strategy-centered management meeting in Chapter 11.

Step Ten: Develop the Ongoing Balanced Scorecard Implementation Plan

Steps one through nine are reminiscent of a proud college graduate receiving a diploma—a significant accomplishment has indeed been marked, but to get the most from the seed that has been planted there is much work ahead! The same applies with the Balanced Scorecard. At this point you will have a Strategy Map that powerfully communicates your strategy and a Scorecard of measures, targets, and initiatives you can use to drive accountability for results. However, for real prosperity to find you, like our newly-minted college graduate, you need to go out into the world, taking the tools you have and expanding them to reach your potential. Later chapters in this book will show you how to do just that, outlining in detail what must be done in order to have your Scorecard act simultaneously as a powerful communication tool, measurement device, and strategic management system.

The time it will take you to complete these steps depends on a number of factors, including: the sense of urgency to create a Balanced Scorecard, the amount of resources dedicated to the implementation, the knowledge of key staff, and of course, executive support. Strategy Maps are literally built in a day at some organizations, while others will labor over the task for weeks. The Scorecard is not something to be "picked away at" as time permits. As with any change-related project, sustaining momentum is critical. Exhibit 3.8 presents a proposed development plan lasting 20 weeks. With focused effort and support, the vast majority of organizations should be able to comfortably craft a Scorecard within this timeframe.

Exhibit 3.8 A Balanced Scorecard Development Plan

Steps / Week	1	2	3	4	5	6	7	8	9	10	11	12	13	14	15	16	17	18	19	20
Planning Phase																				
Step 1. Develop a guiding rationale for your BSC	■																			
Step 2. Secure executive sponsorship		■																		
Step 3. Form your BSC team			■																	
Step 4. Determine where to build your first BSC				■																
Step 5. Determine resource requirements and availability				■																
Step 6. Develop a training and communication plan					■															
Development Phase																				
Step 1. Gather and distribute background material						■														
Step 2. Provide BSC education						■														
Step 3. Develop or confirm mission, values, vision and strategy						■														
Step 4. Conduct executive interviews							■													
Step 5. Develop Strategy Map								■												
Step 5a. Executive workshop									■											
Step 5b. Gather employee feedback									■											
Step 6. Develop performance measures										■										
Step 6a. Executive workshop											■									
Step 6b. Gather employee feedback											■									
Step 7. Establish targets and prioritize initiatives													■							
Step 8. Gather data for your first BSC report															■					
Step 9. Hold your first BSC meeting																	■			
Step 10. Develop ongoing implementation plan																				■

NOTES

1. Paul R. Niven, *Balanced Scorecard Diagnostics: Maintaining Maximum Performance* (Hoboken, NJ: John Wiley & Sons, 2005), pp. 24–25.
2. Interview with Nancy Foltz, September 19, 2002.
3. Interview with Jeff Celentano, June 2002.
4. John Hamm, "The Five Messages Leaders Must Manage,"*Harvard Business Review*, May 2006, pp. 114–123.
5. Phred Dvorak, "How Understanding the 'Why' of Decisions Matters,"*Wall Street Journal*, March 19, 2007, p. B3.
6. Interview with Bill Ryan, September 17, 2002.
7. Robert Simons and Antonio Davila, "How High is Your Return on Management?"*Harvard Business Review*, January–February 1998, p. 70.
8. Ram Charan and Larry Bossidy, *Confronting Reality: Doing What Matters to Get Things Done* (New York: Crown Business, 2004), p. 195.
9. Tony Simons, "The High Cost of Lost Trust,"*Harvard Business Review*, September 2002, p. 18.
10. Robert S. Kaplan and David P. Norton, *The Strategy-Focused Organization*, (Boston: Harvard Business School Press, 2000).
11. Andra Gumbus, Bridget Lyons, and Dorothy E. Bellhouse, "How Bridgeport Hospital Is Using the Balanced Scorecard to Map Its Course,"*Strategic Finance*, August 2002, p. 46.
12. Rudolph W. Giuliani, *Leadership* (New York: Hyperion, 2002).
13. Jeffrey A. Sonnenfeld and Andrew J. Ward, "Firing Back,"*Harvard Business Review*, January 2007, pp. 76–84.
14. Margaret C. Plantz, Martha Taylor Greenway, and Michael Hendricks, "Outcome Measurement: Showing Results in the Nonprofit Sector,"*New Directions for Evaluation*, Fall 1997.
15. Pamela A. Syfert and Lisa B. Schumacher, "Putting Strategy First in Performance Management,"*Journal of Cost Management*, November–December 2000, pp. 32–38.
16. Best Practices Benchmarking Report, *Developing the Balanced Scorecard* (Chapel Hill, NC: Best Practices, LLC, 1999).
17. Laura Downing, "Progress Report on the Balanced Scorecard: A Global Users Survey"*Balanced Scorecard Report*, November–December 2000, pp. 7–9.
18. Adapted from Paul R. Niven, *Balanced Scorecard Step by Step: Maximizing Performance and Maintaining Results, 2nd Edition* (Hoboken, NJ: John Wiley & Sons, 2006), p. 46.
19. Dale Carnegie, *How to Win Friends and Influence People, Revised Edition* (New York: Pocket Books, 1981), p. 34.
20. Jim Collins, *Good to Great and the Social Sectors, A Monograph to Accompany Good to Great* (Jim Collins, 2005), pp. 9–11.
21. Paul R. Niven, *Balanced Scorecard Step by Step: Maximizing Performance and Maintaining Results, 2nd Edition* (Hoboken, NJ: John Wiley & Sons, Inc., 2006), p. 47.

22. Harold L. Sirkin, Perry Keenan, and Alan Jackson, "The Hard Side of Change Management"*Harvard Business Review*, October 2005, pp. 108–118.

23. Business Intelligence, "Driving Corporate Culture for Business Success," 1999.

24. Quoted in: Michael Hammer, "The 7 Deadly Sins of Performance Measurement,"*MIT Sloan Management Review*, Spring 2007, pp. 19–28.

25. Best Practices Benchmarking Report, *Developing the Balanced Scorecard* (Chapel Hill, NC: Best Practices, LLC, 1999).

26. John Hamm, "The Five Messages Leaders Must Manage,"*Harvard Business Review*, May 2006, pp. 114–123.

27. Michael Allison and Jude Kaye, *Strategic Planning for Nonprofit Organizations* (New York: John Wiley & Sons, 1997), p. 35.

28. Dan S. Cohen and John P. Kotter, *The Heart of Change* (Boston: Harvard Business School Press, 2002).

29. Nick Wreden, "Executive Champions: Vital Links between Strategy and Implementation,"*Harvard Management Update*, September 2002.

30. David P. Norton, "Change Agents: The Silent Heroes of the Balanced Scorecard Movement,"*Balanced Scorecard Report*, May–June, 2002, pp. 1–4.

31. Ibid.

32. Paul R. Niven, *Balanced Scorecard Step by Step: Maximizing Performance and Maintaining Results, 2nd Edition* (Hoboken, NJ: John Wiley & Sons, 2006), p. 54.

33. Robert S. Kaplan and David P. Norton, *Alignment* (Boston: Harvard Business School Press, 2006), p. 185.

34. Janice A. Klein, "Why Supervisors Resist Employee Involvement," *Harvard Business Review*, September–October 1984.

35. Paul R. Niven, *Balanced Scorecard Step by Step: Maximizing Performance and Maintaining Results, 2nd Edition* (Hoboken, NJ: John Wiley & Sons, 2006), pp. 38–43.

36. Ibid, p. 58.

4

Training and Communication Planning for Balanced Scorecard Success

Roadmap for Chapter 4 Scorecard creators Kaplan and Norton have occasionally referred to the concept as "simple" but not "simplistic." Unfortunately, many organizations that choose to develop Scorecards hear the "simple," but somehow manage to tune out "not simplistic." If the Balanced Scorecard is simple, they reason, it probably doesn't require a huge investment in training. Sadly, this is not the case. While the Scorecard concept itself is relatively straightforward, the tool has many subtleties and hidden complexities. It is the exploitation of these subtle elements such as cause-and-effect linkages, linkages to management processes, and so on, that will drive the breakthrough results the Scorecard has become famous for. Training has the ability to unlock the power of the Scorecard by placing everyone involved in its development on a level playing field of knowledge. This chapter will provide you with everything needed to design and deliver a comprehensive Scorecard training program.

Without a proper base of Scorecard training, your employees may not have the understanding necessary to take full advantage of this concept. Equally as detrimental is a lack of communication. Missed opportunities, inconsistent expectations, and confusion may appear should you not actively and effectively communicate your Scorecard initiative. Many change initiatives fail to deliver on their promised results. This is a sad and reluctantly accepted reality of organizational life. While there are many causes, lack of communication is consistently cited as a surefire way to short-circuit any change program. In the second half of this chapter, we'll explore the role of communication planning in Balanced Scorecard success. We'll determine precisely why communication is so critical, consider the role of communication objectives, outline the elements of any productive communication plan, and discuss how you can evaluate your success.

TRAINING IS CRITICAL FOR BALANCED SCORECARD SUCCESS

Let me share with you a situation I encounter from time to time at organizations wishing to pursue the development of a Balanced Scorecard. Someone reads an article or hears about the Balanced Scorecard from a colleague. This individual then does some cursory research and learns that the Balanced Scorecard is a relatively straightforward and commonsense solution. Given that and the need for improvement within their organization, the person suggests the development of a Balanced Scorecard.

With the decision to construct a Scorecard completed, a team is put together. They read the same article, maybe even a book, after which they are still convinced it's a simple concept. They hold awareness sessions during which the Scorecard is trumpeted as a measurement system featuring financial and nonfinancial measures, but little is offered regarding the many subtleties and complexities of the model. Then the team begins the difficult work of translating strategy, developing objectives on a Strategy Map and measures for the Scorecard, and hypothesizing about cause and effect, only to realize it's not that simple! However, at this point they're into the implementation stage and don't want to slow their momentum with training. The cost of this decision will frequently manifest itself in Strategy Maps with far too many (or too few) objectives, poorly designed measures, lack of use, and weak alignment within the organization. The resulting tool will most likely contain an ad hoc group of financial and nonfinancial objectives and measures but in no way tells the strategic story of the organization's strategy.

It's often the deceptive simplicity of the Scorecard that makes people very susceptible to the false notion that in-depth training is not required. Feeling the Scorecard can be simply mastered, the organization will sponsor a one-time, high-level training and then trust their employees' business instincts to kick in and fuel the development of powerful new performance objectives and measures.

This chapter will provide you with the materials you need to ensure your organization doesn't suffer the misfortune that often results from a lack of Scorecard training.

Training Generates Tangible Benefits

Management guru Tom Peters is famous for his "pull no punches" style and simple, practical advice. Here is his not so subtle message for organizations that don't invest in regular employee training: "Companies that don't encourage employee education of all kinds are dumb!"[1] I told you he didn't pull any punches. While "dumb" is a subjective evaluation, many researchers have objectively confirmed that training not only leads to a better-educated and motivated workforce, but can also produce dramatic improvements in bottom-line results. In one recent study conducted by the Governmental Accounting Standards Board (GASB) "training for management and staff about performance measurement development and selection" was cited by a majority of respondents as an important aspect of a successful performance management system.[2]

For those of you who invest in the stock market, you may be interested to know that investments in employee training have been positively correlated with financial results. Knowledge Asset Management (KAM), an investment firm in Bethesda, Maryland, tracks organizations that make large investments in training and education. The combined performance of companies in KAM's research portfolio consistently outperformed the Standard & Poor's 500 index.[3]

There are many stories in organizational folklore surrounding the benefits of training. A favorite of mine concerns Dow Chemical founder, Dr. Herbert H. Dow. One day while riding his bike to work, Dr. Dow was stopped by a company supervisor who presented him with a classic good news–bad news scenario. The bad news was that a spill that would cost the company $50,000 had occurred. The good news, remarked the supervisor, was that he had fired the employee who caused the spill. Upon hearing the news, Dr. Dow remarked, "you better get him back here, because I just spent $50,000 to train him."[4]

DESIGNING YOUR BALANCED SCORECARD TRAINING PROGRAM

Most training professionals, and more importantly most training participants, would probably agree that a training event is considered successful when three conditions are met: the training is *effective, efficient,* and *engaging.*[5] Effective implies accomplishing relevant objectives that lead to participant success. Making the best use of participants' time and energy characterizes efficiency. Engaging training sessions and workshops draw the participant into the event and ensure their unique experiences are part of the process. The following sections outline the key steps in designing Balanced Scorecard training sessions that ensure effectiveness, efficiency, and engagement.

Working with Adult Learners

The unique characteristics of adult learners cannot be overestimated when designing a training event. Materials, training flow, and activities must reflect the broad spectrum of learning styles and individual experiences each learner brings to the event. Training experts Milano and Ullius have produced six key principles related to adult learning:[6]

- *Experience is the richest resource for adult learning, therefore, the core methodology of adult education is the analysis of experience.* Adults bring a lifetime of experiences to the learning event and learn best when they're able to draw on their past events. Training design must contain activities that allow the adult learner to analyze the new material in the context of their individual experience. For many, this will entail examining past measurement efforts and discussing them in light of the Balanced Scorecard and strategic measurement.

- *Adults are motivated to learn as they experience needs and interests that learning will satisfy.* Most adult learners see learning as a means to an end of meeting a current need. The more immediate the need, the greater the motivation to learn. As a result, the training session's goals and activities should directly relate to a legitimate need of the participants. Always begin with the end in mind. What is the need that must be satisfied and how does this event do so? What does your team need to be able to do in order to take advantage of Balanced Scorecard opportunities?

- *Adults have a deep need to be self-directing, therefore, the role of the facilitator is to engage in a process of mutual inquiry with them rather than to transmit his or her knowledge to them and then evaluate their conformity to it.* Adult learners may value the trainer's opinions, but ultimately they will decide on the value of what is being discussed. The design should acknowledge this analysis and encourage it by including activities that encourage participants to openly analyze what they are learning and make an evaluation. Rather than stifling the potential conflict that may arise, facilitators should welcome it and encourage frank discussions that often lead to breakthroughs. For example, participants may feel there are other or more established ways to measure performance than the Balanced Scorecard. Facilitators should draw this out and be ready to discuss the differences and the benefits conferred by using the Balanced Scorecard methodology.

- *If the environment does not feel safe to the learner, personal energy will be directed towards self-protection, leaving little for inquiry, analysis, and learning.* The challenge is to create an environment that encourages honest dialogue while protecting the self-esteem of the adult learner. Training sessions must be designed with this in mind, for example, by ensuring appropriate content for the audience, activities that encourage an exchange of ideas, and clarification when one "right answer" is appropriate.

- *Adults have clear expectations about training (based on past experiences), and these expectations will largely determine participants' behavior.* The training's design must manage the expectations of those in attendance. Facilitators should attempt to determine expectations of participants in advance, perhaps by including some participants in the training design process. Goals and objectives of the event should be written from the perspective of the learners and their needs, rather than from the viewpoint of the facilitator. And, finally, participant needs must be acknowledged and built into the session. When developing new training sessions, the design team should analyze the specific needs of the participants and any certain issues they may have. These needs and issues must form the basis for the event.

- *Adults learn in a variety of ways and have preferences in learning styles.* All adults have preferred ways of learning new information based on their past experiences, hereditary makeup, and current environment. Training sessions must be designed to balance the many preferred learning styles participants bring to the event. For example, content should have a mix of "how" and "why" and materials should engage all learners by including an appropriate mix of text and graphics. Designers must be cognizant of their own learning preferences to ensure all activities are not simply reflecting personal appeal and comfort.

Conducting a Training Needs Assessment

In order to improve in any subject, you must first determine where gaps exist between current and desired levels of performance. Needs assessment asks questions (and provides answers) that help you determine skill gaps that must be filled during the training event.

Here is a list of questions you should consider regarding the skill level of Scorecard training session participants:

- What skills and knowledge do participants possess regarding Balanced Scorecard and, more specifically, developing objectives and measures?

- What new skills and knowledge are necessary for participants to be able to develop a Strategy Map of objectives and Balanced

Scorecard performance measures that will help you execute your strategy?

- Will any existing skills or knowledge of participants need to be modified or enhanced for them to develop a Balanced Scorecard system?

You should also conduct a more general analysis of the groups attending your training sessions. Here are a number of items to consider:[7]

- *Number of participants attending each session.* This will ensure you design appropriate activities for the audience size.

- *Level of expertise.* As discussed previously.

- *Positions/titles/reporting relationships.* Open discussions can sometimes be hampered if individuals are attending the session with their superiors.

- *Diversity (age, gender, culture, etc.).* Many organizations have a diverse employee base and training design should respect this diversity.

- *Politics.* Two issues here: First, are there potential politics or conflicts between individuals attending the session? Second, are there political "hot buttons" that should not be pushed during the workshop?

- *Anticipated participant response.* Are attendees likely to welcome the event or be resistant to what is being offered?

Needs assessment allows you to draw a portrait of the participants attending your event. Having defined their needs, and considering the gap you must close, you can now develop goals and key topics for your training session.

Developing Objectives for Your Balanced Scorecard Training

Chapter 3 discussed the importance of developing a guiding rationale for your Balanced Scorecard program. An overarching *raison d'être* is also critical to training design since it will provide the foundation for all other elements of the session. Everything that is designed subsequently, including materials, handouts, and evaluation tools, must align with the guiding reason for holding the training session.

The rationale for your training session answers the question, "why are we conducting this training?" An obvious response may be, "to increase knowledge of the Balanced Scorecard." Though certainly true, it is also quite broad and vague. After reviewing the outcomes of your needs assessment, you should attempt to develop a statement that more accurately captures the spirit of your specific event. For example, it could be "to provide our core team with the skills and knowledge necessary to develop our high-level organizational Strategy Map and Scorecard within 12 weeks."

Agenda for Your Training Session

At this point we are ready to construct the flow of the training event, including the selection and sequencing of agenda items to support your rationale. The topics you choose to present should be engaging, inviting learners to participate actively in the event. Participants should interact with one another, with the facilitators, and with the content itself. The following are a number of criteria for selecting effective and engaging agenda items:[8]

- *Support the guiding rationale.* The activities chosen must directly relate to the overall aims of the session.

- *Offer variety.* Avoid repetition of similar activities.

- *Respect various adult learning styles.* The activities should fit with a variety of learning styles, balancing use of both text and graphics, for example.

- *Transfer learning.* The activities should mirror the real world of the participants as closely as possible. Even though the session may be introducing new material, the learners will bring past experiences that are similar and can be drawn upon to support the learning. Always attempt to build on or enhance what participants already bring to the event. For example, you should attempt to use examples and cases that most participants will easily and comfortably relate to.

- *Reflect the number of participants.* The size of the group will dictate not only the type of activity chosen but also the amount of time allotted.

Sample Balanced Scorecard Training Agenda   As noted, the agenda and activities you develop for Scorecard training should reflect your unique needs and objectives. For many public and nonprofit organizations, however, the following items would most likely form part of a typical Balanced Scorecard training session:

- *Begin with an introductory activity or story.* We've all heard the old adage, "You never have a second chance to make a first impression." So it goes with your Scorecard training session—it's very important to get off to a good start. Design an opening activity that relates to the topic, supports your rationale for training, and "grabs" the attention of participants. I will frequently start my training sessions by sharing with participants a clever riddle that challenges their assumptions about performance measurement or a story that demonstrates the importance of change. Whatever you choose to do, this short activity or story can help create a need to know, assess the knowledge of the Scorecard currently possessed by participants, and start them thinking about how the Balanced Scorecard relates to them.

- *Describe your "burning platform."* What specific challenges do you face (or opportunities do you have) that require you to change, and change now? In this portion of the training event, you will articulate the challenges inherent in your current environment and discuss why change is imperative if you hope to ultimately achieve your mission. You may also wish to include more "macro" considerations (e.g., new laws or regulations, demographic swings, and changing economic prospects).

- *Give background on the Balanced Scorecard.* Provide participants with the history of the Balanced Scorecard—how it has evolved over the past 17 years to become a universally accepted business tool.

- *Provide an overview of Balanced Scorecard fundamentals.* In this component of the event, you should review the specifics of the Scorecard methodology. Begin with the model as originally conceived with the for-profit world in mind and describe how it can be easily adapted to fit the nonprofit or public sectors. Each of the four perspectives should be discussed in detail with particular emphasis placed on common objectives and measures. And don't forget to have some fun with your presentation: Do whatever it takes to make it relevant and enjoyable for your audience. The San Marcos campus of the California State University system has been working with the Balanced Scorecard since 2001 and keeping the Scorecard light has been an important ingredient of their success, as they described to me: "We took a lot of the theory out, and basically said "Hey we've got these issues facing our university, our division and here's a tool we think can help us align our organization to the strategy We used some comical examples to get the point across." Exhibit 4.1 displays their witty depiction of what can happen when you don't meet your customers' needs![9]

- *Answer the question "How does the Balanced Scorecard benefit us?"* Once participants have learned about the Scorecard system, it's time to return to the issues your organization faces. Facilitate an open discussion of how the Scorecard can assist in meeting the challenges and opportunities in front of you.

- *Share success stories.* I could talk until I'm blue in the face (and believe me I can!) about the value of the Balanced Scorecard. But for most people, it all comes down to this: who else in our sector has used the Scorecard successfully? Spend some time discussing Scorecard use in other public and nonprofit organizations. To generate examples, use some of the organizations discussed in this book, speak with colleagues, or conduct your own research. You'll find more examples than you expect!

Exhibit 4.1   Importance of Determining Customer Needs

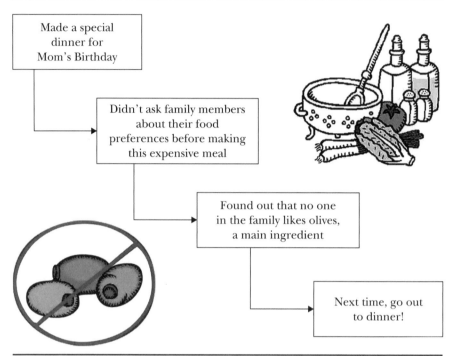

Made a special
dinner for
Mom's Birthday

Didn't ask family members
about their food
preferences before making
this expensive meal

Found out that no one
in the family likes olives,
a main ingredient

Next time, go out
to dinner!

From http://www.csusm.edu/bsc/10

- *Use a case study.* There is no substitute for learning by doing. Nothing
  accelerates learning faster than a case study that forces participants
  to begin grappling with the Balanced Scorecard concept and applying its core principles. Though it's important to devise a case study
  that will be meaningful to your audience, it's not necessary to base
  the case on your own situation. To facilitate the case study, break
  your audience into teams and have each develop a Strategy Map
  of objectives in the four perspectives for your fictional case. Time
  permitting, the teams can also translate the objectives into performance measures. Each team should have the opportunity to present
  their work to the larger group.

Plan on spending a half-day conducting your training session. Assuming
that equates to an event of three hours, I suggest you allot at least one of
those hours to the case study. The discussion and learning generated from
a well-designed case study is unparalleled by other agenda items. In my
workshops with clients, I use a number of different cases based on the audience. I've developed fictitious airlines, nonprofits, local governments, and a

number of others. The creativity and enthusiasm these cases engender never ceases to amaze and inspire me. Over the years, in addition to Hall of Fame caliber Strategy Maps and measures, I've had groups develop new logos and taglines for the case study organization that would make Madison Avenue envious, and even had some compose songs for the case study organization that were sung with pride during their presentation.

A case study is also a terrific way to satisfy a number of adult learning styles. The case should include a narrative outlining the mock organization. This will appeal to those participants whose preferences run toward learning through text presentations. The group will also draw their Strategy Map on a flip chart, which should prove enticing to those who prefer visual learning. Finally, the group will share their output, which will be attractive to members who enjoy verbal learning opportunities. Exhibit 4.2 provides a number of other options for learning materials you may use in your training session.

Unless you have an in-house Scorecard expert in your midst, I would strongly suggest using an outside facilitator or consultant to lead at least your initial training session. A seasoned consultant will be able to spark group thinking and apply proven concepts to ensure you achieve your goals for the event. He or she will also deliver that most critical of currencies—credibility—to your Scorecard initiative at this most important juncture.

Evaluating the Success of Your Training Session

Training evaluation is often an afterthought consisting of a simple form distributed at the end of the event as participants are on their way out the door. Taking a more strategic approach to training evaluation can lead to insights regarding actual transfer of knowledge and application of skills learned. Four levels of evaluation may be considered:[10]

- *Reaction*. At this level you seek to evaluate participants' feelings, thoughts, and perceptions about the training session itself. There are a number of specific factors on which you can solicit reactions: perceived usefulness of what was learned, the physical environment, participant materials, learning aids, activities used, the trainer, times, and content.

- *Learning*. Here you attempt to gauge what participants have actually learned during the event. Comparing behaviors demonstrated during the training with the learning objectives will help you determine whether or not the event has been successful. "Tests" conducted at the end of the event will help reveal whether the participants have developed new skills. Additionally, focus groups or interviews after the event may be used to evaluate learning.

Exhibit 4.2   Choosing Materials for Your Balanced Scorecard Training
Sessions

The materials chosen for the Balanced Scorecard training session are the
tangible, physical items needed for the learning event. Participant materials
could include any combination of the following:

- Prework assignments

- Reading materials: books,
  articles, etc.

- Participant workbooks

- Worksheets for skills practice

- Case studies

- Directions for activities

- Forms for note taking

- Job aids

- Bibliographies

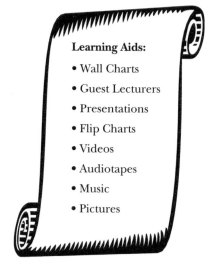

Learning Aids:
- Wall Charts
- Guest Lecturers
- Presentations
- Flip Charts
- Videos
- Audiotapes
- Music
- Pictures

In designing the materials, the following points should be considered:

- Consider organizational culture: Some organizations, for example,
  prefer simple black-and-white text with few graphics. You should always
  adhere to the organizational norms.

- Adult learning. Remember to balance text with graphics, how and why,
  etc., to ensure all learning styles are accommodated.

- Ensure the amount of written material is consistent with what is being
  presented. Don't overwhelm the participants with written material they
  may not use and could find intimidating.

Based on material presented in *Designing Powerful Training,* by Michael Milano and
Diane Ullius (San Francisco: Jossey-Bass, 1998).

- *Behavior.* Our aim here is to measure whether the new skills are
  being applied on the job or on the team. The challenge of course
  is isolating the relationship between the workshop learning and on-
  the-job performance. Also, timing is important since this evaluation
  is necessarily done after the training event.

- *Results*. With this item we are essentially evaluating the workshop's "return on investment." In other words, what was the impact of the training on overall organizational objectives?

Typically, the simplest level to capture in evaluation forms is reaction. Unfortunately, most of us tend to solicit reactions after the training event has ended. This, of course, provides great feedback for future sessions, but does little to quell issues raised by the current group. Consider tracking reactions throughout the event. For example, at a break, do a "spot check" of participants to gauge their reactions to the session. Or have participants write their comments on index cards, and hand them in as they leave for a break. Making "course corrections" and showing your ability to adapt to meet learners' needs is a great way to win their trust and support.

Final Thoughts on Balanced Scorecard Training

It's important to remember that for the majority of employees within your organization, the team you assemble will be the embodiment of the Balanced Scorecard. If the team members don't come across as knowledgeable and credible sources of information, you can be certain that skepticism for the initiative will increase. Some members may come to the implementation with a background in Performance Management and Balanced Scorecard concepts while for others it may be the first exposure. Either way, to ensure a level playing field for the entire team, you have to invest heavily in up-front training. Fairfax County, Virginia is one organization that takes the subject of training very seriously. Its efforts are chronicled in Exhibit 4.3.

One of the most important aspects of training is the questions it raises. When I work with a client and conduct my training sessions, I want the participants thinking not only about Strategy Maps and Scorecards of measures in an isolated academic sense, but also what the initiative will mean at their organization. Following this specific logic path leads them to consider just how they might cascade the Scorecard, how they'll define their terms, and why they even want to use a Balanced Scorecard system. These are all important questions that must be answered before a successful implementation can take place.

Finally, just as your Balanced Scorecard grows and evolves, so too should your training curriculum. The steps described so far in this chapter will help you get off to a solid start, but continuous training is a core ingredient of your Scorecard implementation that must never be neglected. Be sure to add new "modules" that correspond to the maturing nature of your implementation. Sessions on cascading the Scorecard, budget and management reporting linkages, and of course technology (should you choose a software reporting solution) will all pay dividends in greater understanding and use of the system.

Exhibit 4.3   Fairfax County Trains for Measurement Success

Located in northern Virginia, Fairfax County is home to more than 1 million people. The county employs over 11,000 and has been recognized as "one of the best-managed jurisdictions in America" according to *Governing Magazine* and the Government Performance Project. This notable achievement is based on results in a number of areas, one of which is termed "Managing for Results." Fairfax County received an "A−", one of only three awarded in this category that looked at strategic planning and performance measurement.

The County began their performance measurement initiative by research-ing other jurisdictions. They quickly learned that many of those using perform-ance measurement systems had invested in cursory training efforts and, as a result, achieved only limited results from their systems. Fairfax County vowed to make a significant investment in training their core team, and later, all employees.

Training of team members focused on both basic performance meas-urement techniques and concepts, and also on how these concepts affected the County. The curriculum contained sections on measurement basics, data collection, surveying for customer satisfaction, and managing for results. To ensure the training was relevant, facilitators guided team members through exercises that encouraged them to consider how they would actually measure performance in a number of specific county departments. This "hands-on" application was an excellent complement to the new language of performance measurement being introduced to the team.

Once the core team was well versed in performance measurement tools, they took their show on the road. The team offered to help agencies through-out the County develop their own strategic performance measures. It was later discovered that those agencies that requested help early and often developed better measure than those that attempted to "go it alone."[i]

Fairfax County's training initiative has evolved in step with changes to their performance measurement system. For example, recognizing that not all employees can fit formal training sessions into their schedules, the per-formance measurement team is in the process of developing online courses that can be accessed at the convenience of learners. One thing that hasn't changed over the years is the County's commitment to training. Performance Measurement Program Coordinator Barbara Emerson explains the impor-tance of training for performance success: "The better agency staff under-stand performance measurement concepts and tools, the more likely they will be to develop measures that will lead to improvements in service delivery."[ii]

[i] Barbara Emerson, "Training for Performance Measurement Success," *Government Finance Review,* April 2002, pp. 22–25.
[ii] Ibid.

Fairfax County graphic from http://www.co.fairfax.va.us/

DEVELOPING A COMMUNICATION PLAN TO SUPPORT YOUR BALANCED SCORECARD INITIATIVE

Communication: A Vital Link to Success

How do you feel about the communication that takes place within your organization? What's your opinion of the effort that's expended on communication? Any better? Most organizations feel they do a decent job of the latter but aren't pleased with the overall results. Neither, apparently, are employees. In a Harris Interactive poll of 23,000 workers, only 17% felt their organization fostered open communication that is respectful of differing opinions and that results in new and better ideas.[11]

Needless to say, this is an enormous problem since new and better ideas are the lifeblood of today's organizational success, and as previously noted, their development is a direct product of effective communication. Speaking on the essential role of communication, Peter Drucker has said that the most important thing a nonprofit organization can do is "to build itself around information and communication instead of around hierarchy."[12]

Before we go any further, I have to relate to you this story that is very indicative of the sorry state of communication that exists in many organizations. Standing in line for a flight a while back, I overheard two people behind me talking about recent job experiences. It didn't take long for them to note some pretty significant weaknesses with previous employers. Of course, the usual suspects were bandied about: pay, benefits, and working conditions, but for one of them it was the people running the ship that caused him to make the leap to greener pastures. As he put it, "they didn't know what they were doing. . . . there was no leadership, literally. They called themselves 'Leadegment,' leadership and management. Any time you have to make up a word you know how Dilbertesque the situation is!" As a consultant for the past 10 years or so, and a long-time corporate employee, I thought I'd heard it all, but *Leadegment!* Never before, and I hope never again! I'm sure this, leadership/management team had their hearts in the right place when they concocted this unique moniker, but to their employees it was probably seen as just the latest in a long series of smoke and mirrors attempts to keep them utterly confused.

Why Communication Is Critical to Your Balanced Scorecard

Quick quiz: The Balanced Scorecard is___? I'm sure you recall—without referring back to Chapter 1—that a Scorecard is three things: a measurement system, strategic management system, and a communication tool. All of these represent significant changes in how the organization gauges its success. Hence, the Balanced Scorecard more than anything else represents a *change initiative*. And we all know change is tough, really tough, especially when you're introducing something that is potentially threatening. Change can be unsettling, frightening, confusing, and painful for those affected. In other words, something to be avoided at all costs.

Change efforts struggle for many reasons, but fundamentally, the vast majority of organizations struggle with change because of their inability to answer these five questions on the part of those undergoing the change:

1. What do you want me to do?

2. What's in it for me?

3. How will this change affect me?

4. What will you do to help me make the change?

5. How am I doing?

Communication planning holds the key to unlocking many of the answers. A well-conceived, designed, and delivered communication strategy and plan gives you the opportunity to proactively shape your message, ultimately making change, if not pleasant, at least palatable. This is the chance to sell your message of change, improvement, and success to all your stakeholders. Jack Welch, former CEO of General Electric, is someone who knows a thing or two about what it takes to make change happen within organizations. He suggests, no, bellows that he "learned that for any big idea you had to sell, sell, and sell to move the needle at all."[13]

A Guiding Rationale for Your Communication Plan

By now you should be getting the impression that I take the idea of determining the reasons for doing something pretty seriously: a guiding rationale for your Balanced Scorecard program, for your training sessions, and now for your communication plan. Whatever you're doing, the first step should always be a careful and critical exploration of why you're engaging in the activity in the first place. What is the purpose and what are your overriding objectives? This is especially critical for communication planning since this process centers on the delivery of key messages and information that can literally make or break the success of your implementation.

The guiding objectives you select for your communication plan should represent your unique situation. The following list contains a number of objectives commonly cited by organizations developing communication strategies and plans:[14]

- Build awareness of the Balanced Scorecard at all levels of the organization

- Provide education on key Balanced Scorecard concepts to all audiences

- Generate the engagement and commitment of key stakeholders in the implementation
- Encourage participation in the process
- Generate enthusiasm for the Balanced Scorecard
- Ensure team results are disseminated rapidly and effectively

The Michigan Department of Transportation (MDOT) considered the following as its objective for communication planning: "The purpose and focus of the communication strategy will be the explanation of the Scorecard and its value to MDOT, its linkage to our Business Plan and current goals, its incorporation of existing measurements, and its application and value in the future."[15] Notice the inclusion of the words, "its value to MDOT." A specific reference of this nature ensures the team never loses sight of one of the key communication-related questions I posed at the outset of this section: What's in it for me? They will ensure their communications clearly articulate why this change is taking place and its value to employees, and thus worthy of their time and attention.

Setting objectives for the communication plan will often lead you to the establishment of a theme or metaphor you can use to creatively "trademark" your implementation. Some people like slogans and themes while others think they're hokey and convey little if any value. Whatever your opinion, there is little doubt that themes are colorful and often memorable. And memorability is a huge weapon in the arsenal of communication. When Bridgeport Hospital began their campaign a number of years ago, the communication theme was "Journey to Destination 2005," using the analogy of a bus trip to the future. Highways represented the hospital's five strategic imperatives, landmarks represented the objectives, and mile markers represented the performance measures.[16] One client termed their Balanced Scorecard "LENS," an acronym for learning, execution, navigation, and strategy. Whatever moniker you choose should reflect your organization, culture, and aspirations.

Key Elements of a Communication Plan

One simple and effective method of designing your communication plan is to take advantage of the "W5" approach—who, what, when, where, and why. Each is discussed below in the context of communication planning.

Who: The Target Audiences   The size of your organization and scope of your implementation will help you define the specific audiences for your communication plan. In general, you should consider each of the following groups: senior leaders, management (those with direct reports), all employees, the Balanced Scorecard core team, a steering committee (if you use one), boards of directors, and elected officials.

Who: The Communicator Once you've determined your target audiences, you can match them with appropriate message providers. Each group will have different needs and require specific messaging. A board of directors, for example, would likely receive more formal communications consisting of presentation material and oral updates typically delivered by senior leaders. In contrast, a newsletter written for the employee body may connote a more casual attitude and be written by a member of the implementation team.

What and Why: Defining the Key Messages Every communication plan will contain a number of key messages that are translated from your plan objectives and should be aimed at your target audiences. Let's revisit the MDOT communication plan objectives and consider how they may be translated into key messages. "The purpose and focus of the communication strategy will be the explanation of the Scorecard and its value to MDOT, its linkage to our Business Plan and current goals, its incorporation of existing measurements, and its application and value in the future." Based on these objectives, we would expect messaging centered on how the Scorecard can help solve current issues facing MDOT, how it builds on current measures at the department, and how it will prove beneficial both now and in the future as conditions change.

When: Frequency of Communication All effective communication shares one common trait: targeting specific needs. The frequency of your communication will vary depending on the needs of your target audiences. For example, you'll want to keep your senior leaders well informed on a frequent basis. Your core team also requires up-to-date information. However, you could meet the information needs of a board of directors with less frequent communiqués. Having said that, I should remind you of what leading change expert, John Kotter, said about communication. "Without credible communication, and a lot of it, employees' hearts and minds are never captured."[17] Heed this advice and, if anything, err on the side of too much, rather than too little, communication.

Where (and How): Communication Vehicles Ahh, now the fun part: the communication vehicles! Have you ever opened a greeting card and been serenaded with a song or other musical accompaniment? A friend once told me the computer power offered in that card's tiny chip would have matched the output of the world's greatest computers of just 50 years ago. Urban myth perhaps? The point is, we've made tremendous technological advances in the past few decades. Today, with even the humblest of office software packages, you possess a plethora of graphical and communication options. Add to the mix some good old-fashioned creativity and imagination and you're off to the communication races.

Despite the technological leaps I've just touted, face-to-face communication remains the most reliable form of interchange among us. Getting out and speaking directly to your target audiences is your best chance of truly influencing attitudes and stacking the deck of change in your favor. But, if you're going to get on your Scorecard soapbox, you've got to be prepared to answer the tough questions you're sure to get from a sometimes skeptical, and typically apprehensive, audience. Honesty is, naturally, the best policy and you should answer all queries to the best of your current ability. It's also very helpful to develop your key messages, thereby ensuring the responses you're broadcasting are consistent across time and audience groups. Dennis Madsen, former CEO of outdoor gear store REI, understands the power of effective face-to-face communication. He notes: "I spend most of my time staying in front of employees, engaging them in dialogue. The executive team and I do quarterly 'town hall meetings' with groups of 200 employees at a time, where forty minutes of the hour is devoted to questions and answers. Employees won't always tell you what's on their minds if they're forced to raise their hand in a public forum. So we leave three-by-five inch index cards and pencils taped to every chair in the auditorium. Employees can write their questions, the cards are collected and brought up, and we answer them on the spot."[18] Leaving the index cards for shy employees is a simple gesture but it connotes a strong commitment to ensuring every employee's voice is heard.

Two increasingly popular communication vehicles are the Internet and the organizational intranet. Both are reliable, relatively inexpensive, and easy to use. The Finance and Administrative Services department at the San Marcos campus of California State University has used the Internet to provide all interested parties with the latest updates on their Balanced Scorecard efforts. Its home page is featured in Exhibit 4.4.

Not all organizations will possess the technical or financial resources necessary to develop a sophisticated intranet, but, fortunately, alternative communication vehicles abound; it's a matter of finding what works best for your audiences, given cultural preferences, demographics, and so on. Consider any or all of the following as possibilities: group presentations, implementation plans, newsletters, workshops, brown bag lunches, video presentations, message kits, e-mails, news bulletins, raffles and contests, pay-stub messages, demonstrations, road shows, town hall meetings, maybe even instant messages. Just think, you could IM your BFF about your BSC.

Recall from our discussion of training earlier in the chapter that adults tend to have different learning proclivities. Keep that in mind as you design your communication vehicles and attempt to provide a balance of media, ensuring you make a connection with everyone in your target audience. Rick Pagsibigan of the Red Cross of Philadelphia understands the importance of using a variety of communication channels. He explains:

> Different people learn in different ways. Some like to read, some like to hear, some like to feel and touch, some prefer to see practical applications, some enjoy conceptual or theoretical constructs. Essentially what I was trying to do

Exhibit 4.4   Balanced Scorecard Home Page from Cal State San Marcos

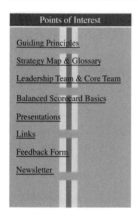

The Finance & Administrative Services
Division Has Begun Our Balanced Scorecard
Journey to . . .

- Improve our Division's effectiveness
- Focus efforts across the Division towards a single strategy
- Improve the culture and climate of our division
- Help us prioritize daily activities
- Assist us with making choices while continuing to deliver
  services to the campus community
- Measure our progress towards improvement in these
  areas

From http://www.csusm.edu/bsc

was to appeal to as many audiences as possible. We did that by using a variety of channels. One method is our Change Management group. The task of this group was to understand the strategic plan and the Balanced Scorecard, and communicate them to the rest of the organization in a way that makes sense. They used a series of meetings, handouts, presentations, and so on.

A second way is through e-mails, informing staff of what's happening with strategic planning and the Balanced Scorecard process. I use the CEO to deliver the message to staff on our latest development. Another channel is the

Board of Directors. We had our board present the strategic plan and Balanced Scorecard. To do so they needed to understand it in order to effectively communicate it to their peers.[19]

Evaluating the Effectiveness of Your Communication Efforts

Earlier in the chapter, I reviewed the process of evaluating training efforts. I described the effort as one that is "often overlooked." When it comes to evaluating the outcomes of communication plans "often overlooked" would probably be a charitable estimation. "Don't even consider it" is probably more reflective of what actually takes place. But the good news is, even anecdotal evidence can help you gauge the effectiveness of your communication efforts. For example: Are groups completing their Scorecard tasks on time? Are you receiving questions about the Scorecard? Have requests been made for Scorecard presentations? Are teams looking for the guide you've prepared on the subject at budget time? These are all indications that your messages are probably reaching a receptive ear.

For those that have the means and the inclination, a formal survey of audiences is recommended. Using survey data, you can assess your efforts on the following criteria:[20]

- *No contact.* Has not heard of the Balanced Scorecard implementation.

- *Awareness.* Has heard about the initiative but doesn't know what it is.

- *Conceptual understanding.* Understands the Balanced Scorecard and any individual effects.

- *Tactical understanding.* Understands both the personal and organizational effects of the Balanced Scorecard.

- *Acceptance.* Will support the Balanced Scorecard and the changes it promises.

A simplified communication plan is shown in Exhibit 4.5.

Final Thoughts on Communication Planning

Writer and aviator Anne Morrow Lindbergh once remarked that "good communication is as stimulating as black coffee and just as hard to sleep after." Today, we are awash in communication, but, how much of what passes for communication would meet Lindbergh's standard of "good?" Your challenge is to cut through the clutter that can surround a new initiative such as the Balanced Scorecard and focus on delivering the right message to the target audience at the right time and in the appropriate manner so that it resonates with your audience.

Let me conclude this chapter with the story of a leader who understood the power of communication to generate understanding and support

Exhibit 4.5   Simplified Communication Plan for Your Balanced Scorecard
Implementation

Audience	Purposes	Frequency	Delivery Vehicle	Communicator
Senior Leadership	• Gain commitment • Remove obstacles • Report progress • Prevent surprises	Bi-weekly	Direct contact	Executive Sponsor
Elected Officials	• Gain commitment • Remove obstacles • Report progress	Monthly	Direct contact	Executive Sponsor
Management	• Convey purpose • Explain concepts • Report progress • Gain commitment	Bi-weekly	• E-mail • Mgt. meetings • Articles • Intranet	Champion/ Team Members
All Employees	• Convey purpose • Introduce concepts • Eliminate misconceptions • Report progress	Monthly	• E-Mail • Newsletters • Town-Hall meetings • Intranet	Core Team Members
Core Team	• Track progress • Assign tasks • Review expectations	Weekly	• Team meeting • Status memos • Intranet	Champion

Adapted from *Balanced Scorecard Step-by-Step: Maximizing Performance and Maintaining Results, 2nd Edition,* Paul R. Niven (John Wiley & Sons, 2006).

for change in a very tumultuous time.[21] When Paul Levy became CEO of Beth Israel Deaconess Medical Center (BIDMC) in 2002, he faced an organization truly on the brink. Formed by the 1996 merger of Beth Israel and Deaconess hospitals, both of which had very distinguished reputations, noted global experts, and dedicated staffs, BIDMC's troubles began almost immediately after the union. By the time Levy arrived, the hospital was losing $50 million a year, relations at all levels were strained, and a once proud and devoted team of employees was deeply demoralized by the precipitous fall their once legendary institutions had suffered.

Facing a turnaround challenge of epic proportions, Levy knew his actions had to be bold and swift. True to that vision of change, during his very first morning on the job, he delivered an all-hands-on-deck e-mail to staff that contained four broad messages: the proud history of the organization, the very real threat of a sale to a for-profit chain if the situation did not improve, the actions staff could expect him to take in the face of this threat, and finally, the open management style he would adopt, including an abundance of direct and open communication.

Throughout the challenging period of change, Levy continued to communicate openly and effectively with all staff, always putting the organization's cards on the table and using simple language that left little possibility of creative interpretation. During one critical juncture, he issued a lengthy e-mail to employees that accompanied the several hundred-page change plan that had been devised by the organization's leaders and a team of consultants. This note, consistent with his day-one missive, began on a positive and uplifting note, emphasizing, among other things, the uncompromising values the institution held dear. The note went on to outline key points of the turnaround plan, including some of the sure-to-be-unpopular measures that would ultimately become necessary. Levy also used the note to directly respond to anticipated concerns the staff would likely harbor, openly acknowledging past missteps leadership had taken. He went on to reiterate his key points at every possible opportunity: meetings with employees, interviews with the press, and public speeches among them. His ceaseless communication efforts convinced all stakeholders of the very real threat they faced and the necessity of change for survival, helping everyone clearly understand the steps that must be taken.

By any yardstick, Levy's tenure at BIDMC has been remarkably successful. The original restructuring plan noted a three-year improvement process, transitioning from a $58 million loss in 2001 to breakeven in 2004. By the conclusion of the 2004 fiscal year, performance was tracking well ahead of plan with the organization reporting a $37 million gain from operations. Revenues were up, costs down, and morale reached premerger levels. Open, candid, and frequent communication, while not a panacea for all that ails a modern organization, is, as this case illustrates, a powerful tonic in the fight to ensure alignment and execution of strategy.

NOTES

1. Bob Nelson, *1001 Ways to Energize Employees* (New York: Workman Publishing, 1997), p. 181.

2. Governmental Accounting Standards Board, "Performance Measurement at the State and Local Levels: A Summary of Survey Results," 2001.

3. Martin Delahoussaye, Kristine Ellis, and Matt Bolch, "Measuring Corporate Smart,"*Training,* August 2002.

4. Ibid.

5. Michael Milano and Diane Ullius, *Designing Powerful Training* (San Francisco: Jossey-Bass, 1998).

6. Ibid., p. 24.

7. Ibid., p. 67.

8. Ibid., p. 159.

9. Interview with Abbi Stone and Katy Rees, September 18, 2002.

10. Donald Kirkpatrick, *Evaluating Training Programs* (San Francisco: Berrett-Koehler, 1994).

11. Stephen R. Covey, *The 8th Habit* (New York: The Free Press, 2004), p. 3.

12. Peter F. Drucker, *Managing the Non-Profit Organization* (New York: Harper Collins, 1990).

13. Jack Welch and John Byrne, *Jack: Straight From the Gut* (New York: Warner Business Books, 2001).

14. Paul R. Niven, *Balanced Scorecard Step by Step: Maximizing Performance and Maintaining Results, 2nd Edition* (Hoboken, NJ: John Wiley & Sons, 2006), p. 64.

15. Interview with Nancy Foltz, September 19, 2002.

16. Andra Gumbus, Bridget Lyons, and Dorothy E. Bellhouse, "Journey to Destination 2005," *Strategic Finance*, August 2002.

17. John P. Kotter, *Leading Change* (Boston: Harvard Business School Press, 1996).

18. "Gearing up at REI," *Harvard Business Review*, May 2003, p. 20.

19. Interview with Rick Pagsibigan, September 19, 2002.

20. Paul R. Niven, *Balanced Scorecard Step by Step: Maximizing Performance and Maintaining Results, 2nd Edition* (Hoboken, NJ: John Wiley & Sons, 2006), p. 67.

21. David A. Garvin and Michael A. Roberto, "Change through Persuasion," *Harvard Business Review*, February 2005, pp. 104–112.

5

Mission, Values, and Vision

Roadmap for Chapter 5 Thousands of organizations around the world have used the Balanced Scorecard to successfully implement their strategies. But before a strategy is formulated or implemented, the organization must contemplate its mission, values, and vision (see Exhibit 5.1). These concepts are at the core of any effective organization—inspiring all stakeholders, guiding decisions, and aligning the actions of every employee. The Balanced Scorecard will ultimately translate the mission, values, vision, and strategy into performance objectives and metrics you can use to gauge your success in meeting your overall aims.

In this chapter, we'll examine each of these building blocks in detail; consider what they are and how to determine their effectiveness, review tips on developing them, and identify their vital linkage to the Balanced Scorecard. As a Scorecard practitioner you'll need to determine if the Balanced Scorecard you've developed is truly aligned to your mission, values, and vision. This chapter equips you with the tools to make that critical determination.

MISSION

What Is a Mission Statement and Why Is It So Important?

Anyone encountering your organization, whether it's a customer, funder, potential employee, or partner, will undoubtedly have a number of questions in mind. Who are you as an organization? Whom do you serve? Why do you exist? It is the mission of your organization that provides the answers to these vital questions.[1]

Exhibit 5.1   The Balanced Scorecard Translates Mission, Values, Vision, and Strategy

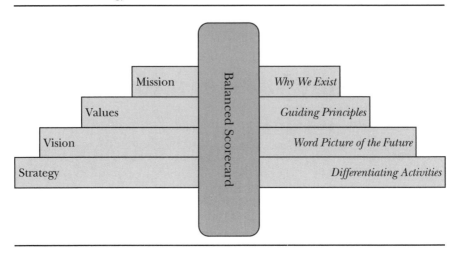

A mission statement defines the core purpose of the organization, its *raison d'être*. The mission also reflects employees' motivations for engaging in the company's work. In the for-profit world that is dominated almost exclusively by shareholder concerns, a mission should provide the rationale for a company's existence beyond generating stockholder wealth. Interestingly, corporate charters of the nineteenth century were regarded as a privilege, with which came the corporate obligation to serve the public interest. Even in today's Wall Street–driven "meet the numbers or else" markets, the mission statement should describe how an organization is indeed serving the public interest—the true responsibility of any organization, be it private, public, or nonprofit in structure.

Nonprofit and public sector agencies of course do not share the profit imperative. This has always been a world dominated by the quest of service provision. A mission statement clarifies the true purpose of these organizations and clearly articulates it to all stakeholders. The mission isn't just window dressing; in fact, the very success of public and nonprofit enterprises is often dependent, at least in part, on the development of a crystallizing mission. Researchers from the Independent Sector found that, "a clear, agreed upon mission statement is one of the four primary characteristics of successful nonprofit organizations."[2] The evidence is clear that public sector organizations also benefit from the declaration of a distinctive mission, as David Osborne and Ted Gaebler reported in *Reinventing Government:* "The experience of hashing out the fundamental purpose of an organization—debating all the different assumptions and views held by its members and agreeing on one basic mission—can be a powerful one. When it is done right, a mission statement can drive an entire organization from top to bottom."[3]

Whichever field of endeavor we choose, one thing is clear: We all strive to make a contribution. Purpose and fulfillment in life are not gained from the collection of a paycheck, but rather from contributing to something greater than ourselves. The organization's mission is the collective embodiment of this most basic of human desires. Hewlett-Packard cofounder David Packard held this belief deeply and made it the cornerstone of his management philosophy. This is how he described mission in a 1960 speech that is as relevant today as it was almost a half century ago. "A group of people get together and exist as an institution that we call a company so they are able to accomplish something collectively that they could not accomplish separately— they make a contribution to society . . . do something that is of value."[4] The best of our organizations offer us the opportunity to accomplish something of value, to attain true meaning and fulfillment through work.

Unlike strategies and tactics that may be achieved over time, you never really fulfill your mission. It acts as a beacon for your work, constantly pursued but never quite reached. Consider your mission to be the compass by which you guide your organization. And just as a compass can lead you to safety when you're lost in unfamiliar terrain, a powerful mission can serve as your guide in times of organizational uncertainty. Consider the case of Bon Secours Health System.[5] Several years ago this healthcare provider that has existed since 1824 was considering the purchase of a group of nursing homes. The deal looked good on paper, but some additional research on the acquisition revealed a troubling source of the potential good fortune. Low pay and inadequate employee benefits were the true driving force of the nursing home company's profits. Bon Secours reconsidered the acquisition in light of its mission statement. In addition to providing a caring environment for patients, the mission also stressed the same treatment for employees. Investing in the nursing homes would clearly have violated this component of Bon Secours' mission, and thus the deal was rejected.

Effective Mission Statements

Now that we know what they are, let's look at some of the attributes that make for an effective and enduring mission statement:

- *Simple and clear.* Peter Drucker has said one of the greatest mistakes organizations make is to turn their missions into "hero sandwiches of good intentions."[6] I've read thousands of pithy quotes over the years but this may very well be my all-time favorite. It's short, colorful, and most important, 100% accurate. I have yet to share this nugget of sage advice with a public sector or nonprofit audience and not have the entire room nod in unison or chuckle somewhat apologetically, as if to say, "okay, you got us on that one." This is a truly extraordinary metaphor that conjures up layer upon layer of societal good to be accomplished by the organization. As admirable as such intentions may be, they aren't practical. You can't be all things to all people and still expect to maintain the focus necessary to accomplish specific goals. The mission must mirror your chosen field of endeavor.

- *Inspire change.* While your mission doesn't change, it should inspire great change within your organization. Since the mission can never be fully realized, it should propel your organization forward, stimulating positive change and growth. Consider the mission of the Partnership for a Drug-Free America: "To help kids and teens reject substance abuse by influencing attitudes through persuasive information." As drug use habits and preferences change, this mission will remain relevant and motivate the group to direct their resources towards attitudinal adjustments of teenagers.

- *Long-term in nature.* Mission statements should be written to last a hundred years or more. While strategies and plans will surely change during that time period, the mission should remain the bedrock of the organization, serving as the stake in the ground for all future decisions. The mission of the Internal Revenue Service is "to provide America's taxpayers with top quality service by helping them understand and meet their tax responsibilities and by applying the tax law with integrity and fairness to all." This would be as appropriate decades from now as it is today.

- *Easy to understand and communicate.* Nobody would argue that our modern organizational community is one saturated with jargon. Buzzwords abound in offices around the world as we invent new and curious words and phrases to describe the world around us. While many people react negatively to buzzwords, others say they simply represent a sign of "words in action and a culture on the move."[7] Regardless of your opinion on the role of buzzwords in our modern life, they really have no place in a mission statement. The last thing you want to do is turn this exercise into a game of "buzzword bingo:" leading-edge, quality first, proactive, good to great . . . Buzzword bingo! Your mission should be written in plain language that is easily understood by all readers. A compelling and memorable mission is one that reaches people on a visceral level, speaking to them and motivating them to serve the organization's purpose.

Developing Your Mission Statement

"The first question is always, what's the mission? Ask yourself what you'd like to achieve—not day to day, but your overarching goal."[8] This is the advice offered by Rudy Giuliani. But how do we answer that question—how do we develop the mission? In the sections that follow, I'll provide you with a number of options for creating your own mission statement.

As you'll see, most exercises are designed to help you develop a mission center on posing a number of key questions. When creatively combined, your thoughtful answers to these questions will lead to a galvanizing mission statement for your organization.

The "5 Whys" A very effective method for developing your mission is based on a concept known as the "5 Whys" developed by Jim Collins and Jerry Porras.[9] Start with a descriptive statement such as "we make X products or deliver Y services." Then ask, "Why is this important?" five times. A few "whys" into this exercise and you'll begin to see your true mission emerging. This process works for virtually any product or service organization. A waste management organization could easily move from "we pick up trash" to "we contribute to a stronger environment by creatively solving waste management issues" after just a couple of rounds. A market research organization might transition from "provide the best market research data" to "contribute to customers' success by helping them understand their markets." An accounting department might begin their deliberations by suggesting "we keep the books." One or two whys later, that stale notion can be transformed to the significantly more meaningful and inspiring mission of "we help all leaders make better, more informed decisions through accurate and timely financial reporting."

You'll discover that with each round of "why," your true reason for being as an organization becomes clearer and the value or contribution you strive to create or make becomes apparent. This process is powerful because it builds on the notion of *abstraction* that I define as moving to a different level, leaving characteristics out. We humans are great abstractors; just ask anyone about him- or herself and chances are the first thing you'll hear is, "I'm an attorney" or "I work in high-tech." We tend to let these descriptions define us and we perceive the world around us through that particular lens. Why not move down the abstraction ladder a bit and see yourself as a husband or wife, neighbor, movie lover, baseball fan, and so on. Doing so opens up a world of possibility in our lives.

Similarly, most organizations focus intently on the micro details of their operations, failing to see the bigger issues that underlie their purpose. The "5 Whys" force us to abstract to different levels, thereby leaving behind the myriad specific characteristics of our organizational being and unearthing our true meaning.

From "5 Whys" to 6 Questions Let's move from the "5 Whys" to the following six questions. Your responses to these queries will help you frame the fundamentals of your mission:[10]

1. *Who are we?* The answer to this seemingly innocuous question should provide stakeholder opinion on what makes the organization different, and why it will endure. It's important not to restrict yourself when

answering this query. Don't focus on what is written on your organization's stationery, instead, expound on the central themes that define you.

2. *What basic social or political needs or problems do we exist to meet?* The answer to this question will provide justification for your existence.

3. *How do we recognize, anticipate, and respond to these problems or needs?* Look outside yourself and consider the wider environment when tackling this question. Liaising with other organizations, conducting research, sharing best practice information, all these activities are geared toward an external orientation that permit the organization to stay in constant touch with developments in the field.

4. *How should we respond to our key stakeholders?* Satisfying stakeholder needs is central to the success of public and nonprofit organizations. When contemplating this question, consider all your stakeholders, their varied needs, and how you propose to respond to these needs.

5. *What is our guiding philosophy and culture?* Once you've developed a mission, values, vision, and a strategy will follow. To successfully implement the strategy, it should be consistent with your guiding philosophy and culture. Therefore, it's important to consider these items now and clearly articulate them in your statement of core purpose—the mission.

6. *What makes us distinctive or unique?* Competition is shaping our global economy and has had a tremendous impact not only on the private sector, but the public and nonprofit arenas as well. Any nonprofit that is unable to demonstrate unique competencies or advantages will soon be overlooked as irrelevant. In the public sector, the cry of "privatization" of services is an all too familiar refrain. Organizations must determine exactly what elevates them from others willing and able to provide similar services in order to truly distinguish themselves in the eyes of stakeholders.

Gast's Laws

The late business professor Walter Gast formulated a series of principles in the 1940s and 1950s that suggested organizational success was not just a function of simply generating profitable returns, but was in fact something deeper. His principles have been adapted and used to help many organizations develop mission statements. Here are the six questions based on Gast's Laws:[11]

1. What *"want-satisfying"* service do we provide and constantly seek to improve?

2. How do we increase the quality of life for our customers and stakeholders?

3. How do we provide opportunities to productively employ people?

4. How do we create a high-quality work experience for our employees?

5. How do we live up to the obligation to provide just wages?

6. How do we fulfill the obligation of providing a return on the financial and human resources we expend?

A Simpler Approach   Each of the techniques outlined has significant merit and will undoubtedly lead to the creation of an inspiring mission. In keeping with the 80/20 rule (80 percent of the value with 20 percent of the effort), Exhibit 5.2 provides a simple template that can help you get the mission ball rolling within your organization.

Who Writes the Mission Statement?

An important consideration when writing your mission statement is who should be involved in the process. There are different schools of thought on this subject. Some argue the mission should be crafted by the senior leader

---

Exhibit 5.2   Simplified Mission Statement Template

We exist to (primary purpose, need served, or problem solved):

_____

_____

_____

For (primary clients or customer):

_____

_____

_____

In order to (core services offered):

_____

_____

_____

So that (long-term outcomes determining success):

_____

_____

_____

or other executives, sent out for comments and revisions, and finalized without any meetings or committee involvement. Others believe the mission statement, with its inherent focus on capturing the hearts and minds of all employees, cannot possibly be drafted without employee involvement. Being the good fence-sitting consultant that I am, I'll come down somewhere in the middle on this debate.

Mission statements require the broad and high-level thinking of an executive to consider the many possibilities available to the organization. Charismatic leaders often possess the enviable ability of crystallizing the organization's place and future goals in compelling terms to be shared with all employees. Don't deny yourself the opportunity of gleaning your executives' wisdom and foresight. At the same time, you should also involve as many people as possible in *reviewing* the draft mission statement. Let employees at every level of the organization have the chance to "kick the tires" of this most important document. The mission must serve to rouse everyone toward an exciting future, and without involvement in the process, commitment will be difficult if not impossible to acquire.

If You Already Have a Mission

As mission-driven organizations, many of you probably already have mission statements. Some might be proudly adorning office walls throughout your organization, while others might be gathering dust on a shelf, or tucked out of sight in a desk drawer somewhere. If yours falls into the latter category— that is, you haven't seen or heard much about your mission for a while—that's a good sign that it is time to reexamine it.

Start by evaluating your mission in the context of the attributes presented earlier in the chapter. Does your statement contain all of these attributes? Here are some additional questions to ask if you're uncertain about the efficacy of your current mission:[12]

- *Is the mission up to date?* Does it reflect what the organization actually does and what it is all about?

- *Is the mission relevant to your clients and constituents?* Does a compelling reason for your existence present itself from a review of your mission?

- *Who is being served?* Should you rewrite the mission to more accurately reflect your current customer base?

Exhibit 5.3 contains sample mission statements from a diverse group of organizations.

Why Mission Is "Mission-Critical" to the Balanced Scorecard

The Balanced Scorecard was not designed to act as an isolated management tool; rather, it is part of an integrated approach to examining your

---

Exhibit 5.3   Sample Mission Statements

The City of Charlotte: The mission of the City of Charlotte is to ensure the delivery of quality public services that promote safety, health, and quality of life for its citizens.

American Association of Retired Persons (AARP): AARP is dedicated to enhancing quality of life for all as we age. We lead positive social change and deliver value to members through information, advocacy, and service.

Society for Human Resource Management (SHRM): SHRM serves the needs of the human resource management professional by providing the most essential and comprehensive set of resources available. In addition, the Society is committed to advancing the human resource profession and the capabilities of all human resource professionals to ensure that HR is an essential and effective partner in developing and executing organizational strategy.

American Institute of Certified Public Accountants (AICPA): Provide members with the resources, information, and leadership that enable them to provide valuable services in the highest professional manner to benefit the public as well as employees and clients.

Police Bureau of Portland, Oregon: The mission of the Police Bureau of Portland is to reduce crime and the fear of crime by working with all citizens to preserve life, maintain human rights, protect property, and promote individual responsibility and community commitment.

Public Radio International: Public Radio International's mission is to serve audiences with distinctive programming that provides information, insights, and cultural experiences essential to understanding a diverse, interdependent world.

---

organization and providing you with a means to evaluate your overall success. Above all, the Scorecard is a tool designed to offer faithful translation. What does it translate? It decodes your mission, values, vision, and strategy into performance objectives and measures in each of the four Scorecard perspectives. Translating this "DNA" of your organization with the Balanced Scorecard ensures all employees are aligned with, and working toward, the mission. This represents one of the great benefits of the Scorecard system as the mission is where you begin your translating efforts. A well-developed Balanced Scorecard ensures the objectives appearing on the Strategy Map and the measures you track on the Scorecard are consistent with your ultimate aspirations and it guides the actions of employees in making the right choices.

When developing objectives and measures, you must critically examine them in the context of your organization's mission, to be certain they are consistent with that purpose. Let me give you an example. Exhibit 5.3 includes the mission of Public Radio International that reads: "Public Radio International's mission is to serve audiences with distinctive programming that provides information, insights, and cultural experiences essential to understanding a diverse, interdependent world." Would an objective of "Increase entertainment programming" accompanied by a corresponding measure of "Number of entertainment items broadcast" make sense for Public Radio International? Only if they've decided to fundamentally shift their purpose.

The Balanced Scorecard is *descriptive*, not *prescriptive*. In other words, there are no hard and fast rules. So you could build and implement a Balanced Scorecard without a mission statement for your organization. It would still contain a mix of financial and nonfinancial objectives and measures linked together through a series of cause and effect relationships. But consider for a moment the tremendous value and alignment you create when developing a Scorecard that truly translates your mission. Now you have a tool that can act as your compass, and guide the actions of your entire employee team. If you have a mission, make certain the Balanced Scorecard you develop is true to the core essence reflected in the document. If you don't have a mission statement, I would strongly encourage you to develop one and see for yourself the focus and alignment you create when translating your mission into a Balanced Scorecard framework.

VALUES

What Are Values?

Modern organizations have a multitude of ways in which to reach their goals. You may use a method of innovative service delivery to distinguish yourself. Or perhaps the customer service ethic at your shop is legendary and propels you towards success. For some organizations, it's the way they behave that makes the difference and provides their source of strength. We've all experienced situations that demonstrate this. For example, perhaps a hotel employee provided you with a missing essential you forgot to include in your suitcase; or an amusement park worker showed up to help you at the exact moment the combination of stress and joy (that only an amusement park can bring) became too much for you to bear. Chances are, these acts didn't result from reading the latest management guru's book or from a desire to get a promotion. No, they simply represent the way things get done at that organization—in other words, its *values*.

Values are the timeless principles that guide an organization. They represent the deeply held beliefs within the organization and are demonstrated through the day-to-day behaviors of all employees. An organization's values make an open proclamation about how it expects everyone to behave. Genuinely held values can prove to be dramatically galvanizing in times of prosperity and crisis alike. Take the case of the United Parcel Service (UPS). In 1997 the company experienced a devastating strike that nearly paralyzed the company. "Brown," as they are now known in their ubiquitous ads, survived that calamity and Chief Executive Mike Eskew believes their values had a lot to do with it. He said "it was a hugely difficult time, like a family feud. Everyone had close friends on both sides of the fence, and it was tough for us to pick sides. But what saved us was our noble purpose. Whatever side people were on, they all shared a common set of values. Those values are core to us."[13] Notice Eskew uses the words "core to us." In the following section, we'll examine why it's critical that the values you hold are truly representative of your organization.

Values Must Represent Your Unique Organization

What would you think of an organization that listed the following as their corporate values: communication, respect, and integrity? They sound pretty admirable, don't they? These simple yet powerful words seem to suggest an organization in touch with what is necessary to achieve success. Perhaps you can see your own organization in these distinguished terms. Well, if you can, be careful. These were the values proudly espoused by Enron! Of course, Enron is not alone in using values like respect and integrity. 55% of Fortune 100 companies proclaim integrity as a core value.[14] As high as this percentage appears, it is undoubtedly much higher at public and nonprofit organizations for which these terms are often a way of life.

There is absolutely nothing wrong with holding respect, communication, integrity, and many of the other "greatest hits of the values collection" as part of your culture. The danger is in publicly stating these values while following a different rulebook to guide your actions in practice. Research has suggested that employees will quickly brand as a hypocrite any leader whose actions are not consistent with publicly stated values. Potentially more troubling for today's leaders is the fact that it's not just their actions that matter, but their *perceived actions* that really drive employee sentiment.[15] As a result, it's critical that all leaders undertake a campaign to ensure organizational values are well-understood from the boardroom to the front lines. Allowing employees to develop their own perceived meanings is, at the very least, a recipe for confusion and, at worst, for all-out insurrection.

Management consultant and author Patrick Lencioni suggests an organization's values should be "aggressively authentic."[16] Authentic in this context means developing values that are consistent with your organizational objectives, not writing something that would be well suited for the inside of a greeting card. He cites Siebel Systems, a Silicon Valley-based developer of Customer Relationship Management Software. Siebel distinguishes itself from many of its Northern California peers by listing professionalism as its top value. This is in stark contrast to many technology companies where basketball courts, cappuccino machines, and t-shirts are the norm. At Siebel, employees are not permitted to eat at their desks or decorate their walls with more than one or two photographs. This sends a clear message to all Siebel associates of what is necessary (and expected) to succeed.

In *Built to Last*, authors Collins and Porras suggest that visionary organizations decide for themselves which values to hold, independent of the current environment, competitive requirements, or management fads. They quote Johnson & Johnson CEO, Ralph Larsen on values: "The core values embodied in our credo might be a competitive advantage, but that is not why we have them. We have them because they define for us what we stand for, and we would hold them even if they became a competitive disadvantage in certain situations."[17] "What we stand for" is an important part of the quote. As discussed previously, no universal set of right or wrong values exists; instead, each organization must determine or discover the core values that comprise its essence and hold importance to those within it. Organizations tend to have a small number of core values that truly reflect their very essence. A large number may indicate confusion between values and practices. While practices, processes, and strategies should change over time in answer to the many challenges that come our way, we expect values to remain the same, providing an enduring source of strength and wisdom.

Heinrich von Pierer, CEO of mega industrial giant Siemens, an employer of over 480,000 people in 190 countries, sums this topic of values continuity very nicely: "Siemens has been a great company for over 157 years, and I think we have stayed true to our values, particularly during the new-economy hype of the late 1990s. We were not seduced or pressured into doing what everyone else was doing. We charted our own course because we had our own values. A company needs this type of compass. But the interpretation of those values has always to be done anew. Globalization, innovation, financial solidity—all of these force a company to keep changing."[18]

In many organizations, the core values represent the strong personal beliefs of the founder or senior leader (e.g., Walt Disney's belief in imagination and wholesomeness). Just as we would expect parents to exert great influence over the developing values of their children, the organization's leaders should set the tone for values within an organization. Therefore, they must constantly strive not only to develop appropriate values, but more importantly to consistently mirror the values in their words and actions. As the Swiss Philosopher Henri Amiel once said, "Every man's conduct is an unspoken sermon that is forever preaching to others.[19] One leader who did a great job of living the company's values is Herb Kelleher, former Chief Executive of Southwest Airlines, which has been consistently named among the best companies to work for in America by *Fortune* magazine. The values of maintaining a sense of humor and having fun at your job are two that were deemed critical by the CEO, and he ensured these values were shared by the entire workforce through careful recruiting efforts. Some industry observers believe Southwest's values and culture lie at the heart of the company's remarkable financial record which, among other achievements, is punctuated by the distinction of producing the highest return to investors of any U.S. company between 1972 and 2002. According to *Money* magazine, a $10,000 investment in Southwest back in 1972 would have yielded more than $10 million by 2002.[20]

Establishing Values

Every organization has a set of values that are demonstrated everyday. The question is, do they reflect the true essence of the organization or simply the thinking at the top of its current regime? I've noted previously that an organization's core values should not change capriciously but should act as the organization's guiding principles as it reacts to the world around it. In addition, we must also recognize that, like virtually everything else, some values within an organization will remain long after they cease to provide any benefit, and may become a hindrance to the ongoing success of the organization. Some values may even prove unethical or unacceptable in the larger societal context. This doesn't imply a wholesale change of values every few years; it simply suggests an honest evaluation of your organization and the recognition of which values truly represent the core of your organization and are the keys to your enduring success.

The solution to changing values and the underlying culture of an organization lies in open and honest identification of the current value systems that exist and are rewarded in the organization. A tool developed by author and consultant Richard Barrett to help you in this endeavor is known as the "corporate value audit instrument."[21] Individuals in the organization use three templates of values/behaviors: the ten values that best represent who they are (*personal values*), the ten values that best describe how their organization/team operates (*organizational values*), and the ten values they believe are most critical for a high-performance organization/team (*ideal organizational values*). This very illuminating diagnostic tool is used to evaluate the strengths and weaknesses of existing values and culture. Organizations are able to assess the degree of alignment between personal values, existing and ideal organizational values, and identify the changes that are necessary to develop a successful and enduring value system.

For additional assistance in identifying values, try these questions developed by author and consultant Jim Collins:[22]

- What core values do you bring to work—values you hold to be so fundamental that you would hold them regardless of whether or not they were rewarded?

- How would you describe to your loved ones the core values you stand for in your work and that you hope they stand for in their working lives?

- If you awoke tomorrow morning with enough money to retire for the rest of your life, would you continue to hold on to these core values?

- Perhaps most important, can you envision these values being as valid 100 years from now as they are today?

- Would you want the organization to continue to hold these values even if at some point one or more of them became a competitive disadvantage?

- If you were to start a new organization tomorrow in a different line of work, what core values would you build into the new organization regardless of its activities?

One final caveat regarding values: While the topic exudes a "warm and fuzzy" feeling, you should not feel compelled to involve your entire employee body in the creation of values. Remember that values should support your mission and help you achieve your organizational objectives. This process is not a matter of polling the entire organization and adopting the top five values suggested. Rather, it's the very demanding work of critically examining your organization and determining the behaviors you need to see demonstrated on a day-to-day basis to drive the results you desire.

Values and the Balanced Scorecard

The preceding section addressed the possibility of changing the values of an organization and the mechanisms for achieving this result. The Balanced Scorecard represents the best solution for broadcasting your values, reviewing them over time, and creating alignment from top to bottom in the organization. The real key is *alignment*, enabling all employees to see how their day-to-day actions are consistent with the values of the organization and how living those values is contributing to overall success.

In Chapter 9, I'll discuss the concept of cascading the Balanced Scorecard, driving it down to lower levels of the organization while ensuring alignment throughout. When we cascade, we allow employees at all levels to develop objectives and measures that represent how they influence the highest ranking agency goals. The objectives and measures selected must be consistent with the values of the organization to ensure consistency of action and results. Reviewing or "auditing" the objectives and measures on lower-level Scorecards provides a great opportunity to determine if the values you espouse are those held by your employees up and down the organizational ladder. If you value collaboration, for example, but your departments have no objectives citing collaboration or associated measures, then perhaps they don't truly value it as a guiding principle of their operations. Conversely, if all lower-level Strategy Maps and Scorecards contain objectives and measures relating to customer service, but this value is not captured on the high-level organizational Scorecard, then perhaps you've missed a core value that is important to all of your employees.

Pragmatically, the Balanced Scorecard may also be used to track the extent to which your organization really "lives" its values. For organizations undergoing changes to values or suffering from turmoil, metrics that gauge adherence to stated values may be of great benefit. That said, developing meaningful value-based metrics may prove challenging to even the most creative Scorecard builders. You could use "mystery shopper" or casual observation techniques to determine if employees are behaving in accordance with your values. Calculating the percentage of employees who can recite your core values without prompting could also be used, but this would prove very difficult to track and would undoubtedly raise the ire of those being asked to spontaneously list the company's values. Another possibility is to identify behaviors consistent with your values and base at least part of the annual performance appraisal on the demonstration of these behaviors by employees.

The Power of Values

For millions of Americans, Tuesday, September 11, 2001 began like any other day: sharing breakfast with their family, commuting to work, and settling into the routine of their daily tasks. Shortly after, however, the day was transformed into one that would forever be etched into the collective consciousness of a shocked nation, if not the entire world. As word of the devastating terrorist attacks emerged, virtually all businesses ceased operations for the day with employees rushing home to comfort loved ones and somehow trying to explain the horrific events to confused children. One of the organizations that shut down early that day was the Cleveland Symphony Orchestra, whose talented ensemble of musicians had been rehearsing Mahler's Fifth Symphony, which was to be performed that Thursday, the 13th of September.

America came to a standstill in the days following September 11th: no flights, no sporting events, and only the most vital of services in operation. In this environment of stunned silence and national mourning, Tom Morris and Christoph von Dohnanyi, respectively the Executive and Music Director of the Cleveland Symphony Orchestra, faced a choice: In line with virtually every other event in the country, should they cancel their upcoming performance or was forging ahead exactly what their audience needed most— the healing tonic supplied by music? Morris and von Dohnanyi reasoned that staging the performance, despite a small minority of dissenting voices, was the best choice for the city and for the Orchestra's musicians. But what to play? Should they abandon Mahler's majestic and sweeping tones in favor of a strictly American program? Such a gesture was certain to strike an approving chord with their audience given the rising tide of patriotism that was sweeping the country.

After a solemn moment of silence, at precisely 8 P.M. on the evening of September 13th Dohnanyi raised his baton, and with the flick of his wrist the decision became clear as the silent air was shattered with the opening trumpet salvo of Mahler's Fifth. Austrian conductor Herbert von Karajan, perhaps one of the most powerful figures in classical music, once suggested that a great performance of the Fifth is a "transforming experience," and "the fantastic finale almost forces you to hold your breath."[23] A transforming experience was precisely what the crowded audience at Severance Hall needed during that haunting week; the strains of Mahler's masterpiece offering a cathartic celebration of birth, life, death, and renewal. Reflecting later on the performance, Morris said, "There is absolutely nothing we could have done to be of better service at that moment than to stick with what we do best, standing firm behind our core values of great music delivered with uncompromising artistic excellence."[24]

VISION

The Role of Vision through History

Human history has been marked by momentous events that have forever changed the way we think, act, and live. Let's assume for a moment that time travel is possible and you suddenly have the chance to take a front-row seat at any of these history-altering occasions. Which would you choose? Lincoln's Gettysburg address? The downing of the Berlin Wall? I could list hundreds. If I had the opportunity, there are two legendary addresses I would have loved to hear in person. The first is Martin Luther King Jr.'s "I Have a Dream" speech delivered on the steps of the Lincoln Memorial on August 28, 1963. Here is a small portion of that stirring oratory:

> I say to you today, my friends, that in spite of the difficulties and frustrations of the moment, I still have a dream. It is a dream deeply rooted in the American dream.
>
> I have a dream that one day this nation will rise up and live out the true meaning of its creed: "We hold these truths to be self-evident: that all men are created equal."
>
> I have a dream that one day on the red hills of Georgia the sons of former slaves and the sons of former slave owners will be able to sit down together at a table of brotherhood.
>
> I have a dream that my four children will one day live in a nation where they will not be judged by the color of their skin but by the content of their character.
>
> I have a dream today.

In my opinion, it's virtually impossible to read these words conceived with clarity and delivered with passion and eloquence, and not feel compelled toward action.

My second window-on-history choice would be President John F. Kennedy's impassioned plea to have the United States commit to sending a man to the Moon, delivered to the U.S. Congress on May 25, 1961. Here is a small portion of the president's remarks:

> Now it is time to take longer strides—time for a great new American enterprise—time for this nation to take a clearly leading role in space achievement, which in many ways may hold the key to our future on Earth.

> I believe that this nation should commit itself to achieving the goal, before this decade is out, of landing a man on the Moon and returning him safely to the Earth.

With these words President Kennedy inspired a generation of citizens and won their commitment to a seemingly impossible task. You may not have to shoulder the responsibility of inspiring millions, but you do have a duty as leaders to help yourself and your employees find meaning in their work and be compelled toward great things.

What Is a Vision Statement?

A vision statement provides a word picture of what the organization intends ultimately to become—which may be 5, 10, or 15 years in the future. Notice the vivid canvas Dr. King paints with his words. He transports the listener to a new and exciting future. While mission statements are often abstract, the vision should contain as concrete a picture of the desired state as possible and provide the basis for formulating strategies and objectives. President Kennedy certainly observed this criterion with his very specific dictum of landing a man on the moon and returning him safely to earth. He uses simple language leaving little room for doubt. With his vision secure, strategies and objectives could easily follow.

The vision you create may not change human relations or put a person in space, but it can forever alter the way your organization does business. A powerful vision provides everyone in the organization with a shared mental framework that helps give form to the often abstract future that lies before us. The vision can inspire every employee and stakeholder to test their boundaries, always stretching to achieve more in pursuit of your overall mission. As Organizational Learning expert Peter Senge has observed, "vision translates mission into truly meaningful intended results—and guides the allocation of time, energy, and resources. In my experience, it is only through a compelling vision that a deep sense of purpose comes alive."[25] And creating a vision may even represent the mark of a "healthy" company, as researchers recently noted in *The McKinsey Quarterly*. In describing the attributes of a healthy corporation, they suggest: "In our experience, healthy companies, however scattered and disaggregated physically and organizationally, generally work toward a common cause. They usually achieve this kind of alignment when they sketch a compelling vision of the future for everyone connected with them.[26]

Let's look at the elements of a vision statement that will serve to enliven the passions of all your stakeholders.

Elements of Effective Vision Statements

Everything discussed in this chapter is critical to your organization and your Balanced Scorecard implementation, but the most critical component is the vision. Why? Because it acts as a conduit between your reason for being (as reflected in the mission), the values representative of your culture, and the strategy you'll put into execution to reach your desired future state. Without a clear and compelling vision to guide the actions of all employees, you could wind up with a workforce lacking direction and thus unable to profit from any strategy you put in place, no matter how well conceived. Let's look at some characteristics of an effective vision statement:

- *It is concise.* The very best vision statement is one that grabs your attention and immediately draws you in without boring you from pages of mundane rhetoric. President Kennedy didn't mince his words; he simply stated his vision of landing a man on the moon by the end of the decade. If everyone in your organization is expected to act and make decisions based on the vision, the least you can do is create something that is simple and memorable. Consider it your organizational campaign slogan for the future.

- *It balances external and internal elements.*[27] The external elements of the vision focus on how your public or nonprofit agency will change or improve the world (or your piece of it) should you fulfill your purpose. Rather than saying, "we will have double the current capacity," the external elements of your vision should force you to articulate how the world will be a better place as a result of your efforts. For example, "all children will have access to quality health care." Conversely, the internal elements of your vision describe how you will appear as an organization when all the elements you need to meet your external vision are present. Use of staff, service and product mix, partnerships, and technology could be included in the internal portion of your vision. For example, "we will have a 100,000-square-foot gallery that has all the great neon artworks of the twentieth century on display" (Museum of Neon Art).

- *It appeals to all stakeholders.* A vision statement that focuses on one group to the detriment of others will not win lasting support in the hearts and minds of all constituencies. The vision must appeal to everyone who has a stake in the success of the enterprise: employees, funders, elected officials, customers, and communities, to name but a few.

- *It is consistent with mission and values.* Your vision is a further translation of your mission and the values of underlying importance to your organization. If your mission suggests solving community problems, and one of your core values is constant innovation in service delivery, then there should be a reference to service delivery innovation in your vision statement. Remember, in the vision, you're painting a word picture of the desired future state that will lead to the achievement of your mission, so ensure the two are aligned.

- *It is verifiable.* Using the latest business jargon and buzzwords can make your vision statement very nebulous to even the most trained eye. Who within your organization will be able to determine exactly when you became world class, leading edge, or top quality? Write your vision statement so that you'll know when you've achieved it. While mission and values won't change, expect the vision to change, since it is written for a finite period of time.

- *It is feasible.* The vision shouldn't represent the collective dreams of senior leadership; rather, it must be grounded solidly in reality. To ensure this, you must possess a clear understanding of your environment, its key players, and emerging trends.

- *It is inspirational.* Don't miss the opportunity to inspire your team to make the emotional commitment necessary to reach your destination. The vision statement should not only guide, but also arouse the collective passion of all employees. To be inspirational, the vision must first be understandable to every conceivable audience from the boardroom to the front lines. Throw away the thesaurus for this exercise and focus instead on your deep knowledge of the business to compose a meaningful statement for all involved. Notice again the simple yet powerful language employed by both President Kennedy and Dr. King.

- *It paints a word picture.* By my count, this is at least the third reference to a "picture" when developing a vision statement, so you know I consider it pretty important. Creating a vision statement should not be reduced to an academic exercise of analysis, data slicing manipulation, and construction, resulting in a stale paragraph or two of unrelated terms and concepts that lead straight to a dead end of confusion. Rather, the words should awaken all our senses, allowing us to literally see the desired future. Regardless of what you think of his politics, it's difficult to recollect Ronald Reagan's time in office without tipping your hat to his brilliant communication skills. Employing techniques and lessons honed over the years on Hollywood backlots and later on the campaign trail, Reagan knew how to weave a yarn, drawing people in with simple and descriptive language that painted a clear and cogent picture. For example, when faced with explaining our budgetary woes to the nation, he rejected the standard menu of graphs and dizzying charts, instead looking straight into a camera and declaring that a trillion dollars amounted to a stack of bills as high as the Empire State Building. How's that for a visual: 1,250 feet of greenbacks. With that reference he made Americans see that federal spending amounted to real money.[28]

Developing Your Vision Statement

A rich body of literature exists on the subject of creating a powerful vision. As you might expect given this abundant supply of material, there are many possible ways to craft this important document. In this section, I provide you with a few alternatives. Consider using one of the following or combining those elements of each that appeal to you.

Ten Key Questions   This exercise challenges a small group of people to formulate answers to ten important questions. The questions each relate to a specific area of vision creation. Reviewing, combining, and synthesizing your responses will help you document your vision.[29]

1. How would the world be improved or changed if we were successful in achieving our purpose?

2. What are the most important services that we should continue to provide, change, or begin to offer in the next three years?

3. What staffing and benefits changes do we need to implement to better achieve our purpose?

4. How will our elected officials or board of directors assist us in achieving our purpose?

5. What resource development (funding) changes do we need to influence to better achieve our purpose?

6. What facilities and technology changes do we need to implement to better achieve our purpose?

7. What infrastructure, systems, or communication changes do we need to implement to better achieve our purpose?

8. How could we more effectively or efficiently provide our services? If you could only make three changes that would significantly impact our ability to provide quality services to our clients/customers, what would these changes be?

9. What makes us unique?

10. What do our clients/customers consider most important in our provision of services? What do our clients/customers need from us?

Interview Method   As you might have guessed, senior management interviews are a key component of this technique for developing your vision. Each senior leader of your organization is interviewed separately to gather his or her feedback on the future direction of the organization. I suggest using an outside consultant or facilitator to run the interviews because a seasoned consultant will have been through many interviews of this nature and possess the ability to put the executive at ease, ensuring that the necessary information flows freely in an environment of trust and objectivity. The interview should last about an hour and include both general and specific questions, as well as a mix of past, present, and future-oriented queries. Typical questions may include:

- Where and why have we been successful in the past?

- Where have we failed in the past?

- Why should we be proud of our organization?

- What trends, innovations, and dynamics are currently changing our environment?

- What do our clients and customers expect from us? Our funders and legislators? Our employees?

- What are our greatest attributes and competencies as an organization?

- Where do you see our organization in three years? Five years? Ten years?

- How will our organization have changed during that time period?

- How do we sustain our success?

The results of the interviews are summarized by the interviewer and presented to the senior leader. At this point, the leader will have the opportunity to draft the vision based on the collective knowledge gathered from the senior team. Once the draft is completed, the entire team convenes and debates the leader's vision to ensure it captures the essential elements they discussed during their interviews. You would not expect the first draft to be accepted by everyone, and that's the idea—to involve the whole team in the creation process. However, by mandating the leader with the initial responsibility for declaring the vision, you ensure his or her commitment to the vision and have a working draft from which to begin the refinement process. Once the team has hammered out the vision statement, it should be reviewed and accepted by people from as many levels in the organization as logistically possible—and with today's technology, that should include just about everyone!

Borrowed Heroes[30]   I opened this section with a short review of two passionate addresses from Dr. Martin Luther King Jr., and former President John F. Kennedy. These two erudite and articulate men aren't the only ones known to stir a crowd with their oratorical genius and powerful visions. Each of you may have your own heroes from the worlds of politics, science, sports, spirituality, or entertainment. In this next exercise, you'll create a dialog on your vision by drawing on the words of those who have inspired you.

Here's how it works: First have the group listen to or read a stirring and inspirational speech from your borrowed hero. It could be Martin Luther King Jr.'s "I Have a Dream" speech, President Kennedy's "landing a man on the Moon" address, or any other you choose. Next, discuss the fact that you've just heard this leader at a specific point in time. Notice that he or she did not address the current state of affairs but instead tapped the aspiration of all by painting a vivid word picture of future events. What was so inspiring, and why?

Use the discussion to develop a vision for your organization. Imagine that *Governing Magazine* or *The Nonprofit Times* is writing a story about your organization 5, 10, or 15 years from now. You've achieved your vision and the reporter asks how you accomplished the impressive feat. Discuss and record what you've accomplished, how the world is better off, who you've served, and how you did it. This open and creative discussion should lead you to the elements of a powerful vision for your organization.

The Power of Vision

The preceding are just some of the methods I've found very useful in developing a vision statement. Fortunately for all of us, abundant literature and practice exists on this subject, so you have many resources at your disposal.

Once you've developed your vision you'll be amazed at the power it provides. Here's how Michael Kaiser, President of the Kennedy Center for the Performing Arts in Washington, DC, describes the power of vision for this renowned performing arts center: "I think what leaders have to do is to provide a vision for the future. And what has been remarkable to me . . . is the power of a vision. If you can present (that vision) to people, either to people inside the organization who have been damaged or people outside the organization who have lost faith in what the organization can do, the power is remarkable."[31] There is little doubt that a powerful vision will confer many benefits to your organization. A summary of potential benefits is outlined in Exhibit 5.4.

Vision Statements and the Balanced Scorecard

Vision statements often describe the desired scope of activities, how the agency will be viewed by its stakeholders (customers/clients, employees, funders, regulators, etc.), areas of leadership or distinctive competence, and

---

Exhibit 5.4   Benefits of a Vision Statement

- *Provides guidance.* A clear and succinct vision statement provides all stakeholders the opportunity to see how they fit into the organization's "big picture." The vision supplies clear and compelling guidance of what the future looks like, and what is necessary for success.

- *Creates positive tension.* While realistic and feasible, the vision must stimulate people to reach new heights of collective performance. This creates a constructive tension between "what is" and "what could be" if we work to achieve the vision.

- *Complements leadership.* A clear and inspirational vision can empower people to make decisions in accordance with the best intentions of the organization in mind. While leaders cannot, in a practical sense, meet and discuss organizational goals with every stakeholder, the vision can portray the organization's ultimate aims, and guide actions accordingly.

- *Forces the discussion of trade-offs.* Even the clearest vision will be open to some interpretation depending on how and where you fit into the overall organizational structure. Visions should be focused enough to guide high-level decision making but flexible enough to encourage active dialog and individual initiative. Achieving the mission should facilitate cooperation and collaboration, not promote isolated win-lose scenarios.

- *Appeals to a variety of senses.* A well-crafted vision taps into the entire human experience. You can literally see, feel, and hear the future as it is elegantly laid out before you. This is why the language of visions is so important. How effective would Dr. King Jr.'s "I Have a Dream" speech have been if he began by saying, "I have a business strategy?" The best visions resonate within us and appeal to all that is human.

---

strongly held values. When writing a vision for the organization, you're attempting to move away from a paradigm of "either/or" thinking to embracing the power of "and." It's no longer a matter of satisfying one group using certain competencies at the expense of another. The vision has to balance the interests of all groups and portray a future that will lead to wins for everyone involved. The Balanced Scorecard is the mechanism you use to track your achievement of this lofty goal. The principle tenet of the Scorecard is balance—more accurately, using measurement to capture the correct balance of skills, processes, and customer requirements that lead to your desired future as reflected in the vision.

The Balanced Scorecard will provide a new, laser-like focus on your organization's results, and as such the potential problems represented by a misguided vision are significant. We've all heard terms like "what gets measured gets done," "measure what matters," and many others. The Scorecard is essentially a device that translates vision into reality through the articulation of vision (and strategy). A well-developed Balanced Scorecard can be expected to stimulate behavioral changes within your organization. The question is, are they the sort of changes you want? Be certain the vision you've created for your organization is one that truly epitomizes your mission and values because the Scorecard will give you the means for travelling first class to that envisioned future!

NOTES

1. Michael Allison and Jude Kaye, *Strategic Planning for Nonprofit Organizations*, (New York: John Wiley & Sons, 1997), p. 56.

2. E.B. Knauft, Renee Berger, and Sandra Gray, *Profiles of Excellence* (San Francisco: Jossey-Bass, 1991).

3. David Osborne and Ted Gaebler, *Reinventing Government* (Reading, MA: Addison-Wesley, 1992).

4. James C. Collins and Jerry I. Porras, "Building Your Company's Vision,"*Harvard Business Review*, September–October 1996.

5. Tom Krattenmaker, "Write a Mission Statement that Your Company is Willing to Live," *Harvard Management Update*, March 2002.

6. Peter F. Drucker, *Managing the Non-Profit Organization* (New York: HarperBusiness, 1990), p. 5.

7. Julia Kirby and Diane L. Coutu, "The Beauty of Buzzwords," *Harvard Business Review*, May 2001.

8. Rudolph W. Giuliani, *Leadership* (New York: Hyperion, 2002).

9. James C. Collins and Jerry I. Porras, "Building Your Company's Vision," *Harvard Business Review*, September–October 1996.

10. John M. Bryson, *Strategic Planning for Public and Nonprofit Organizations* (San Francisco: Jossey-Bass, 1995), p. 76–78.

11. Tom Krattenmaker, "Write a Mission Statement that Your Company is Willing to Live," *Harvard Management Update*, March 2002.

12. Thomas Wolf, *Managing a Nonprofit Organization in the Twenty-First Century* (New York: Fireside, 1999), p. 347.

13. Diane L. Coutu, "How Resilience Works," *Harvard Business Review*, May 2002.

14. Patrick M. Lencioni, "Make Your Values Mean Something," *Harvard Business Review*, July 2002, pp. 113–117.

15. Amy C. Edmondson, "When Company Values Backfire," *Harvard Business Review*, November 2002, pp. 18–19.

16. Patrick M. Lencioni, "Make Your Values Mean Something," *Harvard Business Review*, July 2002, pp. 113–117.

17. James C. Collins and Jerry I. Porras, *Built to Last* (New York: HarperBusiness, 1997).

18. Thomas A. Stewart and Louise O'Brien, "Transforming an Industrial Giant," *Harvard Business Review,* February 2005, pp. 115–122.

19. Henri-Frederic Amiel, *Amiel's Journal: The Journal Intime of Henri-Frederick Amiel* (1852), Mrs. Humphry Ward (trans.) (Macmillan & Co, Ltd., 1889).

20. Jon Berger, "30-Year Super Stocks," *Money,* October 9, 2002.

21. Richard Barrett, *Liberating the Corporate Soul* (Boston: Butterworth-Heinemann, 1998).

22. Jim Collins, *Leader to Leader* (San Francisco: Jossey-Bass, 1999).

23. From www.wikipedia.com Entry: Symphony No. 5 (Mahler).

24. Jim Collins, *Good to Great and the Social Sectors: A Monograph to Accompany Good to Great* (Jim Collins, 2005), pp. 27–28.

25. Peter Senge, "The Practice of Innovation," *Leader to Leader,* 9 (Summer 1998): 16–22.

26. Aaron De Smet, Mark Loch, and Bill Schaninger, "Anatomy of a Healthy Corporation," *The McKinsey Quarterly,* May 2007.

27. Michael Allison and Jude Kaye, *Strategic Planning for Nonprofit Organizations,* (New York: John Wiley & Sons, 1997), p. 69.

28. W. Warner Burke, *Organization Change: Theory and Practice* (Thousand Oaks, CA: Sage Publications, 2002), p. 256.

29. Michael Allison and Jude Kaye, *Strategic Planning for Nonprofit Organizations,* (New York: John Wiley & Sons, 1997), p. 73.

30. Adapted from material developed by Robert Knowling, in "Why Vision Matters," *Leader to Leader,* 18, Fall 2000, pp. 38–43.

31. Interview on National Public Radio's *Morning Edition,* March 26, 2001.

6

Strategy: The Core of Every Balanced Scorecard

Roadmap for Chapter 6 In writing this book, my hope is that readers will find it relevant for years to come—just how many years is anyone's guess. Of course, I can only dream about having the staying power of Sun Tzu, the Chinese General who authored a collection of essays on military strategy. The essays, best known to Western audiences by the title *The Art of War,* have been adapted to suit the needs of businesspeople, athletes, and politicians alike. The book, written over 2,300 years ago, has been a bestseller for years, and Sun Tzu is perhaps the most quoted Chinese personality in history outside of Confucius. Such is the power of strategy. Whether you wrote something valuable yesterday or 2,000 years ago, you're sure to find a ready audience.

As the title of this chapter implies, strategy is truly at the core of every Balanced Scorecard. Essentially, the Scorecard is a tool for translating a strategy into action through the development of performance objectives and measures. My purpose in this chapter is to crack the quizzical code of strategy, demystify the concept, and providing you with tools to review your current strategy or enable you to craft a new and exciting future through the development of a freshly minted strategy.

To do that, we'll explore the brief yet prodigious history of the subject, and examine what strategy is and, equally important, what it is not. Then, in case you're still not convinced of the value of a strategy, we'll examine some of the benefits a strategy can confer. We'll then consider some of the many schools of strategic thought, and I'll share with you one straightforward method of strategy development. The chapter concludes with a discussion of why the subject of strategy is so central to the Balanced Scorecard.

STRATEGY IS EVERYWHERE

As I was writing my first book, *Balanced Scorecard Step-by-Step: Maximizing Performance and Maintaining Results*, my wife and I were in the middle of a move to a new house. So, while conducting research and transcribing notes, I was simultaneously attempting to catalog the business archives of a lifetime in order to facilitate easy packing and unpacking—no easy chore for a self-described packrat! I observed, by means of a not-so-scientific calculation, that approximately 90% of the documents in my possession made at least some passing reference to the subject of strategy. Now comfortably situated in our new home, my accumulation of business materials continues unabated. According to my "strategy meter," I can tell you that the topic continues tov be at least casually addressed in virtually nine out of ten documents that come my way.

Strategy truly is everywhere. Interestingly, though, the formal field we label "strategic planning" has a relatively short history. The topic as we know it began to emerge in the 1950s and gained momentum in the 1960s and 1970s. As we moved into the 1980s, global competition became an increasing threat, especially to the very vulnerable United States.[1] To regain the advantage they once enjoyed, American businesses moved away from formal planning per se and focused instead on making processes more efficient, eliminating "nonvalue added" activities, and simply recognizing the new competitive landscape. Many operational improvements ensued but leaders recognized that simply developing more efficient operations did not represent the path to long-term success. They began to realize the road not taken—one that would lead to sustainable competitive advantage—was paved by a differentiating and defensible *strategy*.

WHAT IS STRATEGY?

Producing a universally acceptable definition of strategy is truly a Herculean task, so as a mental warm-up, let's start with something a little less controversial: what strategy is *not*. Speaking on the current state of strategy development at many nonprofits, author and consultant Bill Ryan says, "some nonprofits develop a big pile of well-intentioned programs, ideas and directions that try to respond to every need and opportunity that comes along and might vaguely fit under their mission. There is always a reason to do something that no one else is willing to do if it relates to your mission. The harder thing as is often pointed out in strategy discussions is to have enough of a strategy to know when to say no, when to drop things, and when to pass up opportunities. Understand that yes, a need might be real, but you might not be the best response to it."[2] Before you move on, think about that quote, reread it if you have to, and critically examine your own organization's approach to strategy development. Is Ryan talking about you? He's putting a deep stake in the ground with this quote, specifically noting that strategy is not about being all things to all people. Deciding when to say no, and determining what you should *not* do is a critical component of strategy.

Public sector firms are not exempt from the temptation to serve everyone. Scorecard codeveloper Robert Kaplan suggests, "strategy can be a foreign concept to a public sector organization. These agencies have little incentive to take a longer-term view of their role. They may attempt to do everything for everyone, and can end up doing not much at all."[3] Virtually all public sector agencies could fall into this trap, but for the sake of illustration, consider the case of public education in the United States, an industry that has seen spending double in the past 30 years to over $450 billion in 2005. Researchers examining the performance of public school districts had this to say about strategy in the education arena: "The term 'strategy' is widely used in public education . . . but it generally doesn't mean much . . . About a third of districts studied trotted out thick binders that they called their strategic plans, which were loaded with pages of activities that lacked rhyme or reason."[4]

If strategy is not about being the same as everyone else, what is it about? Commonly quoted strategy expert Henry Mintzberg provides this excellent synopsis of the subject: "My research and that of many others demonstrates that strategy making is an immensely complex process, which involves the most sophisticated, subtle, and, at times, subconscious elements of human thinking."[5] Maybe so, but that doesn't help us much in nailing down a definition! The difficulty with defining strategy is that it holds different meanings to almost all people and organizations. Some feel strategy is represented by the high-level plans management devises to lead the organization into the future. Others would argue strategy rests on the specific and detailed actions you'll take to achieve your desired state. To others still, strategy is tantamount to best practices. Before I offer a definition of strategy, let's look at some of the key principles of this subject:

- *Different activities.* As explained in the preceding paragraph, strategy is about choosing a different set of activities, the pursuit of which leads to a unique and valuable position in the environment.[6] If everyone were to pursue the same activities, then differentiation would be based purely on operational effectiveness and cost. Some organizations venture well beyond different in their pursuit of carving out a defensible strategic position. Take Canon, for instance. Their CEO, Hajime Mitarai says: "We should do something when people say it is 'crazy.' If people say something is 'good,' it means that someone else is already doing it."[7] Reaching beyond the ordinary and casting your net into the unknown and unproven can often generate the breakthroughs that strategy promises.

- *Trade-offs.* Effective strategies demand trade-offs in competition. Strategy is more about the choice of what *not* to do than what to do.

Organizations cannot compete effectively by attempting to serve everyone's needs. The entire organization must be aligned around what you choose to do and create value from that strategic position.[8]

- *Fit.* The activities chosen must fit one another for sustainable success. Many years ago Peter Drucker articulated the "Theory of the Business." He suggested that assumptions about the business must fit one another to produce a valid theory. Activities are the same; they must produce an integrated whole.[9]

- *Continuity.* Generally, strategies should not be constantly reinvented, with emphasis on the word constantly. While we would expect a strategy to evolve in the face of dramatic changes in your operating environment, a continuous preoccupation with updating strategy is certain to lead to confusion and skepticism. The strategy crystallizes your thinking on basic issues such as how you will offer customer value and to which customers. This direction has to be clear to both internal (employees) and external (customers, funders, other stakeholders) constituents.[10] Changes may bring about new opportunities that can be assimilated into the current strategy—new technologies for example.

- *Various thought processes.* Strategy involves conceptual as well as analytical exercises.[11] As the Mintzberg quote earlier in this section reminds us, strategy involves not only the detailed analysis of complex data, but also broad conceptual knowledge of the organization, environment, and so on.

Using the preceding discussion as a backdrop, I offer my, admittedly succinct, definition of strategy: Strategy represents the broad priorities adopted by an organization in recognition of its operating environment and in pursuit of its mission. Though short on words, this definition is long on implications.

"Broad priorities" means just that: the overall directional areas the organization will pursue to achieve its mission. For many, there is a tremendous appeal of turning their strategy document into an endless wish list of programs or initiatives. Robert Kaplan has seen this in action: "Most nonprofits don't have a clear succinct strategy. Their 'strategy' documents often run upwards of 50 pages, and the so-called strategy consists of lists of programs and initiatives, not the outcomes the organization is attempting to achieve."[12] Outlining every conceivable action that somehow marginally fits with your mission is undoubtedly seductive to public sector and nonprofit organizations alike. After all, such an approach allows you to cover all the bases, please all possible stakeholders, and consider every potential circumstance. What it does *not* do, however, is allow even a hairline crack of opportunity to execute the outcomes most representative of what constituents desire.

I worked with a nonprofit recently that had just completed a strategic planning exercise and wanted to take the opportunity to implement a Balanced Scorecard to assist with the execution of the plan. One glance at the *War and Peace*-sized document and I knew their hopes were about to be grounded. Absent from the tome were any true priorities. Instead, the "strategy" contained specific tactics by the hundreds, all dutifully accompanied by dates, responsible parties, and pages of sub-tasks. What's so bad about that, you ask? This organization was staffed by less than 30 people. By my estimation, they would have to work literally day and night for several years to approach completion of even a fraction of the plan.

Consider a small, local AIDS organization. Its strategy could detail every initiative it plans to undertake for the upcoming year. A better approach would be to inform its stakeholders and employees as to what overall approach it will take in serving the community. Perhaps it would choose to focus on education, or prevention, or building community support. These are strategies. They set direction and provide a context for the development of objectives and measures, which will follow with the Strategy Map and Balanced Scorecard.

In addition to the content of strategic plans, nonprofit and public sector agencies would be well-served in casting a critical eye on the order of items that make up the document. Frequently, these organizations will outline their mission, then a number of specific initiatives, and finally key goals and objectives. In my opinion, this is backwards. Mission always begins the process, on that we agree. However, next comes values and vision, then strategy which represents the broad, overall priorities of the organization. Translating that strategy is accomplished through the development of objectives on a Strategy Map, followed by measures and targets on a Balanced Scorecard. Finally, specific initiatives are put in place to help the organization achieve its Balanced Scorecard targets.

DO WE NEED A STRATEGY?

I recently had a very telling conversation with a consultant to nonprofit organizations. He continually encounters boards of directors who haven't accepted that their organizations need to develop a strategy. This is quite ironic to him since in the nonprofit model, it is the board that is charged with setting the direction of the organization. The irony is extended when you consider the fact that most leaders are expressing a desire to spend more time on strategic issues and less on operational demands.

The uplifting words contained in a mission, values, and vision represents nothing but wishful thinking unless accompanied by a strategy. The strategy gives life to the lofty aims declared in these documents. While mission, values, and vision dwell in the realm of "why" and "who," the strategy burrows into the trenches of "how." A well-conceived and skillfully executed strategy provides the specific priorities on which you'll allocate resources and direct your energies.

Here are but a few of the many benefits that arise when you develop and commit to executing a strategy:[13]

- *Strategic thought and action are promoted.* Rather than focusing on the rote details of the moment, a strategy directs the energies of all employees towards what is truly important within your organization.

- *Decision making can be improved.* The important decisions in your organization can be considered through the prism of strategy, not the glare of urgent activities.

- *Performance is enhanced.* A strategic focus ensures your entire organization is focused on achieving overall goals. Add to this potent mix aligned processes for decision making, resource allocation, and performance management, and performance is almost certain to improve.

Of course, strategy is central to the Balanced Scorecard. To grab hold of the maximum benefit the Scorecard has to offer, you should use it as a mechanism for translating your strategy into action. The final section of this chapter will detail the vital link between strategy and the Balanced Scorecard.

MANY APPROACHES TO STRATEGY FORMULATION EXIST

Part of the confusion surrounding strategy stems from the fact that the field is as crowded with approaches and methodologies as a beach with people and umbrellas on the 4th of July. Military applications notwithstanding, never has a field with such a relatively short history spawned such a multitude of techniques. Just a partial listing of strategic modes would include: strengths and weakness analysis, portfolio approaches, shareholder value, economic value added, real options, core competencies, strategic intents, profit zones, and disruptive technologies. New entrants are constantly joining the fray. One of the latest techniques is known as "Blue Ocean Strategy." Developed by Professors Chan Kim and Renee Mauborgne, this approach seeks to "push for a quantum leap in buyer value while simultaneously lowering the industry's cost structure."[14] Is your head spinning yet? Well, to really get it going, I'll reintroduce a book I first mentioned in Chapter 1, *Strategy Safari.* It extensively documents a whopping ten different schools of strategic thought, for those intrepid enough to make such a journey. The ten schools are presented in Exhibit 6.1.

Unfortunately, no single "right" method exists. What works for one organization at a distinct point in time may not work for another organization

Exhibit 6.1   Ten Schools of Strategic Thought

Design School: Proposes a model of strategy making that seeks to attain a fit between internal capabilities and external possibilities. Probably the most influential school of thought, and home of the SWOT (strengths, weaknesses, opportunities, and threats) technique.

Planning School: Formal procedure, formal training, formal analysis, and lots of numbers are the hallmark of this approach. The simple informal steps of the design school become an elaborated sequence of steps. Produce each component part as specified, assemble them according to the blueprint, and strategy will result.

Positioning School: Suggests that only a few key strategies (positions in the economic marketplace) are desirable. Much of Michael Porter's work can be mapped to this school.

Entrepreneurial School: Strategy formation results from the insights of a single leader, and stresses intuition, judgement, wisdom, experience, and insight. The "vision" of the leader supplies the guiding principles of the strategy.

Cognitive School: Strategy formation is a cognitive process that takes place in the mind of the strategist. Strategies emerge as the strategist filters the maps, concepts, and schemas shaping their thinking.

Learning School: Strategies emerge as people (acting individually or collectively) come to learn about a situation as well as their organization's capability of dealing with it.

Power School: This school stresses strategy formation as an overt process of influence, emphasizing the use of power and politics to negotiate strategies favorable to particular interests.

Cultural School: Social interaction, based on the beliefs and understandings shared by the members of an organization lead to the development of strategy.

Environmental School: Presenting itself to the organization as a set of general forces, the environment is the central actor in the strategy-making process. The organization must respond to the factors or be "selected out."

Configuration School: Strategies arise from periods when an organization adopts a structure to match to a particular context that give rise to certain behaviors.

Adapted from *Strategy Safari,* by Henry Mintzberg, Bruce Ahlstrand, and Joseph Lampel (New York: The Free Press, 1998).

at a different juncture. Conversely, I could also say "fortunately" there is no single right approach because the importance of strategy has stimulated never-ending research, and despite some confusion and head-scratching around the lexicon produced by the field of strategy, we're all better for the efforts. In the next section, I present the most common elements of a strategic planning effort.

STRAIGHTFORWARD APPROACH TO
STRATEGY DEVELOPMENT

Entire books, seminars, and MBA courses have been dedicated to this topic, and though formal and detailed strategic planning techniques are beyond the scope of this book, strategy and the Balanced Scorecard are so inextricably linked that it would be a disservice not to share at least the basics of strategic planning for those of you with limited experience in this area. Therefore, consider this a primer on the subject. It will serve you well in assessing your current process against common practice, as it provides the essentials of developing a unique strategy for your organization.

The strategic planning method that is outlined here represents a composite of many different techniques advocated by a wide range of practitioners, consultants, and academics. The six steps are: getting started; performing an environmental scan; conducting a stakeholder analysis; analysis of strengths, weaknesses, opportunities, and threats (SWOT); identifying strategic issues; and developing strategies. When developing a strategy, most pundits suggest you first develop your mission, values, and vision that set the foundation for your strategy work. We covered those building blocks in Chapter 5, so for the purposes of this discussion, I'm making the assumption they are present when you begin your strategy efforts.

Step 1: Getting Started

As with your overall Balanced Scorecard implementation, you must ensure your organization is ready to embark on a strategic planning process. As a first step, you should review the effectiveness of your current planning efforts. Exhibit 6.2 provides a number of questions to consider regarding your current processes. Items with lower scores are ideal candidates for improvements that can be addressed in the current strategy development endeavor.

Strategic planning requires the commitment of time and attention from your top leaders as well as a willingness to provide ample resources for the effort. If your leaders are mired in current crises or anticipating a key legislative change, then perhaps this isn't the best time to embark on the task of developing a new strategy. To make the decision, you'll have to weigh the importance of the undertaking against the probability of success resulting from limited leadership involvement.

Once you're ready to plan, it's time to consider your *objectives* for drafting a new strategy. Any gap you've uncovered as a result of answering the questions in Exhibit 6.2 may provide an impetus for developing a new plan. You could be facing any number of issues that necessitate the development of a new strategy. However, it's important to distinguish between issues of truly strategic significance and those of operational dilemmas. Any crisis situations or issues with a time window of less than a year fall into the latter category. Fundamental issues of a longer-term nature that relate to your core service are more likely to be strategic.

Exhibit 6.2   Evaluating Your Current Strategy Process

---

1. Our strategy efforts result in a clear picture of organizational priorities for the future.

2. Our strategy works as a unifying force for the entire organization.

3. Senior leaders within the organization view our strategy process as valuable and relevant.

4. As a result of our strategy, all employees know our key priorities, and how we intend to serve customers/clients.

5. Our strategy has been the basis for the development of new initiatives to take advantage of opportunities or safeguard current operations.

6. If we execute our current strategy, our operational efficiency will increase.

7. Accountabilities are clear, whether individual or shared, for each aspect of our strategic plan.

8. We have developed performance measures to track our progress in executing our strategic plan.

Assign a score to each of the questions using the following scale:
1 – No value on this goal
2 – Some help on this goal
3 – Quite helpful on this goal
4 – Extremely valuable on this goal

Once you've answered the questions, total your ratings. A value under 16 suggests there is much room for improvement in your strategy process. A score between 18 and 24 would indicate value in your current process, but also room for improvement. If your total was over 24 you are most likely enjoying the benefits of a well-coordinated strategy management process.

Adapted from Bob Frost, *Crafting Strategy* (Dallas, TX: Measurement International, 2000).

Do you know your formal and informal *mandates*? The formal mandates of your organization spell out in detail what it is you are specifically required to do and not to do. Laws, ordinances, articles of incorporation, and charters are likely sources of information on this topic. No less important are the informal mandates or expectations key stakeholders require from you. Since we defined strategy as the broad priorities adopted by an organization in recognition of its operating environment and in pursuit of its mission, be sure any strategy you develop is consistent with the mandates you're required to observe.

The final step in getting started requires you to take a step back. To develop context for your effort, it's often illuminating to view your organization from an *historical perspective*. Chronicle the history of your public or nonprofit agency from its earliest developments to the present day realities you face. Along the way, you can document programs and services you've offered and the challenges and successes of days past. We all know experience is the best teacher and you can use the history of your own organization to learn from both past missteps and successes alike.

Those engaging in an exercise such as this frequently have a tendency to magnify past transgressions and to focus primarily on faults of the organization. If you find this is the case at your agency, consider using the Appreciative Inquiry approach to balance the deck. Developed in the early 1990s by David Cooperrider at Case Western University, Cleveland, Ohio, this approach focuses on an organization's achievements rather than its problems.[15] Participants are encouraged to share personal accounts of the organization operating at "peak performance." The stories describe the organization at its most alive and effective state. Based on this inspirational task of organizational archeology, workshop attendees then seek to understand the conditions that made peak performance possible—values, relationships, enabling technologies, and so on. From this input, a strategy is developed that draws on the very best the organization has to offer its customers, clients, employees, and all other stakeholders. As an old song says, you have to Accentuate the Positive.

Step 2: Performing an Environmental Scan

The Center for Association Leadership recently conducted a groundbreaking study with a very lofty aim: determining what attributes make a "great" association. In the spirit of similar efforts in the private sector, including the work chronicled in the book *Good to Great*, the research team used a matched-pairs approach, studying nine associations that had achieved consistent success over a multiple-year period and compared them on several criteria with associations that had similar missions or had served similar memberships, but had not experienced enduring success. The study revealed many insights, including the fact that successful organizations consistently scanned their environments in a relentless effort to acquire information they could use to better serve their membership.[16]

This step involves the painstaking acquisition of data from a variety of sources within your organizational orbit, and analyzing that material to assist you in coming up with a unique strategy. Outlined are a number of potential sources for your investigation:

- *Societal Trends*. How are the needs and experiences of your customers changing?

- *Demographics*. In most Western countries, the population is aging rapidly. What impact does this have on the products or services you deliver? And how will an aging workforce impact your ability to meet service demands in the future?

- *The Economy.* Economic tides can wreak havoc with public sector and nonprofit agencies dependent in large measure on third parties for funding. The vicissitudes of market conditions must be considered as you plot your fiscal plan and paint your broader strategic canvas.

- *Technology.* In a macro context, how is popular technology, for instance the Internet, shaping the way you conduct your business?

- *The Political Situation.* How would a new government and their positions affect the way you work towards your mission?

- *Changing regulations.* Is there impending legislation that may cause you to reconsider how you serve your constituent base?

- *Competition.* Who else does what you do? What are their competencies, strengths, weaknesses, opportunities, and threats? Should they grow in scope, size, or both, how will you react?

Mining these sources will inevitably lead to many stimulating discussions, spirited debates, and, hopefully, moments of clarity as you transform the raw data into strategic insights. As you grapple with these questions, be mindful of your current product and services and critically examine them in light of the conclusions you're drawing. Based on what you've discovered, are there offerings you should abandon—things that simply don't fit with the environment as it is presenting itself to you today? As much as we'd like to, we simply can't configure the world to always be consistent with our wants and preferences. We need to be ruthlessly realistic and face the facts. Dare to be bold when conducting these thought experiments, throw away the sacred cows, and listen to what the data is telling you. A rather dramatic example of such thinking is the story of Spanish explorer Hernando Cortez who landed with his soldiers at Veracruz, Mexico in 1519. As the troop headed inland, conditions deteriorated rapidly: disease, deplorable living conditions, and a resolute enemy. Orienting himself to this, and realizing his demoralized soldiers could give up the fight at any moment, Cortez took an extraordinary step—he burned the ships. No turning back now, only the grim face of reality staring menacingly and the necessity to adapt or perish.[17] Have you burned your ships? What dramatic action can you take to forever alter the course of your organization's fate?

Step 3: Conducting a Stakeholder Analysis

You could develop the most insightful strategy ever conceived, but unless it is responsive to the needs of your stakeholders, it isn't worth the three-ring binder it's bound to end up in. All organizations, whether private, public, or nonprofit exist primarily to serve and satisfy the needs of key stakeholders. Only by meeting their needs, and in some way improving their lives, will an organization be able to work towards the fulfillment of its mission.

Exhibit 6.3   Partial List of Public and Nonprofit Stakeholders

Adapted from *Strategic Planning for Public and Nonprofit Organizations* by
John M. Bryson (San Francisco: Jossey-Bass, 1995).

The first step in any stakeholder analysis is to identify specifically who
your key stakeholders are. This can prove to be a complicated endeavor for
any organization, but given the web of relationships that exist for most public and nonprofit agencies, it can be a substantial challenge. Exhibit 6.3
outlines some of the many stakeholder groups that may apply to your
organization. When compiling your list of stakeholders, it's best to cast the
net as widely as possible. Don't limit yourself to the obvious choices; instead,
attempt to identify all those who are touched by your organization.

With stakeholder groups identified, you can move on to a determination of their requirements. Interviews and surveys are proven methods for
gathering this intelligence. Of course, experiences gleaned from working
directly with these groups should also provide you with some excellent
insights you can capture. While canvassing these sources, look for shared
requirements from disparate stakeholder groups. Universal customer requirements will significantly ease the task of forming strategies. When the converse appears, and you encounter stakeholders with vastly different
requirements, the true challenge of strategy has been thrust upon you. Recall
from our earlier discussions that strategy is not about being all things to all
people—that results in chaotic efforts yielding dissatisfied customers and few
results. In the face of various and sometimes conflicting demands, you must
make the determination, based on your resources, the skill sets of your staff
and volunteers, and any mandated requirements, truly aligned with your

mission, which you are the best equipped to meet. Conducting that exercise will peel away layers of confusion and lead to the development of a galvanizing strategy.

One final caveat: Be sure to challenge your assumptions when considering stakeholder requirements, because what you *think* stakeholders require and what they *actually* desire could be two very different things. A light-hearted example comes from the U.S. Forest Service. You might think the average visitor to a national forest would be looking for easy-to-read maps and lots of recreational opportunities, right? That could be part of it, but what years of complaint data has yielded is the enlightening finding that visitors just want toilets that don't smell! In response to this most critical of stakeholder needs, the U.S. Forest Service dubbed 1990 "The Year of the Sweet Smelling Toilet," as it adopted the latest research and science to construct state of the art "facilities" that expunged the air of any malodorous offenses.[18]

Step 4: The SWOT Analysis

Strategies emerge out of a deep understanding of your organization's place in its current and anticipated operating environment. An excellent tool to help complete this assessment is the *strengths, weaknesses, opportunities, and threats* (SWOT) analysis. This widely recognized methodology is simple to administer and facilitate and can yield swift and profound results. The SWOT analysis consists of finding answers to four fundamental questions:

- What are our organization's strengths?

- What are our organization's weaknesses?

- What opportunities are present for our organization, the pursuit of which will lead us toward our mission?

- What threats do we face that may endanger the pursuit of our mission?

When discussing *strengths* you should ask what it is you really do well or what advantages you have that others cannot easily duplicate. *Weaknesses* represent areas in which improvements are necessary if you are to work towards fulfilling your mission. Changes in your environment, be they demographic, legislative, or pertaining to public opinion may represent *opportunities* to the organization. Finally, *threats* represent the converse of opportunities and can be viewed as changes that may potentially hinder your ability to serve stakeholders.

Typically, strengths and weaknesses relate to issues residing within the organization. Among the subjects frequently encountered in a discussion of strengths and weaknesses are: employee competencies, organizational structure, customer and client service, agency reputation, governance, facilities and equipment, fiscal position, technology, communication, culture, and values. Opportunities and threats are normally considered to be external issues that affect the organization. Discussions on these topics will often yield comments relating to: changing client needs, demographic shifts, economic stability (or instability), competition, legislative changes, and technology.

While SWOT is well known and universally utilized, many organizations forget the suffix "analysis" that forms such a crucial part of this process. Perhaps the ritualistic listing of strengths, weaknesses, opportunities, and threats serves enough of a cathartic purpose that no energy is reserved for the important task of analyzing these findings. However, insights will often bloom out of a critical examination of the interplay among the elements. Two intersections are of particular interest: strengths and opportunities and weaknesses and threats. When crafting strategy, it makes great sense to exploit the matching of particular strengths with outstanding opportunities. That's how breakthroughs in performance are born. Consider the example of one prenatal health clinic. Among the many strengths it cataloged during a SWOT exercise was "highly knowledgeable workforce." It was also fortunate enough to list a number of opportunities, one of which was, "new prenatal care techniques that can greatly help our clients." Until this point in its evolution, the clinic had focused almost entirely on service delivery. But when analyzing the results of the SWOT, the clinic's leaders saw the potential for a new strategic direction to emerge: Why not combine the core strength of knowledgeable workers with the opportunity presented by new prenatal techniques and focus on providing education services? They recognized they were in the unique and enviable position of employing some of the brightest professionals in the field who could quickly assimilate the latest research and effectively articulate it to their clients. They hypothesized that by providing education services and increasing awareness of the latest techniques available, clients would be armed with the knowledge required to make better health choices. Ultimately, the clinic's leaders believed this would lead to a reduction in prenatal care issues later in a pregnancy. A new strategy was born.

SWOT analyses are by necessity "point in time" exercises. Given the many insights you can garner from this process, consider making it part of your ongoing Performance Management process. While you wouldn't want to engage in a SWOT every month, it's not unreasonable to suggest, given the unprecedented pace of change in today's world, a review at least annually, if not semiannually.

Step 5: Identifying Strategic Issues

Thus far in the process, you've considered our objectives for developing a strategy, reviewed your organization's mission and mandates, scanned the environment, identified key stakeholders, and considered strengths, weaknesses, opportunities, and threats. Some may consider these steps almost academic in nature, hence not "real," since they do not reflect a bias toward action. All that will change in step five as you carefully analyze the material you've captured to date and frame the key strategic issues facing your organization.

Strategic issues can be defined as "fundamental policy questions or critical challenges that affect an organization's mandates, mission, and values; product or service level and mix; clients, users, or payers; or cost, financing, organization, or management."[19] Thus a strategic issue could be anything from "a shortage of long-term office space requirements" to "potential funding shortfalls" to "changing demographics of key clients." When documenting issues, it's important to phrase them as a challenge facing the organization and outline the specific ramifications that await you should you choose to ignore the issue. Given the input you have at your disposal to help you generate issues—mission, environmental data, mandates, SWOT, stakeholder needs—it should not come as a surprise to learn that many organizations can quickly compile dozens. Distinguishing between the truly strategic issues and merely operational ones will assist you in keeping the list at a manageable level. Strategic items are those that:

- Appear on the agenda of your board or elected officials and leaders.
- Are longer term in nature.
- Affect the entire organization.
- Have significant financial ramifications.
- May require new programs or services to address.
- Are "hot buttons" for key stakeholders.
- May involve additional staff.

Identifying the key issues facing your organization may be accomplished in a number of ways. Brainstorming as a group is one option. Using this technique, a facilitator will instruct the strategic planning team to generate as many possible issues as they can within a limited timeframe. All issues are captured on flip charts or a computer, with the contents projected onto a screen in the room. Once all issues have been identified, the group begins the sometimes arduous task of clarifying and classifying the issues, ensuring there is a common understanding among the team of exactly what the issue is, why it is an issue in the first place, and what the consequences are of not directly addressing it.

Another possible method of capturing issues is a derivative of the Appreciative Inquiry approach presented earlier in the discussion of chronicling the organization's history. Recall that this approach focuses on an organization's achievements rather than its problems. This exercise may be applied to the discussion of issues. Participants are encouraged to envision the organization operating at peak performance and then consider any obstacles standing in the way of their achievement. The obstacles will represent strategic issues that must be mitigated in order for the organization to reach its desired state.

Step 6: Developing Strategies

With the issues facing the organization clearly enumerated, it's now time to develop strategies that directly address the issues and allow you to work towards fulfilling your mission. One effective method of producing strategies centers on providing responses to five key questions relating to each of your strategic issues:[20]

1. What are the practical alternatives we could pursue to address this issue?

2. What potential barriers exist in the realization of the alternatives?

3. What action steps might we take to achieve the alternatives or overcome the barriers to their realization?

4. What major actions must be taken within the next year (or two) to implement the action steps?

5. What actions must be taken in the next six months, and who is responsible?

Have you ever heard the term *green-field brainstorming*? It suggests an activity in which people engage in the purest form of the art of brainstorming, assuming nothing and simply listing any and all aspects of a particular situation or issue. Generating strategies using this technique may yield many options, but as you know, it's the implementation of strategy that produces real benefits. Therefore, your goal should be to elicit strategies that have a reasonable chance of successful execution. Using the five questions presented will stack that deck in your favor. The first question is straightforward and is reminiscent of the brainstorming technique just discussed. However, beginning with the second question, the level of pragmatism is quickly escalated. Discussing barriers at this point will lead to open and frank discussions about the real probability of successfully implementing the proposed strategy. Not that barriers should be considered insurmountable brick walls; in fact, question three promotes the use of creative thinking in overcoming the barriers to success. The final two questions prompt the team to consider specific steps necessary in implementing the strategy, and equally important, assigning ownership for results.

In the discussion of the SWOT technique, I emphasized the use of the word "analysis," by suggesting you look at the interplay among the elements. So it is with strategy. While some strategies will stand on their own, you may find some will tend to form clusters that emerge into themes. Public and nonprofit organizations will often find their strategies contain overarching

Exhibit 6.4 Sample Strategic Priorities for Each BSC Perspective

Customer Perspective	Financial Perspective
Become a more customer-focused organization and heighten visibility in every way.	Grow financial resources available for programs.

Internal Process Perspective	Employee Learning and Growth Perspective
Continuously improve systems to achieve operational excellence.	Maximize people resources.

strategic themes that converge around broad service areas within the organization. For example, the Southeastern Pennsylvania chapter of the American Red Cross has identified four strategic "priorities." These priorities emerged after conducting both an internal and external assessment of strategic challenges and opportunities. The four priorities are:

- Become a more customer-focused organization and heighten visibility in every way.

- Grow financial resources available for programs.

- Continuously improve systems to achieve operational excellence.

- Maximize people resources.

Did you notice anything about the Red Cross's strategic priorities? All are extremely noble and admirable themes, indeed. But what jumps out at me is how nicely they map to a Balanced Scorecard framework. And, in fact, that is exactly what this chapter of the Red Cross did: It made each of these priorities the cornerstones of the four Scorecard perspectives, as depicted in Exhibit 6.4.

While the situation presented in Exhibit 6.4 is convenient, don't feel you have to "force-fit" your strategies to the Scorecard perspectives. That said, it certainly doesn't hurt to keep in mind that success is a product of strategy execution, and the vehicle of that execution is the Balanced Scorecard. I'll conclude the chapter with a look at precisely why strategy is so important to the development of the Balanced Scorecard.

STRATEGY AND THE BALANCED SCORECARD: A CRITICAL LINK

A couple of holiday seasons ago, I had the chance to read a newspaper article chronicling some of the many New Year's resolutions one reporter discovered when speaking to patrons at a particular nightclub. (Appropriate choice of venues for such an assignment, don't you think?) I can just hear the resolutions becoming more grandiose with each passing hour (and drink). The list was replete with the usual suspects: quit smoking, lose weight, get my financial house in order, and so on. But one gentleman's account stood out from the crowd: he resolved to get in shape, had decided to buy books on fitness, join a health club, and cook more balanced meals. I was impressed by the specific accounting he made of what he was going to do and thought it lent an air of authenticity and legitimacy to his resolve. But then I realized that deciding is not doing. He could buy a thousand books on fitness and watch the Food Network from dusk til' dawn and still not get in any better shape. Execution is the key. So it goes with organizations. While the formation of a strategy may initially impress your stakeholders, it's the results borne of strategic execution that really get their attention. The Balanced Scorecard helps you turn the good ideas and potential of strategy into tangible results.

The Scorecard provides the framework for an organization to move from *deciding* to live their strategy to *doing* it. A well-constructed Strategy Map and Balanced Scorecard will describe the strategy, breaking it down into its component parts through the objectives and measures chosen in each of the four perspectives. Far from an academic exercise, this process will force you to specifically articulate what you mean by terms frequently residing in strategic plans, such as "excellent customer service," "continuous improvement," or "enhanced staff competencies." Using the Scorecard as a lens through which to view these terms, you may determine that "excellent customer service" equates to "meeting client requests within 24 hours." Now you have created a focus for the entire organization. While "excellent customer service" could be debated endlessly, depending on your personal point of view, "meeting requests within 24 hours" is objective, measurable, and can act as a focal point for channeling the energy of employees across the agency.

Can you develop a Balanced Scorecard without a strategy? Sure, and some organizations will do just that. But consider for a moment what such a Scorecard would consist of. You would still have a mix of financial and nonfinancial indicators straddling the four perspectives. What you would not possess, however, is a common linkage or theme running through the Scorecard. Your strategy is the common thread that weaves through the Scorecard tying the disparate elements of customers, processes, employees, and financial stakeholders into one coherent whole. Without the unifying theme represented by your strategy, you're left with a collection of good ideas that lack a coherent story or direction. The Balanced Scorecard and strategy truly go hand in hand. Kaplan and Norton sum up this subject very well. "The formulation of strategy is an art. The description of strategy, however, should not be an art. If we can describe strategy in a more disciplined way, we increase the likelihood of successful implementation. With a Balanced Scorecard that tells the story of the strategy, we now have a reliable foundation."[21]

Earlier in the chapter, while discussing environmental scans, I referenced a study conducted by the Center for Association Leadership on the attributes of extraordinary associations. The researchers note in their findings that "remarkable associations don't just emphasize thinking strategically. They find it equally important to act strategically; they consistently implement their priorities . . . In other words, among remarkable associations, it matters what you do, not just what you say."[22] Words to live by.

NOTES

1. Bob Frost, *Crafting Strategy* (Dallas, TX: Measurement International, 2000), p. 7.

2. Interview with Bill Ryan, September 17, 2002.

3. Robert S. Kaplan, BSC Report, vol. 2, no. 6.

4. Stacy Childress, Richard Elmore, and Allen Grossman, "How to Manage Urban School Districts," *Harvard Business Review*, November 2006, pp. 55–68.

5. Henry Mintzberg, "The Fall and Rise of Strategic Planning,"*Harvard Business Review,* January–February 1994.

6. Michael E. Porter, "What is Strategy?" *Harvard Business Review*, November–December 1996.

7. Tom Peters,*Re-imagine* (London: Dorling Kindersley Limited, 2003), p. 302.

8. Michael E. Porter, "What is Strategy?" *Harvard Business Review*, November–December 1996.

9. Ibid.

10. Keith H. Hammonds, "Michael Porter's Big Ideas,"*Fast Company*, March 2001.

11. E.E. Chaffee, "Three Models of Strategy," *Academy of Management Review*, October 1985.

12. Robert S. Kaplan "The Balanced Scorecard and Nonprofit Organizations," *Balanced Scorecard Report*, November–December 2002, pp. 1–4.

13. John M. Bryson, *Strategic Planning for Public and Nonprofit Organizations* (San Francisco: Jossey-Bass, 1995), p. 7.

14. W. Chan Kim and Renee Mauborgne, *Blue Ocean Strategy* (Boston: Harvard Business School Press, 2005), p. 12.

15. Based on a paper delivered by Gervase R. Bushe at the 18th Annual World Congress of Organizational Development, Dublin, Ireland, July 1998.

16. Michael E. Gallery, Chair, Measures of Success Task Force, 7 *Measures of Success* (Washington DC: ASAE, 2006).

17. Tom Peters, *Re-imagine* (London, Dorling Kindersley Limited, 2003), p. 302.

18. John M. Bryson, *Strategic Planning for Public and Nonprofit Organizations* (San Francisco: Jossey-Bass, 1995), p. 74.

19. Ibid., p. 30.

20. Ibid., p. 139.

21. Robert S. Kaplan and David P. Norton, *The Strategy-Focused Organization* (Boston: Harvard Business School Press, 2001).

22. Michael E. Gallery, Chair, Measures of Success Task Force, *7 Measures of Success* (Washington DC: ASAE, 2006), pp. 53–54.

7

Strategy Maps

Roadmap for Chapter 7 This is a good point in the book to pause and reflect both on where we've been and where we're going. The early chapters provided background on the Balanced Scorecard, and how you can adapt the model to fit your government or nonprofit agency. We then explored the elements necessary to construct a solid foundation for your Scorecard effort: determining your "burning platform," building your team, gaining executive support, and training, to mention just a few. Then we turned to the building blocks of any Balanced Scorecard: mission, values, vision, and strategy. Now, it's on to Strategy Maps!

Describing his North African adventures, Mark Jenkins had this to say about maps in his book *To Timbuktu*: "Maps encourage boldness. They make anything seem possible."[1] And you thought a map was just something to get you from point A to point B! For many organizations, executing strategy can feel like an impossible task, one in which boldness, while often in short supply, is in great demand.

In this chapter, we'll discuss the development of *Strategy Maps*. We'll explore how these devices provide a powerful method of graphically describing your strategy, bringing your performance objectives to life, and boldly proclaiming your intent to implement your strategy. We'll outline what a Strategy Map is, why you need one, and determine which perspectives are right for you. We'll then conduct a deep dive into how you'll construct your own Strategy Map. Step by step, instructions will be provided on everything, from whom to invite to the session to how to create objectives in each perspective to how you can review the completed Map with your stakeholders.

WHAT IS A STRATEGY MAP?

To help answer the question just posed, let's break it down into two parts. First, we'll examine the word "map," and then we'll take another look at "strategy."

A map provides a graphical representation of the whole or part of an area. As we all know, a good map is essential to help us navigate unfamiliar terrain. Speaking of unfamiliar terrain, although I make my home in California, I'm originally from the province of Nova Scotia, in Canada. Perhaps some of you have visited my beautiful homeland. For those of you who have not, consider this an invitation. Let's say for a moment you decide to follow my suggestion and plan to visit Nova Scotia during your next vacation. I suggest that if you fly to Nova Scotia, drive from Halifax, the provincial capital, to my hometown of Sydney, on Cape Breton Island. You'll find the scenery breathtaking. Now look at the two maps I've provided of the province in Exhibit 7.1. With the map on the left, do you think could you find your way from Halifax to Sydney? Without some advance knowledge of the province, the answer is probably no. The picture becomes much clearer with the graphic on the right, because now, in addition to a map of the province, you have landmarks to guide you from place to place, simplifying your navigational challenges significantly. Following the landmarks will lead you to your chosen destination.

Let's now return to the word "strategy." Like your fictional visit to Nova Scotia, strategy is a new destination for most organizations, one to which they have never traveled. As much as it is discussed and debated, it is frequently not implemented with any degree of success. In many ways, strategy is reminiscent of the map on the left side of Exhibit 7.1. It's a guide of where we would like to go, but the landmarks to guide us on our journey are missing. This is where performance objectives come in. The objectives on a Strategy Map serve as the landmarks on the road to strategy execution. Scorecard architects Kaplan and Norton explain: "Strategy implies the movement of an organization from its present position to a desirable but uncertain future position. Because the organization has never been to this future place, the pathway to it consists of a series of linked hypotheses. A strategy map specifies these cause and effect relationships, making them explicit and testable."[2] The "linked hypotheses" Kaplan and Norton reference are represented by the performance objectives you choose as translations of your strategy. With a Strategy Map in place, you possess a clear and concise one-page graphical representation, outlining what you believe is most critical in the effort to execute your strategy.

What are Performance Objectives?

Before you begin the development of your Strategy Map, I want to clarify the meaning of the term *objective*, since it is objectives that comprise a

Exhibit 7.1   Landmarks are Critical to Any Map

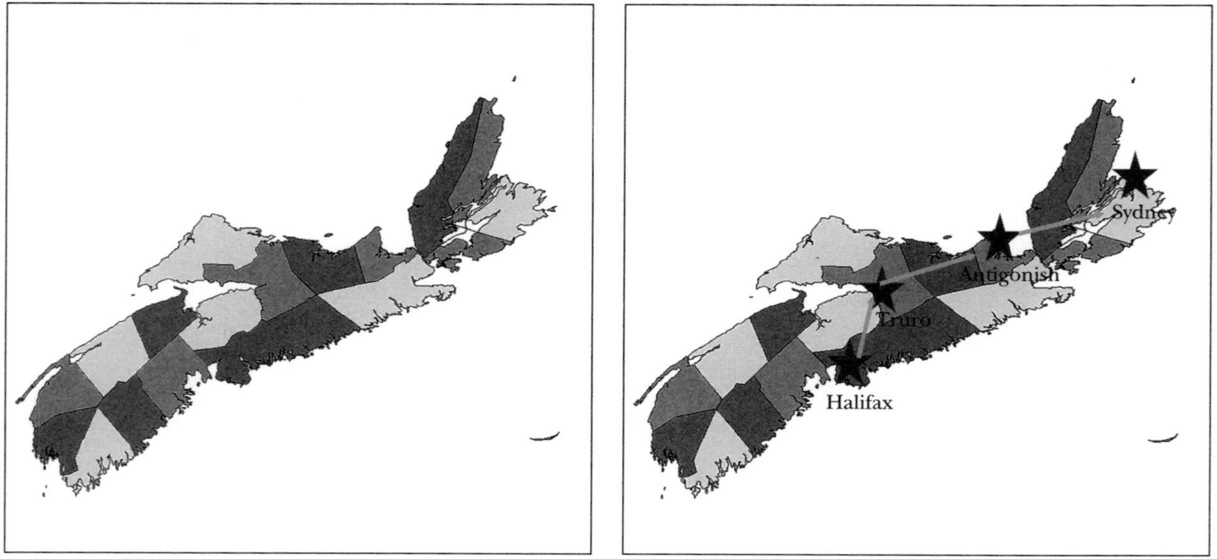

Strategy Map. Consider objectives a bridge that spans your strategy of broad overall priorities and measures, which are the quantitative means by which you will gauge success. Performance objectives describe what you must do well in order to effectively implement your strategy. They are more specific than what is contained in your strategy, but less precise than performance measures. Objectives typically begin with an action verb.

Objectives translate strategic priorities that are often vague and nebulous into directional and action-oriented statements of what must be done to execute the strategy. The objectives are then further translated into more granular performance measures. It would be quite difficult to develop meaningful performance measures without the context established by objectives. For example, it is not uncommon for an organization to adopt a strategy of "maximizing people resources." Given that approximately 75% of value in today's organization is driven by intangible assets, developing the people in an organization makes great sense. Consider the dilemma facing Scorecard developers at an institution should they be required to leap directly from a strategy as broad as this to specific performance measures. Their choices are practically unlimited, and those measures ultimately selected may not represent the true essence of the strategy. In contrast, a focused discussion of what must be done well to capture the essence of the strategy—in other words, the objectives on a Strategy Map—will lead to more focused and refined performance measures. Upon reflection, this organization might determine that maximizing people means "increasing skill sets," "improving communication," and "building organizational alignment." These objectives on the Strategy Map now set the stage for precise measurements appearing on the Balanced Scorecard.

Exhibit 7.2 graphically displays the bridging function of objectives and provides a sample of action verbs.

Why You Need a Strategy Map

As discussed in Chapter 1, Strategy Maps are powerful communication tools, signaling to everyone in the organization the critical drivers of success and providing a means for all stakeholders to determine how they will contribute to strategy execution. Well-constructed Strategy Maps breathe life into the stale rhetoric that tends to populate most sleep-inducing strategic plans, those with 50 to 100 pages of graphs, charts, and endless eight-point font-composed paragraphs. Most employees will probably never have the chance to thoroughly examine your strategic plan, but even if they were granted that privilege, given the state of most plans they'd probably take one suspicious glance at the weighty tome, make sure nobody in their vicinity was looking, and then toss the thing in the nearest dusty corner.

A Strategy Map, on the other hand, can transform employee understanding and buy-in of your strategy since a well-designed map combines text and graphics, as well as colors, and is consistent with your culture.

Exhibit 7.2   Performance Objectives

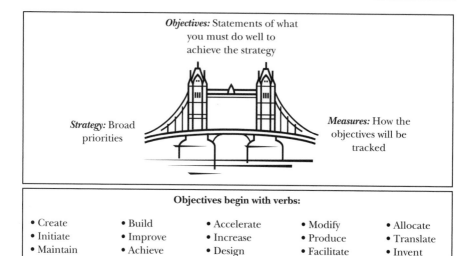

Objectives: Statements of what you must do well to achieve the strategy

Strategy: Broad priorities

Measures: How the objectives will be tracked

Objectives begin with verbs:

• Create	• Build	• Accelerate	• Modify	• Allocate
• Initiate	• Improve	• Increase	• Produce	• Translate
• Maintain	• Achieve	• Design	• Facilitate	• Invent
• Develop	• Activate	• Sustain	• Navigate	• Coordinate
• Devise	• Reduce	• Encourage	• Reach	• Hire
• Excel	• Assist	• Identify	• Supply	• Maximize

I'm not suggesting your employees need pretty pictures with small words, not at all. I'm simply putting forth the notion that, given the "noise" in most organizational environments, people need something that cuts through the clutter, a tool that dismisses with the usual jargon-filled memos and presents your story in a clear, compelling, and simple fashion. Strategy Maps do just that!

Author John Gardner suggested that "most ailing organizations have developed a functional blindness to their own defects. They are not suffering because they cannot resolve their problems but because they cannot see their problems."[3] In a very literal fashion, working in concert with the measures on a Balanced Scorecard, Strategy Maps bring problems and issues from darkness into light, allowing them to be combated and mitigated. The Map acts as an early warning system for the organization's strategy, signaling trouble when indicators suggest a problem with any element of the plan that has been designed to elevate the organization to prosperity.[4]

An example Strategy Map of a city library is shown in Exhibit 7.3. I emphasize the word "example" because as you'll discover, no two Strategy Maps look the same, which is exactly what we would expect since each document should faithfully translate the unique strategy of the organization it represents.

Exhibit 7.3 Example Strategy Map of a City Library

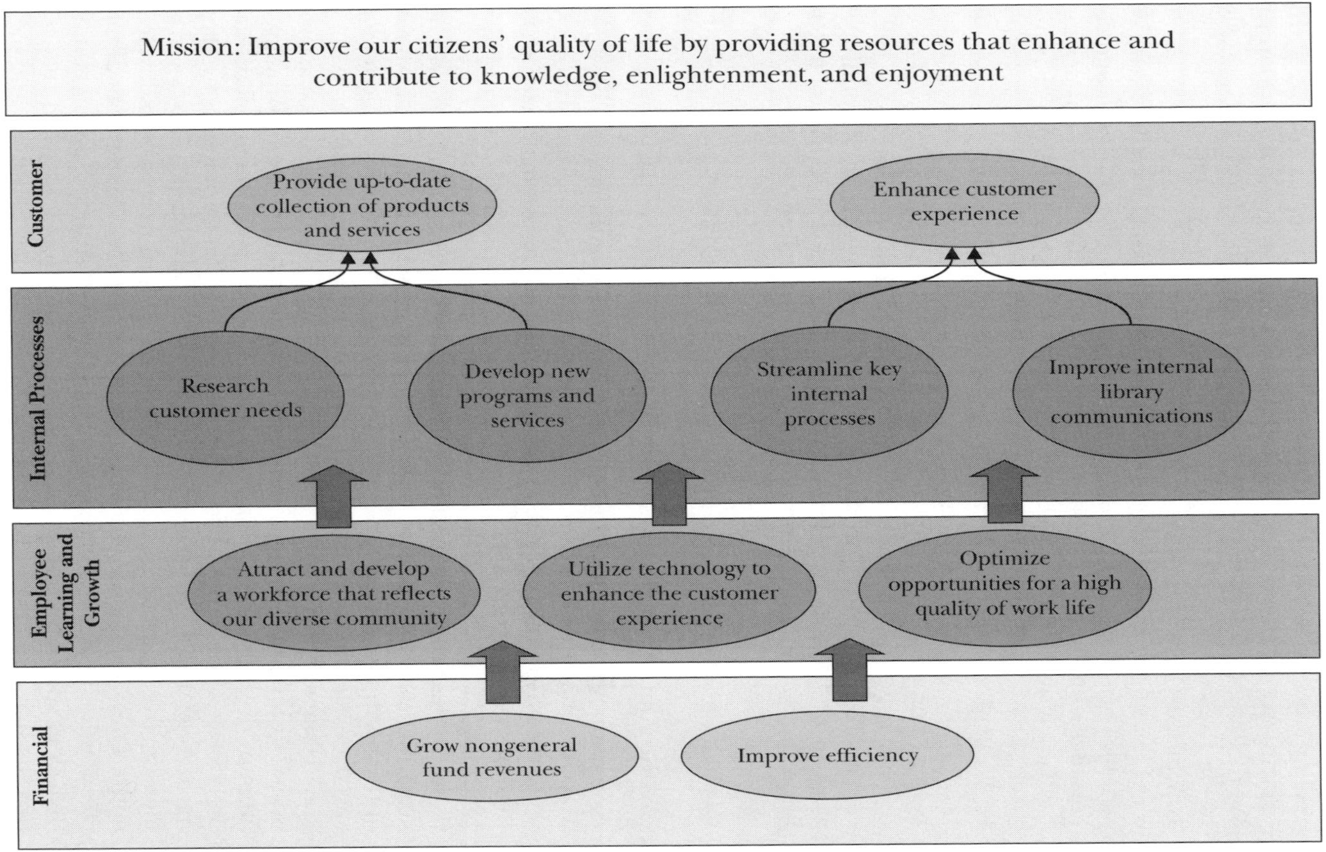

Mission: Improve our citizens' quality of life by providing resources that enhance and contribute to knowledge, enlightenment, and enjoyment

155

DEVELOPING YOUR STRATEGY MAP

Feeling a little parched? I've got a fire hose of information coming your way over the pages ahead that will definitely quench your Strategy Map thirst. We're going to completely dissect this topic into its critical parts, providing all the tools you'll need to develop a powerful Strategy Map that clearly and convincingly tells your story.

I'm sure you're anxious to build your Map, but before the first scented scribbles of a marker hit a flip chart in your mapping workshop, we need to consider some prerequisites to that process. Our first step is pondering the fundamental question whether in fact the four perspectives of performance are right for you. With that issue put to rest, we'll engage in a review of background materials, the careful deciphering of which will greatly ease the task of creating your Strategy Map. The bulk of the chapter is devoted to helping you develop objectives in each of the four standard perspectives of the Strategy Map, and we'll look at possibilities and anecdotes for each. The concluding sections of the chapter are devoted to critically examining your work of art, considering how many objectives are appropriate, and most importantly, the value of simplicity in telling your strategic story.

CHOOSING YOUR STRATEGY MAP PERSPECTIVES

Are the Four Perspectives Right for You?

A fundamental question to ask prior to building your organization's Strategy Map is, "which perspectives will we use to tell the story of our strategy?" As you know, Scorecard architects Kaplan and Norton originally conceived of four perspectives: Financial, Customer, Internal Processes, and Employee Learning and Growth. However, they did so with the private sector in mind. As use of the Scorecard methodology has evolved and expanded over many years, the founding fathers realized their original perspectives may not be appropriate for all organizations. They have since suggested the four perspectives "should be considered a template, not a straitjacket."[5]

Ultimately, the choice of perspectives should be based on what is necessary to tell your strategic story. When you examine your strategy and attempt to translate it, who or what are the key constituents necessary to describe it? The original four perspectives are broad enough to capture most constituents. However, if you feel your advantage derives in large measure from a group or area not represented, you may wish to develop an entirely new perspective. For example, you may conclude that your ability to create value results from your innovative use of strategic partnerships. In that case, you may choose to include a perspective devoted to that topic, thereby signaling its extensive worth to your agency. Suppliers and elected officials represent other groups that could, depending on their importance to your success, be assigned distinct Scorecard perspectives.

As important as the articulation of custom perspectives is, don't make the mistake of creating a "stakeholder Strategy Map." This model outlines everyone even remotely connected to your organization and virtually ignores the other Scorecard perspectives. The danger in doing this lies in missing the "how" of success. You may list noble objectives related to every group, but remember that a well-constructed Strategy Map dictates *how* you'll achieve success through the interplay of processes in the Internal Processes Perspective, resources in the Financial Perspective, and enabling infrastructure in the Employee Learning and Growth Perspective. When combined, these objectives will drive the success you desire for identified stakeholders. The true test is whether you can easily intertwine your perspectives to tell a coherent story. Stand-alone perspectives that describe a constituent group but fail to link together with the other perspectives don't belong on a Strategy Map.

Interestingly, one study of public sector Balanced Scorecard usage discovered that approximately two-thirds of respondents used the same four perspectives typically found in the corporate world.[6] However, as noted, many organizations find it necessary to make modifications to the Scorecard perspectives in order to fit their culture or unique circumstances. Frequently, the changes are in name only, with new monikers more readily accepted within the organization. For example, the Customer Perspective may be referred to as "Serving the Customer," or the "Client Perspective." The Financial Perspective is frequently renamed the "Budget Perspective," or "Resources Perspective." Internal Processes are sometimes labeled "Operations," or "Enabling Processes." Finally, the Employee Learning and Growth Perspective may be repositioned as "People Enablers," "Building for our Future," or "Internal Infrastructure."

One potential change to the Strategy Map nomenclature warrants special treatment—the placement of a possible Mission perspective at the top of the Map. That provocative topic is addressed in the next section.

Mission May Appear at the Top of the Strategy Map as a Fifth Perspective

Unlike your colleagues in the private sector, public and nonprofit organizations don't exist to produce wealth for shareholders. Financial objectives still have a place in your Strategy Map, and financial measures should be a part of your Balanced Scorecard, but they don't represent the final destination you are striving toward. You exist to serve a higher purpose, for example, to "improve the prospects of youth living in low-income communities," or "reduce discrimination." Therefore, you might consider placing a mission objective at the top of your Map and Balanced Scorecard to signify the socially important goals you are striving toward.

Some public and nonprofit agencies may hesitate to include such lofty objectives on their Strategy Map, claiming "we don't have total control over our mission," or "we can't influence the outcomes." Both points have merit, but should not preclude you from citing such objectives on your Strategy Map and subsequently attempting to measure the impact you are having on your key constituencies through your Balanced Scorecard. It's only through the act of measurement that you can gauge real difference in the lives or circumstances of those you aim to serve. Of course, you won't achieve your mission overnight, and in fact may see only periodic movement. This is precisely why the other perspectives of the Strategy Map and Balanced Scorecard are so vital. Monitoring performance, and learning from the results, in the Customer, Internal Process, Employee Learning and Growth, and Financial perspectives will provide you with the short- to medium-term information you require to guide you ever closer to achievement of the mission.[7]

REVIEWING BACKGROUND MATERIALS ON STRATEGY MAP RAW MATERIALS

Gathering Background Information

Very soon, you and your team will gather enthusiastically around a conference room table, and someone will say, "Okay, so what are our key objectives?" The first few will come with great ease—after all, you're experts on the operations of your organization and undoubtedly have years of experience. However, after the initial euphoria that results from identifying the "no-brainer" objectives, the room will get quiet. Identifying the true drivers of your success is more difficult than it first appears. For that reason, it's important to provide the team with as much background on the organization as you can reasonably muster given your time and staff resource constraints. Each of the sources outlined here will provide input that may be used when developing the Strategy Map:

> *Mission statement.* Chapter 5 outlined the importance of mission to the Balanced Scorecard system. Your objectives should act as faithful translations of the sentiments reflected in the mission.
>
> *Values.* Has your organization established its guiding principles?
>
> *Vision.* The vision represents a word picture of what the organization ultimately intends to become. Use this picture of the future to help populate your Map.
>
> *Strategic plan.* Chapter 6 was dedicated to the discussion of strategy and strategic planning. Use the broad priorities articulated in your strategy to guide the development of your Strategy Map.
>
> *Annual plans.* Many nonprofits, and an increasing number of public agencies, will issue annual plans or reports to key constituents. The

document will outline key stakeholders, financial resources, and current metrics used to gauge success. All can be considered raw materials for the Strategy Map.

Consulting studies. Consultants have been known to generate their fair share of paper. Fortunately, a lot of it contains valuable information that may provide relevant background material for your review process.

Mandates/bylaws. What are the parameters that guide the operations of your organization? Your Strategy Map should be firmly rooted in reality, as reflected by the mandates within which you've been chartered to operate.

Organizational histories. Chapter 6 discussed the importance of developing context for the strategic planning effort by looking back at your organization's history. The story often reveals programs and services you've offered, milestones reached, any shifting priorities, and external events such as demographic or legislative changes. When time comes to populate your Strategy Map, this trek down memory lane may yield many useful insights.

Customer surveys. Taking the pulse of your key customers is a popular and proven technique in the private, public, and nonprofit sectors. Information gleaned from these surveys may lead directly to Strategy Map objectives.

Published studies. Both the nonprofit and public sectors are closely scrutinized by ravenous watchdog groups waiting to pounce on your tiniest of missteps. Despite the often-critical nature of the material these groups produce, it will undoubtedly come in hand during the development of a robust Strategy Map.

Benchmarking reports. One of the best attributes of the public and nonprofit sectors is their willingness to openly share and learn from colleagues. This is a refreshing change from the secretive and hyper-competitive world occupied by most for-profit enterprises. Benchmarking studies are available on a wide variety of sectors and functional specialties. While these documents provide useful background, and may stimulate discussion of potential objectives, I caution against a reliance on them. Your Strategy Map should tell the story of *your* strategy. The objectives you choose to represent that strategy may in some cases mirror those of other organizations, but it's the determination of the *key drivers* for *your particular organization* that will ultimately differentiate you from other agencies.

The sources of information cataloged above are not intended to represent an exhaustive list, but they will definitely provide you with a much needed leg up as you begin to contemplate the objectives that will comprise your Map. As you begin collecting this material you'll notice its volume increasing rapidly, and before you know it, you're surrounded by a wall of reports, plans, and studies reaching halfway to the ceiling. Managing the prodigious pile of virtual and tangible material you'll accumulate throughout the implementation requires a filing system of its own. I have provided ideas for a filing structure you can quickly establish to tame the data beast before it's unleashed upon you and your team:

A Filing System for Your Balanced Scorecard Implementation

No matter how small or large your organization, any initiative of this magnitude is sure to generate a lot of information. Simplify your efforts by creating both paper and electronic filing methods to capture, store, and share the knowledge you develop. I suggest creating binders and electronic file directories that mirror the specific steps in your plan. For example, you may have a directory or binder titled "Background Information." Tabs in your binder and subdirectories on your computer could be labeled, "Executive Interviews," "Strategy Information," and so on.

The electronic filing is especially important since each member of your team will have preferred methods of naming and storing files. Develop a process everyone can agree on and insist that all relevant files be posted on a shared drive the whole team can access. Consider adding a date to every file created, or use another form of version control, to ensure you're always working with the most recent copy of your document.

For those of you with the resources, why not create a portal to capture all of your Balanced Scorecard information. That's exactly what the Information Technology Division of Worcester Polytechnic Institute did, creating a shared space that houses all Scorecard information including discussion groups and the latest announcements. A screen shot from their portal is provided in Exhibit 7.4.

This may seem like a small and logical step, but in my experience it is often overlooked until an abundance of documentation has been created and nobody seems to know where anything is located. Developing a Balanced Scorecard is tough enough; don't make it even tougher by hampering your efforts through poor data management.

One final caveat regarding the review of background information: Look for consistency in the messages you've discovered. For instance, if yours is like most organizations I've either worked for or consulted with, you'll unearth a number of documents that reference your mission or vision statement. Do they all say the same thing? Some discrepancies are easily swept aside in the name of timing, newer documents simply containing revised

Exhibit 7.4 Screen Shot from "My WPI," the Scorecard Portal Created by the IT Division of Worcester Polytechnic Institute (Graphic courtesy of Worcester Polytechnic Institute)

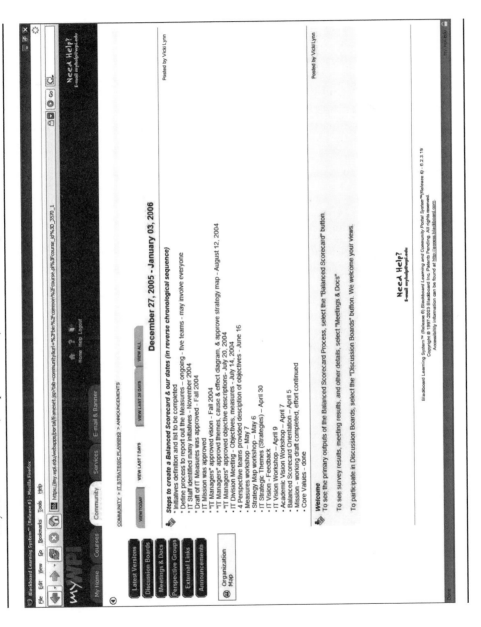

and updated statements. If, however, you dig a bit deeper and find there has been no reconsideration of your mission for the past ten years but you've found at least two different versions, it's time to toss the red flag in the air. Inconsistency is the silent killer of organizations: saying one thing but doing another, providing mixed messages, and so on. In crafting a Strategy Map, and later a Scorecard of measures, you're attempting to create a harmonious strategic story that faithfully translates your mission, values, vision, and strategy, the critical building blocks we covered in Chapters 5 and 6. If you're finding multiple versions of each, you should give serious consideration to calling a time-out on the Scorecard implementation and going back to the drawing board with these raw materials. To invoke one last cliché in ending this section, everyone has to be singing from the same sheet of music should you hope to create a system that truly guides thought and action within your four walls. If you've discovered inconsistencies, correct that deficiency now.

Conducting Interviews to Gather Executive Input

The sources outlined in the previous section will help you unearth many possible objectives for your Strategy Map, and, later, measures for your Balanced Scorecard. But there is one additional source that may be more potent than any other: the knowledge, experience, creativity, and desire that resides within the minds of your senior leadership team.

Interviewing your top leaders provides a number of benefits: First, as noted previously, you'll receive your leaders' input on the key drivers of your success. Second, this is a tremendous opportunity to directly engage your leadership in the process. To earn their support for the Balanced Scorecard implementation, they must first learn what this tool is all about, how it can produce results, and what specifically it can do for your organization. This is your chance to answer all these questions, and more—whether they're asked or not! Interviews are also a great way to detect potential trouble spots that may lie ahead. You'll be able to tell after a short period of time whether a leader is truly committed to the idea of performance measurement and the Balanced Scorecard system or is merely paying it lip service. A quorum of lip servers will necessitate action on your part to demonstrate the value of the tool.

To get the most out of these interviews, it is absolutely critical that your leaders feel comfortable and be willing to share. For that reason, it's preferable to have the interviews conducted by an outside facilitator or consultant. While the questions are certainly not controversial, the answers provided could shed light on some sensitive topics and lead the executive to take a position of reticence should they not feel psychologically safe in divulging such information to a Scorecard team member. Using a consultant is not a steadfast requirement, however. Many fruitful executive interviews have been conducted by members of Scorecard teams. Again, the key to success lies in ensuring that the executive feels psychologically safe in sharing information with the individual. A Balanced Scorecard team member who is well respected throughout the organization, and has ample experience liaising with senior leaders, will normally be welcomed openly.

I suggest this outline for your interviews, discussed in the following subsections.[8]

Review Purpose   In most implementations, your executive team will be among the first people in the organization to receive Balanced Scorecard training, and you don't want to expose this time-constrained team to 20 slides of theory. However, it is important to at least display the Scorecard framework you'll be adopting and to solicit questions. Perhaps this executive was unsure about the meaning of an objective, or didn't quite grasp what was meant by a Strategy Map. This is the time to win his or her support by providing clear and concise answers to any and all outstanding questions. Also take the opportunity to share the objectives for the interview (receiving the executive's input); briefly outline what will be covered and define the expected duration.

Mission, Values, Vision, and Strategy   These are the building blocks of the Strategy Map and Balanced Scorecard so it's important to determine how executives feel about each. Unless directly asked, don't share what you've uncovered in your research. You're attempting to determine how your leaders view these items and, as discussed earlier, whether alignment exists among your senior team. Ask the following questions:

- Has the mission for the organization been defined? If so, what is that mission?

- What core values are essential in pursuit of the mission?

- Has the organization developed a vision statement? If so, what is the vision?

- Which key strategies will lead us to the achievement of our vision?

You may need to define specifically what you mean by these terms in order to receive any feedback. *Mission, values, vision,* and *strategy* are often confused even at the highest echelons of the organizational hierarchy. If confusion seems to be reigning, consider directly asking these questions:

- Why do you feel we exist as an organization? (mission)

- What core values do we hold? (values)

- Where do you see us in 5, 10, or 15 years? (vision)

- What must we do to reach that desired future? (strategy)

The goal of this component of the interview is to determine the level of consensus that exists across the organization in relation to mission, values, vision, and strategy. Should you find that every executive is saying something different, it will be exceedingly difficult to engineer a Strategy Map that suits all of their individual preferences and perceptions. In this case, reverting back to a discussion of mission, values, vision, and strategy at the senior level may be necessary before the implementation can continue.

Balanced Scorecard Perspectives   By this point in your implementation, you should have determined the perspectives that will comprise your Strategy Map and Balanced Scorecard. Ask the executive for his or her input on each of the four (assuming you're using four) perspectives. Use this component of the interview to compile the executive's thoughts on which objectives and measures are critical to the organization's success.

- *Customer.* Who are our customers (or clients), and what must we do well to satisfy them?

- *Internal Processes.* At which processes must we excel if we are to meet customer and client needs?

- *Financial.* Financially, what is most critical to us; growing revenue, enhancing productivity, utilizing our assets more efficiently?

- *Employee Learning and Growth.*

    ○ What skills or competencies do we require to succeed and execute our strategy?

    ○ Do our employees have the technology tools they require to meet customer requirements, and execute our strategy?

    ○ Do we have the proper organizational climate (culture, alignment, teamwork) necessary for success?

    ○ Which measures do we currently use to gauge our success?

The last question does not relate to an individual perspective but seeks to determine how this executive currently tracks success. Objectives and measures repeated consistently here should form part of your Strategy Map and Scorecard.

Implementation and Use   In this phase of the interview, you're attempting to move away from the Scorecard implementation as an academic exercise to probe what it will actually mean for your organization. A constant communication theme for Scorecard-implementing organizations has to separate the idea of the Balanced Scorecard as a theoretical construct from that of the tool as a practical management solution. Ask these questions:

- How would you like to see the Balanced Scorecard used here?

- What are some of the barriers we may face in implementing the Balanced Scorecard, and how do we overcome them?

Chances are, unless they campaigned for the Scorecard, this is the first time your executives will be pressed to consider how they would like to use the tool and how the roadblocks might be overcome. This is valuable input for a couple of reasons. One, the answer to "how would you like to see the Scorecard used?" will provide some parameters for the actual Strategy Map and Scorecard the team designs. If, for example, five out of five executives say they want a complex management reporting tool, then your Scorecard development team will most likely construct a Map and Scorecard consisting of many objectives and measures. Conversely, if "communication tool" is the answer most commonly cited, a Strategy Map and Scorecard with fewer objectives and measures will most likely satisfy executives. Asking executives which barriers you face not only challenges them to enumerate issues, but puts psychological pressure upon them to be part of any solution.

Interviews should be scheduled for one hour, and questions limited to between 10 and 15. Always choose questions that are most vital for your implementation. You don't want to lose the rapport you're establishing with an executive by stopping them midsentence with, "Okay, I'm sorry but we have to move on now." Of course, you have to ensure the interview remains focused as well, which can sometimes prove to be a delicate balancing act. For example, I like to start my interviews on a casual note, engaging the executive on a comfortable topic like the weather, general business news, or sports. This method can be a great icebreaker, but there have been occasions in which 15 minutes have passed and I'm still hearing about the executive's last round of golf! Be on guard for "hot button" issues as well. One executive I interviewed felt passionate about a casual dress policy. Suffice to say that at the end of our time together I knew far too much about the organization's dress code and too little about its key objectives!

Once all of the interviews have been completed, have your consultant or Scorecard champion sort, summarize, and compile all responses. Names, of course, will be removed, as will any quotes that could easily identify a specific individual. Distribute the condensed notes to the Scorecard team for reference purposes during your development sessions. Executive interviews can prove to be tricky business. To help you through the process, a number of tips are provided in Exhibit 7.5.

Exhibit 7.5 Tips for Conducting an Effective Interview

Hold the interview in the executive's office. In order to receive candid feedback, it's critical that the executive feel comfortable. People tend to be most comfortable on their own "turf." Therefore, whenever possible conduct your interviews in the office of the executive. In addition to putting them at ease, by holding the interview in their office you have the opportunity to learn more about them based on their furniture, pictures, desk decorations, etc. Undoubtedly, something in their environment will provide the spark for an "ice-breaking" conversation.

Don't interrupt. I've learned this the hard way. Some people are measured in their comments, taking time to formulate an appropriate response. Ensure the executive has completed their thought before jumping in, or moving on to the next question. When you derail them, even if just for a second, it may throw the rhythm of the interview off significantly.

Consider having a designated note-taker. I have yet to have someone say yes to the following question: "Do you mind if I take some notes while we speak?" However, I have noticed that some people feel distracted by the note-taking. Therefore, if possible, have one person asking the questions and a second person in the room solely to take notes. That way the interviewer can establish a comfortable rapport with the executive.

Be prepared to deviate from the "script." It's crucial to have questions prepared in advance, but be ready to move from topic to topic as the conversation flows. You may pose a question about financial objectives to which the executive replies, "We have to focus on growing revenue, and we'll do that by educating our employees on the latest customer service skills." Not only have you received a financial objective, but an employee learning and growth objective as well. Be sure you capture that information, and either follow up immediately or return to it when the time is right.

Be aware of body language (both yours and theirs). Establishing a comfortable rapport is critical in receiving open, honest feedback. Your body language can either facilitate or inhibit this. Be sure to show interest through appropriate eye contact and facial expressions. You must also be on the lookout for potential clues emanating from their body language. Do they physically back up or cross their arms with certain questions? If so, you've stumbled into an area either they're not comfortable discussing with you, or they have strong feelings on. Either way, tread carefully here to ensure you maintain the level of safety and comfort you've worked hard to establish.

Adapted from *Balanced Scorecard Diagnostics: Maintaining Maximum Performance, 2nd Edition,* Paul R. Niven (John Wiley & Sons, 2005).

DEVELOPING STRATEGY MAP OBJECTIVES IN EACH PERSPECTIVE

In the pages ahead, each perspective of the Strategy Map will be explored. Based on my years of experience in the field, during which I've seen hundreds of Strategy Maps, I will provide suggestions for possible objectives to populate each perspective. Don't feel, however, that your Strategy Map must include the objectives I cover. While I would expect a degree of overlap, since the observations that follow are based on extensive practical experience, you must never forget that your Strategy Map is just that, *yours*. The objectives you choose for each perspective must represent translations of your strategy, and depict the story you're telling. Thus, it won't be surprising to discover that you've created unique objectives or considered elements of the Mapping experience not outlined here.

DEVELOPING OBJECTIVES FOR THE CUSTOMER PERSPECTIVE

Who is the Customer?

First things first. Prior to outlining possible objectives for this perspective, you have to wrestle with what may be the most difficult question you'll have to answer throughout the entire Balanced Scorecard process: Who is your customer? Back in Chapter 2, I noted that in the public and nonprofit world, unlike the for-profit arena, different groups design the service, pay for the service, and ultimately benefit from the service. This web of relationships makes determining the customer a considerable challenge.

The initial, and most simple, step to take in answering the question of who is your customer is to list all possible candidates for your nonprofit or public sector agency. Six short hours later and you're ready to move on. Just kidding . . . sort of. Once you have the inventory of possibilities exhausted, I would offer the following two questions to serve as filters through which you should analyze your list:

1. **Which of those listed fit the actual definition of a customer?** To answer that, you'll need a definition of customer, and I would suggest you use this: "A person or group that directly benefits from our products or services." The emphasis in that definition rests squarely on the word "directly." There are many people or groups who may indirectly benefit from the important work you're undertaking, but your task here is to raise the intellectual bar to a much higher level and critically examine who is directly impacted by your work. An example should help clear things up. I once worked with the head office of an international relief agency that was charged with, among other things, fundraising and then dispersing those dollars and goods. The actual

work of the agency was carried out by national offices situated on the ground in the mostly third world where they operated. When constructing their head office Map, the spirited debate duly began: Was the customer the poor child in a developing nation that ultimately received the food or clothing provided? Or, was it the national office that knew the situation and was able to allocate available resources based on that knowledge? After lengthy discussions, the team decided it was the national office that directly benefited from their service, in this case fundraising and support. Their rationale was convincing: If they provided the national offices with resources (money, people, support, information), the national offices could then effectively serve the children that urgently needed the care. This was the most efficient chain of events to ensure an effective use of donor funds and, most importantly, positive outcomes for the children. The Girl Scouts of the U.S.A. (GSUSA) offer another example. Stroll the corridors of their headquarters and you'll discover cubicles decorated with scouting paraphernalia, walls adorned with pictures of girl scouts, and materials throughout that leave little doubt about whom they exist to serve—the girls. Yet, those same girls are not their customers. Rather, their target customer is the local council that facilitates delivery of the Girl Scout program.[9]

2. **Which person's or group's disappearance would cause us to be irrelevant or unnecessary?** Many organizations, for instance, will include funders as part of their potential database of customers, and some will argue vehemently that since this group is providing the actual cash necessary to sustain operations on a day-to-day basis, they have to be customers. But if your current funders or donors went away, would that force you to close your doors for good? I will argue that it would not. Chasing alternate revenue streams is a distinct possibility for most, if not all, public and nonprofit agencies. Pursuing grants, selling products or services, and offering consulting assistance, are just a few of myriad possibilities for enhancing coffers that deviate from traditional sources. Apply this filter to all of your potential customers and you are sure to winnow the list in a hurry.

To borrow once again from our discussion in Chapter 2, tackling this question head-on and arriving at consensus on an answer may represent one of the most significant benefits you'll derive from implementing the Balanced Scorecard. A failure to determine the true customer could lead you right down the slippery slope to an "all things for all people" approach that eventually means mediocre service for everyone. However, opening the envelope and finding the answer to this query will be as refreshing as a cool breeze on a stifling mid-summer afternoon. Allocating resources will be clearer, assigning people to tasks can be done in a more focused and strategic manner, and all organizational conversations can center on serving the identified customer.

I love being a consultant: There's always a "but" conveniently located somewhere at the periphery of every possible discussion, just lurking about waiting for the right time to pounce. This situation, I'm afraid, calls for the unleashing of a "but." Having said everything I did about isolating *the* customer, I'm not suggesting you must engage in protracted discussions that could take days and many cases of Red Bull to finally experience the "aha!" clarity that comes from finding the one final answer to the question of who is the customer. Some clients will determine more than one customer group that is vital to their success and thus include two in the Mapping and measures discussions. I know of at least one nonprofit Balanced Scorecard Hall of Fame member (yes, there actually is a Balanced Scorecard Hall of Fame, but it's virtual—no stately museum-like building, guided tours and a gift shop—yet) that has included three customers in their Strategy Map. The point is this: Don't dilute your efforts by introducing on the Strategy Map every single person or group that holds even a remote stake in your success. The Balanced Scorecard is concerned primarily with translating strategy, and at the core of strategy we find an elusive pearl, one all organizations should strive to uncover: focus.

What Do Customers Expect or Demand?

Once you've tamed the "who is the customer" beast, and assuming your team members are still on speaking terms, you're ready to move on and create objectives for your target audience. Start the process by simply asking what those customers expect or demand from you as an organization. Timely service, access to information, low costs of doing business, enhanced functionality of products and services, and knowledge are all possible contenders.

Completing this exercise will require you to have a deep knowledge of customer wants and preferences, and distinguishing between those two elements is an important area to contemplate as you're devising your Map. Once again, the issue is focus: Recall that strategy is as much about what *not to do*, as it is what *to do*. As you're getting to the bottom of say, your fifth flip chart page of customer demands, hopefully someone will stop the dance and say, "We can't possibly do all this!" No you can't and no, you don't want to because doing so would be in direct violation of the laws of strategy to which you're most likely precariously clinging at this point. Go back and review your list with the precision of a Swiss watchmaker, carefully considering each item to determine whether it is a legitimate customer expectation and fits with your ongoing strategy.

Assumptions should be continually challenged as you ransack your way through the pile of possible customer expectations lying before you, with all preconceived notions left at the doorstep. As an illustration of assumption busting, I'll end this section with a story about one Los Angeles entrepreneur who discovered that fixing a leaky pipe isn't the only thing people want from a plumber.

Mike Diamond was frustrated. He had established himself as technically savvy—able to fix in a jiffy anything that leaked, burst, or ruptured—but his plumbing business was stagnant. That's when he had an epiphany. Diamond recalled the image of plumbers in popular culture, epitomized by the Dan Akroyd character in *Saturday Night Live* famous for his, how shall we say this delicately, "plumber's smile." Plumbers were often considered wrench-wielding Neanderthals with all the polish and refinement of a Roman Gladiator. Diamond decided the industry, or at least his company, was ripe for an image change—the "Smell Good" campaign was born. All Mike Diamond plumbers would now show up at your house on time, clean-shaven, wearing a crisp white shirt, and donning fresh white booties lest they leave a stain on your floor. The response was astounding. Mike Diamond has become the largest plumbing contractor in Los Angeles and has been called "L.A.'s most famous plumber." Customer referrals are now the number one source of new business. Determining what customers really want unlocked the mystery, as Diamond notes: "The key to this growth is that we listened to our customers and began to measure ourselves like they did: fixing the leak was the least important part of the service."[10]

Customer Value Propositions

Value proposition is a term frequently bandied about in the for-profit world. In that sector, many organizations have embraced the work of Michael Treacy and Fred Wiersema, as articulated in their book *The Discipline of Market Leaders*. Exhibit 7.6 outlines the following three value disciplines they have seen used in practice:

1. *Product Leadership.* These organizations constantly push the envelope of product and service design. While you might expect to pay a little more for their offerings, you expect a superior product or experience. Sony is an example of a product leader.

2. *Operational Excellence.* Wal-Mart is the classic operationally excellent company. You probably don't shop there for outstanding customer service or cutting edge products. What you expect is a huge selection and great prices. They can offer you this value because of flawless execution of hundreds of operational processes affecting your store experience.

3. *Customer Intimacy.* Organizations pursuing a customer intimacy strategy strive to provide total solutions to customer needs. Rather than focusing on a transaction as a one time event, they strive to build long-lasting relationships with customers. Home Depot prides itself on providing helpful solutions to customers' needs.

Exhibit 7.6 Customer Value Propositions

Product Leadership	Customer Intimacy	Operational Excellence
Product leaders push the envelope of their firm's products. Constantly innovating, they strive to offer simply the best product in the market.	Doing whatever it takes to provide solutions to unique customer's needs help define the customer intimate organization. They don't look for one-time transactions, but instead focus on long-term relationship building.	Organizations pursuing an operational excellence discipline focus on price, convenience, and often "no frills."
Sony 3M Intel	Nordstrom	Costco McDonalds Wal-Mart
Most Innovative Product	**Best Solution**	**Best Total Cost**

Adapted from material developed by Michael Treacy and Fred Wiersema, *The Discipline of Market Leaders* (Reading, MA: Perseus Books, 1995).

171

The question is, do the value propositions apply to nonprofit and public sector organizations? The answer is yes. All organizations, regardless of structure, must attempt to forge meaningful bonds with their customers. This is the case even if your service is currently a monopoly. Hence, customer intimacy readily applies to governments and nonprofits. Operational excellence too, is a natural fit. Given shrinking funding and increasing demands, efficient internal operations are a must should you hope to continue to garner the support of your constituents. Finally, even product leadership is possible in public and nonprofit sectors. Approaching your customers in a new way, providing new services to meet demands, and creatively applying technology to simplify the customer experience are all examples of product leadership propositions. The Michigan Department of Transportation used the notion of value propositions when developing their Balanced Scorecard. They described the benefit this way: "Using the value proposition concept was one of the most insightful pieces for us. We learned a lot about things we could do more of, and it drove home more quickly the importance of building relationships, communicating value, and focusing on innovation. It's not only applicable, but was one of the real benefits of doing this."[11]

Do We Need to Focus on One Value Proposition?

When the idea of value propositions hit the mainstream in the mid- to late-1990s, it was quickly applied by those organizations developing Strategy Maps and Balanced Scorecards. The challenge of identifying a value proposition and determining appropriate objectives and measures seemed very well suited to the demands of the Customer Perspective. However, organizations quickly realized they could not focus exclusively on one value proposition to the exclusion of the other two. Rather, they concluded, at least a baseline of acceptable performance must be achieved in two propositions, with a focus of efforts devoted to the third.

Take Wal-Mart as an example. They have to be considered the very exemplar of an operationally-excellent organization, with their laser-like focus on costs and productivity. However, in a strategic shift that signals a transition to the borders of both customer intimacy and product leadership, they recently announced a plan to drop their one-size-fits-all approach at stores across the country. Now, the retailer will custom-fit their merchandise based on demographic patterns of the communities they serve. Specific store designs and product placements have been selected for African-American shoppers, Hispanics, empty-nesters, suburbanites, rural residents, and even affluent customers.[12]

Engaging in the value proposition discussion and, inevitably, debate is an important component of the Customer Perspective objective setting experience. In my travels, I've found that most organizations have not sufficiently examined this enabler and thus have not exploited the value that comes from a clear emphasis on how you choose to create value for your customers.

As with mission and vision, the shared understanding of a value proposition can serve to energize the entire workforce and provide the impetus for improved decision-making, resource allocation, and strategy execution.

DEVELOPING OBJECTIVES FOR THE INTERNAL PROCESS PERSPECTIVE

If your aim is to drive continuous value for customers and clients, and ultimately work towards your mission, process excellence is a must. Every organization is unique and will derive value from a different combination of processes. However, there are several core processes you should consider when developing objectives for the Internal Process Perspective. Each is discussed on the pages that follow.

Understand Your Customers

A researcher in the private sector recently conducted an online survey of a number of well-regarded companies asking them, among other things, "Do you understand your customers?" A paltry 25% of the respondents believed they did. In a related study, participants were asked to identify the most important capabilities that companies could acquire to trigger a new wave of growth. Topping the list of responses was "capabilities to understand our core customers more deeply."[13] It's a fundamental, but often disregarded, premise of successful operations: To develop meaningful products and services, and to satisfy customer expectations and demands, the first step is to simply understand customers—their composition, wants, preferences, and trends. Pulling back the curtain on this baseline exercise creates context for product and service development and delivery.

Innovate Constantly

Your customers are changing, the environment in which you operate is changing, your own staff is undoubtedly changing, the question is; Are you responding? Constant innovation must be built into every organization, from the smallest local nonprofit to the largest federal government department. Embracing the status quo is no longer an option for organizations that wish to be relevant today, tomorrow, and years into the future. Here are some characteristics practiced by organizations excelling at the art of innovation:[14]

- *Innovation is treated as a process.* A structured process is put in place for the systematic practice of innovation. This imposes a discipline and allows for measurement, and ultimately, improvement.

- *Cross-functional teams are used.* Leading innovators recognize that creative insights are often struck from the eclectic exchanges among participants representing every discipline.

- *Customers are at the center.* Organizations committed to innovation learn primarily from their current customers and clients, analyzing their needs, wants, and "must-haves."

- *Support passion and creativity.* Some pundits describe the role of leadership as that of establishing the conditions for success to flourish, and then getting out of the way. Innovating organizations recognize this tenet of leadership and put in place structures and environments conducive to creativity.

Organizations excelling at innovation also tend to value the concept of experimentation, recognizing that while not every new idea will represent a potential breakthrough, many seeds must be planted if you hope to reap a bountiful harvest. As one staffer at the National Association of Counties (NACo) colorfully put it: "We think of programs as pancakes. You ought to be able to throw the first two away."[15] These agencies are willing to burn a few flapjacks in the quest for the next big thing. Of course, not all ideas prove to be successful. Even those occupying the loftiest positions in corporate America occasionally stumble. Take IBM that once patented a system for taking airborne restroom reservations. U.S. patent #6329919—now, sadly, the former patent #6329919—was granted on December 11, 2001, bearing this summary: "The present invention is an apparatus, system, and method for providing reservations for restroom use. In one embodiment, a passenger on an airplane may submit a reservation request to the system for restroom use. The reservation system determines when the request can be accommodated and notifies the passenger when a restroom becomes available. The system improves airline safety by minimizing the time passengers spent standing while an airplane is in flight."[16] I don't know, from the cramped confines of 23B in which I often find myself, this sounds like a great idea to me. The point is: With their storied history of novel ideas and approaches that can be traced all the way back to founder Thomas Watson, IBM didn't let this minor setback derail their innovation engine in the least.

We tend to focus on the end result of innovation: the tangible item that exits the process such as shiny new function-packed gadgets, or transformative services executed flawlessly by extensively trained personnel. What precedes these breakthroughs, of course, is innovation in thought. Our challenge every single day we roam this planet is to critically examine the landscape around us, eyeing it with a fresh perspective in the quest to perhaps see what really lies before us for the very first time. Doing so can yield remarkable results. Television personality and *über entrepreneur* Donald Trump describes how such a paradigm shift once saved him millions of dollars.

Overlooking Trump's golf course in California and offering unobstructed views of the Pacific Ocean is a beautiful ballroom, designed to accommodate high-end corporate functions and society weddings. Unfortunately, the room was unable to house many of the functions originally conceived during the design phase because it was simply too small, holding less than 300 people. Wishing to avoid the now famous cry of "you're fired!" delivered in a dark and cavernous boardroom from their demanding boss, Trump's eager management team set about to solve the problem. Their solution: Enlarge the ballroom. Sounds simple enough, but Trump recognized that this fix would translate to months of chasing down permits, construction nuisances for guests, and millions of dollars drained from his coffers. Contemplating his options in the ballroom one sunny afternoon, Trump noticed a woman experiencing difficulty getting up from her chair. The chair was very large and she was having a hard time extricating herself from it while simultaneously moving it away from the adjacent table. Trump looked around and immediately noticed the room was filled with these oversized chairs. Why not remove them and bring in smaller chairs? This simple solution not only saved him millions but in the end enhanced revenue. The company earned more money selling the old chairs than it spent on the new smaller versions, and the room could now comfortably hold more than 440 people. Aspiring Apprentices should keep this story in mind!

As a final tribute to the power of innovation, consider the case of the Youth Voice Collaborative (YVC).[17] An innovative after-school program of media literacy and leadership training, YVC provides young people between the ages of 13 and 18 with the information they need to become critical consumers of media and the skills to create and distribute messages that reflect their realities. This innovative idea was the brainchild of the Boston YWCA, and resulted from their commitment to getting at-risk kids off the streets after school hours. Upon hearing one young woman explain that her life was changed by "walking into a boys and girls club and picking up a camcorder," YWCA president Marti Wilson-Taylor sprang to action. She spoke to other kids, organized a collaborative effort with other youth service agencies, and set about to develop a program dedicated to the natural attraction of kids and media. The YWCA had never done anything quite like this in the past, but was committed to improving society and used innovation to help them achieve their goals.

Market and Brand Yourself

Getting the word out about your organization has never been more important. However, it seems every organization is clamoring for attention these days, leaving precious little room for individual voices to cry out above the din. Marketing is a long-standing method of telling your story, your way. Here are the "four Ps" of marketing, each of which could lead to important performance objectives on your Strategy Map:[18]

- *Product.* The product of service offered. In order to stand out, it must at least live up to, if not exceed, what customers and clients demand.

- *Promotion.* Going from the best-kept secret in town to a household name is the goal of promotion. Products, services, and image are all potential targets of promotional campaigns.

- *Price.* Price in this context refers to perceived value. Ironically, in the nonprofit world, bewildered consumers often associate greater value with higher price.

- *Place.* Where the product or service is delivered. Public and non-profits must ensure they develop an effective distribution system for their products and services. In other words, if clients can't come to them they should go to the clients.

The goal of your marketing efforts is to distinguish your unique brand from all of the others screaming at your customers from a hundred different channels every single day. Traditionally, the view of marketing and branding was that of a carefully constructed image delivered mainly through advertising, and to that end companies have spent billions promoting their brands each year. Today, however, the notion of *brand equity* is emerging as the rallying cry of organizations attempting to leverage this most valuable of intangible assets, with a concentration on the brand's image, performance, and added value.[19]

Offer a Quality Product or Service

Total Quality Management, or TQM, became a household (or at least organizational) word in the 1980s. This unrelenting focus was long overdue as many organizations saw eroding results due to substandard quality. As with many things, however, the quality movement bore an unintended consequence for some devotees. Their maniacal attention to this one variable of performance led to less attention on customer satisfaction, innovation, and in many private sector examples, financial results. Many quality standouts of the 1980s paid the ultimate price for their lack of balance and ended up in bankruptcy. Using a Balanced Scorecard approach allows you to mitigate this substantial risk. You can do so by balancing the admirable goals of quality improvement with objectives and measures that demonstrate whether the improvement is leading to increased value for customers or clients.

Work Efficiently

Virtually every organization with which I have consulted over the years—pubic, private, or nonprofit—has included a process efficiency or improvement objective on their Strategy Map. And why not? There is not a single enterprise in business today that would not benefit from squeezing extra productivity out of their operations.

This objective comes with a boulder of a caveat, however: Be realistic when crafting it. I've had organizations over the years brainstorm objectives on this topic and ultimately land on something akin to "improve and streamline all our processes." Inevitably, the discussion this spawns could go on for days as inspired participants recount scores of broken processes just waiting to be sanctioned by the new Strategy Map. And then along I come, carrying my reality prod, which I try to administer gently, but it stings quite a bit when you're contemplating how you're going to reengineer everything that has ever littered your path to success.

Even if your organization is relatively small, you could have dozens of critical processes, each cross-functional in nature and so broken that they've got more band-aids than Mr. Bean after a stint as a sushi chef. Trying to fix them all just isn't realistic. Better to err on the side of caution here and pursue a more manageable objective, such as "identify and improve three key processes this year." Now you can focus on identifying which bottlenecks are in fact preventing you from effectively serving your customers and align your scarce resources on tackling them.

Partner for Success

Partnering has become emblematic of modern private sector organizations. The technology sector in particular has grown in large part due to powerful and synergistic unions between organizations. Partnering offers many opportunities for public and nonprofit organizations as well. One area of emerging interest for nonprofits is the potential link to corporate philanthropy efforts. Private sector organizations are beginning to realize they can use their charitable efforts to improve their "competitive context"—the quality of the business environment in the location where they operate.[20] They are beginning to seek out nonprofit (and government) partners in order to improve their business prospects. Consider for example the State Museum of Auschwitz-Birkenau in Poland. They have partnered with Grand Circle Travel, a leading direct marketer of international travel for older Americans. Grand Circle provides donations to the museum, allowing it to maintain the aging facilities, and offer innovative exhibitions. Grand Circle patrons benefit from the relationship by receiving special visiting and learning opportunities at the museum.

More traditional partnering efforts find public sector and nonprofit organizations attempting to fill voids by reaching out to others who possess specific and complementary skills or offerings. For example, the American Dental Association (ADA) discovered its members had a need for more sophisticated practice-management knowledge. In recognition of this need, and acknowledging its own limitations, the ADA turned to the Kellogg School of Management at Northwestern University to develop a mini-MBA program geared specifically towards dentists.[21]

As partnering has swept briskly into the mainstream for all forms of enterprise, the number of dubious or ill-conceived ventures is correspondingly on the rise. We've all read headlines in the business press lamenting corporate mergers gone horribly wrong, and the millions in shareholder value that evaporated as a result of the weakly-considered unions. But poor matches can just as easily take place in the public and nonprofit domains. Due diligence is critical here; look for partners with complementary missions: organizations that share your core values, hold similar expectations, and can contribute to your ability to better serve your constituency.

Raise Funds Effectively and Efficiently

It would be difficult, if not impossible, to get to know your customers, raise your profile, provide quality products and services, attract potential partners, and constantly innovate without a steady stream of revenue. Many sources of objectives exist throughout the fundraising process—from finding potential donors, to developing proposals, to building budgets.

Monitor Your Reputation[22]

On June 13, 2002, the *Wall Street Journal* ran a story chronicling the insider trading charges brought against Samuel Waksal, the ex-CEO of Imclone. Buried deep within the text was this seemingly innocuous reference to a friend of Waksal's: "Also implicated is Martha Stewart, who sold 3,928 shares on December 27th, the day before ImClone announced the FDA's rejection."[23] Within days, a hurricane of controversy was pounding the domestic diva with cable news shows, the business press, and pundits around the globe glued to the sensational story, transmitting every detail to an absorbed public. As we all know, Martha Stewart was eventually convicted, spent several months in jail, and later underwent several months of house arrest. Stewart's once revered reputation had been crushed in a million little pieces by the arrest; or more appropriately, *hundreds* of millions of little pieces as the market value of her company Omnimedia plummeted in the days following her indictment. Remarkably, thanks to a world willing to give her a second chance and a team of high-priced image consultants longer than a city block, Martha Stewart has re-emerged. But hers is certainly a cautionary tale of the power of reputation risk.

The public and nonprofit sectors are certainly not immune to reputation risk. An entire industry of oversight bodies and watchdog groups, poring menacingly over every line of public information available, stand ready to pounce at the most innocent of your blunders. Creating an awareness of the existence of your reputation as a vital intangible asset and cultivating its positive attributes is critical to every public and nonprofit enterprise.

Manage Your Risks

Beyond the vanilla challenges that present themselves every day, modern organizations are subject to a number of unpredictable and often threatening disruptions: financial-market meltdowns, extreme weather, political tumult, even terrorism. While, admittedly, these are all dramatic examples of risk that can affect your agency, it's critical that you carefully delineate the risks, both mundane and potentially horrific, that could impact your operations. Not calculating your risks can lead to extremely nasty outcomes. For example, the British Automotive company Land Rover put over 11,000 jobs in jeopardy in the 1990s when the sole manufacturer of its chassis went bankrupt.[24]

Other Sources of Internal Process Objectives

Objectives in the Internal Process Perspective should flow directly from your choices in the Customer Perspective. After all, you're attempting to tell the story of your strategy through the objectives you choose, and to do so they must link together in a cause and effect chain throughout the four perspectives. Once you've developed your customer objectives, ask yourself, "At which processes must we excel in order to meet these customer goals?"

Finally, consider adopting a value chain approach to your analysis of this perspective by asking, "Where does the process begin and end for our products or services?" What is the very first thing to occur: raising funds perhaps? What's next, investigating customer needs? And then what? By mapping the entire process from start to finish, you're presented with a menu of potential processes from which to populate your Internal Process Perspective.

DEVELOPING OBJECTIVES FOR THE EMPLOYEE LEARNING AND GROWTH PERSPECTIVE

In his foreword to *The HR Scorecard,* David Norton wrote, "the worst grades are reserved for (executives) understanding of strategies for developing human capital. There is little consensus, little creativity, and no real framework for thinking about the subject . . . The asset that is the most important is the least understood, least prone to measurement, and, hence, least susceptible to management."[25] Research has indicated that upwards of 75% of value in today's organization is derived from intangible assets, principally human capital. However, as Norton aptly asserts, the failure to recognize and respond to this undeniable fact has reached epidemic proportions.

My experience as a consultant echoes Norton's findings. In conducting Strategy Mapping sessions with a wide variety of clients, I have detected a worrisome pattern. Enthusiasm abounds as we discuss customer objectives. Internal processes and financial objectives can be tough going, but the groups consistently remain tenacious and generate active discussion on the points until consensus is reached. Inevitably, Employee Learning and Growth issues will be the last area of dialog. Perhaps I'm mistaking fatigue for disinterest, but in a disturbingly high number of cases, when I introduce this perspective I'll be greeted with, "oh, HR will take care of those objectives for us" accompanied by a chorus of chuckles. The majority of organizations, while paying constant lip service to the importance of employees, have yet to make the realization that the value of human capital truly is the distinguishing feature among today's organizations. Public and nonprofit leaders must pay particular heed to this warning since the yield from human capital and intangible assets in your organizations is particularly high.

In this section, we'll look at three areas that comprise the objective setting challenge of the Employee Learning and Growth Perspective: *human capital, information capital,* and the *organizational capital.*

Human Capital: Aligning People with Strategy

Here is some papal wisdom from his Excellency, the late John Paul II: "Whereas at one time the decisive factor of production was the land, and later capital . . . today the decisive factor is increasingly man himself, that is, his knowledge."[26] There you have it, direct from Vatican City, the late Pope expounding an undeniable fact of modern enterprise. The means of production have swung dramatically over the past century, from screeching, hulking machines in the industrial age to the agile minds of men and women, operating in perfect choreography to the rhythms of modern commerce. The corporate world has long recognized this dramatic shift, investing significantly in knowledge development and sharing systems, to the tune of billions of dollars. On a very encouraging note, public sector and nonprofit organizations, not to be left forlorn at the station in this knowledge revolution, have begun to make similar investments. For instance, as part of the bill that created the U.S. Department of Homeland Security, every federal agency must hire a Chief Human Capital Officer whose responsibility is to ensure their agency's strategic alignment and maintenance and to direct Human Resources policies and programs.[27] Outlined below are some possible candidates for the human capital dimension of your Strategy Map.

Closing Skills Gaps in Strategic Positions   Are all jobs created equal? Every person on every rung of your organizational ladder undoubtedly possesses unique talents and skills, but do they all contribute equally to your ability to execute strategy? Many organizations, predominantly in the private sector, believe the answer is no. While recognizing the worth of all people in their business, they've come to the conclusion that certain positions within the corporation are more vital in the fight to execute their specific strategy. Kaplan and Norton term these vital players and positions "strategic job families,"[28] and suggest that isolating, analyzing, and closing gaps within them is a critical enabler of strategic success. To determine your strategic job families, begin by examining the objectives in your Internal Process Perspective, and critically review the positions necessary to enable those processes. Ask yourself: Are there any high-leverage positions currently not staffed? Do particular employees, while dedicated to the mission and enthusiastic in their endeavors, lack a number of the necessary skills to perform at the highest level in these roles? Closing skill gaps in the most vital positions throughout your organization will spark significant productivity and effectiveness gains.

When people are matched with the right position and equipped with the tools they require to carry out their work at peak-performance levels, you're enabling the possibility of flow to enter the workforce. Flow is a state characterized by complete immersion in a task, during which it's not uncommon to briefly lose the concept of time, with hours seeming to pass in the span of minutes as you apply all your creative energies to solve the challenge that lies before you. We've all experienced flow moments, whether it's settling in under the hood of an old car we're restoring, creating a photo album of digital memories, or getting lost in a dance routine we've been practicing for weeks. Flow can apply to virtually any endeavor, work included, if the conditions are right. Here is the best description of flow I've ever come across. It comes not from a business book or psychology text, but a novel: "For the past two hours he's been in a dream of absorption that has dissolved all sense of time, and all awareness of the other parts of his life. Even his awareness of his own existence has vanished. He's been delivered into a pure present, free of the weight of the past or any anxieties about the future. In retrospect, though never at the time, it feels like profound happiness. This state of mind brings a contentment he never finds with any passive form of entertainment. Books, cinema, even music can't bring him to this. Working with others is one part of it, but it's not all. This benevolent dissociation seems to require difficulty, prolonged demands on concentration and skills, pressure, problems to be solved, even danger. He feels calm, and spacious, fully qualified to exist. It's a feeling of clarified emptiness, of deep muted joy."[29] Imagine the power we could unleash if only we could always enable the conditions of flow to be present in the workplace.

Training for Success   Training is a staple of Strategy Maps spanning the entire spectrum of organization breeds, with virtually every enterprise recognizing the necessity of constantly upgrading skills should they expect to compete in our crowded and ultra-competitive marketplaces. A word of caution is appropriate, however, as you hastily adopt this seemingly obvious objective. Foreshadowing Chapter 8 just a bit, think carefully about the accompanying measure you'll use to gauge your training success. Training is certainly an important component of employee success, but what really drives that success are the results of training, not the simple act of attendance—what is sometimes referred to as the "BIC" metric—butts in chairs. Therefore, measures of employee training must balance participation with results. What specific skills or behaviors do you expect to see demonstrated as a result of the training? Measuring and monitoring those will help you see the whole picture of training. So, before the ink is dry on this objective, look ahead to the next step of measurement, and make an honest assessment of your ability to create a meaningful metric.

Incidentally, that advice holds for every objective we're discussing on these pages. While you certainly don't want to curtail your ingenuity in any way by second-guessing every chosen objective over the perceived lack of potential measures, you should at the very least be cognizant of the fact that every objective must be accompanied by a robust measure in order for this system to produce the value you expect.

Recruiting the Right People   How important is hiring the right people? Here's a story featuring chocolate magnate Milton Hershey that sheds some light on the question:

> In the mid 1890s Milton Hershey turned to a cousin, William Blair, to manage his caramel company. Blair was a competent but bull-headed man who resisted many of his boss's suggestions. He was sarcastic and had a way of speaking that made Hershey lose his temper. After one particularly heated argument, Blair quit. Shortly thereafter, Hershey traveled to New York, where he had dinner with a sugar salesman one evening. The man ordered a house specialty, a big slab of beef served on an oiled piece of hardwood. With a flourish he demonstrated how a planked steak should be carved. Impressed by the man's sophistication, Hershey hired him on the spot to replace Blair. Unlike Blair, the new fellow was willing to innovate. Unfortunately, a key decision of his to use corn syrup and cut back on the amount of cane sugar in Lancaster caramels, backfired badly. Customers could taste the lesser-quality sweetener and soon the wagons that carried freshly made candy to the railroad depot were coming back fully loaded with caramels returned by unhappy retailers. Hershey lost $60,000, a tidy sum in the 1890s. The man from New York was fired. Blair was rehired. And Hershey came to understand the risk of emotional decisions. At one dinner meeting with his top men, Hershey ordered a planked steak and as he started to carve, instructed his men to watch closely because 'it cost me $60,000 to learn this.[30]

In a world dominated by knowledge, relationships, and networks, people are what distinguish outstanding companies from also-rans, and, therefore, getting the right people on the bus, as Jim Collins instructs in his blockbuster bestseller _Good to Great_, is imperative for every organization. Most organizations recognize this, as reflected in an American Management Association survey that revealed a whopping 82.4% of leaders believe recruiting and retaining talent is a top corporate concern.[31]

Of course, getting the right people on the bus can present a substantial challenge for public and nonprofit organizations; even getting people to the bus stop is tricky, considering the sector's lack of financial incentives, and other compensation-related bells and whistles that private sector firms are eagerly waving in front of prospective employees. But, as with all challenges, a dash of creativity, combined with good old fashioned tenacity can lead to tremendous results, as the story of Roger Briggs illustrates.

As he taught in the Boulder, Colorado school district, a persistent nagging accompanied Briggs; the thought that their schools could be much better. But he wasn't superintendent, governor, not even principal; what could he do? When he became head of his school's science department, he made the commitment to change the world by changing his small piece of it, and specifically his tactic of choice was recruiting the right people into the department, people who shared his zeal for teaching, and were 110% committed to their students' success. He then changed the structure of the department so that tenure was not rubber-stamped after three years, but had to be earned by proving yourself an exceptional teacher. The turning point arrived when a good teacher came up for tenure. Good, but certainly not great. Much to the dismay of his colleagues, Briggs denied tenure, and clung to this unpopular stance despite their loud protests. Shortly thereafter, a spectacular young teacher became available and Briggs hired her, sending the crystal clear signal that mediocrity was not to be tolerated. Over time, with each new hire, the system continued to evolve and grow until, like a stone rolling downhill, it reached a critical mass and the culture of the entire department became one of discipline and greatness.[32]

Retaining the Right People and Succession Planning   The federal government in the United States is at its lowest staffing level since 1950. At approximately 1.8 million people, the ranks have been diminished by almost 325,000 since 1993.[33] Proponents of smaller government will applaud, but those of you charged with managing programs realize the tremendous challenges you face. You're not alone. Inspectors General at nine major federal agencies have listed workforce problems among the top ten most serious management challenges facing their agencies. Only 7.5% of the federal workforce is under age 30, while 38% is over age 50. If you've never considered retention and succession an issue, this is your wake-up call.

While the statistics are alarming, they are just that, statistics. You may prefer the approach utilized by the Australian Department of Defense. They too face the challenge of an aging workforce. Their Balanced Scorecard champion recognized this fact and felt it must be addressed in the Department's Strategy Map and Scorecard. Rather than quoting dry statistics to reflect the crisis, she showed the senior leadership team a group picture of themselves. Then she asked what they saw. A picture truly does tell a thousand words, or in this case one word: gray! Faced with the stark reality of their aging ranks, the Department rallied to support her cry for succession objectives and measures.

Information Capital: Aligning Information with the Strategy

In the preceding section, I mentioned that the federal government has significantly reduced its workforce over the past several years. Less people means the government must do everything it can do enhance productivity; do more with less, as they say. In keeping with that credo, the federal government has become the world's largest consumer of information technology (IT). Estimates suggest the government spent a whopping $45 billion in 2002 alone.[34] The problem, a significant one, is that despite this prodigious infusion of IT, there have been no measurable gains in productivity. At least part of the blame can be pinned on the tail of performance management. Agencies tend to assess the performance of their IT applications according to how well they serve the agency's requirements, not how well they meet customer needs. Reversing this situation represents a simple, yet profoundly fundamental shift in perspective. IT serves your organization in order for you to better serve your customers better, it's that simple. Performance objectives and measures must balance the extent to which IT investments improve your ability to serve, and the corresponding influence on customer results.

The Bureau of the Census offers a glimpse into how technology may improve performance. The agency uses an electronic hiring system that provides managers with online access to applicant resumes. Within 24 hours of receipt, managers can be reviewing the latest candidate resumes. Using the new system, the Census Bureau has reduced the time required to fill some positions from six months to as little as three days. The next challenge for the Bureau is developing performance objectives and measures that track customer service in an attempt to ensure their new found internal capabilities are boosting results for their customers.

Information represents more than just the ability to log on to the latest IT applications. Access to information is every bit as critical. Employees must have the ability to access information about key customers, donors, and other stakeholders in order to make informed decisions. However, investments of this nature are considered "overhead" by many nonprofits and as a result are shunned in deference to an allocation of the same funds to direct service provision. This may prove to be a short-sighted decision. In the short-term, funds will be directed towards clients and customers, but in the long run, as conditions inevitably change, if employees don't have critical information on customer trends, funder preferences, and environmental shifts, future service delivery is placed in severe jeopardy.

Organizational Capital: Creating the Climate for Growth and Change[35]

History provides many vivid portraits of men and women toiling against seemingly insurmountable odds and facing what appear to be overwhelming obstacles, only to turn sure defeat into stunning and glorious victory. Military sagas are replete with such tales of heroism and cunning as is the field of exploration—it seems incomprehensible that Lewis and Clark, for example, should lead an expedition into virtually uncharted territory, spanning a vast continent and lasting two years with precious few supplies, to return with a treasure trove of scientific and cultural knowledge and suffer only one casualty! The human spirit is beautifully indomitable and can literally move mountains when inspired by a worthy cause. Within the organizational capital dimension, we are seeking to draw upon the infinite resources of human strength and capture both "the hearts and minds" of our employees, in an effort to make sustainable growth and prosperity a literal reality. Three key elements you may consider when drafting objectives for this section of the Strategy Map are:

Culture   Let's begin our discussion of this most elusive of topics by attempting to define the term. One of the most useful explanations of culture I have come across is that offered by Stan Davis from the Columbia University Graduate School of Business, who suggests "culture is a pattern of beliefs and expectations shared by an organization's members. These beliefs and expectations produce norms that can powerfully shape how people and groups behave."[36] While this is a very helpful definition, we can sweep away a layer of confusion surrounding the term by simply thinking of culture as "the way we do things around here." Using that descriptor as a lens, listen to how a very young John F. Kennedy describes what awaits incoming Senators: "Americans want to be liked—and Senators are no exception. They are by nature—and of necessity—social animals. We enjoy the comradeship and approval of our friends and colleagues. We prefer praise to abuse, popularity to contempt. Realizing that the path of the conscientious insurgent must frequently be a lonely one, we are anxious to get along with our fellow legislators, our fellow members of the club, to abide by the clubhouse rules and patterns, not to pursue a unique and independent course that would embarrass or irritate the other members. We realize, moreover, that our influence in the club—and the extent to which we can accomplish our objective and those of our constituents—are dependent in some measure on the esteem with which we are regarded by other senators. 'The way to get along,' I was told when I entered Congress, 'is to go along.'[37] That is without a doubt the best depiction of culture that I've ever encountered.

If culture isn't the most "touchy-feely" of all management topics, the roll call in its class certainly would not take long to conduct. But how important is culture to an organization's success? Turns out it is a vital contributor. In their book, *Corporate Culture and Performance*, authors Heskett and Kotter discovered that over a 12-year period, firms with effective cultures achieved stock price growth of 901% compared to just 74% for those with ineffective cultures. Over that same span, those with effective cultures saw revenue growth of over 680% while the ineffective group managed only 166% gains.[38]

As a consultant, I have the unique opportunity to peer through the window of culture at each of my clients, and believe me the vistas provided are very enlightening indeed. For example, take this "Tale of Two Clients." At the first client, an organization priding itself on teamwork, positive feedback, and innovation, it is not uncommon for spontaneous rounds of applause to erupt in management meetings as executives note the accomplishments of others in helping the company reach its lofty targets. They openly cite their culture as a competitive advantage in their success. At the other end of the culture spectrum, the second client is characterized by a combative management and meeting style, an insular view of the world, and a CEO who is renowned for withholding information—even from direct reports. Several insiders have confided in me that they believe this culture is holding them back and taking a severe toll on employees, many of whom appear to be actively disengaged. If you accept the proposition that people are your most critical resource, then you owe it to yourself to gauge your current culture and determine whether it is aligned with your strategic direction.

The misalignment of culture and strategy is a volatile cocktail capable of disastrous results, as the story of Encyclopedia Britannica illustrates. For much of the firm's venerable history, its 32 volumes were considered the ultimate repository of knowledge from art to zoology. As the world transitioned from bound books to personal computers in the quest for information, Encyclopedia Britannica was initially well-positioned to make the transition. In 1989 they introduced one of the earliest multimedia CD-ROM encyclopedias, *Compton's MultiMedia*. The culture of the company, however, stood in the way of them maintaining their leadership position. That culture was dominated by a nationwide force of home salespeople, the very force that had made Encyclopedia Britannica a trusted household name. No one dared to tinker with the traditional sales format on which his or her livelihood depended. The sacredness of the direct sale force business model was the company's Achilles Heel. As a result, Encyclopedia Britannica failed to develop a serious strategy for electronic products until it was too late. Annual unit sales collapsed from a high of 117,000 to about 20,000. It took the intervention of an outside investor and the abandonment of the direct sales approach to save what was left of the company.[39]

Although shaping or manipulating a culture, which can take years of habitual and patterned behavior, is well beyond the scope of this book, I can offer a few concrete steps you can take to help manage and change your culture to ensure it exists in harmony with your strategy. The first is recruiting and selecting people you believe embody the culture you are either attempting to sustain or create, as Roger Briggs did in his Boulder, Colorado science department. Who you choose to carry out your work and liaise with your team is completely within your sphere of control, so take the opportunity to select those individuals who will further your cultural aspirations. Second, you can manage your culture through intense socialization and training initiatives, demonstrating what you expect from employees. The means of accomplishing this are many, varied, and sometimes downright bizarre. As an example of the latter, consider the online brokerage and banking firm E*Trade. During their first meeting at this innovative company, new employees are required to stand on a chair and tell everyone in attendance something embarrassing about themselves. Doing so knocks down a lot of barriers and creates a bond between employees allowing them to open up and feel comfortable asking questions of coworkers, since appearing to lack a little esoteric corporate information pales in comparison to the loss of face suffered from revealing deep dark secrets. Finally, culture may be advanced using the formal reward systems of the organization. If you value teamwork, a customer-centric approach and attitude, and innovation, those traits should be tangibly rewarded in an effort to have that culture deeply entrenched.[40]

Our last word on culture comes from Lou Gerstner, the former CEO of corporate titan IBM who saw the company's revenue soar by over $20 billion during his watch. Reflecting on his days at the helm of one of the world's largest and respected companies, Gerstner recalled: "I came to see in my time at IBM that culture isn't just one aspect of the game—it is the game."[41]

Recognition and Rewards   Over the years, I've discovered there are two types of people in the world: those who treat books with the care and reverence of a vase from the Ming Dynasty and those who use them like a bookworm's scribbler, recording every thought even marginally related to the text on its soon to be very worn pages. I fall into the latter category. Given my page-marking proclivities, you should see my copy of Dale Carnegie's classic self-help yarn, *How to Win Friends and Influence People*. There is so much homespun wisdom in that book that, if challenged, I could probably support every notion in *this* book with a supporting quote from Mr. Carnegie. Here is a particular favorite that fits our discussion of recognition perfectly: "I once succumbed to the fad of fasting and went for six days and nights without eating. It wasn't difficult. I was less hungry at the end of the sixth day than I was at the end of the second. Yet I know, as you know, people who would think they had committed a crime if they let their families or employees go for six days without food; but they will let them go for six days, and six weeks, and sometimes sixty years without giving them the hearty appreciation they crave almost as much as they crave food."[42]

In case you find that story a little dramatic, consider this nugget from a recent study of departing employees: 79% of those who resign their positions cite perceptions of not being appreciated as a key reason for leaving.[43] So often, public and nonprofit leaders will lament the fact that many variables are out of their control, and frequently that is the case. Recognition, however, is completely within your direct sphere of control, and is a muscle that should be exercised in a sincere fashion every single day. One article I read in researching this subject spoke about the importance of recognition and appreciation beginning on an employee's very first day on the job, since, as we all know, first impressions last a long time. I put the article down and set about conjuring up all of the first days over my working life. Most were pretty typical: I was shuttled around the office at the speed of a blitzing line-backer, introduced to dozens of people, most of whom gave me tight-lipped half smiles and limp handshakes, given a computer that didn't work, taught how to use the phone, and filled out more paperwork than I need to apply for a car loan. But one first day stood out as brightly as the Las Vegas Strip. At this company, my manager personally guided me through the mundane administrivia, made sure I had a companion all day long, went to great lengths to thank me for joining the company, and at the end of the day presented me with a company sweatshirt. It was a small token, but at that moment it capped what I considered to be a near perfect first day, and I've never forgotten it. Such is the profound value of simple appreciation and recognition.

Alignment[44]   The problems of misalignment are frequently and colorfully reflected by parents of youngsters participating in soccer leagues. If you've ever been to one of these "matches" you know what I'm referring to: a blur of frenzied activity around the ball with not a single player venturing more than a few feet from that maelstrom of action. There is no coordination of activities, just a mad scramble covering a few square yards of the pitch. Of course, this is quite amusing if you're watching from the stands with your camcorder catching the moment for posterity; after all the stakes are relatively minor. But for organizations, a lack of alignment can prove extremely hazardous to any hope of executing strategy. Employee actions must be aligned with mission, values, vision, and most importantly, strategy should you wish to fully exploit the advantages of intangible assets such as culture and knowledge. The first step on the road to an aligned organization is ensuring employee understanding of the building blocks of mission, values, vision, and strategy. Only through understanding will action follow. A simple and effective method of ensuring alignment is reviewing cascaded Strategy Maps and Balanced Scorecards from throughout your organization. While most will rightly contain unique objectives and measures, they should be aligned towards a common strategy should you hope to have all oars rowing in a winning direction. We'll discuss the notion of alignment and cascading in greater depth in Chapter 9.

DEVELOPING OBJECTIVES FOR THE FINANCIAL PERSPECTIVE

It seems as though not a day will pass without newspaper articles and television reports delivering doomsday predictions of how budget shortfalls will inevitably affect public service. For self-preservation alone, public and nonprofit agencies must demonstrate their effective stewardship of what limited financial resources they have to a confused and skeptical public as well as funding bodies.

Objectives in the financial perspective of the Strategy Map demonstrate how you are providing your services in a manner that balances effectiveness with efficiency and cost consciousness. Here are some elements to consider.

- *Cost of product or service delivery.* Operating efficiently and safeguarding resources is critical to all organizations, whether they are private, public, or nonprofit. In an era of diminishing budgets and cries for accountability, cost and productivity objectives take on a prominent role. Analyzing this dimension should force a paradigm shift for pubic and nonprofit Map developers, because as Jim Collins notes: "In the social sectors, the critical question is not how much money do we make per dollar of invested capital? But, how effectively do we deliver on our mission and make a distinctive impact, relative to our resources?"[45] Resource consumption must be considered in the context of your mission.

- *Revenue enhancement.* What opportunities exist for broadening our sources of revenue? Do we currently provide services for which we could charge a fee? How diversified are our funding sources?

- *Financial systems.* Regardless of how you view the accountants in your organization, financial systems are the backbone of most operations. Reliable, relevant, and timely financial information feeds virtually every type of decision you'll make. Financial errors can amount to huge sums of money and waste. For example, the Department of Agriculture estimated $976 million in food stamp overpayments and $360 million in underpayments, for a total of $1.34 billion in erroneous payments in 2000. Their payment error rate was an astonishing 8.9%. Robust and reliable financial systems not only produce accurate data, they can also enhance your credibility.

DEVELOPING A SHARED UNDERSTANDING WITH OBJECTIVE STATEMENTS

By this point, you've reviewed copious amounts of background information, validated your mission, values, vision, and strategy, interviewed your executive team and developed objectives for each of the four Strategy Map objectives. Very impressive! But, you're not quite done yet.

If your Strategy Map in any way resembles the hundreds I've seen over the years, it will most likely contain at least a couple, if not a handful, of objectives that border on the vague and nebulous, such as "enhance productivity." During your animated discussions, the meaning of enhance productivity was undoubtedly clear to everyone in the room as you enumerated the specific issues and potential solutions that ultimately led to including it on your Map. However, the Map is meant to serve as a communication tool for your entire stakeholder body and the vast majority of that group didn't have the good fortune to be at the table when you chose the objective and, thus, although its meaning may be plain to you, to them it could mean countless things.

Even seemingly straightforward objectives such as "cut costs" may engender confusion among your workforce as people apply their own filters of perception and experience to the phrase.

Objective statements clarify and elaborate on the objectives displayed on the Strategy Map. These two to three sentence narratives clearly articulate what is meant by the objective, while providing guidance as to what type of performance measures may be appropriate. Well-written objective statements provide precise clarification of the meaning of each objective, outline why the objective is important, and briefly discuss how it will be accomplished. Here are two examples of well-written objective statements:

From a Nonprofit Industry Association:
Close skill gaps through training, hiring, contracting, or outsourcing
> Our team must possess industry and association-leading knowledge, skills, and competencies. This is critical in our efforts of working towards our mission of helping our customers be professional, successful, and profitable. We will achieve this objective by identifying the skills we need, the skills we have, and then filling gaps by training, hiring, contracting, or outsourcing.

From a government-owned utility:
Innovate to reduce energy cost
> Fuel represents a major percentage of our expenses. Managing this significant expense is the responsibility of everyone in the organization and will require innovative responses to mitigate increasing world energy prices. To achieve this objective we must: minimize fuel acquisition costs, strengthen our hedging, and ensure support functions and services are as streamlined and cost-effective as possible.

As important as objective statements are, getting people to take the time to write them can, admittedly, be like pulling teeth—not a fast and painless process. Some organizations will impose a two-week deadline for the submission of all statements. Though the looming deadline poses some urgency, most people will wait until the fourteenth day to craft something, and the results will often reflect a lack of time and attention. I advocate small teams of two or three people writing the objectives statements as soon after the initial crafting of the Map as possible; while the sentiments and meanings you shared in the workshop are still easily accessible in your memory.

One of my clients came up with an innovative solution to keep objective statements at the forefront of everyone's attention. This organization holds a morning management meeting each day and decided that, until the objective statements were completed, updates would be shared at the meeting. Each day, a small team of two or three was assigned to present at least one objective statement for review with the group. This is a great idea for a couple of reasons: First, and practically speaking, it ensures that objective statements are crafted in a timely fashion; second, and equally important, by following this method, the entire management team can hear and see what is being developed and discuss it as a team. The feedback offered helps the writers tighten their statements, while others in attendance learn the "best practices" of objective statement writing and can apply it to their endeavors.

TIMEOUT

If this chapter were a television show, I'd definitely throw in a commercial or two about now—you deserve a break! I know what you're thinking, commercials are more of an annoyance than a break, and with DVRs and TiVo they're on the road to irrelevance anyway. The point is the break—so put down the book, go grab a coffee, sandwich, shoulder massage, martini, Tylenol, whatever you need. I know this is a long chapter, the longest in the entire book by a healthy margin, but it was important to present you with the entire Strategy Map tapestry; one flowing and interwoven story. Breaking it up into two chapters seemed disconnected to me, and despite a string of words that could span the Great Wall of China, I believe seeing the entire landscape will help you immensely as you create your own Strategy Map. So, hang in there, we're almost home.

CONDUCTING AN EFFECTIVE STRATEGY MAPPING WORKSHOP

Years ago, at one of my first jobs, I recall strolling casually into a colleague's cubicle one morning and being visually assaulted by an enormous banner that read "plan your work, work your plan, your plan will work!" This coworker understood that before the promised land of execution comes the blocking and tackling of careful planning. So it is with the Strategy Mapping workshop: A successful event hinges in large measure on the planning that precedes it. Let's look at what you must consider before, during, and after your session to ensure your team develops a Strategy Map that clearly depicts your story.

What To Do Before the Strategy Mapping Workshop

During his nearly three decades of coaching the men's basketball team at UCLA, John Wooden, affectionately known as The Wizard of Westwood, led his Bruins to an unprecedented ten national championships. In 2000, he was recognized by the National Collegiate Athletic Association (NCAA) as the Coach of the Century and in 2003, the Presidential Medal of Freedom was bestowed upon this humble man. Pretty outstanding credentials, and what was one of the Wizard's secret weapons? Planning. Here's how he describes his philosophy: "When I coached basketball at UCLA, I believed that if we were going to succeed, we needed to be industrious. One way I accomplished this was with proper planning. I spent two hours with my staff planning each practice. Each drill was calculated to the minute. Every aspect of the session was choreographed, including where the practice balls should be placed. I did not want any time lost by people running over to a misplaced ball bin."[46] As you can see, meticulous attention to detail was a hallmark of Wooden's principles for success. Here are some items, conveniently packaged as 5 Ds, you should consider if you hope to plan like a champion:

- *Decide who will facilitate the event.* No, this is not a commercial for the services of my company, The Senalosa Group, but . . . I do believe that you should engage a professional consultant or facilitator to lead your Strategy Mapping (and later, measures development) workshop. A seasoned professional will bring years of experience, proven techniques, and tips for sparking creativity at 4:15 when everyone has one weary eye on the flip chart and one on the nearest exit.

- *Determine who will attend.* Ideally, your executive team should own the Balanced Scorecard, and hence, they should be gathered eagerly around a U-shaped table ready to hammer out your Strategy Map. Or, if not your most senior team, the cadre of folks you've assembled to lead your Scorecarding effort should be leading the charge. Either way, don't turn the workshop into an impromptu town-hall gathering by allowing the participants to bring their own binder-touting entourages, or by including "invited guests." I've been part of Strategy Mapping events in which the leaders felt it was important, as they constructed the Map, to hear the voices of customers, or board members, or citizens. Never in my experience has the end product benefited from their contribution. In most cases, the team, whether intentionally or unintentionally, end up pandering to the isolated views being advocated aggressively by the one or two observers, resulting in a skewed Map that in no way reflects the strategic identity of the organization. As we'll discuss, others will have opportunities to kick the Map's tires.

- *Distribute materials in advance of the session.* If you've followed the advice provided earlier in the chapter, you've already reviewed Hummer-sized piles of background information so you should be well-equipped to hold an intelligent conversation on objectives.

- *Deliberate on where to hold the meeting.* I recently read *The Monk Who Sold His Ferrari*, a great little book with an array of timeless wisdom, and, according to the author's Web site at least, Jon Bon Jovi's favorite book. In the text, a character is given the gift of enduring wisdom from a group of monks living in a beautiful Shangri-la setting high atop a mountain somewhere in the Far East. As the character later expounded his insights to another protégé, I got to thinking: It must have been so much easier to grasp and become one with the teachings in that setting, as opposed to having them delivered during, say, a weekend seminar at a Holiday Inn just off the freeway. The setting does matter, whether you're absorbing the everlasting path to personal liberation and happiness or building a Strategy Map. And while I don't have any statistical evidence to bolster my case, I believe Maps created in offsite locations tend to be of a higher-quality than those cranked out in a sterile corporate meeting room. For many people, office meeting rooms carry with them the stigma of long, dry, and useless information exchanges, and wastes of never-to-be-retrieved time. Why not tip the balance in your favor by taking your group to a fresh new place, one stripped bare of any preconceived notions or baggage, where creativity and insight can blossom? You don't need to go to Tibet, just break up the routine a little, that's all. Over the years, I've held sessions in rustic log cabins, restored manors, country inns, and, of course, many hotel conference rooms. For an amusing look at how setting played a role in the creation of the United States, see the inset following the 5 Ds.

- *Decorate the room.* Plaster the meeting room walls with your mission and vision statements, values, strategy, and any interesting or provocative quotes you captured during your executive interviews. Such visual cues will stimulate creativity, reinforce the purpose of the session, and provide practical guidance when necessary. Also, don't forget the details: Stock up on flip chart paper, markers, tape, pens, and notepads.

In *The Domestic Life of Thomas Jefferson* (1871), author Sarah Randolph recounts this interesting footnote to American history: Mr. Jefferson said, "While the question of Independence was before Congress, it had its meeting near a livery-stable. The members wore short breeches and silk stockings, and with handkerchief in hand, they were diligently employed in lashing the flies from their legs. So very vexatious was this annoyance, and so great an impatience did it arouse in the sufferers, that it hastened, if it did not aid, the great document which gave birth to an entire republic."

Randolph received this anecdote from Mr. Jefferson in Monticello, and noted that he seemed to enjoy it very much, as well as to give great credit to the influence of the flies. "He told it with much glee, and seemed to retain a vivid recollection of an attack, from which the only relief was signing the paper and flying from the scene."[47]

During the Strategy Mapping Workshop

If you were inspired by the setting advice provided above, then perhaps by now your Himalayan Sherpa guide has navigated the treacherous path before you, and you're clearing the lenses of your polarized sunglasses to catch the first glimpse of your impromptu meeting room 5,000 feet above base camp. Or, if you chose a less adventurous course, the barely conscious night auditor at the local Hilton Garden Inn may be directing you down the corridor to the Baja Room that has been fully stocked and ready for your entrance. Whichever the case, the big day has arrived and you're ready to begin drafting your Map. Here are a number of things to consider during the meeting itself:

- *Getting started.* Standard meeting protocol dictates the opening monologue from the facilitator: location of amenities (if you're offsite), a big thank you to all participants for their work thus far, and their commitment to the exciting challenge that lies ahead, ground rules for the session, and timing. Some organizations, and it depends entirely upon your culture, will open meetings of this nature with some sort of game or activity. Personally, I fall in line with the camp led by Gordon MacKenzie, who wrote in his wacky account of corporate life *Orbiting the Giant Hairball*: "Games are the force-feeding of some cockeyed activity to a captive audience with intent to generate joviality."[48] A little hostile and cynical perhaps, but I tend to agree. So the decision rests with you. If you do choose a light-hearted opening activity, ensure it is relevant to the task at hand. For example, one group I worked with gave everyone attending a piece of 8 ½-by-11 paper with one or two words written on it. The words comprised the agency's mission statement and the group's challenge was to assemble themselves in order within 60 seconds to display the statement.

- *Facilitating the session.* In the public and nonprofit sectors, most organizations will begin the process by developing Customer objectives, followed by Internal Processes, Employee Learning and Growth, and finally, Financial. This order helps ensure you're weaving a consistent tale as you progress through the process. I tend to shy away from pure group brainstorming despite its proven effectiveness and widespread use. Too often a few people tend to dominate the proceedings leaving the less verbose mute in their chairs. Even if you have a relatively small team, start by breaking them up into groups to stimulate some good-natured rivalry and create stronger ideas. For example, let's say you have ten people participating in the session, begin by splitting them into three groups: two consisting of three people and the third of four. Each group will have 30 minutes to brainstorm as many objectives as they can muster, but must be prepared to come to consensus on their top four before wrapping up. When the 30 minutes has expired, the deck is shuffled and participants are placed in two groups of five. These groups, given approximately 40 minutes, spend their first several minutes reviewing the various objectives generated in the smaller groups, then brainstorm themselves to come to consensus on what objectives they feel should comprise that perspective. Finally, the facilitator asks each group to volunteer their final objectives, and leads a plenary discussion until the ultimate objectives are determined. If you find yourself struggling with a perspective and reaching an impasse, leave it and move on, with the promise to return later. Many great thinkers throughout history employed this technique; sow the intellectual seeds, and then revisit the problem later and receive a profound harvest. When he felt stuck, Albert Einstein was renowned for vacating his desk full of arcane equations to go off and play his violin. As he explained, "A new idea comes suddenly and in an intuitive way. But intuition is nothing more than the outcome of earlier intellectual experience."[49]

- *Dealing with distractions.* I've lost count of how many times I've been just about to reach the crescendo of an important and inspirational point, one certain to elevate the group to the summit of new creative heights, only to be stopped cold in my tracks by the tinny sounds of the William Tell Overture or Britney's Spears' *Toxic* calling from someone's bag. Cell phones and Blackberries have been an unquestionable boon to business productivity, but their untimely shrieks can quickly derail the momentum of a highly engaged team. Asking people to surrender these must-haves of business combat at the door is pretty much out of the question, I know. However, you should request that all devices be silenced or placed on vibrate, and only the most critical calls or e-mails responded to during the session. If your distractions manifest themselves in the human variety, most notably someone who clings to an argument like a stray dog with a bone, or a participant that insists on leading you down a path you know will yield nothing but discontent, consider the Rat card displayed in Exhibit 7.7. Yes, the Rat card. If you sense the conversation spiraling downward, and heading for a black hole, proudly toss your Rat card in the air, bringing an immediate halt to the proceedings. A client introduced this technique to me at a recent offsite and it worked like a charm. Even the CEO was wary of the rodent interjection device, prefacing one controversial remark with the words, "at the risk of having a Rat card thrown at me . . ." It lightened the mood and served its purpose admirably—a great combination.

One last point on the workshop itself: Start and end it on time. If you say you're going to begin at 8:30 and wrap up at 5:00, then welcome everyone

Exhibit 7.7   The Infamous Rat Card

at 8:29 and start summarizing at 4:30. A couple of reasons for this suggestion, beyond the obvious that it simply represents fundamental meeting
management: First, the people you've selected to delve deeply into your
organizational soul and create this Map will no doubt be your best and
brightest, and you can be sure they all have calendars stocked fuller than a
pantry at Thanksgiving. Respect their time and commitment to the process
by adhering to the established schedule. Second, imposing a timeline will
create a climate of subtle pressure, with people occasionally glancing at the
clock realizing they have a finite amount of time in which to complete this
task and, thus, must remain focused for every comment, question, and point
of consensus.

   In the discussion of planning, I quoted legendary coach John Wooden.
Let's return to the hardwood sage once again to learn how he felt about
sticking to a schedule, and the impact it had on his team: "I discovered that
if practice did not end when it was supposed to end, players would hold
back a little effort and energy. When I saw this happening, I became a stick-
ler for stopping on time. Whether we practiced an hour and a half or two
hours, my players knew exactly when we were going to stop and I stuck to
it. They had no reason to hold anything back. As a result they worked harder
during the scheduled time, and we got more done in a shorter amount of
time."[50]

After the Workshop

Quiz: What is your first assignment upon completing the draft Strategy
Map? No, ransacking the first-aid kit for emergency supplies of pain medica-
tion is not the correct response. Hunting me down for writing all this? Nope,

not even close. Your task is to craft the objective statements we discussed earlier in the chapter. Doing so quickly, while the nuggets you generated are still imprinted prominently on your cerebral cortex, will ensure you develop statements that foster a shared understanding of the objectives spanning your Strategy Map. You'll also want to set in motion your Strategy Map review process that is discussed immediately after the following section.

HOW MANY OBJECTIVES ON YOUR STRATEGY MAP?

I really enjoyed the movie *Finding Forrester*. I saw it just as I had begun to write the *First Edition* of my private sector book, *Balanced Scorecard Step-by-Step: Maximizing Performance and Maintaining Results* (John Wiley & Sons, 2002). At one point in the movie, author William Forrester, played beautifully by Sean Connery, advises his young protégé to always write a first draft "from the heart." I remember very well how that advice, albeit from a fictional character, resonated with me. As I continued my writing, I did just as Forrester/Connery suggested and wrote my first draft from the heart. Fortunately, for you, you didn't have to wade through those first drafts. The problem with writing from your heart is that virtually everything seems critical to the topic, and it's very difficult to leave anything out when that topic is so very important (and close) to you. Like all authors, I benefited greatly from a skilled editor who helped me hone my lengthy drafts into a more concise final version that was bound between the covers of the book.

So, other than providing a movie review, what does the preceding paragraph have to do with your Strategy Map? Well, you and your Scorecard team are the authors of your strategy map. And, as such, that Map will undoubtedly convey the strongest feelings of all involved on what is absolutely important to the organization. Like the writer who feels compelled to empty his or her soul in a work, you won't want to leave anything on the table. As a result, it's not uncommon to see first-draft Strategy Maps that contain 25 to 30 objectives.

A number of factors conspire to see the number of first-draft Strategy Map objectives balloon to an unmanageable number. The atmosphere in the meeting room is generally very positive: after all, you've convened a team that was chosen for both their knowledge and enthusiasm. You're all talking about what you do everyday, about your organization; and, truthfully, how often do you have the opportunity to spend an entire day analyzing your operations? It's exciting, liberating, and fun! I've even seen chief executives get caught up in the frenzy. Prior to one strategy mapping session with a client, the Executive Director stressed to me the importance of keeping the total number of objectives capped at around ten. I agreed that a low number was better for this small organization, and together we vowed to curb any attempts at raising the objective total. But when we got into the session, his tune changed, and changed dramatically. He was the one I couldn't rein in!

Suddenly everything seemed critical to the company's success, and before we knew it, there were 31 objectives on the burgeoning Map.

There is no hard-and-fast rule for the "right" number of objectives, but a useful guideline is "less is more." Keep in mind that every objective on the Strategy Map will spawn an average of one-and-a-half performance measures to accurately capture the intent of the objective. So, for example, 20 objectives on the Strategy Map would equate to 30 measures for one Scorecard. Multiply that by several cascaded Scorecards throughout your organization and you could quickly ascend to hundreds of measures, resulting in a challenging and burdensome process to manage. To harness the power of the Balanced Scorecard system as both a measurement and communication system, you have to keep the number of objectives on your Map to a manageable level. Only you can make the determination of what is manageable, however. That said, I would strongly suggest you cap your objectives between 10 and 15. Doing so ensures a focus on the critical few versus the seduction of the trivial many, and limits the potential number of accompanying performance measures. One final thought on the subject comes to us from author and pioneer of international flight, Antoine de Saint-Exupery who reminds us: "Perfection is achieved not when there is nothing more to add, but when there is nothing more to take away."[51]

REVIEWING THE STRATEGY MAP

Upon completion of the draft Map, it makes sense to test its efficacy in telling your story. A fun and creative method to do so is the "*USA Today* interview." Suggest to your group that you're now three years in the future. A reporter from *USA Today* would like to do a story on your organization because of the great success you've achieved. How would the headline for the story read? Do the objectives on your Map lead you to that headline?

If envisioning the future isn't your thing, try evaluating the map with these probing questions:

- Is the cause and effect logic in the Map complete? Are all the necessary elements to tell our story accounted for?[52]

- Is the logic reflected in the Map theoretically sound? Do all the elements fit together logically?[53]

- Will the objectives outlined on the Map lead to the effective execution of our strategy?

- Does the Map represent balance in our efforts to achieve our vision?

Creating the Strategy Map is intense and fatiguing work. As much as we value the organizations in which we work, plumbing the depths of our knowledge on the subject of key objectives for an entire day can be draining even for the best of us. Therefore, give your Scorecard team some time to reflect individually on the Map before reconvening as a team. Between sessions, each team member can quietly review the Map, critically examine the logic it portrays with a fresh eye, and conjure up any possible modifications.

It's always a good idea to circulate the draft Strategy Map among key stakeholders for review and feedback. Employees, senior management, funders, customers, and partners, to name but a few, should have the opportunity to test the logic of the document. Executive input is especially critical. As we all know, for the Scorecard methodology to gain a foothold in the organization, it must be embraced and viewed as a legitimately valuable tool by the senior management.

An effective Strategy Map should tell the story of your strategy, with the objectives chosen serving to make your story leap from the page. If upon review your stakeholders don't understand or agree on the priorities you're asserting, you should revisit the Map. The Strategy Map can serve as a powerful communication tool, signaling to everyone the key drivers of your success. If your Map is overly complex, poorly designed, or difficult to understand, your communication efforts may be severely compromised.

Once your team has had the opportunity to reflect individually on the Map, and you've gathered feedback from all key stakeholders, reconvene the team for a final discussion. Make any recommended changes and, if necessary, conduct a vote to determine the final objectives.

WHEN ALL ELSE FAILS: KISS

If you're completely frustrated by this process, and just can't seem to escape from a quagmire of confusion and despair, go to a quiet room, close your eyes, and wrap yourself in the soothing sounds of "Beth" by legendary rockers KISS . . ."Beth I hear you callin', but I can't come home right now . . ." You should be back on your feet and reenergized within two minutes and 48 seconds.

Oops, not that KISS, I meant, of course, the phrase rarely absent from the lips of software engineers, military strategists, and planners everywhere: Keep It Simple Stupid. Organizations are complex organisms, no question about it, a galaxy of moving parts, interfaces by the thousands, and enough red tape to adhere the earth to Jupiter. But there are guiding principles and higher callings that rise above the din of complexity and present themselves in a rainbow of simplicity across our skies. This notion of simplicity trumping complexity applies not only to business, but every far-flung field of endeavor from photography to physics.

Speaking of physics (can you tell I just read the new Einstein biography?), do you know how Einstein created the Theory of Relativity in 1905, a discovery that ripped the scientific world from its very foundation?

Countless hours and forests of trees sacrificed to his equation scribbling, yes, but the fundamentals of the idea sprang from a thought experiment. Einstein loved to conjure vivid images in his head, bringing an endless sea of numbers to life in gripping detail, which he did to extraordinary impact with relativity. While sitting at his chair in the Bern Patent Office one day (Einstein was a patent clerk in Bern before becoming the *über*-celebrity and pop culture icon we remember him as today), he suddenly thought of a man falling to the ground, weightless, drifting. From that image came the greatest scientific breakthrough of all time. Einstein possessed the remarkable and enviable gift of transforming theories of mind-bending complexity into startlingly simple reality. Science writer Dennis Overbye describes one of Einstein's most famous papers, "On the Electrodynamics of Moving Bodies" this way: "The whole paper is a testament to the power of simple language to convey deep and powerfully disturbing ideas."[54] Let's conclude our survey of the Strategy Map landscape with the inspiring story of one organization that recognized, and took to heart, the power of simplicity.

THE STRATEGY MAP JOURNEY AT FOOD FOR THE HUNGRY U.S. (FHUS)

Food for the Hungry is an international relief and development organization, guided by the inspirational vision "God called and we responded until physical and spiritual hungers ended worldwide." Founded in 1971, the organization works with churches, leaders, and families in 26 countries to provide the resources necessary to help communities become self-sustaining.

The Case for Change

Recognizing the necessity of change in the face of altered circumstances and increasing demands from all stakeholders, FHUS President Ben Homan issued this passionate directive to his team in July 2006:

> God's high standard of doing justice, loving mercy and walking humbly with Him calls us to steward the enormous blessing and responsibility of taking us beyond our early strategic plans and hoped-for influence. Not only are we in an era in which the world and the way we can best serve people around the world is dramatically different, we continue to face a daunting task that is so difficult and so large that, as an organization, we must not tolerate structural or strategic status quo. We cannot accept actions, assessment and strategy that is isolated by department, dominated by personality or shaped only by historical inertia. We are called to grow, to gain capacity and to reflect the excellent and majestic character of the Lord our God. We have been given much, therefore, much is required (Luke 14).[55]

FHUS exists to serve a towering need, but their work is carried out by human beings operating in an organizational climate, and thus an organizational improvement mechanism was necessary to propel the team forward in this time of great change. After canvassing the landscape of possible tools, FHUS chose the Balanced Scorecard as a performance management system they were certain would allow them to harness their powers of spirit and creativity, ultimately leading them ever closer to their vision of an end to physical and spiritual hungers worldwide.

The Strategy Map

As with most Balanced Scorecard implementations, FHUS began their journey by convening a team of senior leaders, charged with the responsibility of crafting their new management framework. Equipped with decades of combined service and experience, both in the field and at the head office, the dedicated team set forth immediately, scouring the FHUS archives, unearthing all they could find on the building blocks of a Balanced Scorecard: mission, values, vision, and organizational strategy. With those raw materials in place the team met, and over several sessions crafted the organization's initial Strategy Map which is displayed in Exhibit 7.8.

In the spirit of information sharing and open communication, the Strategy Map was shared with managers and employees throughout the organization, and, later, measures were dutifully translated from each objective. The team was traversing the Strategy Map and Balanced Scorecard path, following the steps typically recommended during an implementation, and doing so with rigor and discipline. Yet, the reaction from employees was flat: very little enthusiasm, no breakthrough moments of alignment emanating from Map discussions, just a quiet resignation.

A Fresh Look

Not surprisingly, given the high expectations and allocation of resources devoted to the considerable effort of creating the Strategy Map and measures, FHUS leadership were disappointed by the reaction that greeted their initial model. Too much had been invested to abandon the implementation at this point, and the stakes of failure—both internally and externally—were simply too high: They had to succeed.

FHUS reached out to me in early 2007 to assist them in rejuvenating their Scorecard endeavors, specifically tasking me with reviewing and providing guidance on the Strategy Map they'd created. Shortly after coming to terms on our agreement, an e-mail arrived with the Map attached. I eagerly opened the document, anxious to see what was in store for our work together. Based on what you've read in this chapter, any guesses as to the nature of my reaction? Like a jet crossing a clear bright sky, the sound in my head became more and more resonant: simplicity. This Map had to be redesigned through

Exhibit 7.8 Food for the Hungry U.S. Strategy Map (version 1)

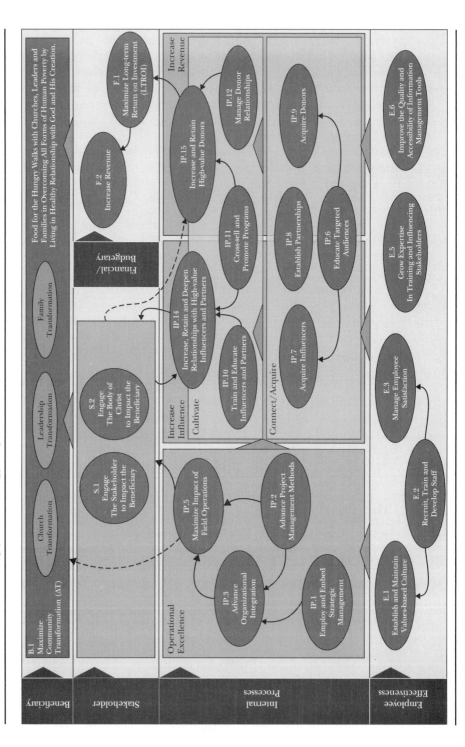

the lens of simplicity. As it stood, there were far too many objectives to meaningfully manage, the perspectives didn't speak to me as they should, and the cause and effect linkages were practically inexplicable: some direct connections, some dotted lines, and some isolated objectives.

When we met in April 2007, the mission was clear: Take advantage of the tremendous work generated by the team in their previous efforts, but apply a chisel to the overcrowded Strategy Map, carving away until FHUS's authentic strategic story emerged. After a number of iterations, the team settled on the Map displayed in Exhibit 7.9.

Business pundit Tom Peters has suggested that any product, process, or service should adhere to the dimensions of beautiful design, which he articulates as simplicity, clarity, grace, and beauty.[56] I believe the Strategy Map of FHUS qualifies on all counts. Let's consider some of the significant improvements in the document:

- *Branding.* It's not labeled a Strategy Map, rather, in the top left corner you see the phrase "Global Poverty Strategy" or "GPS." FHUS recognized that for employee buy-in and support to accompany this work, it required a tagline that fit the culture. Everyone these days is familiar with GPS devices, guiding us to our chosen destination, and so it is with this document, guiding FHUS to the hallowed ground of its mission and vision.

- *Mission and vision.* Everywhere you go at FHUS, you are reminded of the vision; its presence greets you upon entering the building, when meeting with employees, and sitting in their assembly hall. That it was missing from their initial Map was a major omission that was not overlooked in this draft.

- *Perspective names.* During our deliberations over the Customer Perspective, Ben Homan had an epiphany. He realized FHUS doesn't have "customers"; they're working with a group infinitely more valuable: responders. FHUS wants people to respond to God's call, and thus equipping responders was elevated to the very top of the Strategy Map. Additionally, the rather banal Employee Effectiveness Perspective was replaced by the uplifting moniker, Catalyst.

- *Simplicity.* Just ten objectives populate this Map, versus 25 on the original rendering. FHUS has literally seen the light, rejecting the alluring cries of the trivial and responding to the call of the critical few enablers of their success.

- *Beautiful design.* This Map captures the culture and personality of FHUS beautifully, from the simple and organic colors (which you of course can't see) to the dedication in serving those in need as evidenced by the pictures framing the text.

Exhibit 7.9 Food for the Hungry U.S. Strategy Map (version 2)

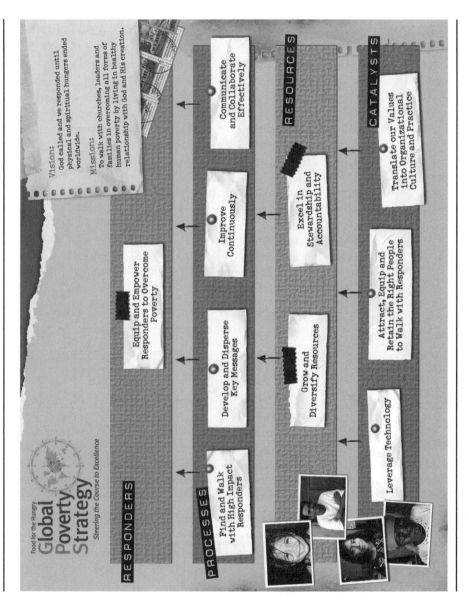

Food for the Hungry
Global Poverty Strategy
Steering the Course to Excellence

Vision:
God called and we responded until physical and spiritual hungers ended worldwide.

Mission:
To walk with churches, leaders and families in overcoming all forms of human poverty by living in healthy relationship with God and His creation.

RESPONDERS

PROCESSES

RESOURCES

CATALYSTS

Find and Walk with High Impact Responders

Develop and Disperse Key Messages

Equip and Empower Responders to Overcome Poverty

Improve Continuously

Communicate and Collaborate Effectively

Grow and Diversify Resources

Excel in Stewardship and Accountability

Leverage Technology

Attract, Equip and Retain the Right People to Walk with Responders

Translate our Values into Organizational Culture and Practice

Okay, so I like it, but that means very little. How did FHUS managers and employees react to the Strategy Map's second take? Soon after finalizing the Map, the Scorecard team held two sessions with FHUS staff, during which a short presentation was delivered on GPS, why it was critical, and what they could expect to see as the rollout evolved over the coming months. Then the Map was outlined in some detail, each objective shared with the group, its meaning and relevance to FHUS related in simple yet powerful language by a member of the Scorecard team.

While the first employee presentation was in full swing, a member of the Scorecard team named Peter, retreated to the back of the room and I noticed he was drawing what resembled two crude lines on a flip chart page. Each line was flanked by what I thought was a number. I had no idea what he was up to and, accordingly, returned my attention to the speaker. The mystery was solved as the session wound to its conclusion. As people were getting up from their chairs after a very fruitful question and answer session, Peter took center stage and asked everyone to do two things before leaving. On the flip chart were indeed two lines with scales from 1 to 10. Each person was to answer two questions: First (the first line), on a scale of 1 to 10 how well does this Strategy Map reflect the strategy of FHUS? And second, using the second line, on a scale of 1 to 10 are you able to see yourself in this Map? In other words, are there objectives appearing on it you feel you are able to contribute to in your daily work?

We held our breath as the first person approached the chart, held a marker to his hand and applied his evaluation to the empty line before him. A little apprehension could easily be understood, after all, months of work and preparation, and hours of debate and deliberation had been poured into this vessel, and the leadership team's credibility was clearly on the line as much as the two questions Peter had penned just moments ago. Within five minutes we had our answer: over 90% of attendees (in both sessions as it turns out) rated the Map at 8 out of 10 or higher on both questions.

FHUS's Balanced Scorecard implementation, while by no means complete—they're never complete as you'll learn later in the text—is progressing rapidly. They've refined their performance measures, have held management review meetings using the Balanced Scorecard, and recently began the cascading process. Amazing what a little simplicity can do.

NOTES

1. Mark Jenkins, *To Timbuktu* (New York: William Morrow & Company, 1997).

2. Robert S. Kaplan and David P. Norton, "Having Trouble with Your Strategy? Then Map It," *Harvard Business Review,* September–October 2000, pp. 167–176.

3. Stephen R. Covey, *The 8th Habit* (New York: The Free Press, 2004), p. 271.

4. Paul R. Niven, *Balanced Scorecard Step by Step: Maximizing Performance and Maintaining Results, 2nd Edition* (Hoboken, NJ: John Wiley & Sons, 2006), p. 101.

5. Robert S. Kaplan and David P. Norton, *The Balanced Scorecard* (Boston: Harvard Business School Press, 1996).

6. Jake Barkdoll, "Balanced Scorecards in the Federal Government," *Public Manager,* Fall 2000, pp. 43–45.

7. Robert S. Kaplan, "The Balanced Scorecard and Nonprofit Organizations," *Balanced Scorecard Report,* November–December 2002, pp. 1–4.

8. Paul R. Niven, *Balanced Scorecard Step-by-Step: Maximizing Performance and Maintaining Results, 2nd Edition* (Hoboken, NJ: John Wiley & Sons, 2006), p. 108.

9. Michael E. Gallery, Chair, Measures of Success Task Force, 7 *Measures of Success* (Washington, DC: ASAE, 2006), pp. 26–27.

10. Chris Denove and James D. Power IV, *Satisfaction* (New York: Portfolio, 2006), pp. 66–68.

11. Interview with Nancy Foltz, September 19, 2002.

12. Ann Zimmerman, "To Boost Sales, Wal-Mart Drops One-Size-Fits-All Approach," *Wall Street Journal,* September 7, 2006, p. A1.

13. Chris Zook, "Finding Your Next Core Business," *Harvard Business Review,* April 2007, pp. 66–75.

14. Jean Philippe Deschamps and P. Ranganath Nayak, *Product Juggernauts: How Companies Mobilize to Generate a Stream of Market Winners* (Boston: Harvard Business School Press, 1995).

15. Michael E. Gallery, Chair, Measures of Success Task Force, 7 *Measures of Success* (Washington, DC: ASAE, 2006), p. 33.

16. Marina Tsipis, "Plucked From Obscurity: Restroom Reservations," *Annals of Improbable Research*, March–April 2007, p. 18.

17. Christine W. Letts, William P. Ryan, and Allen Grossman, *High Performance Nonprofit Organizations* (New York: John Wiley & Sons, 1999), p. 67.

18. Thomas Wolf, *Managing a Nonprofit Organization in the Twenty-First Century* (New York: Fireside, 1999), p. 162.

19. Dean R. Spitzer, *Transforming Performance Measurement* (New York: AMACOM, 2007), pp. 223–224.

20. Michael E. Porter and Mark R. Kramer, "The Competitive Advantage of Corporate Philanthropy," *Harvard Business Review,* December 2002, pp. 56–68.

21. Michael E. Gallery, Chair, Measures of Success Task Force, 7 *Measures of Success* (Washington, DC: ASAE, 2006), p. 61.

22. Paul R. Niven, *Balanced Scorecard Diagnostics: Maintaining Maximum Performance* (Hoboken, NJ: John Wiley & Sons, 2005), p. 9.

23. "ImClone's Ex-CEO Arrested, Charged with Insider Trading," *Wall Street Journal,* June 13, 2002.

24. Aaron De Smet, Mark Loch, and Bill Schaninger, "Anatomy of a Healthy Corporation," *The McKinsey Quarterly*, May 2007.

25. David P. Norton in Foreword to: Brian E. Becker, Mark A. Huselid, and Dave Ulrich, *The HR Scorecard* (Boston: Harvard Business School Press, 2001).

26. Thomas A. Stewart, *Intellectual Capital* (New York: Currency Doubleday, 1999), p.12.

27. Reported in "In the News Briefs," *Balanced Scorecard Report*, September–October 2003, p. 5.

28. Robert S. Kaplan and David P. Norton, *Strategy Maps* (Boston: Harvard Business School Press, 2004).

29. Ian McEwan, *Saturday* (New York: Random House, Large Print Edition, 2005), p. 382.

30. Michael D'Antonio, *Hershey* (New York: Simon & Schuster, 2006), pp. 72–73.

31. Adrian Gostick and Chester Elton, *Managing with Carrots* (Salk Lake City, UT: Gibbs-Smith, 2001), p. 19.

32. Jim Collins, *Good to Great and the Social Sectors: A Monograph to Accompany Good to Great* (Jim Collins, 2005), pp. 13–16.

33. From "The President's Management Agenda," at www.whitehouse .gov/omb/budget/fy2002/mgmt.pdf

34. Ibid.

35. Portions of this section are drawn from Paul R. Niven, *Balanced Scorecard Step-by-Step: Maximizing Performance and Maintaining Results, 2nd Edition* (Hoboken, NJ: John Wiley & Sons, 2006), pp. 129–132.

36. Drawn from an unpublished paper presented by BrassRing LLC, 2005.

37. John F. Kennedy, *Profiles in Courage* (New York: HarperCollins, new edition, 2003), p. 4.

38. John Kotter and James Heskett, *Corporate Culture and Performance* (New York: The Free Press, 1992), p. 78.

39. Haig R. Nalbantian, Richard A. Guzzo, Dave Kieffer, and Jay Doherty, *Play To Your Strengths* (New York: McGraw-Hill, 2004).

40. Jennifer A. Chatman and Sandra E. Cha, "Leading by Leveraging Culture," *California Management Review*, Summer 2003.

41. Tom Peters, *Re-Imagine* (London: Dorling Kindersley, 2003), p. 26.

42. Dale Carnegie, *How to Win Friends and Influence People* (New York: Pocket Books, Revised Edition, 1981), p. 27.

43. Adrian Gostick and Chester Elton, *Managing with Carrots* (Salt Lake City, UT: Gibbs-Smith, 2001), p. 20.

44. This section is drawn from Paul R. Niven, *Balanced Scorecard Diagnostics: Maintaining Maximum Performance* (Hoboken, NJ: John Wiley & Sons, 2005), p. 80.

45. Jim Collins, *Good to Great and the Social Sectors: A Monograph to Accompany Good to Great* (Jim Collins, 2005), p. 5.

46. John Wooden and Jay Carty, *Coach Wooden's Pyramid of Success* (Ventura, CA: Regal, 2005), p. 34.

47. Quoted from *The New Oxford Book of Literary Anecdotes,* edited by John Gross (New York: Oxford University Press, 2006), p. 60.

48. Gordon MacKenzie, *Orbiting the Giant Hairball* (New York: Penguin Putnam, 2006), p. 118.

49. Walter Isaacson, *Einstein* (New York: Simon & Schuster, 2007), p. 113.

50. John Wooden and Jay Carty, *Coach Wooden's Pyramid of Success* (Ventura, CA: Regal, 2005), p. 34.

51. Timothy Ferriss, *The Four-Hour Workweek* (New York: Crown Publishing, 2007), p. 65.

52. John A. McLaughlin and Gretchen B. Jordan, "Logic Models: A Tool for Telling Your Program's Performance Story," *Evaluation and Program Planning,* 1999, pp. 65–72.

53. Ibid.

54. Walter Isaacson, *Einstein* (New York: Simon & Schuster, 2007), p. 127.

55. From internal Food for the Hungry U.S. documentation shared with the author.

56. Tom Peters, *Re-Imagine* (London: Dorling Kindersley, 2003), p. 153.

8

Performance Measures, Targets, and Initiatives

Roadmap for Chapter 8 When Kaplan and Norton originally conceived of the idea for a Balanced Scorecard, they were attempting to solve a measurement problem: How do organizations balance the historical accuracy and integrity of financial numbers with the drivers of future success? Since that time, over 16 years ago, the Balanced Scorecard has evolved from a measurement system to a strategic management system, and a powerful communication tool. Creative Scorecard adopters are finding ever new ways to harness this revolutionary tool. However, at its core, the Scorecard retains a commitment to performance measurement. In this chapter we examine the final pieces necessary to develop a Balanced Scorecard measurement system—measures, targets, and initiatives.

We'll begin the chapter by defining measures and considering the types of measures most used by public and nonprofit organizations. We'll then examine each of the four Scorecard perspectives in detail, providing information and techniques you can use to develop your performance measures. To help you choose the most appropriate measures for your organization, a number of criteria are presented. The chapter also includes advice on the number of measures your Scorecard should contain, gathering feedback from critical stakeholders, and even creating data dictionaries for your new metrics.

The critical role played by targets is the next stop in our Balanced Scorecard journey. Different types of targets will be examined, and sources of target information reviewed. Finally, we'll review organizational initiatives. Initiatives describe the steps, processes, projects, and plans that will bring the targets to life. Using the Balanced Scorecard as a lens, we'll explore a method of determining whether or not your current initiatives are acting as allies in the campaign to execute your strategy, and outline a method for creating entirely new initiatives.

WHAT ARE PERFORMANCE MEASURES?

Modern organizational vocabulary is flooded with references to measurement: "You get what you measure," "measurement matters," "measurement gets results." You've probably heard these and many more in your working life. The truth is, as cliché-sounding as these adages may appear, each is absolutely sound. Measurement does matter and it does drive results.

Performance measures may be considered standards used to evaluate and communicate performance against expected results. Granted, that's a rather banal description when you consider the undeniable power of a good performance measure. Not only do measures provide managers and executives with a tool to gauge organizational progress, but when well-crafted, they can inspire and motivate all employees, set direction for the organization, and encourage alignment from top to bottom.

The idea of measuring performance existed well before Kaplan or Norton conceived of something called a Balanced Scorecard. Organizations have long been devoted to the art and science of tracking performance. However, there is a cavernous gap between the simple act of measurement and measuring the right things. Consider these dubious examples of measurement:[1]

- At one time, the single goal for the Department of Defense (DoD) procurement was the percentage of procurement funds requested and appropriated by congress compared to DoD identified needs. This was a measure of inputs and lobbying success, but talks nothing about results achieved with the appropriated funds.

- The Health Resources and Services Administration provided grants to increase the number of primary care providers, encourage better distribution of health professionals, and increase the number of minorities in the health professions. Program performance was measured, not by the number or distribution of health care professionals, but rather by the number of grants made to academic institutions, hospitals, or students.

Measurement is about more than "counting widgets." Real benefits accrue to those who view the full range of measurement's vast potential, drawing on a range of measurement alternatives. Next, we'll explore several types of performance measures you can draw upon when designing your Balanced Scorecard.

Types of Performance Measures

Traditionally, three types of performance measures have been encountered in practice. Each is discussed in turn.

Input Measures   At the lowest end of the performance measurement spectrum is the tracking of program inputs. Typical inputs include staff time and budgetary resources. Inputs are generally the simplest elements to measure, but provide limited information for decision making and analysis of actual results.

Output Measures   Results generated from the use of program inputs are the domain of the output measure. These metrics track the number of people served, services provided, or units produced by a program or service. They may sometimes be referred to as activity measures. Depending on the nature of the program or service, output measures may provide information on whether or not desired results are being achieved. An immunizations program, for example, would gauge their effectiveness based on the number of inoculations delivered. However, for the majority of agencies, these too fail to disclose whether customers or clients are better off.

Outcome Measures   As noted, input and output measures demonstrate effort expended and numbers served, but reveal little about whether or not these interventions are making a difference—whether the targeted population is any better off as a result. The outcome measure answers this call.

Outcomes track the benefit received by stakeholders as a result of the organization's operations. Whereas inputs and outputs tend to focus internally on the program or service itself, outcomes reflect the concerns of the participants (clients, customers, other stakeholders). Outcome measures shift the focus from activities to results, from how a program operates to the good it accomplishes.[2] Outcome measures offer many advantages:

- Outcomes demonstrate results, and in today's environment that is exactly what everyone from the general public to the world's most generous philanthropists are demanding from public and nonprofit organizations.

- Outcomes provide guidance in resource allocation decisions. Funding can be directed in alignment with those actions that produce documented results.

- Focusing on outcomes, rather than inputs or outputs, serves to guide the entire organization toward its true aims.

- Accountability is enhanced when the focus shifts to outcomes. Administrators cannot hide behind data indicating numbers served, but must outline specifically how targeted audiences are better off as a result of their program or service.

Your Balanced Scorecard will likely contain a mix of input, output, and outcome measures weaving through the perspectives chosen. Exhibit 8.1 provides an example for a prenatal health clinic. In this example, the clinic measures new revenue received in the Financial Perspective. Funding dollars will be used to support their ongoing operations, and is thus considered an input. They will dedicate at least a portion of their enhanced funding to support training of staff on the latest prenatal care techniques. Number of staff trained is a metric chosen in the Employee Learning and Growth Perspective. Trained staff will use their knowledge in the delivery of services, and hence training may be considered an input. Possessing additional knowledge will allow the staff to deliver new and highly informative presentations to their targeted audience of low-income mothers. The number of presentations delivered is the output measure chosen in the Internal Process Perspective. The clinic is hypothesizing—remember a Balanced Scorecard is designed to capture your business hypothesis—that informative presentations will help clients make better decisions, which will ultimately result in improved choices, and clients feeling better about themselves. This will be reflected in an outcome measure of customer satisfaction. Finally, those patients who feel satisfied are more likely to maintain the healthy habits necessary for a safe delivery, which will lead to a greater number of healthy

Exhibit 8.1 Mix of Input, Output, and Outcomes in a Balanced Scorecard

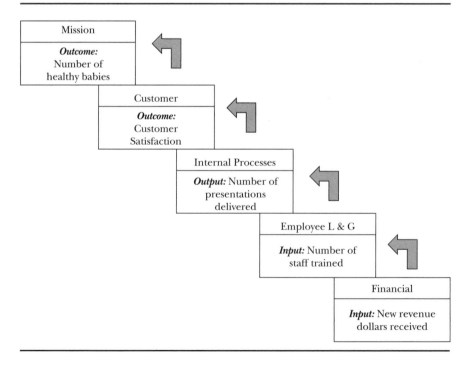

babies. The number of healthy babies is chosen as an outcome under the Mission Perspective of the Scorecard.

You're probably thinking, "Okay, sure, inputs and outputs are easy, they're accessible and simple to count. But tell me, how do I get at the outcome of what I do? It's not like in business where the ultimate outcome is profit." All true—input and output measures don't present the challenges of identifying and monitoring quality outcome indicators. But as Jim Collins writes in his monograph *Good to Great for the Social Sectors*, "to say we cannot measure performance in the social sectors the way you can in a business is simply a lack of discipline. All indicators are flawed, whether qualitative or quantitative . . . What matters is not finding the perfect indicator, but settling upon a consistent and intelligent method of assessing your results, and then tracking your trajectory with rigor."[3]

In Chapter 5, we discussed the Cleveland Symphony Orchestra, and the uplifting performance they staged shortly after the September 11th terror attacks. When Tom Morris assumed control of the organization, he asked board members what they expected of him during his tenure. Their response: Make an already great orchestra even greater, defined by artistic excellence. There is no simple metric you can pick up off the shelf to correspond directly with artistic excellence, but that didn't stop Morris and his team from following Collins's advice and brainstorming a number of consistent and intelligent metrics they could use to serve as proxies for excellence. In the end, they counted the number of standing ovations they received, number of pieces played to perfection, invitations to prestigious festivals, and ticket sales in other venues outside of Cleveland.[4] Perfect metrics? No, but what measure is. School test scores are flawed, customer service data is often unconvincing, even medical tests can prove misleading. What matters is not striving for perfection in measurement, but tracking a small number of simple items, discussing them frequently, analyzing them with rigor to learn from what they're telling you, and tracking your progress towards your mission.

Other Types of Performance Measures: Lag and Lead Indicators

Later in the chapter, when we discuss the Employee Learning and Growth Perspective, we'll explore employee satisfaction. You'll learn that taking the pulse of your employees' attitudes, opinions, and beliefs is immensely popular. While employee satisfaction is an important metric worthy of any Balanced Scorecard, it is essentially a "lag" indicator of performance. Satisfaction will typically be gauged once, maybe twice, a year with findings being incorporated into plans for the following year. By the time you survey your employees, the actions they're reflecting upon and assessing in the survey have already occurred. You need to balance this historical view with a predictive, driving metric that leads to improved employee satisfaction—in other words a "leading" indicator of performance. Perhaps you hypothesize that absenteeism is a leading indicator of satisfaction, and thus you monitor employees' time away from work in the belief that higher absenteeism is an early warning sign that overall satisfaction is falling. This gives you information you can take action upon now, not a year from now when you complete your next employee satisfaction survey. Should absenteeism increase, you must mount a campaign to determine why this is taking place, and enact programs to mitigate it.

Deborah Kerr of the Texas State Auditor's Office describes lag and lead measures this way. "Lag measures tell you basically whether or not you have met your target. Lead measures tell you how you are doing along the way and allow you to adjust performance so that you can be more successful in achieving your goal."[5] An interesting example of lag and lead measurement comes from the Department of Corrections in New York City.[6] Using their performance measurement system, this department tracks commissary sales in its jails. They've determined that if sales of cigarettes and candy suddenly increase, a riot may be in the planning stages. Inmates realize that they'll be confined to their cells immediately after any kind of uprising, and therefore stock up on supplies. A spike in candy and cigarette sales in this case is a leading indicator of the number of prison riots. Knowing this relationship exists allows prison officials to take action and attempt to avert a potentially dangerous confrontation.

The Balanced Scorecard should contain a mix of lag and lead indicators of performance. If you track nothing but lag indicators, historical representations of performance, you know little about the "how" of your operation. Conversely, a preoccupation with leading indicators will not reveal whether improvements are leading to improved process and customer results.

I'll warn you, some people on your Scorecard team may suggest every measure is in effect "lagging" because, by their very nature, all metrics are historical in nature. It's very easy to get off track and engage in a semantic discussion of this nature, but in the end it boils down to a simple principle. When selecting measures ask what drives that measure. Whenever you choose one measure and can hypothesize a relationship with a related metric you feel drives the performance of the first measure, you've determined a lag and lead relationship. Exhibit 8.2 outlines some of the key differences between lag and lead indicators.

DEVELOPING MEASURES FOR EACH OF THE FOUR PERSPECTIVES

The measures appearing in each of the four perspectives of your Balanced Scorecard aren't plucked randomly from thin air, nor are they chosen based on the seniority of the person advancing them. The measures selected to populate your Scorecard serve as direct translations of the objectives comprising

Exhibit 8.2 Lag and Lead Performance Measures

	Lag	Lead
Definition	Measures focusing on results at the end of a time period. Normally characterizing historical performance.	Measures that "drive" or lead to the performance of lag measures. Normally measure intermediate processes and activities.
Examples	• Revenue • Employee Satisfaction	• Grants written • Absenteeism
Advantages	Normally easy to identify and capture.	Predictive in nature, and allow the organization to make adjustments based on results.
Issues	Historical in nature and do not reflect current activities. Lack predictive power.	May prove difficult to identify and capture. Often new measures with no history at the organization.

The Balanced Scorecard should contain a mix of lag and lead measures of performance.

Adapted from *Balanced Scorecard Step-by-Step: Maximizing Performance and Maintaining Results, 2nd Edition,* Paul R. Niven (John Wiley & Sons, 2006).

your Strategy Map, which were also faithfully translated from your strategy. Measures provide insight into whether we are achieving our stated objectives and foster accountability for results, ensuring we maintain the course of implementing our strategy.

No universal set of right or wrong performance measures exists in practice; they will prove beneficial only in the context of your specific objectives and strategy. The critical question to ask when developing performance measures for your Balanced Scorecard is: "How will we know if we are successful in achieving this objective?" On the pages that follow, we'll revisit many of the proposed Strategy Map objectives from Chapter 7 and consider possible measures for each. Along the way, we'll place special emphasis on a small number of metrics that find their way on to virtually all Balanced Scorecards.

MEASURES FOR THE CUSTOMER PERSPECTIVE

When composing objectives for the Customer Perspective of the Strategy Map, we tossed around the following question: "What do our customers demand or expect from us?" Assuming you donned your empathy sneakers for the exercise and trudged a mile in your customer's shoes, you undoubtedly revealed a number of potential candidates. While each customer group may produce different answers to the question, requiring different measurements, they will often fall under one of the following categories:

- *Access.* Metrics relating to the ease with which customers can avail themselves of your products or services.

- *Timeliness.* Time expended, or saved, by clients as a result of your offerings.

- *Selection.* Depending on the nature of your organization, you may be in a position to offer more than one product or service. Are your offerings meeting the expectations of your customers?

- *Efficiency.* Customers of public sector organizations especially value a transaction that can be completed easily and accurately in one stop.

Customer Value Propositions

The concept of value propositions was introduced during our discussion of customer objectives in Chapter 7. The concept suggests that any business should face the market using one of three value propositions, each of which is outlined once again, with possible performance measures provided:

- *Product leadership.* Innovation is at the heart of a product leading enterprise: creating new products and services for which they're frequently able to achieve a higher price. Possible performance measures include: "brand awareness," "brand image," "number of new products or services," "revenue from new products or services," "joint ventures," "time to develop a new product or service," and "number of customer needs satisfied."

- *Operational excellence.* Excelling at what we, the customers, don't see is the hallmark of the operationally excellent organization. The "formula" of their operations leads to standardized experiences and low costs. Among the performance measures correlating to operational excellence are: "average wait times," "number of customer complaints," "yield," "first call resolution" (for call centers), "total cost of ownership," and "defect rates."

- *Customer intimacy.* Providing a total solution to customer needs characterizes the customer-intimate agency. Consider the following potential measures: "number of solutions offered," "reputation index," "number of customer or partner awards received," "customer retention," "number of customers profiled," and "access to key customer information." For something completely different relating to customer intimacy, you may be inspired by the latest techniques to woo car buyers practiced by Lexus in Japan, who have embraced the "Samurai sell." Sales associates have received training in etiquette from the Ogasawara Ryu Reihou Institute, whose teachings have been handed down through the family since the 1300s. Among the new Lexus rules of etiquette in Japan, "The Warrior's Waiting Position:" leaning 5 to 10 degrees forward when a customer is looking at a car, kneeling on the floor with both feet together and both knees on the ground when serving coffee or tea, and practicing "The Lexus Face," a closed-mouthed smile said to put customers at ease.[7]

Taking the Pulse of Your Customer: Customer Satisfaction

I would be very surprised if at some point in your discussion of customer measures—regardless of the objective you're unraveling—someone doesn't scrawl the words customer satisfaction across a flip chart, perhaps underlining it with a thick red mark for extra panache. Customer satisfaction is to the Balanced Scorecard what Paris Hilton is to Las Vegas club openings: always there. In one study, 70% of respondents noted its appearance on their Scorecard.[8] Customer satisfaction that is, not the hotel heiress.

Customer satisfaction surveys have been used successfully in both the public and nonprofit sectors for many years. Prince William County in Virginia, a recognized leader in performance management, has been doing annual telephone surveys of hundreds of community households since 1993. The auditor's office of the City of Portland, Oregon has been even more aggressive, undertaking an annual mail survey of approximately 10,000 households since 1991.[9] At the federal level, customer satisfaction is monitored annually by the American Customer Satisfaction Index.

While many organizations devote significant resources of both money and time to query satisfaction, not all surveys are created equal. Designing an effective evaluation tool requires moving beyond simple questions such as "overall, how would you rate your satisfaction with our services?" to an examination of variables which exist on several levels. Based on interviews with over a billion—that's right a billion—customers, the Gallup organization has identified these four expectations inherent in the study of customer satisfaction:[10]

- *Accuracy.* Whatever your product or service, customers expect it to be delivered accurately every time.

- *Availability.* Services should be available in locations that meet customers' needs.

- *Partnership.* Customers and clients want to feel that you understand them and are "on their side."

- *Advice.* This is the real barometer of nonprofit and public sector success. How can you help your customers in some way, thereby improving their situation in a demonstrable fashion?

Customer satisfaction surveys should attempt to probe customers' feelings about your offerings in each of the four categories.

There are many contradictory statistics and numbers butting heads in the customer experience atmosphere; for example, a recent survey by Bain and Company of customers of 362 companies found that only 8% of those customers described their experience with the company as superior. Yet, a massive 80% of the companies believed they had been providing a superior experience.[11] Given that finding, this following discovery is rendered all the more confusing: A U.K.-based study found that while 95% of all firms collected customer feedback of some type, only 30% used the data to make decisions about service levels, and only 10% deployed the data to their front lines.[12] So there you have it, organizations are confident they're offering a superior experience, which they're not. They go to the expense and considerable effort of gathering data which disproves what they believe, and they choose to ignore it.

Fortunately, there are organizations out there that "get it"; they survey their customers with no preconceived notions, listen with open minds, and put what they hear to good use in the development of future products and services. The Society for Human Resource Management (SHRM) is one such institution. They routinely conduct member and reader surveys, and perform member needs assessments. As one staffer explained, "We analyze as much information as possible as a way of serving them better and understanding their needs."[13]

MEASURES FOR THE INTERNAL PROCESS PERSPECTIVE

The Internal Process Perspective signals an important transition in the Balanced Scorecard, from "what" to "how." In the Customer Perspective, we focus on *what* customers expect or demand from us as an organization, and what our value proposition is in serving them effectively and efficiently. Answering those questions leads us down the path of *how* we will accomplish the outcomes we've set forth for our customers, which is the domain of the Internal Process Perspective.

All objectives on the Strategy Map, and measures appearing on the Balanced Scorecard, must represent direct translations of your strategy, and thus all are vital to your success. However, Internal Process metrics may be elevated to an even higher perch since, upon close examination of your operations, this perspective will sometimes require the drafting of measures never before contemplated—brand new measures you have little experience in gathering, monitoring, and analyzing. Thus, when creating these indicators, it's important to be what I term "ruthlessly realistic," critically examining your ability to actually collect the data without breaking the bank, and equally as compelling, your ability to interpret what the measure is telling you as you begin collecting and analyzing results.

In Chapter 7, we outlined a number of potential considerations for Internal Process objectives. Each is shown in Exhibit 8.3 accompanied by possible performance measures.

MEASURES FOR THE EMPLOYEE LEARNING AND GROWTH PERSPECTIVE

I've already chronicled, at several points, the rising value of intangible assets to organizational success. In today's environment, we rely almost exclusively on the knowledge of our people, robust information systems, and cultures capable of innovation and change to deliver the results we expect. Measures in the Employee Learning and Growth Perspective represent the enabling factors that fuel efficient processes, and ultimately lead to improved outcomes for customers. Let's revisit the three areas of capital we discussed in Chapter 7 with a view of providing potential measure candidates for each.

Measuring Human Capital

I'm sure many of you enjoy sinking deep into your sofa with a bucket of popcorn and watching the Academy Awards each year. I do, and what strikes me as I listen to those accepting Oscars (you're not allowed to say "winners") is that regardless of the picture for which they win, the thanks are always for people.

Think of how movie-making has changed over the decades from silent movies to the first talkies, to the blockbuster technological achievements that the earliest filmmakers couldn't have imagined in their wildest dreams. The difference between a Charlie Chaplin movie and a release like *War of the Worlds* is immense. But for all the technological advancements, it is still people that are at the heart of the experience, as it is with all organizations. Sadly, however, this fact is lost on many organizations, as evidenced by a recent Conference Board study which found that only 12% of the companies they surveyed make use of people measures to meet their strategic targets.[14] But we know that you don't comprise part of that 12%, right? Or, at least you don't want to. To help you avoid being inducted into that dubious class, here are a number of measure suggestions.

Closing Skill Gaps   In our discussion of this topic in the previous chapter, I introduced the term *strategic job families*: the cadre of positions within

Exhibit 8.3 Possible Internal Process Performance Measures

Internal Process Objective	Possible Performance Measures
Understand your customers	–Number of customers profiled –Number of customer meetings held –Percentage of targeted customers purchasing products or services –Number of focus groups held
Innovate constantly	–Amount of budget allocated to research and development –Number of new product or service development teams –Number of lead users identified (lead users are those most willing to share input on product and service enhancements) –Number of new products or services in the pipeline –Number of new products or services developed –Revenue from new products and services
Market and brand yourself	–Brand equity: measured by the following factors:[*] • Distinctiveness (the brand's differentiation) • Quality (reputation and actual performance) • Value (strength of preference for the brand) • Image (extent to which the brand conveys the intended image) • Loyalty (commitment to the brand)
Quality	–Number of product or service defects –Response time –Customer complaints –Rework (e.g., repeat calls)

Work efficiently
—Number of key process improvements
—Number of customer bottlenecks identified
—Number of "handoffs" in a key process (the goal is to reduce the number of people or departments impacting a particular process)
—Operating costs per employee

Partner for success
—Number of new partners
—Partner retention
—Partner satisfaction
—Number of private sector partners

Raise funds effectively and efficiently
—Number or grants proposals written
—Grant success rate
—Number of channels utilized in fundraising
—Revenue by channel
—Response rate to solicitations

Monitor your reputation
—Reputation index
—Number of positive (or negative) press stories
—Audit findings

Manage your risks
—Number of potential risks identified
—Number of risks mitigation strategies identified
—Number of risk management sessions held

*Dean R. Spitzer, *Transforming Performance Measurement* (New York: AMACOM, 2007), p. 224.

your organization contributing the most to strategy execution. Kaplan and Norton recommend you measure skill gaps in these areas through human capital readiness.[15]

The first step in calculating human capital readiness is identifying the competencies, skills, and behaviors required to successfully achieve the objectives in your Internal Process Perspective of the Strategy Map. Achieving these objectives may require new competencies not currently residing within the organization. In step two, you build detailed "competency profiles" for each of the key jobs required to achieve the process objectives. These detailed models can be used by Human Resources when recruiting, training, and rewarding employees. To calculate readiness, assess your current roster of skills and competencies for strategic job families with what is required to execute the strategy. This is typically done on a percentage basis. Techniques for assessing current skills include self-assessments by employees, 360 degree feedback, and job descriptions.

Measuring Employee Training   The roll call of standard training measures includes: hours of training per employee, number of training courses offered, number of training participants, training satisfaction, and dollars invested in training. What these metrics share as a common denominator is a focus on activity rather than effectiveness.

Organizations are separated from billions of their dollars each year by the siren call of training and the seductive promise of improved business results that will surely follow the investment. While everyone agrees there is a correlation between training and business results, very few have taken the intrepid step of actually proving such a link exists. One pioneer challenging the status quo is Dean Spitzer, who developed the Learning Effectiveness Measurement (LEM) while at IBM.[16] The centerpiece of LEM is the concept of "causal chains," diagrams used to trace the impact of learning through a series of causes and effects from: acquisition of skills to behavior change to individual or team performance enhancement to organizational performance improvements. Spitzer suggests the causal chain approach can be utilized to design more powerful training and assess its impact on desired results.

Recruitment   If you've been on an airplane recently, you know that air travel is verging ever closer to contact sport status. Accounts of violence and air rage in the sky are climbing faster than a 737's ascent from the runway, as the number of people flying has exceeded pre-September 11th levels. Southwest Airlines isn't completely immune to the hooliganism more reminiscent of a European soccer match, but generally speaking, their crews seem better equipped to pacify the tempers of frustrated passengers. Of course, a key plank of Southwest's low-cost strategy is ensuring a fun and pleasant atmosphere for their customers.

Southwest's integration of strategy and human capital isn't a lucky coincidence. Customer-facing personnel are selected and trained deliberately to support the company strategy. They operate as a team and will do whatever is necessary to get their planes loaded and into the air as quickly as possible, all in an atmosphere charged not with stress and discomfort, but infused with humor and compassion. Not only does recruiting the right people keep air marshals ensconced comfortably in their seats, but most industry observers attribute the company's cost advantage to the productivity and flexibility of its employees.

Consider the following possible measures for recruiting the right employees: "time to fill open positions," "number of referrals from current employees," "number of applications received," and "cost per hire."

Retention   Nothing complicated here. Track retention rates—you may wish to differentiate between voluntary and involuntary departures—then pat yourself on the back for being so efficient and move to the next objective. Speaking of which . . .

Succession Planning   According to a study by the Conference Board, more than 40% of the U.S. labor force will reach the traditional retirement age by the end of this decade; while the number of workers between ages 35 and 44 is expected to shrink by 7%.[17] This clash of demographic meteors leads to just one conclusion: succession planning must be embraced by every organization concerned with capturing the knowledge of long-term workers and passing the torch to the next generation.

We all know that balanced diets and more exercise will enhance our health, but do we avail ourselves of tofu and treadmills? Not always, and such is the case with succession planning. Most organizations recognize at least intellectually that succession planning should drive leadership development but many fail to take action. Why is that? Here is what experts on the subject suggest: "Many people, from the CEO on down, consider the word "succession" taboo. Planning your exit is like scheduling your own funeral; it evokes fears and emotions long hidden under layers of defense mechanisms and imperceptible habits. Perversely, the desire to avoid this issue is strongest in the most successful CEOs. Their standard operating procedure is to always look for the next mountain to climb, not to step down from the mountain and look for a replacement."[18] I once had a client that slips this description on like a perfectly fitting suit. He is talented, motivated, inspiring, but bring up the word succession in his presence and the rockets begin to flare.

Recognizing the trends, some forward-thinking organizations have begun formal programs to start the succession ball rolling. IBM, for example, encourages its 330,000 employees to post detailed descriptions of their job experiences in an online directory called the "Blue Pages," so that employees far from retirement can find knowledge before it walks out the door.[19] IBM might track "number of submissions to its Blue Pages" as a succession planning metric. Other candidates include: "number of succession plans in place," and "number of candidates ready to assume a promotion."

Measuring Information Capital

Inventor and futurist Ray Kurzweil thinks a lot about change, and argues that fundamental change is occurring at a rate unprecedented in history. Before about 1000 AD, what we consider a paradigm shift, a major shift in the way people think about things, typically took thousands of years to unfold. By 1000, a paradigm shift was taking place about every 100 years. From there, the rate of change continued to accelerate. In the 1800s, there was more change than there had been during the previous 900 years. Fast forward to the year 2000 and a paradigm shift was occurring every decade. Looking ahead, Kurzweil estimates there will be 1000 times more technological change in the twenty-first century than there was in the twentieth century.[20] And I could barely manage to schedule a recording on my VCR before it was replaced by TiVo!

In the days ahead, your ability to harness the power of technology, regardless of the size or type of organization you represent, will become paramount to your success. When discussing human capital I reviewed a measure known as human capital readiness. Strap on your pocket protectors, because it's time to calculate *information* capital readiness.[21] With this metric, we're basically changing the recipe from people to information or technology. Your challenge is to critically assess the information and technology you require to execute your strategy, compare that with what is currently available and design interventions to diminish the gap. Remember that, as with objectives on the Strategy Map, the measures on our Balanced Scorecard should weave together to tell a story. In this case we're hypothesizing that by closing an information and technology gap, we'll be better able to ensure efficient processes and drive greater outcomes for our customers.

Measuring Organizational Capital

Employee Satisfaction   Possibly the single most popular metric appearing in the Employee Learning and Growth Perspective is employee satisfaction. Popular and important as well, as recent studies suggest upwards of 50% of workers here in the United States are not satisfied in their jobs, citing issues ranging from robotic and meaningless work to lack of influence to work/life balance. That could explain a subsequent finding that the average worker spends more than two hours of each working day surfing the Internet, conducting personal business, or just "spacing out."[22]

If you're attempting to create a climate of positive action, one that will improve your performance, and ultimately benefit customers, it's virtually impossible without satisfied and committed staff. As a result, workplace surveys abound in organizations large and small, public, private, and nonprofit alike. Putting your ear to the ground and finding out what your people think is critical, but our methods for gathering that data often leave much to be desired. Survey experts suggest most organizations are applying survey design principles formulated 40 or 50 years ago.[23] To bring your surveying techniques out of the dark ages, here are a number of recommendations:[24]

- *Ask questions related to observable behavior, not thoughts or motives.* This allows respondents to draw on first-hand experience, not inference.

- *Measure only those behaviors that are linked to your organization's performance.* Awareness of your new cafeteria hours may be interesting, but is it relevant to your results?

- *About one-third of questions should lead to a negative response.* This avoids our natural tendency to agree to things.

- *Avoid questions that require rankings.* We tend to remember the first and last things in a list, which may bias our answer to the question.

- *Make sure the survey can be completed within 20 minutes.* Recognize that everyone is busy and taking an hour to complete a 100-question survey may elicit a negative response that shows up in the respondent's answers.

Of course, surveying is one thing, taking action on the findings is another. To generate commitment from employees you must demonstrate a willingness to act on the concerns raised in the surveys. Anything less and your survey efforts will be dismissed as hollow, dust-collecting make-work projects.

Recognition and Rewards   In the private sector, where everything not nailed down seems subject to a study of some sort, researchers recently pointed out that companies that have effective mechanisms for recognizing employees realized a median total return to shareholders of 109% versus 52% for employers that didn't—a two-to-one margin.[25] In many ways, this is reminiscent of employee training, it seems common sense that recognizing and rewarding employees will lead to improved business results. But how to measure it?

Should we count smiles in the hallways? Don't laugh—measuring smiles has actually been undertaken in the private sector (didn't I just say they measure everything there?). And what did they find? The bigger the employee's smile the happier the customer. With the help of trained observers, researchers followed 173 encounters between customers and employees in a coffee shop, scoring the employee's "smile strength" on a scale from "absent" to "maximal" (which features exposed teeth) at various points during the transaction. The researchers then intercepted the customers and asked them about their service experience. Indeed, the bigger the employee's smile, the more likely customers were to view that person as competent and the encounter—averaging just two minutes—as satisfying.[26] Interesting research, but not particularly relevant for our discussion since the study tracked employee smiles and we're looking for managerial grins. And, incidentally, in case you're thinking of mandating smiles from all of your customer-facing personnel, the researchers in the study above cited earlier scholars who determined that forcing employees to act friendly leads to job burnout and depression.

This is a difficult area to track adequately since many proposed measures, such as "number of celebrations," or "number of rewards allotted," appear contrived, simplistic, and more than a bit specious in effectiveness. Your best bet is to create the conditions in which rewards and recognition may flow freely by hiring people that share those values, and using every forum available to share the power of recognition.

Alignment   In my ongoing effort to try and stay in shape, I recently bought a treadmill. It was with great anticipation that I plugged it in for the first time and climbed aboard, anticipating the smooth rubber tread to begin flowing beneath my feet. Unfortunately, when I pressed the start button I was greeted by a horrendous and violent shrieking noise. A quick examination determined the track had been jolted out of alignment during shipping. Things just don't work when they're not aligned. Now, my treadmill was easily remedied, and will undoubtedly provide me with years of service, but if your employees are not aligned to your overall goals, the results can be devastating. Conflicts of interest, misallocated resources, wasted performance management efforts, and missed opportunities can all result from poor alignment. Without a workforce that understands your mission, vision, and strategy, and is aligned toward their achievement, you will never produce the results you desire.

Track alignment in the first year of your implementation by counting the number of cascaded Balanced Scorecards created, and also by assessing the degree of alignment with overall organizational strategy. Once you've cascaded, a quick alignment diagnostic can be performed by evaluating how well your Scorecards work together to tell your strategic story. Alignment is also frequently measured anecdotally through employee surveys: "Do you understand the goals of your department?" "Do you work collaboratively with other groups to achieve success?" and so on.

Communication   In a recent study, less than one-third of respondents believed their company communicates effectively with them.[27] Shakespeare said,

"If music be the food of love, play on." Modern organizations would be well advised to say, "Communication is the food of success, communicate on." Employees are frequently drawn to careers in the public and nonprofit are-nas by the allure to make a difference. That fire behind that bright-eyed idealism can be quickly extinguished without constant communication of the organization's goals, how they fit in, and what is expected of them going forward. In Chapter 12 you'll read the story of Charlotte, North Carolina's journey with the Balanced Scorecard. Among their words of wisdom to Scorecard-adopting organizations is communicate, communicate, communi-cate. They recognize the value of providing constant information to all employees, and have seen the results it can bring. Their advice could be easily expanded into communication regarding all realms of the organiza-tion. Candidates for communication measures include: "communication rat-ing" (normally conducted by employee survey), "number of communication mediums utilized," and "intranet hits."

MEASURES FOR THE FINANCIAL PERSPECTIVE

Good thing we've reached the last perspective in our quest to develop per-formance measures, because I've run out of amusing (I hope) anecdotes, arcane research studies, and silly statistics on this subject. The good news is I've got plenty more for the remaining chapters.

So, with apologies for the brevity of this section to all my bean-counting friends, let's cut right to the chase. Here are a number of measures you may consider for the Financial Perspective of your Balanced Scorecard (but remember, it's not like the dessert aisle at the grocery store—you don't just grab what looks good; the measures must be direct translations of your objectives):

- Net income
- Gross revenue
- Net assets
- Budget variance
- Earned income
- Diversification of income streams
- Percentage of restricted (or unrestricted) net assets
- Timeliness of financial reports
- Income (or expense) per employee
- Budget or forecasting accuracy

FINAL THOUGHTS ON SELECTING PERFORMANCE MEASURES

Great challenges throughout the ages: achieving world peace, eradicating poverty, persuading Britney Spears to wear underwear, and developing performance measures. If you find yourself bogged down in this quest, revert to some basic principles and questions to get yourself un-stuck.

First, when pondering an objective, move beyond a dry and analytical view of the subject to engage all of your senses. If you were to succeed on the objective, what do you physically see people doing; what behaviors are they engaged in? What are they saying, how are they acting? Break out of the cognitive box you're in and peer daringly into the future. You can also ask yourself what behavioral change the objective demands; what improvements are required. Does it entail doing something faster, more accurately, with more customer involvement, with greater knowledge inputs? Another simple technique is to simply imagine what your executives will need to discuss regarding the objective.[28]

Lastly, and straight from the broken record department, strive to keep it simple when designing measures. I recall a client workshop in which we were brainstorming possible measures and became ensnared in the trap of a challenging objective. One team member, a very bright and articulate person, began to opine on a possible metric. Opine is a bit euphemistic, considering she stammered her way through a vague explanation that, when it was finally concluded a good two minutes later, left the rest of us looking straight down not knowing how to respond. I broke the silence a moment later by joking, "Any measure that takes more than 30 seconds to describe probably doesn't belong on the Balanced Scorecard." We all laughed, but the more I reflected on it the more I believed I'd stumbled on a truism. Given the demands we face in our daily lives, it's not much of an exaggeration to suggest that gnats have longer attention spans. So, you've got a very narrow window of opportunity to attain your staff's buy-in on your measures. Keeping them simple will go a long way towards securing the understanding and support you need to see your measures translated into action.

CRITERIA FOR SELECTING PERFORMANCE MEASURES

Not all performance measures are created equal. Effective metrics provide direction, align employees, improve decision making, and serve as a basis for resource allocation decisions. Here are some criteria to consider when attempting to narrow your measures down to the critical few that articulate your strategic story.

- *Linked to strategy.* The Balanced Scorecard was designed to facilitate the description of strategy. It does so by translating your strategy into a set of objectives on the Strategy Map and measures used to evaluate performance. All measures on the Scorecard should serve as faithful translations of objectives, which in turn, have been translated from your strategy.

- *Easily understood.* Congratulations, I think you've reached my last reference to the importance of keeping your metrics simple. A final story to bid adieu to the topic: A fashion retailer needed a way of determining the conversion ratio at its stores (the percentage of shoppers who bought something). Various complex schemes were proposed, involving the use of radio frequency identification tags and various types of sensors. In the end, the company decided on the low-tech approach of hiring high school students to sit outside stores and count the numbers of people who went into the store and the number coming out carrying shopping bags.[29] Clear and elegant in its simplicity.

- *Link in a chain of cause and effect.* The measures you select should link together through the four perspectives of the Scorecard. When you have a coherent story emerging from your measurements, communication efforts will be greatly enhanced, as will your opportunities to learn from performance results.

- *Updated frequently.* Your primary motivation in launching a Balanced Scorecard was most likely to improve results. Results can only be enhanced through the provision of timely information upon which you can take action. Timely in this context refers to measures that are updated frequently—monthly or quarterly. Semi-annual and annual performance measures allow little room for midcourse corrections. By the time you receive your results, the actions that led to the performance are long past.

- *Accessible.* Research suggests that upwards of 30% of your performance data may be unavailable when you launch a Balanced Scorecard. Many organizations are disappointed to learn this until they realize the missing data represent entirely new ways of monitoring performance that had been neglected in the past. Proclaiming a measure as critical enough to appear on the Scorecard, regardless of initial data availability, signals a strong commitment to focusing on what really matters. While 30% is palatable, 70, 80, or 90% is not. Never let the best be the enemy of the good. Sounds profound (maybe), but it simply means a Balanced Scorecard you can use immediately with 70% of data available is better than a Scorecard you have to wait a year for, because of data availability issues.

- *Use averages with caution.* Let's say you pick up your local paper tomorrow and see a headline that reads, "County Incomes Increase by Record Margin." Sounds like great news worthy of celebrating and congratulating your elected officials. But what if you later discovered that in the past year, Bill Gates, Warren Buffet, and Oprah Winfrey all decided to take up residence in the cozy confines of your town. I'm sure you'd be excited, but think about the effect their galactic-sized incomes had on your town's average. Typical townsfolk may be no better off, and perhaps suffered through a year in which income had fallen. Such is the danger of averages. Look for performance measures that portray the true picture of the process or event you're attempting to capture.

- *Avoid "date"-related measures.* It's not uncommon for Scorecard developers to include at least a measure or two to the effect, "Complete project X by September 30." This reflects an initiative—an action taken to assure success on the measure—rather than a measure itself. Should they be fortunate enough to complete the project, does the measure simply vanish from the Scorecard? In this case, the Scorecard creators should ask, "What happens on September 30? How are we better off as an organization? How are prospects improved for our customers or clients?" In other words, "Why are we embarking on this initiative?" Answering these questions may lead to the development of a more appropriate performance measure.

- *Quantitative.* For all the men out there who are fashion-challenged, what would your wife say if you were about to leave for a romantic dinner dressed in a striped shirt and plaid pants? To put it mildly, she might suggest the two just don't go together. And so it is with subjectivity and performance measurement. Evaluation of performance should reflect objectivity as much as possible. Using quantitative indicators ensures any subjective biases are barred from the system. With a little creativity, you can transform even the most challenging measurement issue into a number. I can recall a medical services unit I worked with at a county government. A key performance metric was the distribution of their trauma reports in a timely fashion. Their original measure was "reports issued." In other words, a simple yes or no would suffice as the indication of performance. With a little tweaking, we improved the measure by restating it as "the percentage of trauma-report recipients receiving the document on time."

- *Dysfunctional.* Dysfunctional is a word that has gradually crept into the mainstream. We have dysfunctional families, dysfunctional workplaces, and dysfunctional teams. Basically, anywhere humans congregate seems to breed the potential for dysfunction. Measures can be dysfunctional too, in that they may drive the wrong behavior in your organization. Consider the example of one restaurant chain. Concerned with a large amount of food being thrown away at the end of the day, they instructed their staff not to cook any food within one hour of closing until ordered by a customer. Great for waste, bad for customer service. Customers had to wait an inordinately long period of time for their orders, and soon business dried up. Measuring waste in this case drove the wrong behavior. Consider the behavior your measures will drive before including them on your Balanced Scorecard. Eli Goldratt, author of the popular business novel, *The Goal*, was once asked by a client, "what can we do immediately to improve performance in our company?" Goldratt's reply:"Change one key measure that is driving the wrong behavior."[30]

To help you make the hard choices among competing measure alternatives, I've developed a worksheet, shown in Exhibit 8.4, for ranking your metrics. List your measures under the appropriate perspective, and award a score to it in relation to each criterion. Consider rating each out of a possible ten points.

How Many Measures on a Balanced Scorecard?

This is the $64,000 question: Just how many measures should your Score-card contain? The standard response suggests you employ the number of measures necessary to adequately describe your strategy. If that means 10 measures, great, if it translates to 30 measures, so be it. When discussing objectives in Chapter 7, I suggested you cap your number at between 10 and 15. Ten objectives would equal at least 10 performance measures. However, measures and objectives don't always exhibit a one-to-one relationship. Some objectives may require two measures to adequately capture their essence. For those objectives you do feel comfortable in assigning only one performance measure, a closer examination may reveal it to be a lagging indicator that requires the balance of a leading indicator, again translating to more than one measure for the objective. A minimum of one-and-a-half measures per objective is the rule of thumb we previously established. Therefore, 10 objectives would translate into at least 15 performance measures, 20 objectives would mean 30 measures, and so on.

My bias is towards fewer performance measures, under 20 whenever possible. There is a lot of "noise" in modern organizations, and a good Balanced Scorecard should rise above the ruckus, providing you with a view of the real drivers of success in your organization. Limiting your measures means making the commitment to monitor strategic measures and place less relevance on operational indicators. This can prove to be a vexing challenge, especially in the public sector where measures in the hundreds are not uncommon. You're not alone; recent research from a Hackett Benchmarking study found the typical monthly performance report to contain 140 different measures.[31]

Exhibit 8.4 Worksheet to Select Balanced Scorecard Measures

Balanced Scorecard
Measure Selection Worksheet

Perspective	Linkage to Strategy	Easily Understood	Cause & Effect Linkage	Frequency of Updating	Accessibility	Reliance on Averages	Date Driven?	Quantitative	Dysfunctional	Comments
Customer										
Measure 1										
Measure 2 . . .										
Internal Processes										
Measure 1										
Measure 2 . . .										
Employee Learning and Growth										
Measure 1										
Measure 2 . . .										
Financial										
Measure 1										
Measure 2 . . .										

Adapted from *Balanced Scorecard Step-by-Step: Maximizing Performance and Maintaining Results, 2nd Edition*, by Paul R. Niven (John Wiley & Sons, Inc., 2006).

Concentrating on the strategic doesn't mean the operational necessarily vanish. My car monitors speed, fuel, temperature and a few other critical variables, but that doesn't mean I'm not concerned about what happens under the hood. I just don't need to be monitoring those myriad activities unless something occurs out of a normal range. Your organization is the same; as leaders, you have an obligation to focus on the strategic, the core drivers of performance. Examining performance measures related to activities three levels below you is an inefficient use of your time and the organization's resources. Maximize your time, abilities, and effectiveness by choosing to monitor only those few variables that truly correspond to success.

Gathering Employee Feedback on Your Performance Measures

Creativity tends to flourish in workplaces where employees are informed, inspired, and involved. The Balanced Scorecard can certainly inform all stakeholders of your progress, and positive results will no doubt prove inspiring. The other aspect of this triad is not to be overlooked. Before you can expect employees to embrace and use the Scorecard, you should provide them with the opportunity to provide input on this most critical of organizational documents.

Feedback can be gathered in a number of ways. Here is how the County of San Diego, California accomplished the task.[32] Several years ago, this county, the sixth most populated in the country according to the 2000 census, instituted a wide-ranging performance management program to better serve its citizens. They began their efforts by developing Balanced Scorecards for the Health and Human Services Agency (HHSA). With a budget of over $1 billion and 5,000 employees, the HHSA is larger than many corporations. Given the diverse nature of services offered throughout the agency, the HHSA asked each of its program areas to develop Balanced Scorecards that demonstrated how they successfully serve their customers. A Balanced Scorecard implementation team comprised of county personnel and consultants worked with each program to develop Scorecards over a four-month span. Once preliminary Scorecards were built, the team looked for a way to share what had been developed with all employees and gather their feedback. They decided to hold what they termed "validation sessions."

Upon entering the conference room for these sessions, participants were greeted by Scorecard team staff and given a folder to hold the information they would gather during the event. Each session was kicked off with a short presentation from the team leader who provided an overview of the implementation, benefits to be derived from performance management, and the work that lay ahead. Once the presentation concluded, participants were free to roam the large room and visit any one of the several booths manned by team members. Each booth featured a number of different Scorecards that the participants could review and discuss with the team. A kiosk was also set up, giving employees the opportunity to take a test drive of the Scorecard software that would be used to report results. Feedback forms were distributed and participants were encouraged to provide their input to the team. The events were a great success since employees from across the agency had the chance to participate in the evolution of performance measures, and see how other groups within the HHSA were measuring their outcomes.

Another client took an even more direct approach. After much deliberation, the Scorecard team could not reach a consensus on how to measure the objective of "creating a safe and healthy environment." Rather than debating the topic endlessly, the chief executive used his weekly e-mail message to all employees to seek their input. Here is what he said:

> . . . . Next, I would like to update you on our progress with our Balanced Scorecard (BSC) program. Last week, the executive team met with the implementation team to review the latest version of the BSC as we prepare to bring our five-year and line-of-business scorecards to the board of directors. We had very productive discussions and are close to finalizing the objectives, measures, and targets for the Balanced Scorecard.
>
> One objective, which is very important to our organization and generated significant discussion and dialog, was related to creating an organization that is "well"—including the physical, mental, and emotional well-being of all of our employees. Specifically, our objective is to "Create a safe and healthy environment that supports balance in people's lives." Both the implementation team and executive team have debated a variety of measures—everything from measuring absenteeism to insurance claims to the number of accidents on the job to the amount of wellness programs we offer—and we just can't seem to find the ideal measure for gauging how "well" our organization is. We agreed that with the wealth of knowledge resident across our organization, we would likely be able to find the answer. So, here's what I propose: Please think about what the best way to measure our organization's wellness might be, and drop me a note via e-mail sometime before next week. We'll gather up the responses and attempt to complete our work with your input on this last objective we're struggling with. I'm really looking forward to your input on this one.

Not surprisingly, many possible measures were advanced by employees across the organization. This is the epitome of that well-worn phrase, win-win. Not only does the organization's Scorecard benefit from the input of knowledgeable employees at all levels, but the chief executive reinforced both his commitment to the Balanced Scorecard and his faith in employees to deliver whatever is necessary to succeed.

I'm partial to the interpersonal nature of the techniques shared above, but in the spirit of our earlier review of information capital, a variety of other options are open to organizations wishing to share their measures with employees. Posting measures on an intranet and requesting feedback is a low-cost and highly efficient mechanism for garnering feedback, as is simply generating an e-mail blast to all staff, informing them of the measures and seeking their opinions.

RECORDING YOUR MEASURES IN A DATA DICTIONARY[33]

Creating a Performance Measure Data Dictionary

Once you've settled on a collection of performance measures, you're ready to catalog the specific characteristics of each in a data "dictionary." My dictionary's definition of the word "dictionary" reveals the following: "book that lists. . . . the topics of a subject." That is precisely what you're crafting in this step of the process: a document that provides all users with a detailed examination of your Balanced Scorecard measures, including a thorough list of characteristics.

Creating the measure data dictionary isn't a very glamorous task, but it is an important one. When you present your Balanced Scorecard to senior managers and employees alike, they will undoubtedly quiz you on the background of each and every measure: "Why did you choose this measure?" "Is it strategically significant?" "How do you calculate the measure?" "Who is responsible for results?" These and numerous other queries will greet your attempts to share your Scorecard with colleagues. The data dictionary provides the background you need to quickly defend your measure choices and answer any questions your audience has. Additionally, chronicling your measures in the data dictionary provides your team with one last opportunity to ensure a common understanding of measure details.

Exhibit 8.5 provides a template you can use to create your own measure dictionary. There are four sections of the template you must complete. In the first section, shown at the top, you provide essential background material on the measure. The second lists specific measure characteristics. Calculation and data specifications are outlined in the third component of the dictionary. Finally, in the bottom section, you provide performance information relating to the measure. Let's examine each of these sections in some detail.

Measure Background   At a glance, readers should be able to determine what this measure is all about, and why it's important for the organization to track.

- *Perspective.* Displays the perspective under which the measure falls.

- *Measure Number/Name.* All performance measures should be provided a number and name. The number is important should you later choose an automated reporting system. Many will require completely unique names for each measure, and since you may track

Exhibit 8.5 Balanced Scorecard Data Dictionary

Perspective: Customer	*Measure Number/Name:* C01/Customer Satisfaction	*Owner:* L. Hess
Strategy: Expand program offerings	*Objective:* Increase Satisfaction with Programs	
Description: Customer Satisfaction measures the percentage of surveyed customers stating they are satisfied with our current service offerings. Satisfaction is judged using a number of criteria, including: access to services, timeliness, and overall quality. We feel that only by ensuring current customers are satisfied will we be able to expand our offerings.		
Lag/Lead: Lag	*Frequency:* Quarterly	*Unit Type:* Percentage	*Polarity:* High values are **good**
Formula: Number of quarterly survey respondents feel satisfied with current access, timeliness, and quality of our services **divided** by the total number of surveys received.		
Data Source: Data for this measure is provided by our survey company, "SST." Each quarter they perform a random survey of our customers and provide the results electronically to us. Data is contained in the form of MS Excel spreadsheets (CUST SURVEY.xls, lines 14 and 15). Data is available the 10th business day following the end of each quarter.		
Data Quality: High—received automatically from third party vendor	*Data Collector:* P. Lee	
Baseline: Our most recent data received from SST indicates a Customer Satisfaction percentage of 59%	*Target:* Q1 2001: 65% Q2 2001: 68% Q3 2001: 72% Q4 2001: 75%	
Target Rationale: Achieving customer satisfaction is critical to our strategy of service expansion. The quarterly increases we're targeting are higher than in past years but reflect our increased focus on satisfaction.	*Initiatives:*	
	1. Transportation services for targeted customers	
	2. Customer management software program implementation	
	3. Customer service training	

Adapted from *Balanced Scorecard Step-by-Step: Maximizing Performance and Maintaining Results, 2nd Edition,* by Paul R. Niven (John Wiley & Sons, 2006).

the same measures at various locations or departments, a specific identifier should be supplied. The measure name should be brief, but descriptive. Again, if you purchase software for your reporting needs they may limit the number of characters you can use in the name field.

- *Owner.* Not only does the Balanced Scorecard transmit to the entire organization your key strategies for success, but it simultaneously creates a climate of accountability for results. Central to the idea of accountability is the establishment of owners for each and every measure. Simply put, the owner is the individual responsible for results. Should the indicator's performance begin to decline, it's the owner we look to for answers and a plan to bring results back in line with expectations.

- *Strategy.* Displays the specific strategy you believe the measure will positively influence. This box is customarily used should you have several "strategic themes."

- *Objective.* Every measure was created as a translation of a specific objective. Use this space to identify the relevant objective.

- *Description.* After reading the measure name, most people will immediately jump to the measure description, and it is therefore possibly the most important piece of information on the entire template. Your challenge is to draft a description that concisely and accurately captures the essence of the measure so that anyone reading it will quickly grasp why the measure is critical to the organization. In our example, we rapidly learn that customer satisfaction is vbased on a percentage, what that percentage is derived from (survey questions), and why we believe the measure will help us achieve our strategy of expanding program offerings.

Measure Characteristics   This section captures the "meat and potatoes" aspects of the measure you'll need when you begin reporting results.

- *Lag/Lead.* Identify whether the measure is a core outcome indicator or a performance driver. Remember that your Scorecard represents a hypothesis of your strategy implementation. When you begin analyzing your results over time, you'll want to test the relationships you believe exist between your lag and lead measures.

- *Frequency.* How often do you plan to report performance on this measure? Most organizations have measures that report performance on a daily, weekly, monthly, quarterly, semi-annual, or annual basis. However, I have seen unique time frames such as "school-year" for one government agency. Attempt to limit the number of semi-annual and annual measures you use on your Scorecard. A measure that is only updated once a year is of limited value when you use the Scorecard as a management tool to make adjustments based on performance results.

- *Unit Type.* This characteristic identifies how the measure will be expressed. Commonly used unit types include numbers, dollars, and percentages.

- *Polarity.* When assessing the performance of a measure, you need to know whether high values reflect good or bad performance. In most cases, this is very straightforward. We all know that lower costs and increased employee satisfaction are good, while a high value for complaints reflects performance that requires improvement. However, in some cases, the polarity issue can prove quite challenging. Take the example of a public health organization. If they choose to measure a caseload of social workers, will high values be good or bad? A high number of cases per social worker may suggest great efficiency and effectiveness on the part of the individual workers. Conversely, it could mean the social workers are juggling far too many clients and providing mediocre service in an attempt to inflate their caseload numbers. In such cases you may want to institute a "dual polarity." For example, a maximum of 25 cases per social worker may be considered good, but anything over 25 would be a cause for concern, and necessitate action.

Calculation and Data Specifications   Information contained in this section of the dictionary may be the most important, yet pose the greatest difficulty to gather. To begin reporting your measures, precise formulas are necessary, and sources of data must be clearly identified.

- *Formula.* In the formula box you should provide the specific elements of the calculation for the performance measure.

- *Data Source.* Every measure must be derived from somewhere—an existing management report, third party vendor supplied information, customer databases, the general ledger, and others. In this section you should rigorously attempt to supply as detailed information as possible. If the information is sourced from a current report, what is the report titled, and on what line number does the specific information reside? Also, when can you access the data? This information is important to your Scorecard reporting cycle since you'll be relying on the schedules of others when producing your Scorecard. The more information you provide here, the easier it will be to begin actually producing Balanced Scorecard reports with real data. However, if you provide vague data sources, or no information at all, you will find it exceedingly difficult to report on the measure later. A warning: spend the time you need to thoroughly complete this section. I have seen a number of Scorecards proceed swiftly through the development stage only to stall at the moment of reporting because the actual data could not be identified or easily collected.

- *Data Quality.* Use this area of the template to comment on the condition of the data you expect to use when reporting Scorecard results. If the data is produced automatically from a source system and can be easily accessed, it can be considered "high." If, however, you rely on an analyst's Word document that is in turn based on some other colleague's Access database numbers that emanate from an old legacy system, then you may consider the quality "low." Assessing data quality is important for a couple of reasons. Pragmatically, you need to know which performance measures may present an issue when you begin reporting your results. Knowing in advance what to expect will help you develop strategies to ensure the data you need is produced in a timely and accurate fashion. Second, data-quality issues may also help direct resource questions at your organization. If the information is truly critical to strategic success, but current data quality is low, perhaps the organization should invest in systems to mine the data more effectively.

- *Data Collector.* In the first section of the template, you identified the owner of the measure as that individual who is accountable for results. Often this is not the person you would expect to provide the actual performance data. In our example, L. Hess is accountable for the performance of the measure, but P. Lee serves as the actual data contact.

Performance Information   In the final section of the template, you note your current level of performance, suggest targets for the future, and outline specific initiatives you'll use to achieve those targets.

- *Baseline.* Users of the Balanced Scorecard will be very interested in the current level of performance for all measures. For those owning the challenge of developing targets, the baseline is critical in their work.

- *Target.* Some of you may be saying right now, "At this point in the process we haven't set targets, so what do we do?" Fortunately, some of your measures may already have targets. For example, perhaps you've currently stated an expectation to cut costs by 15% next year. Whenever targets exist, use them now. For those measures that don't currently have targets, you can leave this section blank and complete it once the targets have been finalized. For those of you that have at least some targets, list them based on the frequency of the measure. In this example, I've shown quarterly customer satisfaction targets. Some organizations may find it difficult to establish monthly or quarterly targets and instead opt for an annual target, but track performance toward that end on a monthly or quarterly basis.

- *Target Rationale.* As in Target, this will only apply to those measures for which you currently have a performance target. The rationale provides users with background on how you arrived at the particular target(s). Did it result from an executive planning retreat? Does it represent an incremental improvement based on historical results? Was it based on a mandate? For people to galvanize around the achievement of a target, they need to know how it was developed, and that while it may represent a stretch, it isn't merely wishful thinking on the part of overzealous senior management team.

- *Initiatives.* At any given time, most organizations will have dozens of initiatives or projects swirling about. Often, only those closest to the project know anything about it, hence any possible synergies between initiatives are never realized. The Scorecard provides you with a wonderful opportunity to evaluate your initiatives in the context of strategic significance. If an initiative or project cannot be linked to the successful accomplishment of your strategy, you have to ask yourself why it is being funded and pursued. Use this section of the template to map current or anticipated initiatives to specific performance measures.

TARGETS

What Are Performance Targets? Why Are They Important to the Balanced Scorecard?

Poet, painter, and novelist Kahlil Gibran once noted, "To understand the heart and mind of a person, look not at what he has already achieved, but at what he aspires to do." We all have aspirations that range from the grand—writing the great American novel—to the practical—painting the back fence before the first snowfall. Targets bring our aspirations to life, and give us something to shoot for in the quest for improvement. The young writer may set a target of writing ten pages per day, while the suburban homeowner may vow to paint the fence over two weekends in November. Both actions will lead to improved overall results in their specific situations.

In the context of a Balanced Scorecard, targets represent the desired result of a performance measure. By comparing actual performance results against a predetermined target, we receive information that is imbued with value and meaning. For example, knowing your city can fill a pothole within two days of notice means very little until you know that neighboring jurisdictions can do it in one, and the best organizations can do it in three hours. Armed with this information, you might establish a target of filling potholes within two hours of notification. With the target in place, you have a point of reference towards which to guide your actions, decisions, and resource allocation. As a result, improvement, not the status quo, is reinforced and communicated.

Targets are powerful communication tools, informing the entire organization of the expected level of performance required to achieve success. As a result, they typically drive a focus on continuous improvement as the organization strives to constantly better its performance. Targets also provide a mechanism for the organization and its customers to gauge management effectiveness and foster accountability. The Environmental Protection Agency (EPA) used performance targets when it launched its "33/50" program in 1988. The goal of the program was to work with industry in an effort to have them voluntarily reduce toxic waste levels a full 50% by 1995, with an interim goal of 33% by 1992. Before the deadlines were reached, both targets were accomplished.[34]

Types of Performance Targets

If we define a target as "desired result of a performance measure," there is a strong connotation of an orientation towards the future. Targets represent our goals for some period that has yet to elapse. They may be established by month, quarter, half-year, year, or multi-years. In this section, we'll examine three types of targets, each corresponding to different time frames.

Long-term Targets: Big Hairy Audacious Goals   In Chapter 2 I shared with you a portion of President John F. Kennedy's inspirational May 25, 1961 proclamation: "I believe that this nation should commit itself to achieving the goal, before this decade is out, of landing a man on the Moon and returning him safely to the Earth." That lunar ambition represents the very essence of a Big Hairy Audacious Goal, or BHAG. The unlikely acronym, so often at the lips of senior executives with galactic ambitions, was coined by *Built to Last* authors Jim Collins and Jerry Porras to represent the seemingly outrageous goals established by organizations, serving as powerful mechanisms to stimulate progress.

BHAGs are intended to tear an organization loose from business-as-usual thinking and prompt the innovation and creativity necessary to climb to such an exalted position. They are typically 10 to 30 years in duration, the time frame synchronizing with the level of difficulty associated with reaching the finish line. Private sector firms have embraced the idea of BHAGs for some time, but the idea is catching on in the public and nonprofit arenas as well. For example, in Canada last year, the federal government announced a wide range of long-term targets aligned with closing the gap in the quality of life between native Canadians and the rest of the population. Among the goals to which they've held themselves accountable are: reducing infant mortality, youth suicide, childhood obesity, and diabetes by 50% in ten years, and closing the educational gap so that by 2016, the high school graduation rate for aboriginal students will equal that of other Canadian students.[35]

Midrange Targets: Stretch Goals   Targets established in the three to five (or occasionally longer) period are often termed "stretch" targets. Their purpose is keeping the organization focused on a midrange goal that is in alignment with their vision and mission, and the achievement of which will lead them closer to their BHAG. In the EPA example cited earlier, a 50% reduction in toxic waste over a seven-year period is clearly a stretch target. As with BHAGs, the achievement of stretch targets will often require the organization to abandon the status quo and alter the way they do business in order to meet the dramatic challenge represented by the lofty target.

By their very nature, BHAGs may appear wild in their proportions, with the stratospheric goal meant to stimulate entirely new ways of operating. Stretch targets must be a bit more down to earth in order to captivate and motivate. The caveat with any stretch target is that it contain some semblance of realism. A target that simply reflects the wishful thinking of an overzealous management team is certain to be greeted with tremendous skepticism by employees, and could actually prove debilitating to performance. Before establishing a stretch target you hope will transform your organization consider the following:

- Ensure reaching the target is truly critical to your success.

- Determine whether you possess the skills within your organization to help you reach the target.

- Gauge the organization's willingness to accept a challenge of this magnitude. A workforce lacking the necessary motivation to beat the target will probably result in a Sisyphean endeavor.

Short Term: Incremental Targets   Most organizations will develop annual performance targets for their performance measures. In keeping with the theme of cause and effect which is so critical to the Balanced Scorecard, the achievement of annual performance targets will help lead to the accomplishment of longer-term stretch targets, and ultimately, BHAGs. Whenever possible, it is desirable to decompose annual targets into increments corresponding to your Scorecard reporting frequency. For example, you may have a customer satisfaction target of 90% for the year. If you survey your customers more than once a year, break the target down. Perhaps you'll be shooting for 75% in the first quarter, 80 in the second, 85 in the third, and finally 90 at year-end. Rather than waiting until the end of the year to take action on the results, you can now make customer satisfaction a regular and routine part of your operational decision-making process.

Do You Need All Three Types of Targets?

Based on the discussion in the previous sections, we see that the three types of targets can link together in positively shaping an organization's future. BHAGs set the desired long-term future, maybe decades in the making, stretch targets provide the midrange warning systems designed to propel us towards the BHAGs, and finally, incremental targets supply feedback on the attainment of stretch goals. Sounds great, but in practice just devising incremental targets can pose a significant test to public and nonprofit agencies not historically conversant in the art, and starting with a slate composed of several entirely new measures for which no baseline of performance even exists.

Creating BHAGs for every measure on your Balanced Scorecard, and expecting to achieve them, is about as realistic as me expecting this book to be featured in Oprah's book club. It would be virtually impossible to manage BHAGs for every metric, and almost certainly lead to a diffusion of priorities throughout the organization. One galvanizing BHAG is probably more than enough for most organizations. Stretch targets, on the other hand, should be applied in liberal quantities to your Scorecard effort. They require loosening the grip on the status quo, and their achievement will yield a crop of substantial results. And of course, incremental targets should accompany every Scorecard measure.

Setting targets is a delicate balancing act: become overly optimistic and you'll find a workforce bathed in apathy and confusion. Plunge to the opposite of the target pool, however, by settling for LHMGs—Little Hairless Mediocre Goals[36]—and you miss a golden opportunity to motivate and align your team around a shared goal.

Setting Performance Targets

One survey of more than 500 studies indicates that performance increases by an average of 16% in companies that establish targets.[37] Why have performance targets proven to be so effective? Maybe there is more at work here than just the motivational power of a goal. Actually, social scientists have long argued that humans will always align with their commitments.[38] As a result, when we make public commitments, such as those in a written performance target, we tend to stick with them. A classic 1955 experiment in which students were asked to estimate the lengths of lines on a screen supports this assertion. Some students were asked to write down their estimates, sign them, and turn them over to the researcher. Others were asked to write them down on an erasable slate, then erase the slate immediately. A third group was instructed to keep their decisions to themselves. The researchers then presented all three groups with evidence that their initial choices may have been wrong. By a wide margin, the group most reluctant to shift from their original choices were those who had signed and handed them to the researcher. Those who made a public commitment were the most hesitant to move away from that pledge. This underscores the importance of having written performance targets as part of your Balanced Scorecard. Their achievement may just be human nature!

The advice most often associated with setting targets is keeping them realistic, yet challenging. This is proven and practical advice, especially for closely scrutinized government and nonprofit agencies. Your missteps will not only cause you to lose organizational momentum, but are quite often featured on the local news.

Setting targets can represent new territory for some agencies. Often the challenge lies in knowing where to search for meaningful sources of target information. Here are a number of potential areas to consider when setting your targets:

- *Trends and baselines.* If past data for the measure exists, you can use it to create a trend line or baseline projection into the future. Examining past data and trends will allow you to choose a target representing a meaningful challenge, while staying within the ballpark of reality.

- *National, state, local, or industry averages.* Many organizations monitor the performance of government and nonprofit agencies, and offer a ready supply of potential target information on a wide variety of performance variables. In the public sector, both the Governmental Accounting Standards Board (GASB) and the International City/County Management Association (ICMA) provide relevant performance measurement information.

- *Employees.* Never forget that those closest to the action are frequently in the best position to provide insight on what represents a meaningful target. Involving employees in the process not only makes great sense based on the knowledge they possess, but not approaching them could lead to alienation and lack of buy-in, which in turn may translate to decreased attention on the chosen target. As Samuel Butler wrote nearly 300 years ago, "He that complies against his will/Is of his own opinion still."

- *Other agencies.* While private-sector firms tend to hold their information close to the vest for competitive purposes, public and nonprofit agencies embrace a willingness to share and learn from one another. Talk to your colleagues at other agencies in an effort to glean insights from their experiences.

- *Feedback from customers and other stakeholders.* The goal in all this is improving results for customers, so why not ask them what they expect from your agency?

- *Executive interviews.* When you met with your executives earlier in the process, they may have shared with you what they felt was a required level of performance to achieve success. Similarly, your executive workshops, conducted throughout the process of developing a Scorecard, will likely yield potential Scorecard targets.

- *Internal/external assessments.* If you've recently gone through any kind of strategic planning process you've undoubtedly conducted an assessment of strengths, weaknesses, opportunities, and threats (SWOT). Information from these assessments will help you determine appropriate targets to maximize opportunities and minimize threats.

- *Benchmarking.* Examining best in class organizations and attempting to emulate their results is effective—to a point. It's very important to try and achieve the same level of success as the star performers in your industry, but benchmarking has a downside as well. First of all, most organizations will simply focus on one element of operations when conducting a benchmarking study. Perhaps innovation processes, month-end closing processes, or fundraising. The problem with this approach is that the best in class organization you're studying probably has a number of different activities it combines to drive a unique mix of value for customers (the essence of strategy as espoused by strategy guru Michael Porter). Copying just one element of this formula may lead to isolated improvements in that area but fail to bring about breakthrough performance. Additionally, the organizations you review may have different customers, processes, and resources. Perhaps they allocate significant human and financial resources to the process under the microscope, and that's what accounts for their success.

INITIATIVES

We've covered a lot of ground in these past two chapters. We examined the steps necessary to develop a Strategy Map of performance objectives, translated those objectives into performance measures, and, most recently, considered the role of performance targets. One step that will translate our targets into reality remains in the development of our Balanced Scorecard: initiative setting.

Initiatives are the specific programs, activities, projects, or actions you will engage in to help ensure you meet or exceed your performance targets. An initiative could be anything from building a customer service portal on your Web site to launching a career development program for employees to redesigning your financial management system. While the nature of initiatives will vary tremendously, the common thread that should run through all is a linkage to strategic objectives, measures, and targets.

Most organizations do not suffer from a lack of initiatives. In fact, many government and nonprofit agencies will be bursting at the seams with initiatives, since they frequently begin their performance management efforts with initiative development. The logic works this way: We'll engage in this initiative in order to better meet our needs or our customers' needs, and then we'll develop goals and objectives to track our progress. I believe this approach is fundamentally flawed. Mission, values, and vision always come first. Strategy follows, and outlines the broad priorities necessary for success. Next up are performance objectives and measures, which tell us what we must excel at in order to execute the strategy, and how we'll gauge our progress. Targets supply a star to shoot for, and finally, initiatives are put in place that will help us achieve our targets. Following this logic path will lead to the design and implementation of a manageable number of initiatives directly aligned with your strategy.

Ensuring Initiatives Support Your Strategy

A careful analysis of your current crop of initiatives may reveal the seemingly contradictory finding that you simultaneously have too many and too few.[39] You may have any number of initiatives vying for scarce human and financial resources that have literally no effect on the ability to implement your strategy. Concurrently, your Balanced Scorecard may identify entirely new performance objectives and measures that are not represented by a single initiative.

A useful exercise to undertake upon completing your Scorecard is the mapping of current organizational initiative to your Strategy Map objectives. Any initiative that cannot demonstrate a clear linkage to an objective, and hence, to your quest of strategy implementation, should be considered a strong candidate for removal. If you're searching for a quick economic payoff to justify your investment in the Balanced Scorecard, this step could be it. Consider the potential drain of organizational resources an ineffective initiative represents. Naturally, financial resources have been committed that would be better served elsewhere. Additionally, staff time and attention have been diverted from strategic endeavor in the pursuit of activities that really produce no value. Using the crystal clear focus provided by the Strategy Map, you can put your current initiatives under the microscope and ferret out those that really contribute to value from those that merely drain all-too-scarce human and financial resources.

The first step in mapping initiatives to objectives involves seeking out each and every initiative currently being sponsored within the organization. Since all initiatives entail the allocation of financial resources, your finance team may be able to provide you with a list of current projects. Next you should create a grid similar to the one shown in Exhibit 8.6. Strategy Map

Exhibit 8.6 Mapping Initiatives to Balanced Scorecard Objectives

Perspective	Objectives	Initiatives										
Customer												
Internal Processes												
Employee Learning & Growth												
Financial												

Adapted from *Balanced Scorecard Step-by-Step: Maximizing Performance and Maintaining Results, 2nd Edition,* by Paul R. Niven (John Wiley & Sons, 2006).

objectives are listed on the left side of the document, while initiatives will be outlined across the top. Your considerable challenge is critically examining each initiative in light of all Strategy Map objectives. To conduct such an analysis in a meaningful fashion insists you perform a good deal of "due diligence" on each of the initiatives. Read background on the project, speak with the sponsor, and review financial information to ensure you have a solid understanding of the project's true essence. For those initiatives that support Strategy Map objectives, put a check in the corresponding box of the grid. Any initiatives that do not meet your criteria of being strategic in nature should be carefully reviewed, possibly reduced in scope, or even discontinued.

Eliminating initiatives that don't contribute to your strategy frees up valuable resources within the agency. These resources, both human and financial, can now be directed towards drafting new initiatives that do in fact propel you towards your goals.

Creating New Initiatives[40]

Should you require new initiatives to fill the void created by new performance objectives or measures, develop them on a solid foundation. Ensure there is: an executive willing to sponsor the new initiative, clearly defined plans and project scope, a legitimate budget, and the commitment of resources necessary to successfully complete the initiative. To help you crisply document any new initiatives you are considering, Exhibit 8.7 provides a template outlining the attributes and fields you should consider.

You'll be amazed at how imaginative your team can be when it comes to creating new initiatives. Take the case of the Boston Lyric Opera (BLO).[41] Employees at this performing arts company rose to the call and suggested a number of inventive approaches to achieving targets. The most successful initiative to emerge was the production of "Carmen on the Common." To meet the Strategy Map objective of increasing community support, the BLO staged two free outdoor performances of the classic opera before appreciative audiences of over 130,000 people. What better way to increase community support than to bring opera to the public? For many who took advantage of this unique opportunity, it was their first exposure to opera, but most assuredly will not be their last. Only a creative approach resulting from the discussion of initiatives could lead to such a breakthrough.[42]

Prioritizing among Strategic Initiatives

Now that you have a finite number of initiatives you consider strategic, you must rank them in order to make resource allocation decisions (assuming you don't have unlimited financial and human resources!). The key is basing your decision on a common set of criteria that will determine the most appropriate initiatives given your unique priorities.

Exhibit 8.7   Strategic Initiative Overview Template

Strategic Initiative Overview Template   Date: [   ]

This template is intended as an enterprise-wide tool to enable the Executive to quantify, assess and prioritize proposed strategic initiatives based on their impact on strategic objectives.

Please limit input and commentary to the space provided and use minimum 10 pt. font.

Department [   ]

Strategic Initiative Name: [   ]

Executive Owner: [   ]   Initiative Leader: [   ]

Anticipated Start Date: [   ]   Anticipated End Date: [   ]

Initiative Description/ Scope:

Strategic Impact		Strategic Impact: (H,M,L)
Describe Strategic Impact		
Customer:		
Internal Process:		
Financial:		
Employee Learning & Growth:		

Resource Allocation Requirements

Capital & Operating Budget ($000)	Year One	Year Two	Year Three	Year Four
Capital Spending Profile	$0	$0	$0	$0
Operating Budget Spending	$0	$0	$0	$0

Economic Fit	
NPV: Net Present Value	
IRR% : Internal Rate of Return	
Payback Period	

(continued)

Exhibit 8.7   Strategic Initiative Overview Template *(continued)*

Net FTE Impact (+/−FTE's)				

Key Dependencies

Key Risks to Successful Implementation and Mitigation Activities

Describe Internal Impact (employees/processes) of this Initiative

Describe External Impact (customers/partners/other stakeholders) of this Initiative

Milestones, Deliverables, & Corresponding Due Dates

Key Milestone	Deliverables	Due Date

Key Milestone	Deliverables	Due Date

Key Initiative Resources (Top 5 Involvement)

Name	Time Allocation (%)	Explanation of Time Allocation

Obviously, the initiative's impact on driving strategy is the chief concern, but you can't ignore investment fundamentals like cost, net present value, and projected time to complete. Essentially, every initiative should have a valid business case to support its claim as being necessary to achieve your strategy. Once you've drafted business cases for each of the initiatives you can use a template similar to that shown in Exhibit 8.8 to assist in making the prioritization decision. Each criterion you choose is assigned a weight, depending on its importance within your organization. The assignments are

Exhibit 8.8 Prioritizing Balanced Scorecard Initiatives

Criteria	Weight	Description	Initiative #1		#2		#3		#4	
			Points	Score	Points	Score	Points	Score	Points	Score
Linkage to Strategy	45%	Ability of the initiative to positively impact a strategic objective	7	3.2	1	.45				
Net Present Value	15%	Present value of initiative benefits discounted 5 years	5	.75	10	1.5				
Total Cost	10%	Total dollar cost including labor and materials	5	.50	10	1.0				
Resource Requirements (Key Personnel)	10%	Key personnel needed for the initiative including time requirements	8	.80	10	1.0				
Time to Complete	10%	Total anticipated time to complete the initiative	8	.80	10	1.0				
Dependencies	10%	Impact of other initiatives on the successful outcomes anticipated with this initiative	3	.30	10	1.0				
				6.35		5.95				

Adapted from *Balanced Scorecard Step-by-Step: Maximizing Performance and Maintaining Results, 2nd Edition*, by Paul R. Niven (John Wiley & Sons, 2006).

subjective, but strategic importance should always carry the greatest weight in the decision. Next, each initiative must be scored on the specific criteria listed in the chart. You may use ratings of between 0 and 10, or if you prefer a wider scale, use zero to 100. I've used 0 to 10 in my example. Before assigning points to each, you must develop an appropriate scale. For example, a net present value (NPV) of greater than $2 million dollars may translate to 10 points. NPV of $1.75 million yields 9 points, and so on. Involving more than one executive on a full-time basis may translate to a score of 2 points in the "resource requirements" section since their involvement could impose a heavy burden on the organization. Develop scales that work for you, however, to ensure mathematical integrity, a high value should always represent preferred performance. Those initiatives generating the highest scores should be approved and provided budgets to ensure their timely completion. Notice in our example, initiative #1 generates a higher total score than initiative #2 despite the latter's impressive scores on five of the six criteria. The reason for the discrepancy is the critical variable of strategic linkage. Initiative #1 demonstrates a strong linkage to strategy while #2 is missing that connection.

I recognize that many public and nonprofit agencies have an obligation to serve and may chafe at the inclusion of net present value in the calculation. However, as discussed in our review of the Financial Perspective, you must demonstrate stewardship for the funds with which you've been entrusted. Sound financial management and a mission-orientation cannot be viewed as mutually exclusive endeavors, but must work hand-in-hand as you strive to serve your constituent base.

NOTES

1. "The President's Management Agenda," at www.whitehouse.gov/omb/budget/fy2002/mgmt.pdf

2. Margaret C. Plantz, Martha Taylor Greenway, and Michael Hendricks, "Outcome Measurement: Showing Results in the Nonprofit Sector," *New Directions for Evaluation*, Fall 1997.

3. Jim Collins, *Good to Great and the Social Sectors: A Monograph to Accompany Good to Great* (Jim Collins, 2005), pp. 7–8.

4. Ibid., p. 7.

5. Deborah L. Kerr, "The Balanced Scorecard in the Public Sector" *Perform Magazine*, Vol. I, No. 8, pp. 4–9.

6. Rudolph W. Giuliani, *Leadership* (New York: Hyperion, 2002), p. 87.

7. Amy Chozick, "The Samurai Sell: Lexus Dealers Bow to Move Swank Cars,"*Wall Street Journal*, July 9, 2007, p. A1.

8. Lawrence S. Maisel, Performance Measurement Survey by the American Institute of Certified Public Accountants, 2001.

9. Harry P. Hatry, "Where the Rubber Meets the Road: Performance Measurement for State and Local Public Agencies,"*New Directions for Evaluation*, Fall 1997.

10. Marcus Buckingham and Curt Coffman, *First Break All the Rules* (New York: Simon & Schuster, 1999), p. 128.

11. Christopher Meyer and Andre Schwager, "Understanding Customer Experience,"*Harvard Business Review*, February 2007, pp. 116–126.

12. Dean R. Spitzer, *Transforming Performance Measurement* (New York: AMACOM, 2007), p. 113.

13. Michael E. Gallery, Chair, Measures of Success Task Force, 7 *Measures of Success* (Washington, DC: ASAE, 2006), p. 41.

14. Craig Schneider, "The New Human Capital Metrics,"*CFO Magazine*, February 2006, pp. 22–27.

15. Robert S. Kaplan and David P. Norton, *Strategy Maps* (Boston: Harvard Business School Press, 2004).

16. Dean R. Spitzer, *Transforming Performance Measurement* (New York: AMACOM, 2007), p. 251.

17. Kelly Greene, "Bye-Bye Boomers?" *Wall Street Journal*, September 20, 2005.

18. Jeffrey M. Cohen, Rakesh Khurana, and Laura Reeves, "Growing Talent as if Your Business Depended On It," *Harvard Business Review*, October 2005, pp. 63–70.

19. Kelly Greene, "Bye-Bye Boomers?" *Wall Street Journal*, September 20, 2005.

20. Tom Peters, *Re-Imagine* (London: Dorling Kindersley Limited, 2003), p. 23.

21. Robert S. Kaplan and David P. Norton, *Strategy Maps* (Boston: Harvard Business School Press, 2004).

22. E.L. Kersten, "Why They Call it Work,"*Harvard Business Review*, February 2006, pp. 66–67.

23. Palmer Morrel-Samuels, "Getting the Truth Into Workplace Surveys,"*Harvard Business Review*, February 2002, pp. 111–118.

24. Ibid.

25. Adrian Gostick and Chester Elton, *Managing with Carrots* (Salt Lake City, UT: Gibbs-Smith, 2001), p. 19.

26. Forethought: "Service with a Very Big Smile,"*Harvard Business Review*, May 2007, p. 24.

27. Stephen Taub, "Dazed and Confused," *CFO.com*, September 11, 2002.

28. Andrew J. Pateman, "Five Easy Steps for Developing Your BSC Measures,"*Balanced Scorecard Report*, March–April 2004, p. 16.

29. Michael Hammer, "The 7 Deadly Sins of Performance Measurement," *MIT Sloan Management Review*, Spring 2007, pp. 19–28.

30. Dean R. Spitzer, *Transforming Performance Measurement* (New York: AMACOM, 2007), p. 15.

31. Institute of Management and Administration, "20 Best Practice Budgeting Insights: How Controllers Promote Faster, Better Decisions," 2001.

32. Paul R. Niven, *Balanced Scorecard Step-by-Step: Maximizing Performance and Maintaining Results, 2nd Edition* (Hoboken, NJ: John Wiley and Sons, 2006), p. 173.

33. Ibid., pp. 167–172.

34. Jonathan Walters, *Measuring Up* (Washington, D.C.: Governing Books, 1998), p. 74.

35. Beth Duff-Brown, "Canada Pledges $4.3B for native people," Associated Press release reported in: *North County Times*, November 26, 2005.

36. Peters, *Re-Imagine* (London: Dorling Kindersley Limited, 2003), p. 199.

37. Edwin A. Locke, "Motivation by Goal Setting,"*Harvard Business Review*, November 2001.

38. Robert B. Cialdini, "Harnessing the Science of Persuasion," *Harvard Business Review*, October 2001.

39. Robert S. Kaplan and David P. Norton, *The Balanced Scorecard* (Boston: Harvard Business School Press, 1996).

40. Adapted from Paul R. Niven, *Balanced Scorecard Step-by-Step: Maximizing Performance and Maintaining Results, 2nd Edition* (Hoboken, NJ: John Wiley & Sons, 2006), p. 192.

41. Robert S. Kaplan, "The Balanced Scorecard and Nonprofit Organizations," *Balanced Scorecard Report*, November–December 2002, pp. 1–4.

42. Adapted from Paul R. Niven, *Balanced Scorecard Step-by-Step: Maximizing Performance and Maintaining Results, 2nd Edition* (Hoboken, NJ: John Wiley & Sons, 2006), pp. 192–194.

9

Creating Alignment by Cascading the Balanced Scorecard

Roadmap for Chapter 9 There is a great story about former President Lyndon B. Johnson touring Cape Canaveral during the space race to the moon. During his visit, the President came across a man mopping the floor, and asked him, "What's your position here?" The gentleman looked up from his pail and proudly replied, "I'm helping to send a man to the moon, Mr. President." Such is the power of alignment—when every person, regardless of role or rank, possesses a clear line of sight between their job and the organization's loftiest goals.

You may not be sending a man to the moon, but whatever you're working towards requires the total commitment and alignment of all your people. This chapter will discuss how the Balanced Scorecard framework can be used to drive organizational alignment from top to bottom through the process of cascading. We'll explore what the concept is all about and why it's critical to both employees and the organization, and examine techniques you can use to develop aligned Scorecards at your agency.

WHAT IS CASCADING?

In a recent poll conducted by Harris Interactive, of 23,000 U.S. residents employed full time, only 37% said they had a clear understanding of what their organization was trying to achieve and why. The same study discovered that only 9% believed their work teams had clear, measurable goals.[1] Another report performed by consulting firm Watson Wyatt obtained similar results, with 49% of employees saying they understood the steps their companies were taking to reach new business goals, a 20% drop since 2000. In reviewing the data, one researcher said "there is tremendous positive impact to the bottom line when employees see strong connections between company goals and their jobs. Many employees aren't seeing that connection."[2] Although nonprofits and public sector organizations are not bottom line–driven, you too will benefit greatly when employees see the connection between what they do everyday and how those actions affect overall goals. In fact, considering that many employees are drawn to the public and nonprofit sectors by the strong mission orientation you offer, it's virtually mandatory that your staff see how their work contributes to overall goals in order for them to derive the meaning that attracted them to you in the first place.

Cascading the Balanced Scorecard is a method designed to bridge the considerable learning gap that exists in most organizations. Specifically, cascading refers to the process of developing Balanced Scorecards at each and every level of your organization. When I use the phrase "Balanced Scorecard" in this context, I am referring to the overall process. Some organizations will cascade both Strategy Maps of objectives and Balanced Scorecards of measures from top to bottom, while others will choose to create just one high-level Strategy Map and cascade measures only. We'll return to that debate later in the chapter.

The Scorecards constructed at lower levels will align with your highest-level Balanced Scorecard by identifying the objectives and measures lower-level groups will track in order to gauge their contribution to overall success. Some objectives and measures will be used throughout the organization and appear on every Scorecard. Employee satisfaction is a good example. However, in many respects, the real value of cascaded Scorecards is evident from the unique objectives and measures lower-level groups engineer to signal their specific contribution to overall strategy implementation. When I introduced this concept to one client recently, a participant half-jokingly commented, "So you're not talking about the stuff I use to clean my dishes?" No, we're not talking about Cascade™ dishwasher detergent here, but the cascading process will clean away something far more important: the misunderstanding and confusion existing between employee and organizational goals.

Peter Drucker has commented that "the nonprofit must be information-based. It must be structured around information that flows up from the individuals doing the work to the people at the top—the ones who are, in the end, accountable—and around information flowing down. This flow of information is essential because a nonprofit organization has to be a learning organization."[3] Every organization today must make continuous learning a core competency in order to survive the unprecedented changes we witness on a daily basis. Cascading facilitates learning by fostering a two-way flow of information

Exhibit 9.1   Knowledge and Information Flow Two Ways When Cascading the Balanced Scorecard

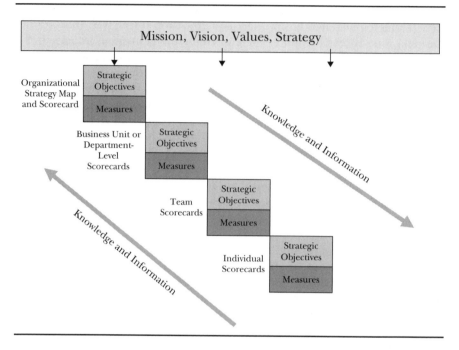

up and down the organizational hierarchy (see Exhibit 9.1). As Scorecards are created at lower levels of the organization, employees of every function and rank are given the opportunity to demonstrate how their actions can lead to improved results for everyone. Simultaneously, as results are analyzed across the agency, leaders benefit from the ability to view results that span their organization. Analysis is no longer limited to a few high-level indicators that must serve as abstractions for an entire agency; instead, cascaded Scorecards provide real-time data for decision making, resource allocation, and most importantly, strategic learning.

In the public sector, cascading should be considered more of a necessity than a luxury or option presented by the Balanced Scorecard. Achieving results in the public domain demands collaboration from a vast web of groups that span levels and service functions. As an example, a family attempting to secure health insurance for their children could simultaneously be interacting with government health insurance specialists, immunization providers, and family counselors. Each of these groups plays a vital part in helping the family achieve its goal of receiving insurance for their children. Therefore, each must document this contribution in the form of performance measures on the Balanced Scorecard. Taken cumulatively, the actions of program providers across the enterprise will move the agency ever closer to achieving its overall mission.

In his book on Olympic rowing, *The Amateurs*, David Halberstam writes that "When most oarsmen talked about their perfect moments in a boat, they referred not so much to winning a race but to the feel of the boat, all eight oars in the water together, the synchronization almost perfect. In moments like that, the boat seemed to lift right out of the water. Oarsmen called that the moment of swing. When a boat has swing, its motion seems almost effortless."[4] I can't imagine a better description of the graceful power that can be achieved when people work together towards a common goal. Cascading holds the promise to bring that same feeling of effortless motion to your organization.

Not only does the cascading process align employee actions to strategy, it is consistently cited as a key factor in the success of Balanced Scorecard programs. Kaplan and Norton have discovered that the greatest gap between Balanced Scorecard Hall of Fame organizations and all others occurs in aligning the organization to the strategy. This, they said, "demonstrates that effective organizational alignment, while difficult to achieve, has probably the biggest payoff of any management practice."[5] Not surprising when you consider that through alignment, you're harnessing the greatest resource known to mankind: the minds and hearts of your employees. Successful Scorecard implementers know that those on the front line must embrace and use this tool if it is to reach the level of effectiveness it's capable of achieving. Cascading the Scorecard allows you to reach your entire organization and supply them with the means of answering the critical question, "How do I add value and make a meaningful contribution to our success?" The answer lies in the objectives and measures embedded in Balanced Scorecards throughout your organization.[6]

The Search for Meaning

Man's Search for Meaning is among the most powerful and gripping books I have ever read. In it, Austrian psychiatrist Victor Frankl describes his experiences as he clung to life in a Nazi concentration camp. He had lost everything and yet it was his discovery that a greater purpose can allow us to rise above even the bleakest of circumstances that led to his psychological emancipation from the Nazis. He used his experience in the development of "logotherapy," which focuses on the meaning of human existence as well as on man's search for such a meaning.[7]

Does man's search for meaning end upon entering the workplace? Does the first ring from the phone on our desk erase any existential cravings? The answer is an unequivocal no. Now, more than ever, people from all walks of life hold high expectations. They demand a higher purpose beyond a paycheck from their jobs. Nowhere is this more evident than in the public and nonprofit arenas where employees are typically compelled by the organization's guiding mission and values. Employees are asking, "Why is my organization important to society, how does it contribute something of value?" A lack of alignment between personal objectives and broad organizational goals obscures any hope of discovering true meaning and contribution through our work. Cascading the Balanced Scorecard restores the pledge of organizations to help all employees find meaning in their chosen professions. The creation of objectives and measures that forge a direct link to high-level goals provides all employees with the opportunity to demonstrate that what they do everyday is indeed critical to success.

THE CASCADING PROCESS

One very successful corporation that grasps the importance of alignment is Honda Motors. This recognition most likely stems from their founder Soichiro Honda, who described the sacred obligations of senior leadership as:

1. Craft a vision: What we will be.

2. Create goals: What four or five things we must do to get there.

3. Alignment: Translate the work of each person into alignment with the goals.

He's really describing the process of cascading performance measures very well. First, we craft the vision that will guide the organization. Next, we develop key performance measures we can track, and finally, we translate the work of each person into alignment with the goals. Mr. Honda didn't go on to say how to create alignment, but we now know the best way to do that is through cascading performance objectives and measures. In this section, we'll examine how you can successfully align employee objectives and measures throughout the organization.

Develop Implementation Principles

Just stop for a moment to reflect upon how far you will have traveled to get to this point in your Balanced Scorecard implementation. It began as an idea—perhaps someone read an article, attended a seminar, or learned of the Scorecard from a colleague. You then undertook the challenging tasks of forming your team; gathering materials; reviewing your mission, values, vision, and strategy; and developing objectives on a Strategy Map and measures on your Scorecard. It would be an understatement to suggest that you learned a thing or two about the Balanced Scorecard and its implementation at your organization along the way. Before you begin your cascading efforts, pause for a moment to reflect on and catalog those key insights.

The Balanced Scorecard system you've created is a true team effort. Your cross-functional team contributed the knowledge that exists in every far corner of your agency to craft a Strategy Map and Scorecard that will clearly articulate your strategic story. However, going forward, the cascading process may represent more of a diffused effort. Your team members may now be tasked with the responsibility of leading the development of cascaded Scorecards within their work group or business unit. Consistent implementation practices across the organization are an absolute must should you hope to gain the benefits offered by true strategic alignment. To ensure your cascading efforts are consistent and aligned, consider convening your Balanced Scorecard team and all those individuals that will have a hand in leading the development of Cascaded Scorecards. A one-day session in which you review the lessons you've learned along the way and specifically document the principles you expect to employ going forward, will go a long way towards ensuring you create Scorecards that paint a consistent picture. Outlined here are several key elements you should consider when developing your cascading plan.[8]

Cascading Strategy Maps and Balanced Scorecards, or Just Scorecards   The initial question to answer is: Will you cascade both Maps and Scorecards or simply Scorecards? My database of clients is split on this, although if pressed to do the math, I would estimate a slight majority cascade both elements of the framework. My recommendation is to cascade both since a Strategy Map provides a powerful communication tool that can be employed in any unit, department, or group to signify the key elements of success, with the accompanying measures providing the link to accountability for results. Most practitioners agree with the value of communication but argue that creating Maps throughout the enterprise represents an unnecessary step leading to "paralysis by analysis"—too many Maps spawning an abundance of unique measures that will unleash a heavy administrative burden to manage.

Balanced Scorecard Perspectives   Will all groups be required to use the four perspectives of the Balanced Scorecard: Customer, Internal Processes, Financial, and Employee Learning and Growth? This assumes you used the standard roster. If not, the question still applies—will you require all groups to adopt the perspectives you've chosen at the highest level of the organization? Or, will individual groups have the liberty to develop their own perspectives and perspective names? "Personalizing" the Map and Balanced Scorecard may produce benefits in the form of enhanced buy-in and local understanding, but dissimilar terms scattered throughout the agency may lead to confusion.

Number of Objectives and Measures   Will you impose a limit on the number of objectives and measures any group may have as part of their Balanced Scorecard? Keep in mind that as you begin cascading the Scorecard, you could quickly generate dozens, if not hundreds, of performance measures throughout the organization. My advice is to avoid choosing one single number and instead focus on a not-to-exceed total of objectives and measures.

Use of "Corporate" Objectives and Measures   Corporate in this case refers to your highest-level Strategy Map and Scorecard. When developing their Maps and Scorecards, will groups be required to use certain corporate objectives and measures or have *carte blanche* in developing unique indicators that tell their story? Some organizations will ask groups to use the same objectives and measures (whenever possible) as those used at the highest level. The goal is to encourage uniformity and consistency throughout the organization. Dell Inc. is one such organization. Founder Michael Dell sees significant benefits in this approach: "Our performance metrics are the same around the world, which allows us to identify the best practices on any given dimension: generating leads, increasing margins, capturing new customers. If a council sees that Japan has figured out a great strategy for selling more servers, its job is to learn how Japan is doing it and transfer the lessons to other countries."[9] A possible disadvantage of this approach is limiting the creativity of groups as they determine how they can best influence high-level objectives and measures. As a compromise, organizations will sometimes impose a limited number of "required" objectives and measures on all groups while also including "shared" between interdependent groups, and of course, allowing "unique" additions as well.

Ensure Understanding of Your Highest-Level Strategy Map and Scorecard before Cascading

You may have hesitated to write objective statements as described in Chapter 7, or bristled at the thought of completing the data dictionaries presented in Chapter 6, but you're about to receive the payback for those arduous tasks. They are just a couple of the tools you can use to ensure everyone involved in the cascading process has a detailed understanding of your highest-level Strategy Map and Balanced Scorecard.

Your "corporate" level Map and Scorecard represent the starting point for your cascading journey. They contain the objectives and measures that weave through the four perspectives, informing everyone of your strategic story. For individuals shouldering the responsibility of leading cascading efforts, in-depth knowledge of the Strategy Map and Scorecard is vital. Imagine someone leading a cascading session in a lower-level department and beginning the workshop with a comment like, "Okay, we say here on the Strategy Map that we're going to delight the customer. I don't really know what that means. What do you think?" Not exactly the stuff oratorical legends are made of. Contrast that with someone who possesses a deep understanding of high-level objectives and measures. He or she is in a position to offer something of this nature: "Delighting the customer is our first customer objective. This is critical to our strategy of expanding into new services since current clients will often be our best source of referral information. We'll measure it using quarterly surveys consisting of five questions. . . . "

Context that will allow for thought-provoking and beneficial conversations about the objective has been established.

Understanding of your Strategy Map and Scorecard is achieved mainly through communication and education. You have a number of tools at your disposal. Consider any of the following: your intranet, presentations from Scorecard team members, Strategy Map and Scorecard brochures, newsletters, or town hall meetings.

"Influence" Is the Key to Cascading

The goal of cascading is to allow all groups within your organization the opportunity to demonstrate how their actions contribute to overall success. In describing this process, I will assume you are cascading the highest-level Strategy Map to all levels of your organization. In other words, lower-level groups will have the opportunity to develop their own Strategy Maps that offer their aligned objectives. Given this assumption, their next step would be the creation of measures for each of the objectives appearing on their Strategy Map. Let's use Exhibit 9.2 to review this concept. To fit the page, the exhibit has been truncated with each perspective displaying objectives (the domain of the Strategy Map), along with measures, targets, and initiatives (found in a Balanced Scorecard).

It all begins with your highest-level Strategy Map—what some would refer to as the corporate-level or organization-wide Map. The objectives appearing on this Strategy Map represent what you consider to be the critical variables driving your success. Therefore, every Map subsequently created at all levels of the organization should link back to this document.

The first level of cascading occurs as business units (as described in Exhibit 9.2; your terminology may differ) examine the high-level Strategy Map and ask themselves, "Which of these objectives can we influence?" The answers to that question will form the basis for their own Strategy Map. Chances are, they won't be able to exert an impact on each and every objective appearing on the high-level Map. After all, organizations build value by combining the disparate skills of all employees within every function. Therefore, each group should rightly focus on the objectives over which they may exert an influence. However, if a group is unable to demonstrate a link to any objectives, you would have to seriously consider what value they are adding to the whole. The business unit may choose to use the language shown in the high-level Strategy Map or create objectives that more accurately reflect the true essence of how they add value to the organization.

Once the business unit has developed its own Strategy Map—one that aligns with the highest-level Map—demonstrating how the unit influences success, their job transitions to the development of accompanying performance measures for each objective. Once again, they should return to the top and determine if measures used on the highest-level Balanced Scorecard are

Exhibit 9.2 The Cascading Process

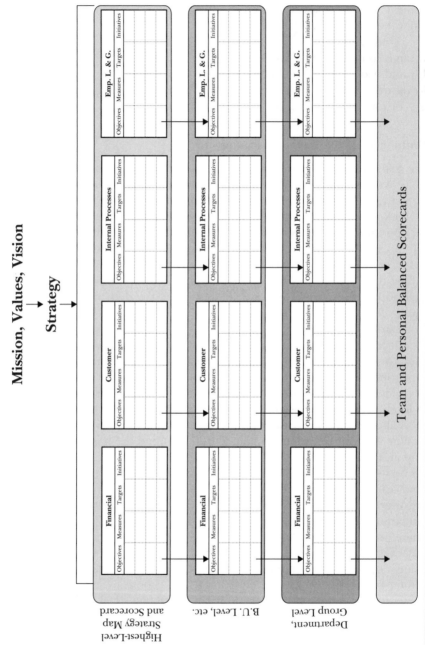

Adapted from *Balanced Scorecard Step-by-Step: Maximizing Performance and Maintaining Results, 2nd Edition,* Paul R. Niven (John Wiley & Sons, 2006).

applicable to their operations. Some objectives and measures, often in the Financial and Employee Learning and Growth objectives, will flow freely from top to bottom in an organization. For example, it's quite common to see an objective such as "enhance employee engagement" appear in the Employee Learning and Growth Perspective of the top-level Strategy Map, with the corresponding measure of "employee engagement score" materializing on the Balanced Scorecard. Every group within the organization could adopt this objective and measure with no change to the wording of either.

Once business units have developed Strategy Maps and Balanced Scorecards, the groups below them are ready to take part in the process. Individual departments will now review the Strategy Map and Scorecard of the business unit to which they report and determine which of the objectives they can influence. Their Map is formed by making that determination. With a Strategy Map formed, they develop performance measures to gauge their success. Again, they may use similarly termed objectives and measures, or develop unique names for their elements.

Let's look at an example of cascading using a fictional city government organization. Exhibit 9.3 provides excerpts from Strategy Maps and Scorecards at three levels of this organization, which will demonstrate the principles of cascading just discussed.

Within the Customer Perspective of their Strategy Map, the city has chosen an objective of providing safe, convenient transportation. To gauge their effectiveness on this objective, they will measure the increase in average ridership of public transportation. A 10% increase for the year is the target.

The Department of Transportation is one of several business units within the city. When developing its own Strategy Map, organizers began by closely inspecting the city's Map to determine which of the objectives they could influence. As is the case with all city business units, the Department of Transportation is anxious to show how their important work links to the city's overall goals. When reviewing the city's Customer Perspective, they see the objective of providing safe, convenient transportation and feel they have a strong impact on this objective. They too have a goal of providing safe and convenient transportation, so they carry the objective forward to their own Strategy Map with no change in the wording. However, the measure of increased ridership is not considered appropriate for them. It's a critical indicator, but they would like to develop a measure that indicates how *they influence* ridership. The team concludes that by ensuring the city's entire fleet of public transportation vehicles is available every day, they can help the city increase ridership. Hence, they measure the percentage of fleet that is available.

Several groups comprise the Department of Transportation, one of which is the Operations Department. Among their many responsibilities is ensuring the city's fleet of vehicles is serviced efficiently. When developing their Strategy Map, they begin by reviewing the Map of the business unit to which they report: the Department of Transportation. Upon review, they see the objective of providing safe and convenient transportation. They feel

Exhibit 9.3 Cascading the Balanced Scorecard

	Excerpt from the City Strategy Map and Scorecard		
Perspective	Objective	Measure	Target
Customer	Provide safe, convenient transportation	Increase in average ridership of public transportation	10%

	Department of Transportation Map and Scorecard Excerpt		
Perspective	Objective	Measure	Target
Customer	Provide safe, convenient transportation	Percentage of fleet available	90%

	Operations Group Map and Scorecard Excerpt		
Perspective	Objective	Measure	Target
Customer	Provide safe, convenient transportation	Percentage of vehicle repairs completed within 24 hours	75%

they can impact this objective, and thus choose it for their own Customer Perspective, again adopting the language used above them with no change necessary. They ask themselves how they might influence the measure of fleet availability and realize that if they're able to complete vehicle repairs in a timely fashion, the Department will have more vehicles at its disposal and the public will be presented with more riding options. They strive to complete at least 75% of vehicle repairs within 24 hours.

Although each of the three Strategy Maps profiled in this example share a common objective, the measure chosen for the Scorecard at each level is representative of what is necessary for the group to contribute to overall success. Those linked objectives and performance measures are the key to ensuring alignment throughout the city. Employees in the Operations Department are now able to conclusively demonstrate how their activities link back to a key goal for the city. Likewise, city officials can rest assured that Operations personnel are focused on the necessary elements to drive value for the city's citizens.

Support Group Balanced Scorecards

Support groups such as human resources, finance, and information technology (IT) often feel like the Rodney Dangerfields of the organization: They get no respect! In truth, some reading this may feel I'm contributing to that predicament by using the moniker "support group." No disrespect intended; we're all well aware that corporate resource groups, shared service, support groups—whatever term you choose—provide valuable offerings, without which actual service delivery to customers would most likely be compromised severely. However, there exists among public and nonprofits, and in many private sector firms, a temptation to label these groups as pure overhead and diminish their valuable role.

The Balanced Scorecard can change all that. Support groups should have the same opportunity as any other department to illustrate their contributions, and the Scorecard provides the forum. Typically, units that have the responsibility for providing services to the entire organization will look to the high-level organizational Strategy Map and Scorecard when developing their own objectives and measures. Their quest is to examine the objectives on the "corporate" Strategy Map and contemplate how the group plays a role in their success.

In addition to demonstrating alignment with the highest-level Strategy Map and Balanced Scorecard, support unit Maps and Scorecards typically display a number of common themes across the perspectives.[10] Within the Financial Perspective, we would expect the group to report on both the efficiency and effectiveness of their operations. The Customer Perspective of a support group outlines how the group will add value to *their* customers—other departments and the organization as a whole—and customarily includes objectives centering on customer knowledge and solution delivery.

Internally, support groups must focus on forging partnerships and working collaboratively with other departments, operating at the upper bands of high efficiency and innovating to produce the solutions their customers demand. Finally, within the Employee Learning and Growth Perspective, the group will turn the spotlight inward, ensuring their team possesses the skills they require, the information necessary to deliver on Internal and Customer objectives, and a supportive work environment.

Unlike their colleagues working with external clients and other stakeholders of the organization, support group employees are often shielded from much of the direct service provision taking place. Cascading the Scorecard to these units lifts the strategy veil and provides a much-needed line of sight between support work and the mission of the organization.

Personal Balanced Scorecards[11]

In a recent survey conducted by Salary.com of 2,000 employees and 330 Human Resource (HR) professionals, the researchers found a glaring, but not entirely surprising, contradiction: 66% of the HR professionals believed their company's performance reviews were effective while only 39% of employees echoed that view.[12] It seems as though the annual performance appraisal process is one fraught with issues for management and employees alike. Companies will expend significant energy in promoting a formal appraisal process, issuing memos, providing templates with information on the competencies and behaviors they desire to see, and training employees on how to develop an effective plan. However, there is often little follow-up beyond this initial splash of activity. Former General Electric (GE) CEO turned corporate curmudgeon, Jack Welch, blames it on the paper chase suggesting that "If your evaluation system involves more than two pages of paperwork per person, something is wrong!"[13] One of Welch's apostles at GE, Larry Bossidy, who has been a very successful CEO in his own right, agrees with the succinct approach to performance reviews advocated by his former boss. He suggests a simple one-page form listing what the employee does well, what he can improve upon, and how they can work together to fill any gaps.[14]

When I discuss the performance appraisal process with new clients, I'm often greeted with rolling eyes and shaking heads. Even organizations that follow-up on the appraisal process and hold review sessions with employees are invariably behind schedule. Amazing how this critical activity involving the most precious of resources tends to get pushed to the back burner. But when we critically examine the process at most organizations, there is little wonder why this sorry state of affairs exists. Very often, the performance ratings are completely subjective and based purely on a manager or supervisor's limited view of employee performance. This does little to engender trust on the part of employees and instead engenders suspicion of the process. Throughout the performance period, there is infrequent feedback to employees, and even when feedback is offered, it typically concerns outcomes and results, not behaviors. But the most egregious omission of the process is the lack of alignment between personal and organizational goals. Employees have little or no idea how success on their performance review will positively impact the company's success.

Cascading the Balanced Scorecard to the individual employee level can mitigate, if not entirely eliminate, many of the issues we find with the normal performance appraisal process. Some of the many benefits derived from having employees develop their own personal Balanced Scorecards are:

- *Builds awareness of the Balanced Scorecard.* Developing Scorecards at the individual level provides yet another opportunity to share with all employees the principles and techniques inherent in the Balanced Scorecard system.

- *Generates commitment to the Scorecard.* There is little doubt that increased involvement in virtually any activity will tend to increase commitment to that cause. So it goes with the Balanced Scorecard. Having employees learn about the Scorecard and develop their own series of linked objectives and measures will certainly boost support from this critical audience.

- *Increases comprehension of aligned Scorecards.* In order to develop their individual Scorecards, employees must first understand the objectives and measures appearing in all cascaded Scorecards from the high-level organizational Scorecard to the business unit Scorecard to their team or department's Card. Thus, cascading supplies an outstanding training opportunity.

- *Offers a clear line of sight from employee goals to organizational strategy.* Developing personal Balanced Scorecards that align to team or department Scorecards allows every employee to demonstrate how their specific actions are making a difference and leading to improved overall results.

- *Builds support for the goal setting process.* Using the Balanced Scorecard can breathe new life into often tired and irrelevant employee goal-setting processes.

The format you follow for personal Balanced Scorecards is limited only by your imagination. Exhibit 9.4 provides one possible version of a template your employees can utilize to develop personal Balanced Scorecards. This template is based on the cascading efforts of a government-owned electric utility organization. The document merges two key areas: cascaded Scorecards and personal development plans. To maximize educational and practical value, it is split into two pages. Page one serves the important purpose of outlining mission, vision, and strategy and establishing a line of sight for the employee. The remainder of the page illustrates the cascading Scorecards

Exhibit 9.4 Personal Balanced Scorecard Template (Page 1)

PERSONAL BALANCED SCORECARD

Name:	Department:	Date Covered:

Our Mission and Vision

Mission: Provide low cost energy to help our communities prosper. *Vision:* Be the #1 Energy supplier by 2010.

Our Strategy

Utilize state of the art technology and human capital principles to maintain low cost energy supply.

Our Balanced Scorecards

Perspective	Corporate Scorecard Measures	Business Unit Measures	Department Measures
Financial	F1. Return on Investment	F1. Manageable Cost Reduction	F1. Lower Administrative Spending F2. Increase Miscellaneous Revenue
Customer	C1. Customer Loyalty Rating C2. Sales Volume	C1. Customer Loyalty Rating C2. Outage Performance Index	C1. Customer Loyalty Rating C2. Meter Reading C3. Call Centre Performance C4. Reliability Index
Internal Process	IP1. Environmental Performance IP2. Number of new products and services	IP1. Environmental Performance IP2. Service Quality Programs in place	IP1. System Maintenance IP2. Inspections IP3. Service Quality Programs
Employee Learning & Growth	E1. Safety Rating E2. Employee Commitment Rating E3. Employee Development	E1. Number of Accidents E2. Employee Commitment Rating E3. Employee Development	E1. Number of Personal Accidents E2. Number of Vehicle Accidents E3. Employee Commitment Rating E4. Employee Development

DEPARTMENT MANAGER
PERSONAL BALANCED SCORECARD

Perspective	Objective	Measure	Target	Related PDP Goals
Customer	Increase Customer Loyalty	Presentations to local trade groups	15	• Develop 5 new professional contacts this year.
	Ensure Outage Reliability	Plant visits	30	• Join 2 trade associations
Employee Learning & Growth	Promote Safety	Departmental Injuries	1	• Attend Safety Training course
	Develop Skill Sets	% Employees completing business education	90%	• Complete facilitator training
	Develop Skill Sets	Complete Personal Development Plan	–	• Complete PDP by mid-year
	Enhance Employee Commitment	Departmental Commitment Rating	80	• Support employee volunteer efforts
Internal Process	Provide Meter Reading & Meter Changes	% on time readings	95%	
	Enhance System Maintenance	Conduct plant audits	40	
Financial	Minimize Administrative Spending	Local Costs	Budget less 1%	• Complete 2 courses in Finance
	Grow Revenue	Increase Departmental miscellaneous revenue	10% increase	• Lead departmental brainstorming sessions on revenue enhancement

relevant to that individual. Summarized versions of the Organizational, Business Unit, and Departmental Balanced Scorecards are provided. Displaying this "individualized cascading" demonstrates the path that has led to this point and greatly facilitates the completion of the personal Balanced Scorecard on page two.

While we might consider page one a learning opportunity, page two has a more specific purpose—allowing the individual employee to define the specific objectives and measures he will pursue to help his department reach its objectives and outline the action steps he'll take to achieve success. The first step for the individual is developing the objectives, measures, and targets that comprise her individual Scorecard. By displaying all linked Scorecards on page one, the development of personal goals should flow quite smoothly with discussion and coaching. Next, the employee may begin to construct a personal development plan (PDP) based on the goals established on their Scorecard. This document may or may not replace the need for a formal PDP, but it will certainly facilitate the development of that document by identifying the key areas of focus for the individual.

This section focused almost exclusively on the benefits employees can derive from developing personal Balanced Scorecards—knowledge of the Scorecard system, understanding of organizational objectives and measures, and alignment with overall goals. However, senior managers also have much to gain from this process. Cascading to this level allows managers to gain a high level of visibility into the specific actions contributing to, or detracting from, overall organizational results. Take the case of one travel agency I worked with. Senior managers at this organization monitor a productivity index that tracks the number of tickets issued per hour by individual agents. The measure appears on the corporate Balanced Scorecard but is also cascaded down to the individual agent level. When actual results begin to lag expectations, senior managers look to their cascading Balanced Scorecards for an answer. Examining regional performance (the first level of cascading) on the productivity index provided little information since most areas were producing similar results. However, when managers examined specific site Scorecards, they found some very interesting deviations that were driving the high-level corporate outcome. It turns out that agents who catered to professional service firms (attorneys, accountants, and consultants) were producing consistently lower results than other groups. When questioned, they noted that clients from these firms were frequently changing plans that made it difficult to actually issue a ticket. Without the questions spawned by the Balanced Scorecard, senior management could have made the faulty and dangerous assumption that these sites were simply poor performers and taken inappropriate action. Armed with the knowledge gleaned from cascaded Balanced Scorecards, managers were able to adjust the targets to more accurately reflect the nature of clients served by different sites.

Checking the Alignment of Cascaded Balanced Scorecards

We all know the many dangers inherent in making assumptions. For me, the point was driven home in a razor-sharp way by a junior high school teacher who made his way to the blackboard one day and wrote a sentence that has remained with me to this day (I'm sure you've heard of it): "When you assume, you make an a** out of you and me." I can't remember if he actually spelled it out or not. Cascading the Balanced Scorecard is no different. The act of developing Scorecards up and down the organizational hierarchy can prove to be an exciting and liberating effort, but you must be sure there is true alignment existing from top to bottom. Assuming alignment where none exists could lead to unrealistic targets, missing measures, departments inadvertently working against one another, misallocated resources, and a whole lot of confused people.

As each level of cascading is completed, pause to review the Scorecards just created to validate the presence of alignment. Each "chain" of Scorecards should be evaluated to ensure the objectives and measures flow in a demonstrable pattern leading towards the objectives and measures embodied in the highest-level Scorecard. Upon conclusion of the critique, your Scorecard auditing team should meet with developers at lower levels and discuss any modifications that would improve the quality of their Scorecards. Exhibit 9.5 provides some additional things to look for when reviewing cascaded Strategy Maps and Scorecards.

Once you've completed your reviews, you should open the feedback process to a wider audience. Give all employees the chance to kick the tires of their colleagues' Scorecards, along the way providing advice and learning a thing or two about what their colleagues actually do! In Chapter 8, I outlined the "open houses" conducted by the County of San Diego. Employees of the Health and Human Services Agency were invited to a session during which they learned more about the Balanced Scorecard and had the chance to view Scorecards from groups across the agency. Not only did those attending provide great input on the objectives and measures they saw, but they began to see how collaboration between groups could drive overall agency results. I overheard, "Oh, I didn't know you did that. . . ." several times during the events. The inevitable reply was always, "We should meet and talk about this." Rome wasn't built in a day, but when people start talking about strategy, they're thinking about strategy, and when they're thinking about strategy, good things tend to happen.

A Final Thought on Cascading

Of those items within your control, cascading may be the single most important ingredient of a successful Balanced Scorecard implementation. You can't control the level of executive sponsorship you receive or predict any crisis that may derail your efforts. You can, however, make the decision

Exhibit 9.5   What to Look for When Reviewing Cascaded Strategy Maps and Scorecards

- *Linkage to Related Maps and Scorecards.* Don't forget the key principle here is cascading—driving the Scorecard process to lower levels in the organization. Each Strategy Map and Balanced Scorecard should contain objectives and measures that influence the next group in the chain.

- *Linkage to Strategy.* The Balanced Scorecard is a tool for translating strategy. The objectives and measures appearing on cascaded Maps and Scorecards should demonstrate a linkage to the organization's overarching strategy, and their achievement should signal progress towards the mission.

- *Appropriate Targets.* Target setting can be a difficult exercise requiring significant professional judgment. Ensure cascaded targets will lead to the fulfillment of higher-level targets throughout the chain.

- *Coverage of Key Objectives.* The chief tenet of cascading is that of influence. What can we do at our level to influence the next Scorecard in the chain. Not every group will influence every high-level objective and measure, but across the agency, the complete population of highest level objectives and measures should receive adequate coverage.

- *Adherence to Cascading Principles.* Ensure cascaded Maps and measures conform to the principles you developed; for example, consistent use of perspective names and number of objectives and measures permitted.

Adapted from *Balanced Scorecard Step-by-Step: Maximizing Performance and Maintaining Results, 2nd Edition,* Paul R. Niven (John Wiley & Sons, 2006).

to drive the power of the Balanced Scorecard system to all levels of your organization.

Developing a high-level Strategy Map and Scorecard is a great start, but how many people are really involved in the effort? Involvement is the key to ownership. If you want your employees to take true ownership of your collective success, let them carve out a share for themselves. Allow them to create a language of success with themselves at the center. Everyone wins as interest, alignment, accountability, knowledge, and results are all enhanced in the process.

NOTES

1. Stephen R. Covey, *The 8th Habit* (New York: The Free Press, 2004), p. 2.

2. As quoted in Stephen Taub, "Dazed and Confused," *CFO.com,* September 11, 2002.

3. Peter F. Drucker, *Managing the Non-Profit Organzation* (New York: HarperBusiness, 1990), p. 182.

4. James Surowiecki, *The Wisdom of Crowds* (New York; Doubleday, 2004), p. 176.

5. David P. Norton and Randall H. Russell, "Best Practices in Managing the Execution of Strategy," *Balanced Scorecard Report*, July–August 2004, p. 3.

6. Paul R. Niven, *Balanced Scorecard Step-by-Step: Maximizing Performance and Maintaining Results, 2nd Edition* (Hoboken, NJ: John Wiley & Sons, 2006), p. 201.

7. Victor E. Frankl, *Man's Search for Meaning* (Boston: Beacon Press, 4th edition, 1992).

8. Paul R. Niven, *Balanced Scorecard Diagnostics: Maintaining Maximum Performance* (Hoboken, NJ: John Wiley & Sons, 2005), pp. 129–130.

9. Thomas A. Stewart and Louise O'Brien, "Execution without Excuses," *Harvard Business Review*, March 2005, pp. 102–111.

10. Robert S. Kaplan and David P. Norton, *Alignment* (Boston: Harvard Business School Press, 2006), p. 139.

11. Adapted from Paul R. Niven, *Balanced Scorecard Step-by-Step: Maximizing Performance and Maintaining Results, 2nd Edition* (Hoboken, NJ: John Wiley & Sons, 2006), pp. 211–215.

12. From "How'm I Doing," *CFO Magazine*, February 2007, p. 21.

13. Jack Welch with Suzy Welch, *Winning* (New York: HarperBusiness, 2005), p. 104.

14. Larry Bossidy, "What Your Leader Expects of You," *Harvard Business Review*, April 2007, pp. 58–65.

10

Linking Resource Allocation to the Balanced Scorecard

Roadmap for Chapter 10 Humorist Will Rogers once remarked that "The budget is a mythical bean bag. Congress votes mythical beans into it, and then tries to reach in and pull real beans out." As long as they've existed, budgets have been a source of monetary pain and controversy for public, nonprofit, and private firms alike. Ostensibly designed to pair dollars with results, most budgeting efforts lack a true "strategic stake," and are instead characterized by chicanery and politics of the highest order. One recent study conducted by CFO Research Services found that 45% of respondents felt budgeting is contentious and political, 72% said the process yields unrealistic numbers, and 53% said budgets make managers behave badly.[1]

In this chapter, we'll examine the role of the Balanced Scorecard in linking resource allocation to strategy. A five-step process will be presented to demonstrate how a series of cascaded Scorecards can drive the budgeting process in any organization. Following the techniques outlined in this chapter will help your agency avoid the dubious distinction of joining 60% of all organizations that do not link budgets to strategy.

HISTORY OF PERFORMANCE AND BUDGETS

Interest in the linkage of performance measures to budgets has been growing in the public sector for many years. The past dozen years in particular have introduced a number of elements improving the environment for a merger of budgets and performance.

276

In 1990, the Chief Financial Officers Act was passed. While the Act's main focus was the improvement of federal financial management, it also referenced the development of performance measures. Following on its heels was the Government Performance and Results Act (GPRA) of 1993. The bill decreed that all federal agencies engage in strategic planning, objective setting, and performance measurement. Going one step further, the GPRA mandated that, beginning in 1999, performance measures be reported in the budgets of federal programs.[2] Budgeting and performance measurement was provided yet another attention boost when then–Vice President Al Gore's National Performance Review issued their findings. The report recommended a conversion from budgets based on inputs to a system focused on results. More recently, President George W. Bush has, for the first time in history, sent a budget plan to congress that will formally assess the performance of government agencies and programs, and to some extent link financing to their results.

All of these initiatives are noble and well intentioned, but results have thus far been less than encouraging. In one study by the General Accounting Office (GAO), it was determined that a majority of federal managers are largely ignoring performance information when allocating resources.[3] Part of the problem can be traced to performance measures that are ill-conceived and poorly designed. As the backbone of any link to resource allocation, measures must accurately and reliably track outcomes.

As you've read throughout this book, the Balanced Scorecard has been proven to surmount many of the obstacles associated with typical performance measurement systems. Therefore, nonprofits and government agencies wishing to pursue the linkage of budgets to performance measures are well advised to first create a Balanced Scorecard system. Assuming you've followed the advice set forth in this book, the remainder of the chapter will itemize the steps necessary to link your resource allocation process back to your Balanced Scorecard.

LINKING BUDGETS AND BALANCED SCORECARDS

The process of aligning budgets and Balanced Scorecard measures is outlined in Exhibit 10.1. As always, the agency's mission, values, vision, and strategy are the starting point in our discussion. These building blocks are translated into a high-level Strategy Map and Balanced Scorecard for the organization, which are then used as the key reference points for cascaded Maps and Scorecards throughout the organization. As we discovered in Chapter 8, all Scorecards include not only objectives, measures, and targets, but equally important, they contain initiatives. These programs, projects, and plans describe how the agency will go about achieving the performance target. As we'll soon learn, it is the initiatives that forge the bond between

Exhibit 10.1 Linking the Balanced Scorecard to Budgeting

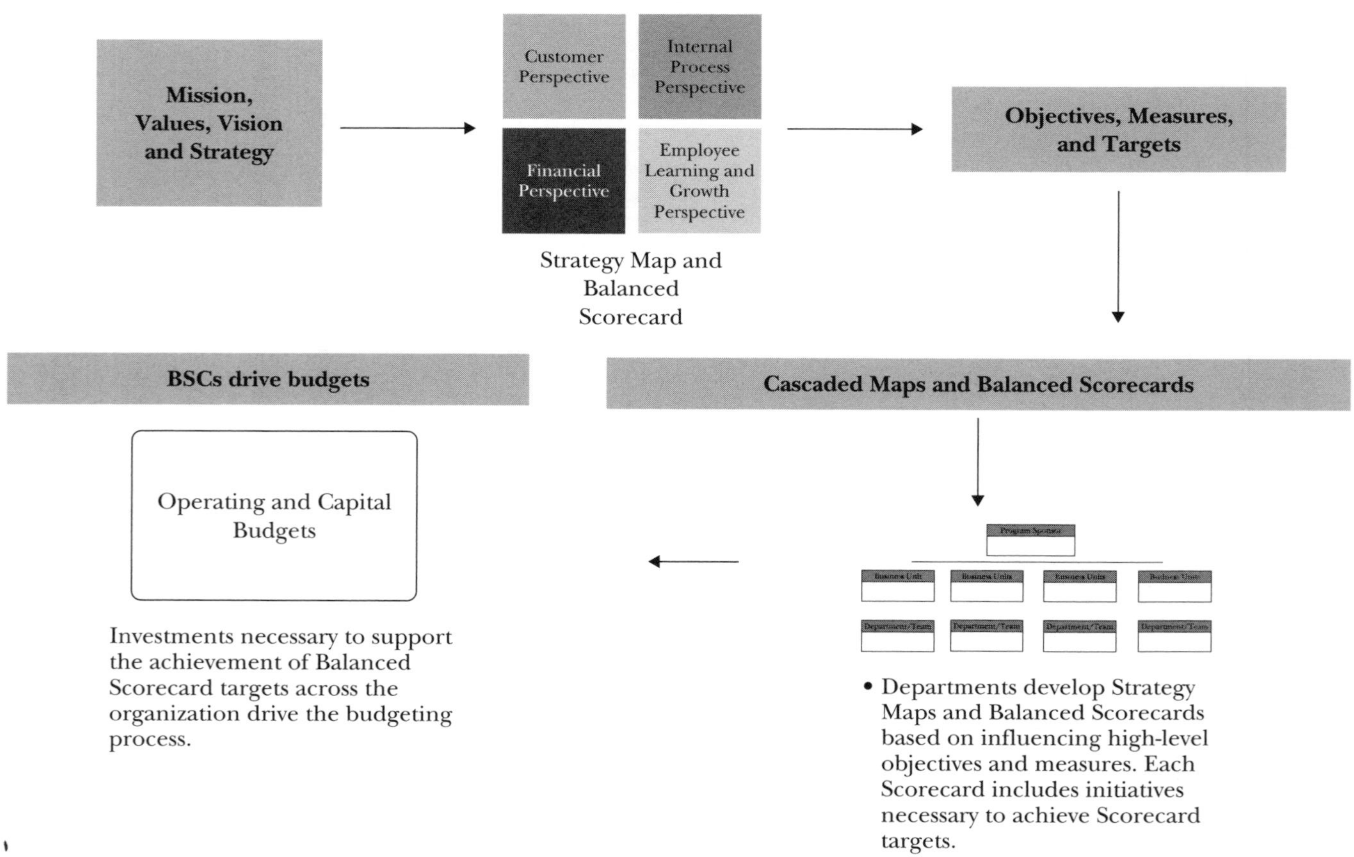

Mission, Values, Vision and Strategy

Customer Perspective

Internal Process Perspective

Financial Perspective

Employee Learning and Growth Perspective

Strategy Map and Balanced Scorecard

Objectives, Measures, and Targets

Cascaded Maps and Balanced Scorecards

Program Signature

Business Units

Business Units

Business Units

Department Teams

Department Teams

Department Groups

Business Teams

Departmental Units

- Departments develop Strategy Maps and Balanced Scorecards based on influencing high-level objectives and measures. Each Scorecard includes initiatives necessary to achieve Scorecard targets.

BSCs drive budgets

Operating and Capital Budgets

Investments necessary to support the achievement of Balanced Scorecard targets across the organization drive the budgeting process.

Adapted from *Balanced Scorecard Step-by-Step: Maximizing Performance and Maintaining Results, 2nd Edition*, by Paul R. Niven

Scorecards and budgets. Quantifying the initiatives will form the basis for operating and capital budget requests. Let's now turn our attention to the specific steps involved in this process.

Step 1: Develop a Plan

Chapter 4 reviewed the topic of communicating your Balanced Scorecard implementation to every person or group with a stake in your organization. Without communication, and a lot of it, even the most well-intentioned change program can die on the vine. The same advice is readily applicable in your quest to transform the budget process. You have to get the word out to everyone involved in the process.

Communication should center on why the change is being made, how it will benefit the organization, recognizing the "WIIFM" (What's In It For Me) principle, and how it will make life easier for budget preparers. The plan doesn't end with communication. Templates that facilitate the capture of budget information in as painless a way as possible must be designed and distributed.

Step 2: Develop or Refine Your Highest-Level Strategy Map and Balanced Scorecard

This method of Scorecard and budget linkage relies exclusively on the development of cascaded Balanced Scorecards. Therefore, a high-level organizational Strategy Map and Scorecard, spelling the key objectives, measures, and targets for the organization must be in place.

Step 3: Develop Cascaded Balanced Scorecards

Cascading, as you learned in Chapter 9, gives every group within your organization the opportunity to clearly signal how their local actions are contributing to overall results—yet another example of the axiom, "think globally, act locally." Each cascaded Scorecard should include not only measures and targets but initiatives as well. Effective initiatives will help you close any gaps existing between current and desired performance as reflected in your performance targets.

The link to budgeting appears when we calculate the monetary investments necessary to launch the initiative. Every initiative, no matter how big or small, will entail the allocation of resources. Budget requests should be based upon the resources required to effectively implement your initiatives, which in turn will drive the successful outcomes you're aiming for in your performance targets. All initiatives should clearly document which local and high-level objective(s) they support, resources required to implement (both human and financial), dependencies with other initiatives, and key milestones.

Organizations pursuing this technique will soon have to answer this question: Should typical budget items that normally do not have supporting initiatives, such as salaries, supplies, and travel, be allocated against the initiatives appearing on the Balanced Scorecard? In other words, how do we support a request for salaries (for example), when there is no supporting initiative? Differences of opinion exist on the subject. Scorecard architects Kaplan and Norton have advocated the use of so-called dynamic budgeting that represents an amalgam of operational and strategic budgeting.[4] They suggest an operational budget be used to allocate resources necessary for typical, recurring operations. Given the large volume of current service offerings, the majority of an organization's spending would be dictated by the operational budget. The strategic budget is reserved for spending designed to close any significant gaps that exist between current and desired performance on critical performance indicators.

Another school of thought suggests that only one budget be used and it should contain the entire mix of operational and strategic elements necessary to reflect a true picture of the organization. Following this advice forces an agency to consider every possible line item on the budget in light of strategy, which could be a Herculean task indeed. Financial innovations such as Activity-Based Costing, which provide input on cost drivers, are helpful in this regard but will not eliminate the specter of subjectivity from creeping into the analysis. Proponents of this school also suggest, with some merit, that challenging managers to relate strategy to even the most mundane of activities will bring the concept to the forefront and promote learning through the exchange of ideas around the agency.

The Scorecard and budget linkage process I am describing will work with either budget school. Your choice will depend on how accurately you can attach costs to strategic initiatives and how motivated your organization is to attempt a change of this magnitude.

Step 4: Compile Spending Requests

Your first task in step four is to provide budget preparers throughout your agency with templates they can use to easily capture resource requirements relating to Scorecard initiatives. Exhibit 10.2 displays a condensed version of such a template. In this example, the Building and Planning department of a city government has proposed three initiatives they feel are crucial in helping them achieve an 80% customer service target. Building a customer service portal will allow citizens to find and purchase permits without visiting a city office, which is sure to improve satisfaction. For those who must travel to a local office, the experience will be more pleasant thanks to newly remodeled facilities. Finally, a records management program will provide all Building and Planning staff with the resources they need to respond to customer inquiries in a swift and efficient manner.

Keep in mind this is just one measure. You'll require documents such as this for all measures (no wonder budgets produce so much paper!). Each initiative must be accompanied by supporting documentation as well—costs, timing, dependencies, key milestones, payback periods, and so on.

Exhibit 10.2   A Simplified Budget Submission Form

Business Unit/Department: City Building and Planning Department

			Resource Requirements	
Measure	Target	Initiatives	Operating	Capital
Customer Satisfaction	80%	Internet Customer Service Portal	$100,000	$50,000
		Remodel of Citizen Service Center	$25,000	$250,000
		Records Management Program	$50,000	$150,000

Adapted from *Balanced Scorecard Step-by-Step: Maximizing Performance and Maintaining Results, 2nd Edition,* by Paul R. Niven (John Wiley & Sons, 2006).

Exhibit 10.3   Budget Requests by Strategy Map Objective

Corporate Strategy: Make Customers the Center of Everything We Do

Objective	Current Scorecard Status	Budget Request Operating $000s	Budget Request Capital $000s
Increase customer satisfaction	Red	$XXM	$XXM
Promote economic opportunity	Green	$XXM	$XXM
Provide new services	Yellow	$XXM	$XXM
Percentage of Total Spending		35%	27%

Adapted from *Balanced Scorecard Step-by-Step: Maximizing Performance and Maintaining Results, 2nd Edition,* by Paul R. Niven (John Wiley & Sons, 2006).

   In keeping with the title of this step, your next assignment is compiling budget requests from throughout the agency. The rollups should be summarized in relation to their corresponding Strategy Map objective. Exhibit 10.3 provides an example. Here, the agency has developed a strategy of "making customers the center of everything we do." Three objectives organizers hope will lead to the execution of this strategy have been developed in the Customer Perspective: increase customer satisfaction, promote economic opportunity, and provide new services.

   The column labeled "Current Scorecard Status" provides readers with a snapshot of performance on the accompanying measure (not shown) in the most recent year. The evaluation uses a traffic light metaphor: green is synonymous with meeting or achieving the target, red indicates performance requiring improvement, and yellow signifies that caution and attention are in order. Thus, it's easy to discern that customer satisfaction is performing below expectations, the promotion of economic opportunities is above expectations, and new services require more attention.

The final two columns of the document provide a summary of the total operating and capital dollars requested across the organization on these objectives. You can see that customer objectives represent 35% of total operating fund requests and 27% of capital. Those responsible for approving budget requests can use this information to determine where the majority of spending requests are being directed, and take action to ensure appropriate balance in the allocation of resources. As is always desirable, this analysis will inevitably produce important questions relating to how funds are expended. In this instance, administrators must determine how much they are willing to spend in order to elevate customer satisfaction to an acceptable level. Similarly, while the promotion of economic opportunities is currently green, how much is necessary to sustain that performance?

Step 5: Finalize the Budget

Once all budget requests have been tabulated, you will almost always discover a gap. Maybe "gap" is too euphemistic a word; "abyss" may be a better description. The abyss to which I am referring is the difference between the funds requested by groups throughout the agency and the funds you have available.

To close the gap and finalize the budget, the head of each group should deliver a formal presentation to senior leaders, outlining the budget submissions from his or her group to include: what they encompass, why they are strategically significant, and how they will positively impact Scorecard targets. By clearly demonstrating how initiatives link to Scorecard targets, the information presented will assist leaders in making appropriate resource allocation decisions.

Now the process becomes iterative in nature, with executives reviewing and questioning the proposals, attempting to determine which are worthy of inclusion in the budget. To ease the decision-making process, you may wish to develop an internal ranking system for the initiatives you propose. A simplified rating system may be devised to represent the potential impact of removing a specific initiative on the Balanced Scorecard. For example, the number 1 might indicate an initiative that could be eliminated and have minimal impact on the ability of the group to achieve its target. A 2 may translate to an initiative that could be cut, but with a definite effect on the group's chances of meeting targeted expectations. Finally, initiatives awarded a 3 could represent projects that are deemed as crucial to the successful achievement of Scorecard targets. The ratings will be necessarily subjective, but they will serve as a powerful impetus for conversations centered on establishing spending priorities.

BENEFITS TO EXPECT FROM THE PROCESS

Have you ever found yourself in a situation where you felt like a fish out of water? It happens to all of us from time to time. An old friend in the consulting business told me this story that demonstrates the surprising outcomes when we find ourselves in a seemingly uncomfortable situation.

Fresh out of graduate school, he was immediately dispatched by his new employer, a large and prestigious consulting firm, to an important client on the East Coast. The consulting firm felt my friend's liberal arts background would serve him well in any and all situations. However, they gave little consideration to the fact that he had only taken one finance course during his entire academic career. They thrust him into a lion's den of financial professionals who were craving instant answers to their budgeting problem. Decked out in his freshly pressed suit, he arrived at the client's office radiating confidence and ready to solve any problem thrown at him. When the meeting began, he quickly realized that it was nothing like the philosophy seminars he attended in school. The topic was budgeting, and hard as he pressed his mental accelerator, he had nothing in the tank. Finally, exasperated and feeling his short-lived consulting career was over anyway, he asked the seemingly simple question "Why do you budget?" The room fell silent. He was preparing for the inevitable tirade focusing on his utter incompetence when suddenly, from the head of the table, a voice was heard. It was that of the company president, who said, "He's got a point; why do we budget?" The next thing he knew, the entire group was engaged in a spirited discussion on the underlying rationale for their budget, and before long, they had developed several recommendations based on an examination of their true purpose. My friend was branded "a brilliant consultant" and never looked back.

The point of the story is this: Sometimes simplicity is the best approach. We have a tendency in modern organizations to make things appear more complicated than they really are. Budgeting is a case in point. Some readers may regard the process I have laid out as unduly simplistic and, as such, not worthy of implementation. But what, I ask, is the fundamental purpose of a budget? To allocate scarce resources among a variety of possible alternatives. What better way to do that than to use the Balanced Scorecard that represents a direct and faithful translation of our strategy. Only those initiatives that provide a meaningful contribution to the fulfillment of strategic objectives should be undertaken. Simple yes, but effective as well. Listed next are some of the benefits associated with this process.

- *Develop budgets based on facts not emotion.* The typical budgeting process is fraught with extensive game-playing, as each department postures and engages in whatever histrionics are necessary to secure adequate funding. Persuasive arguments tend to hold as much weight as strategic needs during these entertaining, yet ineffective, proceedings. The Balanced Scorecard levels the playing field for all participants, forcing all groups to demonstrate a clear link between budget requests and strategic impact. The Ministry of Defence (MoD) in the United Kingdom discovered the difference a Balanced Scorecard can make at budget time. "The MoD now uses its Scorecard during funding negotiations with the Treasury. By removing the emotion from funding discussions and enabling the MoD to dispassionately demonstrate the impact of various funding scenarios, the Scorecard helps focus the conversation on the facts and key priorities."[5]

- *Builds collaboration.* Admiral Raymond A. Archer, former Vice Director of the Defense Logistics Agency, described the use of the Balanced Scorecard in the budgeting process this way: "We decided that the only way to make the Balanced Scorecard work was to put our money where our Scorecard was. So we made a rule: Investment initiatives had to be in the Balanced Scorecard. If they weren't they wouldn't be funded. What used to be a painful investment strategy process became quite simple. In fact, the Scorecard eliminates turf battles."[6] Eliminating turf battles is a tremendous enhancement to the budgeting process, but the Scorecard can take it one step beyond. With strategy at the center of the discussions, an open dialog in which groups actively look for opportunities to collaborate and share resources is encouraged. Perhaps an initiative alone won't be funded, but when combined with another group's plan, there may be synergies that make both more appealing. This facet of the Scorecard and budget link is very appropriate for nonprofits and governments where so many of the outcomes require cross-collaboration.

- *Reinforces the strategy.* In order to effectively create a budget request with a clear link to a strategy, there is an implicit assumption that individuals preparing budgets understand the strategy. A poor grasp of the strategy will be revealed in initiative and budget requests that have little impact on driving overall outcomes. Linking dollars to the Scorecard is a great opportunity to enhance learning, since knowledge of the strategy will become a prerequisite to generating budget dollars.

NOTES

1. Don Durfee, "Alternative Budgeting,"*CFO Magazine*, June 2006, p. 28.

2. Philip G. Joyce, "Using Performance Measures for Budgeting: A New Beat, or Is It the Same Old Tune?"*New Directions for Evaluation*, Fall 1997.

3. "The President's Management" Agenda at www.whitehouse.gov/omb/budget/fy2002/mgt.pdf

4. Robert S. Kaplan and David P. Norton, *The Strategy-Focused Organization* (Boston: Harvard Business School Press, 2001).

5. Lauren Keller Johnson, "Making Strategy a Continual Process at the U.K. Ministry of Defence," *Balanced Scorecard Report,* November–December 2002, pp. 5–8.

6. Raymond A. Archer, "Enabling a Whole New (and Customer-Focused) Structure at the DLA," *Balanced Scorecard Report,* November–December 2002, pp. 8–9.

11

Reporting Results

Roadmap for Chapter 11   Reflecting on the future of management reporting, former General Electric Chief Executive Jack Welch once commented that "Most of the information a manager will need to run a business will reside on a computer screen in a digital cockpit. It will contain every piece of real-time data, with automatic alerts spotlighting the trends requiring immediate attention."[1] Well, the future is here. Today's Balanced Scorecard reporting tools can perform all of Mr. Welch's prognostications plus 101 other tasks. In this chapter, we'll explore the role of technology in reporting your Balanced Scorecard results and look at the steps you should follow when choosing a software solution.

Technology is not for everyone, however, and we'll learn that many Scorecard pioneers used simple paper-based results to drive breakthrough results for their organizations. Key considerations when developing an in-house system will also be provided.

Results can only generate improvement and learning if analyzed and shared. The Balanced Scorecard provides governments and nonprofits with the mechanism to redefine and invigorate an often-tired and ineffective management meeting process. We'll look at the specifics of this new and exciting process, culminating in the discussion of a new, strategy-centered management meeting.

FROM THEORY TO PRACTICE

A public sector client recently introduced me to an acronym I had never heard before: SPOTS. Any guesses? It stands for "strategic plan on the shelf." The term is indicative of organizations that go to great and painstaking lengths to develop a strategy, only to have it sit on a shelf or be used to prop up a projector during presentations—both fairly ignominious results for the much vaunted strategic plan! The last thing you want is a "BSCOTS." Okay, it's not as catchy as SPOTS, but you get the picture.

Developing performance objectives on a Strategy Map and translating them into measures, targets, and later supporting initiatives on a Scorecard, is a challenging task. However, people find it exhilarating and thought-provoking. With a frenetic pace characterizing most organizations, there is precious little time reserved for actually contemplating high-level strategy and how it will be executed. Creating a Balanced Scorecard system provides that opportunity, that mental fresh air, revealing a new perspective on your organization. Beneficial and thought-provoking yes, but it's still largely an academic exercise. Not until you begin reporting your Balanced Scorecard results does the tool transform from a cognitive simulation into a real business solution.

Every organization will launch the Balanced Scorecard for individual reasons. However, improving results and enhancing accountability are frequently cited. These Scorecard traits are not introduced until you begin reporting your results. Only then will you see the true power of the Balanced Scorecard, the power to drive alignment from top to bottom, to improve communication, and to learn about your business through strategic conversations arising from an analysis of reported results.

BALANCED SCORECARD SOFTWARE

The *First Edition* of this book mentioned a Web query I made regarding Balanced Scorecard software. I had typed the words "Balanced Scorecard" and "software" into a search engine to see how many hits I would receive, and within fractions of a second later, discovered 44,000 was the "jaw-dropping" (as I put it then) response. That was in late 2002. I decided to repeat the experiment for this edition of the book, written in the waning months of 2007, so I Googled—notice it's no longer a search engine query, it's "Googled"—the same phrases, and a few less fractions of a second later, the number came back: 2.1 million! Obviously, there isn't an army of over 2 million-strong peddling Balanced Scorecard software, but the enormous number indicates overwhelming evidence of the interest in this topic. In fact, interest may be putting it mildly when you consider that one survey discovered 70% of respondents were using some type of software in their Balanced Scorecard implementation.[2]

When I started working with the Balanced Scorecard over a decade ago, reports generated using an Excel spreadsheet with some clip art added for a stylistic flourish were considered *avant-garde* and often yielded expressions of awe from Scorecard reviewers. Whenever I mention that, I feel as though I'm recounting one of those stories you might hear from your grandfather: "When I was your age, we walked eight miles to school. . . . in the snow. . . . uphill both ways." We weren't suffering in our technology-deprived state, but in retrospect, we could have achieved much more from the Scorecard had we been able to avail ourselves of the many benefits present in even the most modest of Scorecard software systems available today.

As the Balanced Scorecard evolved from a pure measurement system to a strategic management system in the mid-1990s and to a powerful communication tool with the advent of Strategy Maps, the paper-based reports used by early adopters were hard pressed to keep up with progress in the field. Organizations were cascading the Scorecard from top to bottom, linking it to budgeting and in many cases compensation as well. The reporting, analysis, and communication requirements represented by these advances required new tools. Software providers were swift in their response and soon developed a number of sophisticated programs capable of everything from simple reporting to strategy mapping and scenario planning.

Automating your Balanced Scorecard provides a number of benefits and maximizes its use as a measurement system, strategic management system, and communication tool. The advanced analytics and decision support provided by even the simplest Scorecard software allow organizations to perform intricate evaluations of performance and critically examine the relationships among their performance measures. Automation also supports true organization-wide deployment of the tool. Cascading the Scorecard across the enterprise can often lead to the development of dozens of Scorecards if not more. Without the use of an automated solution, managing the process and ensuring alignment can prove difficult. Communication and feedback may also be dramatically improved with Scorecard software. Commentaries used to elaborate on a specific measure's performance may spawn a company-wide discussion and lead to creative breakthroughs based on collaborative problem solving made possible only through the wide dissemination of Scorecard results. Information sharing and knowledge are also enhanced by the software's ability to provide relevant links to interested users. A hyperlinked measure may be just the beginning in the user's journey to a variety of knowledge enhancing sites including the mission statement, the latest comments from a valued customer, or the results of a much anticipated benchmarking study.[3]

Selection of the right software for your organization is a crucial decision. Not only are you shopping for a system to report your Scorecard results and provide a platform for future evolution of the tool, but you must ensure that whatever you buy will suit the needs of your workforce and be accepted as a useful tool. Software selection is typically a sequential five-step process:[4]

1. *Form a software team.* Just as you used a cross-functional team to develop your Strategy Map and Scorecard, so too will you rely on a number of

people to make the crucial software decision. Include your executive sponsor, Balanced Scorecard champion, a representative of your Information Technology (IT) group, and an individual representative of the typical Scorecard user. The team should begin their work by reviewing the current landscape of Scorecard software and speaking to end users regarding their requirements for this tool. Remember that different users will demand specific functionality. Executives may simply be interested in one-page summary reports while analysts may focus on data input, retrieval, and complex reporting. The team should also develop a software project plan outlining key dates and milestones on the path to the software decision.

2. *Develop a short list of candidates.* You'll find dozens of potential vendors ready and willing to supply you with Scorecard software. Use the criteria presented later in this chapter to help you determine three or four finalists.

3. *Submit a request for proposal (RFP).* Compile your needs and specifications into a document for distribution to your finalists. Each organization you contact should provide you with a written summary detailing how their product stacks up to your requirements.

4. *Arrange demonstrations.* Invite software candidates to conduct a demonstration of their product at your facility. To ensure the demonstration is relevant to your needs, send a copy of your Strategy Map and measures to the vendor in advance, and have them base the demonstration on your data. This is important since many vendors will default to manufacturing or service examples that bear little resemblance to the world faced by public and nonprofits.

5. *Create a summary report and make your selection.* Determine which functionality and specifications are most vital to you and rank each product against them. The software program that most closely matches your requirements should be selected.

Exhibit 11.1 displays a screen shot from Corporater, a Balanced Scorecard software provider. One user of that tool summarizes their experience this way: "We chose Corporater for its ease of use and its depth of features. It is made for business users, enabling our managers to easily manage their scorecards. The tool offers the next generation of performance management software that flexibly integrates reporting, initiative management, automated and manual data collection into a single interface. It contains both a clean end-user interface and rich functionality that meets our advanced reporting and scorecard needs."[5] I'm sure most software users would have similar comments, reflecting the value of applying an automated solution to your Balanced Scorecard implementation.

Exhibit 11.1 Screen Shot from Corporater (A Balanced Scorecard Software Program)

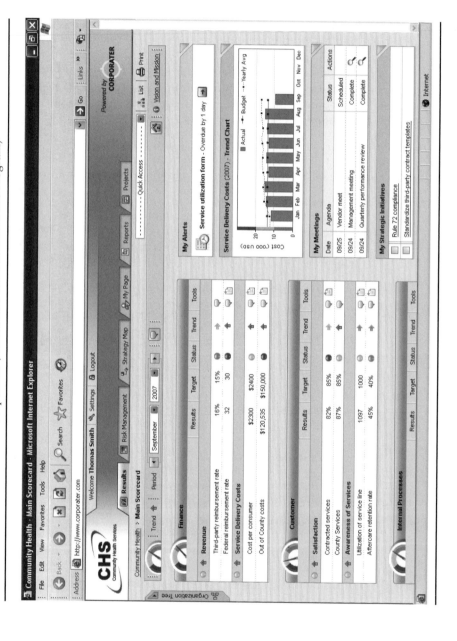

Criteria for Selecting Software

Design Issues: Configuration of the Software   In this section we'll examine a number of the Scorecard software setup and design elements.

- *Setup wizards.* Your software solution should provide easy-to-use and understand "wizards" to guide new users through the initial setup process.

- *Time to implement.* Software programs for the Balanced Scorecard can run the gamut from simple reporting tools to sophisticated enterprise-wide management solutions. Therefore, major differences exist in the time and resources necessary to implement the system. You must determine what your thresholds are in terms of timing and resource requirements necessary to have the system up and running. Carefully consider the resource requirements you have and are willing to dedicate to the Scorecard software.

- *Various Scorecard designs.* This book focuses exclusively on the methodology of the Balanced Scorecard. However, you may at some point wish to track other popular measurement alternatives such as the Baldrige award criteria, Total Quality Management (TQM) metrics, or any number of different methodologies. The software should be flexible enough to permit various performance management techniques.

- *User interface/display.* Most Balanced Scorecard software will feature a predominant display metaphor. It may use gauges similar to those you'd see in the dashboard of a plane, or automobile boxes that are reminiscent of organizational charts or color-coded dials. Some of these simply look better (i.e., more realistic and legitimate) than others. That may sound insignificant, but remember you're counting on your workforce to use this software faithfully. If they find the "instrumentation" unrealistic, or worse, unattractive, that could significantly impact their initial reaction and ongoing commitment.

- *Number of measures.* In all likelihood, you will use the Scorecard software for tracking performance measures from around your entire organization. Ensure your software is equipped with the flexibility to handle a significant volume of measures.

- *Strategies, objectives, measures, targets, and initiatives.* Since it is the backbone of the Scorecard system, you should be able to easily enter all of the above elements in the software. The software should also allow you to specify cause and effect relationships among the objectives and measures.

- *Strategy Maps.* Capturing the Strategy Map with compelling and easy-to-understand graphics is critical should you hope to benefit from the information sharing and collective learning to be derived from the Balanced Scorecard.

- *Multiple locations.* The software should accommodate the addition of performance measures from a variety of physical and nonphysical locations.

- *Descriptions and definitions.* Simply entering names and numbers into the software is not sufficient for communication and eventual analysis. Every field in which you enter information must be capable of accepting textual descriptions. Upon launching the software, the first thing most users will do when looking at a specific performance indicator is examine its description and definition.

- *Assignment of owners.* The Scorecard can only be used to enhance accountability if your software permits each performance indicator to be assigned a specific owner. Since you may also have another individual acting as the owner's assistant and yet another as data enterer, it is beneficial if the software provides the ability to identify these functions as well.

- *Various unit types.* Your performance indicators are likely to come in all shapes and sizes, and descriptors from raw numbers to percentages to dollars. The tool you choose must permit all types of measures.

- *Appropriate timing.* Your performance measures are sure to have differing time increments. Spending may be tracked monthly, while customer satisfaction is monitored quarterly. The software should accommodate varied reporting frequencies.

- *Relative weights.* All measures on the Balanced Scorecard are important links in the description of your strategy. However, most organizations will place greater emphasis on certain indicators. For public and nonprofit organizations, customer indicators are of vital importance and may warrant a higher weight. A good Scorecard tool should permit you to weight the measures according to their relative importance.

- *Aggregate disparate elements.* This description sounds a little complicated, but it simply means your program should deliver the ability to combine performance measures with different unit types. This can best be accomplished with the use of weighting (see the preceding element). Measures are accorded a weight that drives the aggregation of results regardless of the specific unit type of each indicator.

- *Multiple comparatives.* Most organizations will track performance relative to a predefined target (e.g., the financial budget). However, it may be useful to examine performance in light of last year's performance, relative to your peers, or a best-in-class benchmarking number. Look for the software to allow a number of comparatives.

- *Graphic status indicators.* At a glance, users should be able to ascertain the performance of measures based on an easy-to-understand status indicator. Many programs will take advantage of familiar color metaphors using (e.g., red [stop], yellow [caution], and green [go]). Fortunately, they usually offer greater color ranges. This is particularly important to public and nonprofits who may feel hesitant to attach red lights to performance.

- *Dual polarity.* For the software to produce a color indicating measure performance, it must recognize whether high values for actual results represent good or bad performance. Results might be considered good up to a certain point, but they may be a cause for concern beyond a certain threshold. For example, it may be perfectly appropriate for a call center representative to answer 12 to 15 calls an hour, but responding to 30 may indicate the representative is rushing through the calls and sacrificing quality for the sake of expediency. The software solution should be able to flag such issues of "dual polarity."

- *Cascading Scorecards.* Users should be able to review Balanced Scorecards from across the organization in one program. Ensure your software allows you to display aligned Scorecards emanating from throughout the organization.

- *Personal preferences.* "My" has become a popular prefix in the Internet world, with "My Yahoo" and "MySpace" as two prevalent examples. The information age has heralded a time of mass customization. And so it should be with your Balanced Scorecard software. If desired, users should be able to easily customize the system to open with a page displaying indicators of importance to them. Having relevant information immediately available will greatly facilitate the program's use.

- *Intuitive menus.* Menus should be logical, easy to understand, and relatively simple to navigate.

- *Help screens.* Some help screens seem to hinder users' efforts as often as they help them. Check the help screens to ensure they offer relevant, easy-to-follow information.

- *Levels of detail.* Your software should allow users to quickly and easily switch from a summary view of performance to a detailed view comprising a single indicator. Navigating from data tables to summary reports to individual measures should all be easily accommodated. The user community will demand this functionality as they begin actively using the tool to analyze performance results.

Reporting and Analysis

Any software solution you consider must contain robust and flexible reporting and analysis tools. In this section, we'll explore a number of reporting and analysis factors to be considered during your selection process.

- *Drill-down capabilities.* A crucial item, this tool must allow users to drill down on measures to increasingly lower levels of detail. Drill-down might also be considered in the context of Strategy Maps, which should be easily navigable at the click of a mouse.

- *Statistical analysis.* Your software should include the facility of performing statistical analysis (e.g., trends) on the performance measures making up your Balanced Scorecard. Additionally, the statistics should be multidimensional in nature, combining disparate performance elements to display a total picture of actual results. Simply viewing bar charts is not analysis. Users require the opportunity to slice and dice the data to fit their analysis and decision making needs.

- *Alerts.* You will want to be notified automatically when a critical measure is not performing within acceptable ranges. Alerts must be built into the system to provide this notification.

- *Commentaries.* This is particularly crucial for government and non-profit users where much of your work is contextual and requires explanation. Whether a measure is performing at above or below targeted expectations, users (especially management) need to quickly determine the root cause of the performance and be aware of the associated steps necessary for sustaining or improving results. Commentary fields are essential to any Scorecard software program and most, if not all, will include them.

- *Flexible report options.* "What kind of reports does it have?" is invariably one of the first questions you'll hear when discussing Scorecard software with your user community. We're a report-based and dependent culture, so this shouldn't come as a surprise. What may in fact come as a surprise is the wide range of report capabilities featured in today's Scorecard software entries. Test this requirement closely because, simply put, some are much better than others. An especially important area to examine is print options. We purchase software to reduce our dependency on paper, but as we all know it doesn't necessarily work that way. Ensure the reports will print effectively, displaying the information clearly and concisely.

- *Automatic consolidation.* You may wish to see your data presented as a sum, average, or year-to-date amount. The system should possess the flexibility to provide this choice.

- *Flag missing data.* At the outset of their implementation, most organizations will be missing at least a portion of the data for Balanced Scorecard measures. This often results from the fact that the Scorecard development process has illuminated entirely new measures never before contemplated. The software program should alert users to those measures that are missing data, whether it is for a single period, or the measure has never been populated.

- *Forecasting and what-if analysis.* Robust programs will possess the capability of using current results to forecast future performance. It's also very useful to have the ability to "plug-in" different values in various measures and examine the effect on related indicators. This what-if analysis provides another opportunity to critically examine the assumptions made when constructing the Strategy Map.

- *Linked documents.* At a mouse click, users should have the ability to measure results into a larger context by accessing important documents and links. Media reports, executive videos, discussion forums, and a variety of other potential links can serve to strengthen the bond between actual results and the larger context of organizational objectives.

- *Automatic e-mail.* To harness the power of the Balanced Scorecard as a communication tool, users must be able to launch an e-mail application and send messages regarding specific performance results. Discussion forums, or "threads," may develop as interested users add their perspective on results and provide insights for improvements.

Technical Considerations

In this section, we'll examine the technical dimensions of both hardware and software to ensure the tool you select is right for your technical environment.

- *Compatibility.* Any software you consider must be able to exist in your current technical environment. Most employ client/server technology and will run on Windows 95, 98, XP, 2000, NT, Vista, or UNIX.

- *Integration with existing systems.* Data for your Balanced Scorecard will most likely reside in a number of places. Your software should be able to extract data from these systems automatically, thereby eliminating any rekeying. Users who appear reluctant to use the Scorecard software will often point to redundant data entry as a key detraction of the system. Therefore, a big win is delivered should you have the ability to automatically extricate information with no effort on the part of users.

- *Accept various data forms.* In addition to internal sources of data, you may collect performance information from third-party providers. The software should therefore contain the ability to accept data from spreadsheets and ASCII files.

- *Data export.* Getting information out is as important as getting it in. The data contained in the Balanced Scorecard may serve as the source for other management reports to boards, regulators, or the general public. A robust data export tool is an important component of any Scorecard software.

- *Web publishing.* Users should have the option of accessing and saving Scorecard information using a standard browser. Publishing to both an internal intranet and the Internet is preferable.

- *Trigger external applications.* Users will require the capability of launching desktop programs from within the Balanced Scorecard software.

- *Cut and paste to applications.* Related to the preceding element, users may wish to include a graph or chart in another application. Many programs will provide functionality enabling users to simply copy and paste with ease.

- *Application service provider (ASP) option.* An ASP is a company that offers organizations access to applications and related services over the Internet that would otherwise have to be located in their own computers. As information technology outsourcing grows in prominence, so too does the role of application service providers. A number of Scorecard software vendors now offer this service, which gives anyone direct access to the Balanced Scorecard for a monthly (normally) fee based on the number of users.

- *Scalability.* This term describes the ability of an application to function well and take advantage of changes in size or volume in order to meet a user need. Rescaling can encompass a change in the product itself (storage, RAM, etc.) or the movement to a new operating system. Your software should be scalable to meet the future demands you may place on it as your user community and sophistication grow.

Maintenance and Security

Ensuring appropriate access rights and ongoing maintenance are also important criteria in your software decision. Here are a few elements to consider:

- *System administrator access.* Your software should allow for individuals to be designated as system administrators. Depending on security (see the third and fourth entries in the list), a number of these users may have access to the entire system.

- *Ease of modification.* Altering your views of performance should be facilitated easily, with little advanced technical knowledge required.

- *Control of access to the system.* My proclivities are toward open-book management with complete sharing of information across the organization. Agencies practicing this participative form of management give it glowing reviews for the innovation and creativity it sparks among employees. The Scorecard facilitates open sharing of information both through the development of a high-level organizational Scorecard and the series of cascading Scorecards that allow all employees to describe their contribution to overall results. However, not all organizations share this view and many will wish to limit access to the system. Therefore, a software program should allow you to limit access to information by user, and develop user groups to simplify the measure publishing process.

- *Control of changes, data, and commentary entry.* Related to the preceding, not all users will necessarily be required to make changes, enter data, or provide result commentaries. Only system administrators should have the power to change measures, and only assigned users will have access to entering data and commentaries.

Evaluating the Vendor

With the number of players in this market, you'll be presented with a wide array of software choices from both industry veterans and upstarts attempting to make a splash. Either way, performing a little due diligence on the vendor is always a good idea.

- *Pricing.* As with any investment of this magnitude, pricing is a critical component of the overall decision. To make an informed decision, remember to include all dimensions of the total cost to purchase and maintain the software. This includes the per-user license fees, any maintenance fees, costs related to new releases, training costs, as well as salaries and benefits of system administrators.

- *Vendor viability.* Is this provider in for the long term, or will any vicissitudes of the economy spell their demise? Since the vendor is in the business of providing Scorecard software, you would expect it to steer their own course using the Balanced Scorecard. Ask them to review their Scorecard results with you. For confidentiality reasons, they may have to disguise some of the actual numbers, but you should still glean lots of valuable information on the organization's future prospects.

- *References and experience.* By examining the profiles of past clients, you can determine the breadth and depth of experience the vendor has accumulated. While no two implementations are identical, it will be reassuring to know the software company has completed an installation in a public sector or nonprofit environment. References are especially important. When discussing the vendor with other organizations that have been through the process, quiz them on the vendor's technical skills, consulting and training competence, and ability to complete the work on time and on budget.

- *Long-term service.* You'll inevitably have many bumps in the road as you implement your new reporting software. Bugs hidden deep in the program will be detected, patches will be required, and thus a lifeline to the vendor is crucial. How much support are they willing to offer, and at what cost? Do you have a dedicated representative for your organization or are you at the mercy of their call center? These are just a couple of questions to ask. And never forget that software companies owe a lot to us, the users. New functions and features are very often the product of intense lobbying on behalf of function-starved users who sometimes end up knowing more about the product than the vendor. So don't be shy with your requests!

Exhibit 11.2 displays an easy-to-use template that will assist you in ranking various software choices. This example includes only the configuration and design elements, but you can expand it to include all aspects of the decision. In this example, the configuration and design items have been weighted at 50% of the total decision. Specific elements comprising the category are listed in the first column, and the competing vendors are shown in the third, fourth, and fifth columns. Each vendor is accorded a score out of a possible 10 points demonstrating how well it satisfies each element of the decision. For example, vendors 1 and 3 each have easy-to-use setup wizards and are awarded ten points. On many elements of the analysis, subjectivity is sure to make its way into the decision. All vendors may offer the option of graphically displaying your Strategy Map, for example. Your point decision will then be based on ease of importing the Map, graphical appearance, and so on. Once all evaluations have been made, the points are totaled for each vendor. In this example vendor three has scored perfect tens on all points and therefore receives the full 50 points available.

DEVELOPING YOUR OWN BALANCED SCORECARD REPORTING SYSTEM

Investing in a technological solution to report your Scorecard results is neither a guarantee nor a prerequisite of success. Long before software companies sensed the burgeoning Scorecard opportunity, many early adopters were blazing their own trail with paper-based reports created on desktop computers. The success of the Balanced Scorecard today is due in large part

Exhibit 11.2   Ranking the Software Alternatives

Criteria	Weight	Vendor 1	Vendor 2	Vendor 3
Configuration and Design	50%			
Setup wizards		10	9	10
Time to implement		9	10	10
User interface/display		8	8	10
Various Scorecard designs		8	9	10
Number of measures		9	9	10
Strategies, objectives, measures, targets, and initiatives, and cause and effect		8	7	10
Strategy Maps		8	7	10
Multiple locations		8	5	10
Cascading Scorecards		7	8	10
Descriptions and definitions		5	9	10
Assignment of owners		10	10	10
Various unit types		6	10	10
Varied reporting frequencies		6	10	10
Relative weights		10	8	10
Aggregate disparate elements		9	7	10
Multiple comparatives		10	10	10
Graphic status indicators		6	9	10
Dual polarity		5	10	10
Personal preferences		5	10	10
Helpful help screens		9	8	10
Levels of detail		7	8	10
Total		163	181	210
Total Points		38.80	43.10	50.00

to the efforts and tenacity of the pioneers who quickly grasped, and gained, the Scorecarding benefits of alignment, accountability, and strategy execution with nary a thought to "graphic user interfaces" or "data import functions." You may be surprised to learn that the City of Charlotte, North Carolina, widely considered the single best example of using the Balanced Scorecard in a government setting, has never used a software program to report their results since they began using the Scorecard in the mid-1990s. In Chapter 12, you will learn how they've reported results and why they've resisted the allure of technology.

Necessity is the mother of invention, and when it comes to building in-house Scorecard applications, creativity can surge. I've witnessed everything from humble paper reports with a few graphs and charts to large whiteboards custom-designed to hold Scorecard data to relatively sophisticated intranet applications. One client of mine, known for his creativity and often quirky solutions, devised a unique approach to the reporting challenge. He created a three-sided board, about six feet tall, complete with wheels for ease of transport. Results were posted each month on each side of the board: corporate measure updates on one side, key strategic initiatives on a second side, and probably the most viewed of the three, the monthly incentive compensation calculator on the third side. The wheels turned out to be the greatest innovation, transforming the device from a wacky conversation piece to a roaming meeting agenda. The CEO insisted his managers roll the board into conference rooms when conducting meetings, and use the posted results to stimulate discussions on corporate and business unit progress. When not roaming the hallways, the board was posted in common areas such as the company's foyer—where it caused more than one unsuspecting visitor to cast a quizzical double take—and the cafeteria where, coffee stains notwithstanding, the board served as grist for many a lunch-time conversation. The total cost of this investment was minimal but the payback in the form of enthusiasm and frank discussion has been substantial.

When the topic swings to reporting, a phrase that tends to pop up quite frequently in nonprofit and government circles is "dashboard." Although they vary widely in design and content, these reporting tools all focus on one key attribute: displaying performance in a clear and unambiguous way. The Minnesota Department of Transportation (Mn/DOT) has used the dashboard technique to broadcast their performance on a number of performance variables. Its snow-and-ice dashboard is featured in Exhibit 11.3.

Your choice of reporting formats will depend on a number of variables, including the resources you're willing to expend, available expertise to craft the reports, and the preferences of your senior managers. Here are a couple of key considerations to keep in mind before developing any in-house reporting tool:

- *Before producing the first manual Balanced Scorecard report, create a mock-up with dummy results.* Circulate it to the executive group for their approval. This is important since senior leaders may have different style preferences and wishes. By creating a mock-up, the team has the opportunity to incorporate executive feedback into the process and design a reporting tool that satisfies all. And, as I've discussed at other points in the book, involvement tends to breed acceptance.

Exhibit 11.3 Minnesota Department of Transportation Performance Dashboard

Snow and Ice Removal: How are we doing?

The Minnesota Department of Transportation uses dashboards to measure levels of performance in its snow and ice removal operations. These measures help set goals for the timely removal of snow and ice on 12,500 miles of state highways

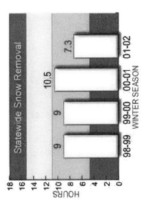

- Slightly over target
- On Target.
- Slightly under target.
- Under target
- Hours to bare lanes

Statewide hours to bare lanes.

Statewide Snow Removal

Average hours on all state highways it takes to get to bare lane after a snowfall.

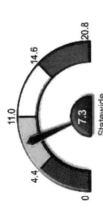

How are target levels determined? Mn/DOT used Market Research to help determine how quickly after a snowfall customers expected to see clear roads, and what their definition of bare pavement was.

We have dashboards for all areas of the state. To view a power point presentation that will show you more click here

- *Be cognizant of the data collection issues that may accompany your in-house solution.* Virtually all software solutions will provide "bridges" from the system to various data sources spread throughout your organization. Should you build your own system, however, manual data entry is a distinct possibility. Perhaps the least favorable association for the Balanced Scorecard is with the word "redundancy." If those charged with the task of loading Scorecard data feel it is a task being duplicated in other areas, resistance, if not downright anarchy, will surely follow. Manual data entry also introduces the attendant risks of errors from the miskeying of performance data. Unreliable data is a huge Scorecard momentum killer.

THE NEW STRATEGY-CENTERED MANAGEMENT MEETING

Story of the Century: Meetings are Flawed!

I know the following dramatization bears absolutely no resemblance to what takes place at your agency, so just for a chuckle at how the other half ambles aimlessly through their days, please follow along as I outline the first 20 minutes or so of a typical meeting at many organizations. The meeting is scheduled to start promptly at 9:00 am. Here goes:

8:55: Room is completely empty, no lights on.

9:00: The first of five invited participants arrives (feeling early), turns on the lights, and sits as far from the head of the table as possible.

9:05: Two more attendees shuffle in looking confused, wondering if there actually is a meeting today, and when assured there is, they take their seats.

9:07: Amid chatter about last night's baseball game, calls are placed to the extensions of the tardy, and the technically savvy of the group begin fiddling with the ancient laptop and Prius-sized overhead projector in the room.

9:08: One of the missing—the meeting organizer as it turns out—arrives with stacks of papers in both arms, apologizing profusely, blaming his belated appearance on a call he had to take. No one really notices, however, because all eyes are riveted on the nonfunctioning projector.

9:10: A volunteer is dispatched to round up Phil, the last missing person. Chatter subsides, and the first pangs of tension: *Why am I here? I have so much work to do today* begin to announce themselves to those present. The projector is suspiciously quiet and one person contorts themselves painfully to ensure its cord is reaching the receptacle under the table. It is.

9:12: General murmuring begins anew, accompanied by griping about the lack of food: *If you have a 9:00 meeting you could at least have coffee.* No sign of the intrepid searcher or Phil.

9:15: Volunteer returns; apparently Phil got called into another meeting (more important being the sub-text) at the last minute and won't be coming. On the plus side, the projector and laptop have been reunited successfully, with the appearance of the Windows logo on the screen signaling once again man's prominence over machine.

9:16: Heads swivel until the person who arranged the meeting calls it to order.

9:17: The first of 44 PowerPoint slides is beamed across the room, but no agenda for the meeting is shared.

9:19: Yawns are concealed, pens are toyed with, and legs are shuffled as the group settles in.

Cynical? You're right, I'm way off base. Actually, the complaints about the food start a lot sooner. Sadly, this tale is a faithful representation of many such gatherings I've had the displeasure to attend over the years. Of course, I'm not alone in criticizing what passes for meetings in most organizations; sessions during which, by one tally, 80% of the time is spent on items creating less than 20% of the organization's value.[6] *USA Today* conducted a poll a few years back and found that over 25% of those asked would prefer to visit the dentist, read the phone book, or mop their kitchen floor than attend a meeting at their company.[7] There is actually an historical precedent for nonproductive meetings that stretches all the way back to the early days of the United States Senate. Listen to this impressive account of the day's activities in the hallowed chamber, recorded by Senator William Maclay on April 3, 1790: "Went to the Hall. The minutes were read. A message was received from the President of the United States. A report was handed to the Chair. We looked and laughed at each other for half an hour, and adjourned."[8] Maybe Frederick Nietzsche had it right when he said "madness is the exception in individuals but the rule in groups."[9]

Why do we suffer from such ineffective meetings, wasted opportunities of enormous proportions? Author and management consultant Patrick Lencioni has suggested that most meetings suffer from two near fatal flaws: they are lacking in both conflict and contextual structure.[10] Let's begin with the paucity of conflict. Unless your organization is a member of the tiniest of minorities, you can probably relate to Lencioni's call to arms. In most management gatherings, the rules of etiquette dictate that only the politest of questions be asked, if any are raised at all, to which vanilla answers of shallow substance are provided in response. And the group moves along, smiling, realizing they are one step closer to the door. The tough questions, the ones that could lead to actual insights, are stifled, the result of participants fearing the wrath of their colleagues should they violate the norms guiding such civilized sessions. Well, it's time to remove the cheap gold plating of silence from meetings, and glaze the process with meaningful queries, bold statements, and heated debate. Lencioni, in his provocatively titled book, *Death by Meeting*, suggests that meeting participants should be jolted within the first ten minutes of a session with topics edgy enough to uncover relevant ideological conflict. Small group research has consistently demonstrated that diversity of opinion is the single best guarantee the group will garner any benefits from a face-to-face discussion. The open confrontation with a dissenting view forces those holding the majority opinion to interrogate their own views more closely, and this can often lead to revelations that spring the entire group forward.[11]

Lou Gerstner, the architect of IBM's turnaround throughout the 1990s, understood the principle of conflict and applied it liberally during his days at the helm of the corporate giant. He tells the story of an early strategy meeting, convened just after he assumed the role of CEO in 1993. At the appointed time, his managers began parading into the room, each followed by legions of binder-touting assistants, and took their assigned space at the large conference room table. When the meeting got into full swing, or perhaps full crawl, Gerstner was bitterly disappointed by the rote slides being presented and the lack of meaningful discussion and debate he knew was necessary to tease out real learning. In what he called the "click heard round the world," he finally jumped from his chair and pulled the plug on the overhead projector, insisting on real dialog and discussion from his team. It set a powerful precedent and laid out his expectations in no uncertain terms.[12]

As for Lencioni's second proposed flaw of meetings—the lack of contextual structure—that's just a nice way of saying most management get-togethers serve up a steaming pot of "meeting stew." Lacking a formal agenda to guide the proceedings, the roll call of discussion topics can often include such disparate points as operational reviews, the annual picnic, or hotly-contested parking spaces. What suffers as this pot of urgent, yet hardly important, topics boils over, is the organization's strategy, which, according to researchers, receives a paltry three hours of coverage each month.[13]

Executing a strategy requires a ceaseless assault on the data coming into the organization: What is it telling us, what does it mean for our people and our processes? Are course corrections required? How should we conduct this strategy audit? The answer: Use the Balanced Scorecard to drive the agenda of your management meetings. Doing so sends a resonant signal to everyone that strategy will now represent the core topic discussed at these sessions, with all background noise aggressively tuned out. In the sections below, I will outline a new management meeting, one with strategy squarely in the cross-hairs, one that uses the Balanced Scorecard to generate candid and progressive discussions of results.

Not to be dramatic, but the longer I work with the Balanced Scorecard, and the more exposure I gain to organizations of all types, from every corner of the globe, the more I'm convinced that reengineering your meeting process to harness the focusing power of the Balanced Scorecard is perhaps the single most important change your organization can make to generate improved results.

The New Strategy-Centered Management Meeting[14]

Because this may be new to you, and issues could abound, I'm going to frame the discussion of our new and improved meeting by offering a series of questions you may have when contemplating this topic.

Who Is Invited to Participate in the Meeting?   I've read and heard others advocate that when filling the seats for management review meetings, you throw away the organizational chart and invite based purely on the criteria of who can meaningfully contribute to the dialog. Follow this seemingly sound and politically correct advice and your meeting will be populated not only by senior executives but, possibly, by those holding lower ranks that have an intimate knowledge of Scorecard results as well.

My populist inclinations cause me to cheer this sentiment. However, the pragmatist dwelling deep within me channels the wisdom delivered in the Boz Scaggs hit, *Breakdown Dead Ahead!* Here's what can happen. You tell a mid-level manager that due to their outstanding erudition on a Scorecard measure, they'll be presenting the results to the executive team at an upcoming meeting. Once the initial shock passes, the chosen employee develops a narrative, rehearses it until he or she can deliver it with the clarity and conviction of a stumping politician, and then waits for the big day to arrive. At the appointed time, they are shuttled into the room—normally they have to wait outside until the exact moment they are to deliver their findings. The first few moments go very well, and why shouldn't they, the speech has been honed to a fine edge thanks to countless sessions in front of a bathroom mirror. About a minute in however, a chink appears, as the perceived enormity of the situation—delivering a presentation to a group of faces they normally see gracing the pages of the annual report—produces a vice in their stomach that won't let go. Their mouth dries, pulse quickens, and then . . . the . . . words . . . just . . . won't . . . come . . . out.

An overactive imagination is not the source of the woeful story above. I've seen it play out in three dimensions many times. In fact, I can still recall witnessing such a meltdown many years ago. It was very early in my career, and a colleague and I had been invited to a senior team session to deliver updates. I was the first person to speak, an enormous boon because the nervous germ had virtually no time to penetrate my wafer-thin defenses. I just got up there, did my thing, and retreated swiftly to a waiting chair at the back of the room. My friend wasn't as fortunate. His talk was scheduled for the very end of the session, leaving ample time for the projector in his mind to flash every doomsday outcome imaginable. No more than a minute or two into his scheduled ten minutes, it happened. He went completely blank. Actually, not completely blank, as he was muttering something completely incoherent, trying desperately to find his way back to the track of pure thoughts he'd delivered a thousand times in his head. I could have jumped in, tossed him a softball question that would surely have righted his mental ship, but I, like everyone else in the room, sat transfixed. It was like driving past a car accident; you know you shouldn't, but you just have to crank your neck and take a look. Or, opening the fridge for a glass of milk, only to discover it expired a week before. You take it to the sink, but before pouring it down the drain you've just got to take a little sniff. And so it was for my friend, the sour milk we all had to take in.

The intentions of casting lower-level managers in starring roles at these sessions may be honorable, but the execution can lead to a long-lasting, foul taste in the mouth of those unaccustomed to such gatherings. Thus, feel free to invite managers with a point of view who can contribute, and perhaps call on them with questions of clarification, but at its core strategy, execution is the responsibility of the senior management team and they must actively engage in and ultimately own this process.

How Do You Prepare for the Meeting? Stepping back a bit, before preparation comes scheduling of the meetings that should be done well before you sip coffee at your first Scorecard review. In fact, given the hectic calendars of most time-starved executives, you will be doing yourself an immense favor by placing these sessions on their calendars months in advance of the actual dates.

Sharing materials prior to the session is an absolute must should you hope to derive the benefits these meetings are capable of delivering. Snappy and clever spontaneous dialog is delivered effortlessly in movies and on television, but back here in the real world, your participants will need some help in framing the discussions you hope will lead to creative tension and breakthrough discoveries. That assistance comes in the form of materials delivered approximately one week in advance of the meeting, including your Strategy Map, Balanced Scorecard measure results, commentaries on performance, and updates on key strategic initiatives.

Who Should Facilitate the Meeting? Practitioners are mixed on this point, with some tapping their Balanced Scorecard Champion or team leader to guide the review session and others rotating the assignment among the senior management team. Both options have merit. Using the Scorecard

Champion ensures the meeting will be led by a guiding hand well-schooled in the mechanics of the Balanced Scorecard's principles and functions, thereby helping the group avoid digressing into the weeds of the organization's operations and missing the big picture being portrayed by Scorecard results.

Having a member of your senior management team conduct the session can also prove beneficial since one of your aims in pursuing the Balanced Scorecard is to drive ownership and accountability for strategy execution throughout the highest ranks of your organization chart. An additional benefit of employing this option is challenging the senior manager facilitator to step out of his or her usual silo and think broadly about organizational success, engaging in dialog with other business unit leaders and brainstorming creative solutions to cross-functional challenges.

How Do You Review Results during the Meeting?   There are a variety of options from which to choose when considering how you will actually review your Scorecard results. Let's consider some of the more popular alternatives:

- *Worst to first.* In this method, designed to take advantage of the time-tested power of peer pressure, the owner whose measure results are poorest is the first to present and explain the deficient state of affairs to the group. This technique has been employed with effect by New York City, and industrial giants General Electric and Siemens. Each has noted the impetus placed on poor performers to improve their performance lest they open the show each and every month.

- *The strategic story.* If your Strategy Map and Scorecard have made good use of cause and effect linkages, weaving a powerful strategic story through the four perspectives of the model, you may choose to use these causal paths as your roadmap in reviewing performance. You might begin with the Customer Perspective and work through the chain evident in the other perspectives, all the while challenging the hypothesis suggested by the linkages you created when developing the Map and measures.

- *No stone unturned.* This process features the sequential review of all four perspectives, beginning with Customer and dutifully scanning performance on each objective and measure right on down through the Employee Learning and Growth Perspective.

- *Exception-based.* Those employing this approach look first to measures operating significantly out of a predetermined range of acceptable performance and take a deeper dive to the inner workings of the metric in an attempt to ferret out the root causes of the aberration and get things back on track. It is similar to the "worst to first" method without the associated psychological pressure.

- *Five questions.* Scorecard cocreator Robert Kaplan suggests you pose these questions during your review:[15]
  - ○ Why did we miss the target?
  - ○ What correcting actions should we consider?
  - ○ Are initiatives on schedule?
  - ○ Do we need more resources?
  - ○ Would a multifunctional task force help?

- *Three questions.* If five questions seem like too much of an ordeal, follow the path worn by a client of mine that focuses on just three simple questions for every Balanced Scorecard measure:
  - ○ What happened?
  - ○ Why did it happen?
  - ○ What are we going to do about it?

As with most things Balanced Scorecard, there is no absolute method for running your review meetings. In fact, the modus operandi of the session runs a distant second to the actual conversation produced by the investigation itself. Regardless of the tack you use to steer the ship, what really matters is the discussion spawned along the way. The primary task of the facilitator is to use the results simply as a spark lighting a flame of intense discussion during which conventional views are challenged, assumptions exposed, and hypotheses about the strategy tested. Allow yourself some room for experimentation as you begin to structure your meetings using the Balanced Scorecard as the agenda, making alterations and improvements as you find a style that suits your culture and meets your unique needs.

How Do We Set an Appropriate Tone for the Meeting? The make or break variable of a successful meeting is the tone, or overall atmosphere that pervades the session. Your challenge, and it's a considerable one, is to infuse the room with a spirit of open and honest debate, challenging everything in your quest to unlock the truth and move further down the path of strategy execution. That path to truth and strategic enlightenment can quickly transform to a painful road of thorns, however, should you choose to push the envelope of inquiry and enter the territory of blame.

To experience the cleansing fresh air of open dialog and debate that leads to breakthroughs, your people need to feel psychologically safe—able to unearth sacred cows and previously taboo subjects without fear of sanctions, be they rendered in the form of stinging criticism, telling silence, or informal reprimands levied back in the workplace. An interviewer once asked *former* Dell CEO Kevin Rollins what would happen to a Dell manager whose product or sales region falls off track and starts losing money. Without missing a beat, Rollins replied smugly that "they'd become a pariah."[16] Dell has tumbled from its perch atop the computer mountaintop recently, but they may ascend again one day, I don't know. What I do know is that a culture characterizing underperformers as "pariahs" is most likely never going to reap the benefits of true strategic learning. The Rollins quote was drawn from an article titled, "Execution without Excuses." At the risk of never being hired by those of you subscribing to this no-holds-barred, wild-west method of management, I think it stinks! You can intimidate people into performing for awhile, and short-term results will surely follow as the career of Chainsaw Al Dunlop, and his trail of destruction in the private sector, will attest. But with every criticism and each belittling remark, long-term damage is being sewn into the culture and a toxin of fear and mistrust is being spread throughout your organization that will one day manifest itself as an organizational cancer ready to exact its revenge.

Contrast the punitive environment at Dell with the more nurturing mood at data storage firm Adaptec. During his tenure as the firm's CEO, John Adler drove the company's valuation from $100 million to over $5 billion because he had a very healthy attitude about business goals and financial results. For him, results were not a punitive weapon but a useful diagnostic and learning tool. When the firm, at one point, missed a quarterly goal, he and his management team calmly analyzed all the factors contributing to the shortfall. They discovered that, as a result of an unusual quality-control issue, the company had been unable to make some end-of-quarter shipments. Instead of reacting emotionally and assigning blame, Adler asked rigorous questions of the senior management team, which was able to uncover the root cause of the problem. He then communicated this information broadly to ensure organizational learning.[17]

Learning, and not the assignment of blame, must always be the primary objective of the strategy-centered management meeting, should you hope to create a culture in which continuous learning about the strategy is truly seen as everyone's job. Albert Einstein was once asked about his inspiring genius. The iconic scientist paused, then earnestly replied: "I have no special talents, I am only passionately curious."[18] This is what we should all strive for, in life as well as business: a hunger to uncover the truth, to move beyond the shiny veneer of simple answers often masquerading as the truth, and penetrating deeper until we reach the core essence of any challenge.

How Often Do We Hold the Meeting?   I know you want fewer meetings not more, so I'm risking a good deal of page tearing and muffled expletives when I suggest you hold your strategy-centered meetings *at least* quarterly, but preferably monthly. Before you angrily toss this book across the room shouting "No, not more meetings, please!!" hear me out. Circumstances change so rapidly in our modern business world that you simply cannot afford to let as many as 90 days pass without holding a rigorous review of the results you hope will propel you toward strategy execution. Customer requirements may be subtly shifting, the political landscape may be altered, and the economic environment in which you operate may be undergoing seismic shifts. Ignoring the warning signs, not to mention the opportunities, in front of you is done entirely at your peril.

The good news is that using the Balanced Scorecard may actually shorten the duration of your review meetings. Where before you launched a painstaking examination of every operational issue occupying even the outer reaches of the periphery, in addition to airing as much dirty personnel laundry as you could squeeze in, now your sessions will benefit from the structure of a tool with strategy at its core, with strategy as the guiding force behind your discussion and your exploration of the truth of your organization.

How Do We Ensure Accountability?   On the subject of accountability and making the most of time spent in meetings, authors Bossidy and Charan are crystal clear in their excellent book, *Execution*: "Never finish a meeting without clarifying what the follow-through will be, who will do it, when and how they will do it, what resources they will use, and how and when the next review will take place and with whom."[19] Ideas are the currency of the knowledge economy and during these sessions they will be flowing as freely as promises at a political convention. But as we all know, ideas are only as good as their execution, and they require directed action to reach fruition. Always compile a list of action items flagged during the meeting and ensure updates are provided at the next gathering.

Concluding Thoughts on Management Meetings

My assessment of meetings in this chapter has been quite cynical, even bordering on acerbic, from my parody of a typical meeting to begin the section, to the perils of inviting lower-level managers to participate, to most recently, the diatribe against playing the blame game. I don't think we need to call in a psychologist; it's probably all a thinly-veiled attempt to mask my frustration with what could be the most beneficial activity managers engage in each and every day.

We've all spent countless hours in meeting rooms during the course of our careers and unless there is a drastic upending of the way we conduct business, we are destined to spend many more in the years to come. As a leader in your organization, and you don't need to be the CEO or executive director, I urge you to follow the advice offered in this chapter. From the seemingly benign act of beginning and ending your sessions on time, all the way to the pinnacle of embracing a spirit of inquiry and learning, seize the opportunity that is staring you in the face and transform the meeting experience today. You, your organization, and dare I say the world, will all be better for it.

NOTES

1. Jack Welch with John A. Byrne, *Jack, Straight from the Gut* (New York: Warner Business Books, 2001).

2. Raef A. Lawson, William G. Stratton, and Toby Hatch, "Scorecarding in North America: Moving Towards a Best Practices Framework, Part I," *Cost Management*, July–August 2005, pp. 25–34.

3. Paul R. Niven, *Balanced Scorecard Step-by-Step: Maximizing Performance and Maintaining Results 2nd Edition* (Hoboken, NJ: John Wiley & Sons, 2006), p. 262.

4. Christoper Palazzolo and Kent Smack, "The Four Steps to BSC Software Selection,"*Balanced Scorecard Report*, November–December 2002, pp. 15–16.

5. Corporater.

6. Michael C. Mankins, "Stop Wasting Valuable Time,"*Harvard Business Review*, September 2004, pp. 58–65.

7. Julia Neyman and Julie Snider, "USA Today Snapshots,"*USA Today*, November 14, 2004.

8. John F. Kennedy, *Profiles in Courage, New Edition* (New York: Harper Collins, 2003), p. 27.

9. James Surowiecki, *The Wisdom of Crowds* (New York: Doubleday, 2004), p. xv.

10. Patrick Lencioni, *Death by Meeting* (San Francisco: Jossey-Bass, 2004), p. 228.

11. James Surowiecki, *The Wisdom of Crowds* (New York: Doubleday, 2004), pp. 183–184.

12. Michael Beer and Russell A. Eisenstat, "How to Have an Honest Conversation About Your Business Strategy,"*Harvard Business Review*, February 2004, pp 82–89.

13. Michael C. Mankins, "Stop Wasting Valuable Time," *Harvard Business Review*, September 2004, pp. 58–65.

14. Portions of this section are drawn from, and are adaptations of Paul R. Niven, *Balanced Scorecard Step-by-Step: Maximizing Performance and Maintaining Results, 2nd Edition* (Hoboken, NJ: John Wiley & Sons, 2006), pp. 275–278.

15. Robert S. Kaplan, "Using the Balanced Scorecard in the Public Sector,"*Government Summit*, 2006.

16. Thomas A. Stewart and Louise O'Brien, "Execution without Excuses,"*Harvard Business Review*, March 2005, pp. 102–111.

17. John Hamm, "The Five Messages Leaders Must Manage," *Harvard Business Review*, May 2006, pp. 114–123.

18. Walter Isaacson, *Einstein* (New York: Simon & Schuster, 2007), p. 548.

19. Larry Bossidy and Ram Charan, *Execution* (New York: Crown Business, 2002), p. 128.

12

The City of Charlotte: A Balanced Scorecard Success Story

Roadmap for Chapter 12   The City of Charlotte, North Carolina is widely considered the best example of Balanced Scorecard success in a public or nonprofit setting. An early adopter, the city implemented their first Balanced Scorecard in 1996. Adhering to a firm belief that "measurement matters," they have continuously fine-tuned their efforts, maximizing the benefits of the Scorecard as a measurement system, strategic management system, and communication tool. Their success has resulted in a long list of accolades, including: University Best Practice from the International City/ County Manager's Association (2001), and entry into the Balanced Scorecard Collaborative's Hall of Fame (2002). Charlotte's former City Manager, and Scorecard guiding force, Pam Syfert, was named a top ten public official in 1999 by *Governing* magazine.

When writing the *First Edition* of this book in 2003, I had the distinct pleasure to conduct a wide-ranging interview with three people instrumental in Charlotte's Balanced Scorecard success: Lisa Schumacher, Tiffany Capers, and Matt Bronson. Lisa has been with Charlotte's Budget and Evaluation Office for over 20 years and has worked with the Balanced Scorecard since its inception in 1996. She has spoken on the Charlotte experience at seminars and conferences throughout North America and has coauthored articles on the use of the Balanced Scorecard. Tiffany and Matt are also key players contributing to the success of Charlotte's ongoing Balanced Scorecard implementation. They have shared the Charlotte story with conference audiences in the United States, Canada, Ireland, and Singapore.

312

The original interview, which is contained on pages 313 to 324, was structured so that topics flowed in a pattern resembling the subject matter of this book. Readers interested in specific subjects may refer to the italicized text, which outlines the key topic represented in each question. However, I would highly recommend enjoying the entire learning experience.

Recently, as I was writing this *Second Edition*, I had the opportunity to reconnect with Lisa Schumacher and a new addition to her team, Kim Eagle, Evaluation Manager for the city. Kim has worked in local government administration for over 12 years and has published on topics including public finance, managed competition, administrative reform, and performance measurement. Lisa and Kim were kind enough to share with me the latest developments in Charlotte's ongoing and highly successful Balanced Scorecard implementation during our interview. On pages 324 to 329, you'll discover how the Scorecard pioneers at the City of Charlotte sustain their momentum, keeping the Scorecard fresh, relevant, and top of mind for all city staff.

2003 INTERVIEW

Paul Niven (PN): Who *introduced the Balanced Scorecard* to the City of Charlotte, and when?

City of Charlotte (CC): Pam Syfert was Deputy City manager in 1994, and at that time she read the first *Harvard Business Review* article on the Balanced Scorecard.

PN: Did she just happen to come across the article or was there interest in the topic of performance measurement, and specifically, the Balanced Scorecard at that time?

CC: We were interested in a new Performance Management system. We had been doing management by objectives (MBO) since the early 1970s and had been looking at what other cities were doing. We were kind of "shopping around" for a better and more meaningful way to approach performance management. The article Pam read in 1994 was the first we heard of the Balanced Scorecard.

PN: Were you concerned that this was a tool conceived for, and used primarily by, the private sector, and therefore it wouldn't be *appropriate for a public sector organization*?

CC: The initial reaction was intrigue. The idea of being able to measure and report on your strategy was something that we had never really attempted with our Performance Management system. I think we knew that it would be a leap, in the sense that it was designed for the private sector and most of the literature and training available was designed for the private sector. So that was a bit of an adjustment in the beginning to take a private-sector idea, private-sector language, and figure out how to make that work and be meaningful for a city organization.

PN: Were you able to get *executive sponsorship* for implementing the Balanced Scorecard? And, how did you win the *support of your mayor and city council*?

CC: When we implemented the Scorecard in 1996, Pam Syfert, who had originally introduced the concept to us, had become the city manager. So she was our most visible champion. We also had a mayor and city council who had been urging us to emulate the best practices in the private sector whenever possible. When they learned the Scorecard would help us become more strategic and give them better information for making decisions, they were onboard.

PN: What were your *objectives* in launching the Balanced Scorecard?

CC: In the past, any links between our Performance Management system and strategic plan were coincidental. So we wanted to tie our Performance Management system and city strategy together. We wanted the ability to measure our strategic plan.

PN: How did you *adapt the Kaplan and Norton model of the Balanced Scorecard* to fit the City of Charlotte?

CC: If you look at our Scorecard, you'll see the first thing we did was to move the Customer Perspective to the top. We initially attempted to develop the Scorecard with the Financial Perspective on top but found that we were spinning our wheels because financial results don't represent our "bottom line." Financial measures are important, but the customers' view of our performance is much bigger in government.

Putting the Financial Perspective at the top of the Scorecard would also have sent the wrong message. Being a public sector organization, we are funded by citizens, by taxpayers, so we didn't want to send a message that we were in this "for the money," that is, for a profit. We really wanted to convey that we were providing services as an organization to meet the needs of our citizens, meet the needs of our customers. By reorganizing the perspectives, it conveyed a more accurate and more appropriate message to our customers and our organization on how we view our customers and deliver services to them.

A more recent adaptation for our 2004/2005 Scorecard is renaming the perspectives. We recommended changing the names of the perspectives so that they were more consistent with the language we use internally. For example, the city manager doesn't talk about "Internal Processes," instead, she talks about "Running the Business." Similarly, rather than simply using the word "Customer," we say "Serve the Customer." The perspectives are now more representative and more consistent with our organizational culture and management expectations (see Exhibit 12.1).

PN: Did you use the typical Kaplan and Norton terminology of objectives, measures, targets, and initiatives?

CC: For the most part we were very consistent with using the terminology that's presented in the original Balanced Scorecard book. We use objectives, measures, targets, and initiatives. However, we expanded the types of measures. Specifically, we use four types of measures: activity measures, input measures, output measures, and outcome measures.

Outcome measures, the results measures, were a struggle for us initially—understanding them conceptually, and then actually trying to define and describe what an outcome would be for a city organization in a fiscal year, or even within two fiscal years. There was a learning curve, and to some extent, we still have opportunities in those areas. We've done a lot over the past year or so to make sure our vocabulary, our definitions, our lexicon is consistent.

PN: Can you describe some of the methods you've used to educate employees about key Balanced Scorecard concepts and terms?

CC: We've done several things. Discussing the Scorecard in our newsletter is one method we've used. We've also developed a glossary of all the terms we use in describing performance measurement. We conduct Balanced Scorecard training sessions through our organization training department. Finally, we developed a Balanced Scorecard Handbook that includes a lot of useful Scorecard information.

PN: Where did you build your first Balanced Scorecard? Was is a high-level Scorecard for the city or did you choose a department to "pilot" the Balanced Scorecard?

CC: It was a combination. At the outset we did build a Corporate Scorecard. After we had the initial 21 objectives described for the Corporate Scorecard, there were two other processes that went on simultaneously. Focus-area cabinets developed Scorecards and four key business units (KBUs) also built Scorecards.

PN: Can you describe what is meant by a focus-area cabinet?

CC: In 1991, our current City Manager, Pam Syfert, had a conversation with the city council during one of their retreats and essentially shared with them that the city organization can't be all things to all people. She strongly suggested a need to define and describe the areas that we could most impact as a city organization. That conversation

Exhibit 12.1   City of Charlotte's Focus Areas and Objectives (2003)

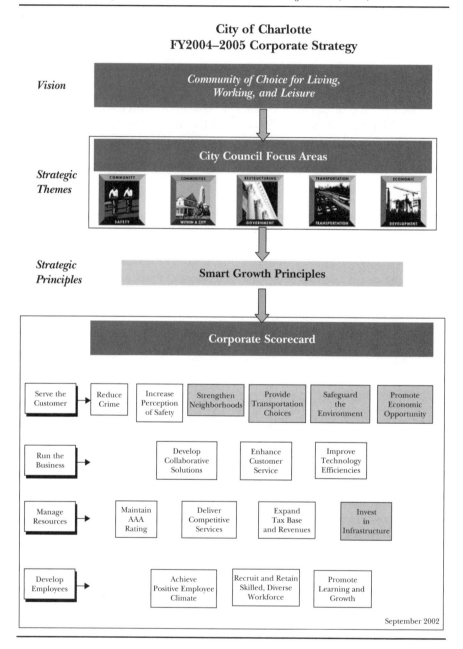

ultimately resulted in what we know as our five focus areas: community safety, city within a city (now communities within a city), transportation, economic development, and restructuring government.

Each of the focus areas has a cross-functional staff team that meets on a regular basis to discuss the corporate strategy relative to the respective focus areas and how the city as an organization can impact, influence, and achieve the overall vision for the focus areas by identifying strategic initiatives and measures. During our initial rollout of the Balanced Scorecard, those teams were responsible for developing focus-area cabinet Scorecards.

PN: What process, or processes, did you use to actually develop your Scorecards?

CC: We contracted with a consulting firm that, over a period of weeks, gave us a crash course on the Balanced Scorecard as a concept, as a tool, and how we could use it in the city organization. We then adopted a train-the-trainer model and facilitated the development of KBU Scorecards. Initially, two staff members, Lisa Schumacher and Nancy Elliot, were primarily responsible for facilitating the implementation of the Balanced Scorecard for the organization. Nancy Elliott spent over a year working with each key business unit. Now, the Balanced Scorecard is administered by a team of five members from the Budget and Evaluation Office.

PN: Public and nonprofit organizations often have a difficult time determining what to measure in their Customer Perspective. Who or what did you measure in your Customer Perspective and how did you make that determination?

CC: I don't think we had as much difficulty because we had our focus areas in place, which represent strategic focus. I think for a lot of nonprofits and governments, implementing a Balanced Scorecard requires some conversation at a high level in the organization to decide the organization's strategy—what is it that the organization wants to accomplish? What is the organization's focus, mission, and vision? To what end or for what outcomes should we be dedicating our resources? We had wrestled with these questions and more before deciding to implement a Balanced Scorecard.

PN: By looking at your Scorecard, it's apparent you don't advocate focusing on one customer group. You look at the broad spectrum of customers.

CC: That's correct. We look at the broad spectrum of customers. We view our customers as the donor, the taxpayer, as well as the service recipient. So in defining and describing our Customer Perspective, we really try to think about what it is we want to accomplish. Quite honestly, we try to answer the fundamental questions the Balanced Scorecard poses, which are: "At what must we excel to satisfy our customers?" "At what must we succeed to satisfy our customers?" The objectives appearing in our Customer Perspective represent what the citizens and city council have indicated as being critical to providing customer and taxpayer value—value in terms of what they pay and the services they receive.

PN: How many measures do you have on your Balanced Scorecards?

CC: Before the Balanced Scorecard, we had about 900 measures across 13 key business units. After we implemented the Scorecard, that number dropped down to about 260. Right now we have approximately 375 measures across all 14 of our key business units. We felt a little apprehensive when we saw the number of measures gradually increasing; however, our concerns subsided because we were getting a better balance of measures. Government is process-oriented. Oftentimes it takes more than a fiscal year to achieve or to accomplish the ultimate goal. We had to become more comfortable with the fact that we're not going to have only outcome measures on our Scorecard or in key business unit business plans. There will undoubtedly be some process measures as well (see Exhibit 12.2).

PN: Did you *cascade the Balanced Scorecard* across the City, and if so, how did you accomplish that task?

Exhibit 12.2　Sample of Charlotte's Corporate-Level Scorecard Measures (2003)

Perspective	Objective	Sample Measure	Target
Serve the Customer	Strengthen Neighborhoods	Number of stable neighborhoods as measured by the Quality of Life index	102 Stable Neighborhoods
Run the Business	Develop Collaborative Solutions	Percent of strategic transportation and land use projects utilizing integrated land use and transportation planning	100%
Manage Resources	Expand Tax Base and Revenues	Percent change in tax valuation in targeted neighborhoods	10% increase in tax valuation
Develop Employees	Recruit and Retain Skilled, Diverse Workforce	Percent increase in City average turnover rate	<5% increase in turnover

CC: Yes, we designed the Scorecard to really cascade the corporate strategy and vision down to the departments. We focused on translating the five focus areas into tangible objectives that could then be adopted by departments in guiding their initiatives. We began with the four pilot KBUs Tiffany mentioned, and then we rolled it out to other departments over an 18-month period.

There were varying degrees of success in developing KBU scorecards. All of the departments developed Scorecards, but with mixed results. Some departments really grabbed onto the concept of taking those objectives and developing meaningful and specific measures. Other departments found it more difficult. Over the past year and a half, we've really reinvigorated the KBU Scorecard development process. We have been leading a number of retreats and discussions, and facilitating brainstorming sessions—really challenging the departments to look at the Scorecard, identify which of the corporate objectives they relate to, and develop some key measures and targets based on those objectives (see Exhibit 12.3).

PN: Have you *linked the Balanced Scorecard to budgeting* and if so, do you think that link has proven effective?

CC: Very timely question because that's an area we're spending a lot of time on right now. In the past, we've always had some linkage between budgeting and performance management, particularly with the focus areas. For many years we've been able to say, for example, "because of council's priority in community safety, we've identified $X million in community safety initiatives in the recommended budget." What we haven't always done is really to show how service-level changes and resource requests tie back into specific Scorecard objectives. For example, "How does X request tie back into 'strengthen neighborhoods'?" "How does this request tie back into 'deliver competitive services'?" That's the missing piece that we were always faced with.

Another complicating factor is the fact that our budget requests were developed in the fall and winter while departmental Scorecards and business plans were developed in the spring. So, in essence, you have the budget driving the business planning. We're changing that now by developing a "strategic operating plan" that integrates business planning and budgeting. The strategic operating plan starts off with developing KBU Scorecards and business plans with departments, then identifying the resources necessary to carry out these strategic priorities.

PN: Who *owns or manages* the Balanced Scorecard process at the city?

CC: The Scorecard is primarily managed and coordinated by the Budget and Evaluation office. This office has been the traditional home of Performance Management at the city. Three of us, in addition

Exhibit 12.3 Charlotte's Strategy Pyramid

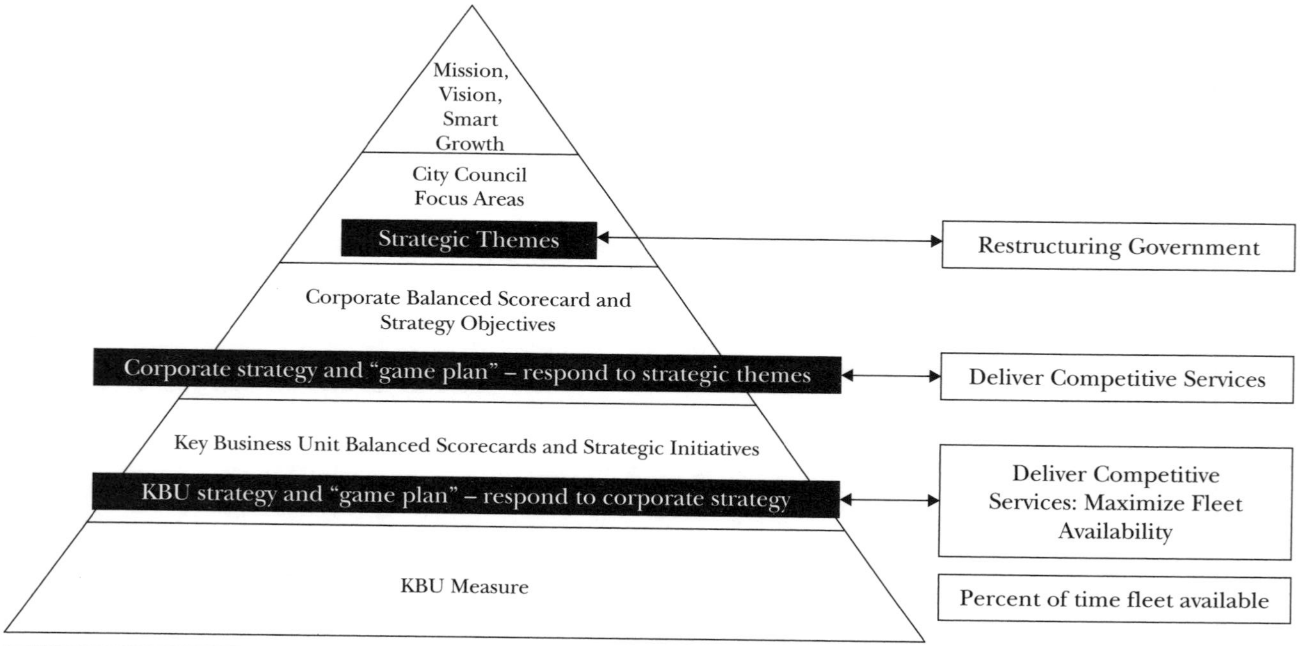

Mission, Vision, Smart Growth

City Council Focus Areas

Strategic Themes → Restructuring Government

Corporate Balanced Scorecard and Strategy Objectives

Corporate strategy and "game plan" – respond to strategic themes → Deliver Competitive Services

Key Business Unit Balanced Scorecards and Strategic Initiatives

KBU strategy and "game plan" – respond to corporate strategy → Deliver Competitive Services: Maximize Fleet Availability

KBU Measure → Percent of time fleet available

to two other analysts, are the primary Scorecard coordinators for the organization. We're charged with helping implement corporate strategy throughout the organization, monitoring performance, advising the leadership team on Scorecard-related issues, and consulting with departments across the organization.

PN: How do you *report your Balanced Scorecard results*? Are you using an off-the-shelf software package? Is it something you built in-house? What do you use?

CC: We've taken a look at a couple of off-the-shelf systems and our dilemma has been that those systems tend to be extremely quantitative in their orientation and in the reports they generate. As I was alluding to earlier, because of the processes involved with government work, there wasn't really a good fit with what we were seeing from off-the-shelf providers and what we felt we needed to provide as management information. We've also explored trying to develop something internally that allowed for more qualitative and more anecdotal data collection and data retrieval, but we've not landed on a perfect solution for how to automate that, yet. At the present time, our reporting system is paper-based. We produce mid-year and year-end reports.

We really wanted to get it right on paper. A big part of our challenge has been defining and describing those measures that provide management information. That's really where we're trying to move our organization: to being a strategy-focused organization that uses data to make decisions to move forward.

We've used Word and Excel because we have to report a good bit of narrative. If we do have a number to report, we usually need to give context. You can't just look at spreadsheets of columns and numbers and make judgments of whether that was particularly outstanding or not. That's one of the things people are often surprised about us, that we've not wanted technology or a system to drive the Scorecard. We've wanted to have it right on paper and then automation will come whenever automation comes.

PN: What has been the *effect of new administrations coming in*, a new mayor if that has occurred, or new city council members? How has that affected the Balanced Scorecard, if at all?

CC: We have been fortunate to have a good deal of consistency in our elected leadership. There have been some new faces on our city council in the last six to eight years, but there has also been a lot of consistency as far as people serving for six and more years on city council, as well as the mayor who is now in his fourth two-year term. So that has certainly helped us.

I also think if you look at our strategic themes, in some ways they are timeless. I don't know that we'll ever raise the flag and say that we have conquered community safety or that we have arrived at economic development. Maybe that is a test of good strategy. As council members change, the only thing that really changes is agreement on the initiatives. It's not that they disagree with the ultimate outcome of economic development, but there can be some disagreement about what the appropriate role of government is. So you see some adjustment in the initiatives we may be undertaking.

PN: What do you feel have been the biggest *benefits to using the Balanced Scorecard* at the City of Charlotte?

CC: This can be a very challenging question because it's often difficult to identify tangible, specific benefits from the Balanced Scorecard in terms of cleaner streets, a safer neighborhood, or other tangible services citizens expect of government. The benefits we point to are more internal in nature—really developing a strategy-focused organization.

The first benefit we tout is emphasizing strategy throughout the organization—taking the five themes of city council and really articulating what those mean. Community safety to us means reduced crime and increased perception of safety. The Scorecard has also been an important tool to help us integrate strategy with budgeting. It's really helped us view the budget as those resources necessary to achieve the community goals articulated through the Scorecard.

The Scorecard also represents a one-page game plan that shows what we're about as an organization. We can take that one-page sheet and say this is who we are as the city of Charlotte. This is our direction for the next two years. Additionally, the Scorecard helps us develop consensus through the process of coming up with these objectives and developing the measures and initiatives.

It helps improve management decisions by developing more relevant performance measures based on strategy, on our council focus areas, and our key themes. Lastly, it reports outcomes to elected officials and the community. We can show exactly what we're doing to achieve those key Balanced Scorecard objectives: reducing crime, creating economic opportunity, and so on.

Another benefit to using the Scorecard is an understanding of the city's strategy. In our 2002 employee survey, 57% reported that they understood what the city's overall goals are. And I believe almost 70% reported that they understood the goals of the specific business unit that they work in. We think that's a good baseline; it actually increased from the 2000 survey, but our goal is to see that number go up over time. The Scorecard also gives nonprofit and government organizations a platform to discuss employee growth and development. Sometimes a tenuous subject to broach in nonprofit and government organizations, the Scorecard clearly positions the employee as being integral to the successful achievement of organizational strategy. By doing so, it allows organizations to ask: "What do employees need to be successful, and in turn help the organization succeed?" The Balanced Scorecard truly "balances" success on the four critical pieces—the customer, the business, the resources, and the employees.

PN: What *roadblocks did you face in your implementation,* and how did you overcome them?

CC: We faced some initial challenges from KBUs in trying to develop the Balanced Scorecard. One KBU had a director who really viewed this as a "flavor of the month," a management tool that had come up in a magazine, and he wasn't quite sold on it. I will say, however, that this particular director has since become a strong champion and ally of the Scorecard, which is a testament to the time and effort we have invested into making the scorecard meaningful for the organization. It was also perceived by some as too top-down, as coming from the top of the organization, being pushed down to those in departments, particularly at a time when the organization was moving towards more of a decentralized format. We have worked with departments to see how they can be creative in selecting key strategic initiatives and measures based on a set of core organizational objectives.

We mentioned the private-sector orientation earlier. It can be challenging with terminology: Lead and lag measures are one example. Trying to familiarize these terms in a public-sector organization has been a challenge for us.

"Strategic selection" is another challenge. A Scorecard can't include everything we do as a city. Some departments had difficulty finding themselves in the Scorecard, and felt they were strategically ignored. Pam's [City Manager, Pam Syfert] challenge to the departments was: Find where you support the organization internally in a way that helps us all deliver those services to our customers. The Scorecard can't include every particular service that we provide to the community, but we can still build the organization internally. It can be very difficult to strike the right balance of measures to really show meaningful performance; particularly with so many of our measures being multi-year measures, we also need to keep working on developing shorter-term measures to give us information to make decisions.

PN: What *advice would you have for other organizations,* particularly nonprofit and government, who are just starting out on their Balanced Scorecard journey?

CC: I'd say it looks easier than it is. It is hard work. You should begin with a commitment to devote time to it. Our implementation period was longer than was desirable, but that was a result of juggling competing priorities. If you have staff available who can jump on it and spend six months, that's terrific. Our reality was that we didn't have that level of resources to devote to it, so we had to do a slower implementation than we would have liked. But even if you can launch a quick implementation, it still takes time and commitment. There will be some bumps and frustrations. Also, don't hold out for the perfect Scorecard the first time around; but get the first one on paper, and then in the next year build and improve from there.

It's also critical to have a high-level champion, an executive champion visible throughout the organization. The Balanced Scorecard has to have this kind of champion to be a success. Team members can do the legwork and coordinate, but unless you have the high-level champion visible and supporting it, the Scorecard will not go far.

Another key is this: You can't over-communicate the Scorecard to employees. We've built partnerships with Corporate Communications, our Training Team, and the City Manager's Office to really communicate the importance of the Scorecard and strategic planning, and how it's part of everyone's job. That is one of our biggest ongoing challenges—communicating the Balanced Scorecard and communicating strategy.

Finally, the Balanced Scorecard is ultimately a tool for change—it's a change agent. With change you have potential benefits and risks. Organizations should not underestimate the extent to which the Balanced Scorecard can and will and should change the way they think about strategy, the way they view strategy, and hopefully the way they evaluate the successful achievement of strategy.

2007 INTERVIEW

Paul Niven (PN): You have been working with the Balanced Scorecard for over a decade. How do you share your Balanced Scorecard and your measurement philosophy with new employees?

City of Charlotte (CC): At our new employee orientation training, we talk about city strategy and have ongoing training programs throughout the year that we call "City Strategy 101," which any employee in the organization can attend. Also, when supervisors or employees are promoted to supervisory and management positions, we have special training for them, and strategy and performance management are part of that training.

PN: How do you integrate the Balanced Scorecard with Personal Development Planning?

CC: Using their Key Business Unit (KBU) Scorecard, employees sit down with their supervisors and develop objectives that are related to the work they are doing, and to how their department responds to city strategy. So there is a direct link all the way down to the front line employee.

PN: You've had very few changes to your objectives over the last several years. Do you try to promote stability of objectives and city council focus areas or, does the constancy reflect a lack of change in your environment?

CC: We don't explicitly promote stability, but it seems to have worked out that way because we were very deliberate and specific when we identified the objectives at the outset of our Scorecard implementation. They remain constant for that reason. However, we do make changes when necessary. For example, last year we re-examined, from a comprehensive viewpoint, how we're serving our citizens. Based on that examination, we added the objective of "Optimize Business Processes" within our "Run the Business" perspective (see Exhibit 12.4).

PN: According to your Web site, you have 426 measures scattered across the 14 KBUs of the city. Of those, approximately 55% would be lagging indicators and 45% lead. Can you talk about the number of measures within the city?

CC: We are currently updating the measures inventory, and a more recent count of measures reveals a total of about 350. What we're seeing is that business units that have in the past tracked 30 or more have reduced that number. We encouraged that. There were some business units that initially had real difficulty believing 20 measures covered all facets of their business. However, we're now seeing a comfort level that some measures may not be appropriate at the KBU level and are better suited to a personal Scorecard (for example).

One of the messages we use consistently is that the information included on the Scorecard needs to be used for decision-making purposes, and therefore needs to be critical. However, just because something doesn't appear on the Scorecard specifically, doesn't mean it's not still important and there's not a place for it. It could be on a work plan or on an individual personal Scorecard at a different level. The understanding of what best fits on a Scorecard has been part of our continual message and we believe the more folks hear that and the more we practice it, the more comfortable they get.

PN: When cascading, do the KBUs have the option to develop their own objectives or, are they required to choose only city objectives that they can influence when they build their Scorecards?

CC: We ask that they use corporate objectives because it demonstrates how the work in the KBU supports the overall city strategies. That's the

Exhibit 12.4   City of Charlotte Focus Areas and Balanced Scorecard Objectives (2007)

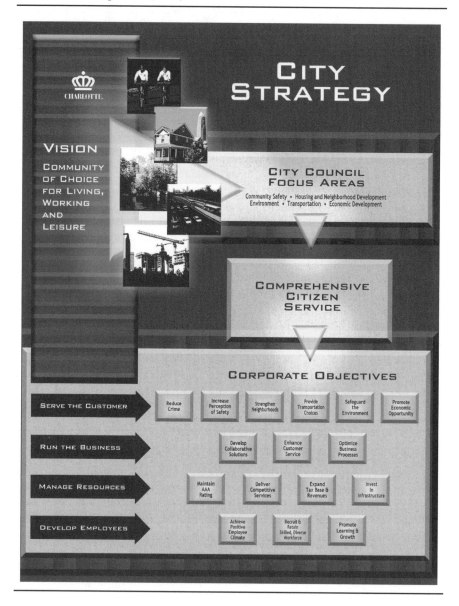

first thing we have to look for: How are they (the KBU) supporting overall city strategy and what council has said is important from a policy stand-point? Of course, there is the chance to "personalize" their Scorecard by adding unique measures, targets, and initiatives. But the primary goal is to demonstrate how they link back to the corporate level objectives.

Learning and alignment are two-ways streets though. You can also look at the process from the reverse view, think about what's going on in the business units, and use that as an opportunity to see where you may have gaps at the corporate level. That's what happened when we added the corporate objective "optimize business processes." We started looking at the way the KBUs did their work and we saw issues and opportunities that resulted in adding a corporate objective. So in this way, the cascading process informed the corporate level Scorecard.

PN: When we spoke back in 2003, you were really starting to focus on the Balanced Scorecard and budgeting link. Can you describe your efforts in this area?

CC: When we first talked about the budgeting and Balanced Scorecard link during our initial interview with you, we were just beginning to look at this area and trying to align how we conducted the strategy and budgeting processes. We now have the two on a common calendar, resulting in a singular process. Resource requests are based on KBU strategy as outlined in their Scorecard.

PN: As we all know, budgeting can be a fairly political process; there can be game-playing, politics, and so on. Was there any hesitation from your KBU leaders or was the process embraced?

CC: I think it was embraced. There was always some level of concern or question as to why the two processes were not put together. That we performed them separately was not always comfortable for people, and we recognized that you can't have a conversation regarding strategy separate from budget. Thus, it made sense to put them together. I would not say that folks were apprehensive at all from that standpoint. I think our KBUs are eager to tell us what resources they need, and put that in the framework of the strategy context. At the point we put the processes together and focused on the linkages between budget and strategy, the Balanced Scorecard had been around long enough for people to see that the union made sense.

PN: Kaplan and Norton have advocated for an Office of Strategy Management (OSM)—a group responsible for strategy execution through the use of the Balanced Scorecard. Would you say that your Office of Budget and Evaluation fulfills the duties of an OSM perhaps without using that title?

CC: I think so. For more than 30 years, the Budget office has had responsibility and ownership of performance management and when we adopted the Balanced Scorecard we became the facilitators for strategy discussions. We worked with the consultants who helped us develop our first Scorecard.

The Budget Evaluation office has been the city manager's resource and owner/champion of the Scorecard from the very beginning. It probably helped us in that we were familiar and were doing similar work even before that. We'd been doing performance management for more than 30 years, so the Balanced Scorecard was just an evolution of that for us. One of the things we have done recently is to reorganize our Budget Evaluation office to add Kim's [Kim Eagle] position, the Evaluation Manager. Previously we had a five-member team within our office that worked on strategy in addition to other responsibilities. By adding the Evaluation Manager, we feel we've enhanced our ability to lead strategy, particularly the integration of strategy and budget. So that has been a refinement we have made and we think an improvement in our own structure to champion and lead the effort for the organization.

PN: Let's talk about Balanced Scorecard reporting. When we spoke in 2003, you had not been comfortable with an off-the-shelf reporting package for the Balanced Scorecard and were using Excel. Any changes?

CC: We've continued to see some demonstrations and look at software packages. In late 2007, we are planning to pilot a software program in one of our business units, so it's possible that by the spring of next year (2008) we will make a decision to use software throughout the city if we feel the tool is right for us.

PN: An abundance of literature suggests that in order for performance measurement, specifically Balanced Scorecard, to be successful, when you examine and measure results you've got to use them for learning and not for punishment. It's imperative to talk about results, challenge people to improve them going forward, without laying a lot of blame. Can you talk about how you've been able to do that at the city?

CC: I think the mindset of learning from measure results, as opposed to punishment, has always been part of the culture here in the city. We try to engage KBUs when they're developing their measures and their targets. We encourage them to include stretch targets and reemphasize that message. Given our culture, it hasn't proven difficult to convince people there won't be retribution for missing targets. As a learning organization, the emphasis really is on using the information to take the best path moving forward and make the best decisions whether you end up with a green light or a red light at the end of the day. People are at a point where they understand that either one is okay as long as they learn from their results.

PN: In 2003, I asked you about the impact of new elected officials on the Scorecard. You replied that consistency had worked in your favor, as well as the constancy of your focus areas. Any new insights?

CC: The Balanced Scorecard has become very ingrained and institutionalized for us, and we've been able to demonstrate positive benefits to incoming officials. Therefore, they are accepting of the Scorecard as a tool the city employs in executing its strategy.

PN: Perhaps the most important question: How do you sustain the momentum for performance management on a broad scale and the Balanced Scorecard specifically?

CC: One of the things that has helped us is the consistency of leadership—we had the same city manager for ten years. The city manager said "Let's try the scorecard," and was here for ten years to champion it in that position. I believe that was a real key. If we had experienced changes in our top leadership and that interest or commitment to the scorecard wasn't evident, we might have been one of those who derailed and started again later.

Also, we've benefited from taking a phased approach to the Balanced Scorecard. We sit down as an evaluation team once a year and think about what's going well, what our next steps are, what can we do better, and when do we introduce changes to the organization. I think that phased approach has worked very well for us. I often suggest to people that they take a phased approach in implementing it.

Over time, people have embraced the Balanced Scorecard and are very comfortable with it. The elected officials, even the new elected officials who come in and see it for the first time, appreciate that such a system is in place. They say, "There IS a strategy and that's something I can go out and share with my constituents. Here's our performance report. The next neighborhood meeting I'm invited to, these are my speaking points. Or I can take the city's strategic focus area plan and develop my speaking points for the Rotary Club next week." They recognize the Balanced Scorecard is a tool that can help them.

13

Sustaining Balanced Scorecard Success

Roadmap for Chapter 13   A Balanced Scorecard journey is more akin to a marathon than a sprint. To ensure your Scorecard has the staying power of a champion, this chapter begins with an examination of what is necessary to update the Scorecard's core elements as conditions inevitably change. In addition, you'll learn about a critical emerging discipline within organizations committed to making strategy a core competency: the Office of Strategy Management (OSM). I'll discuss how and why this promising function has emerged, outline considerations in establishing an OSM, and provide a case study of one organization's Balanced Scorecard and OSM journey.

UPDATING THE BALANCED SCORECARD

"Does our Balanced Scorecard stay the same?" is a question I often hear from those who have recently developed Scorecards. Some fear that, once established, the Strategy Map of objectives and Scorecard of measures are cast in stone, never to be altered. Fortunately, that is definitely not the case. The Scorecard system was designed to help you navigate the changing tides your organization must ride and as such must be occasionally updated to ensure it remains relevant and effective.

Prudent organizations will critically examine their Scorecard framework at least annually to determine if its core elements are still appropriate in telling an accurate strategic story. A "best practices" benchmarking study suggests a majority of Scorecard practitioners do just that. In the study, 62% of participants updated their Balanced Scorecards annually, 15% updated every 6 months, while 23% updated every 3 months.[1] Let's look at the core elements comprising a Balanced Scorecard system and consider how they may change over time.

- *Mission, values, and vision.* The mission defines your core purpose and, as a result, will seldom change. In a similar fashion, values reflect the timeless and deeply held beliefs of your organization and guide day-to-day actions. Unless you determine your value system to be undermining your efforts, it is unlikely you would advocate a wholesale change. The vision represents a word picture of what the organization intends to become, maybe 5, 10, or 15 years into the future. Unlike the mission, which is foundational and permanent, the vision can be accomplished and may change. Should you feel you've reached the aspirations articulated in your vision, it will be time to retool it for the next generation of your existence. The Strategy Map and Balanced Scorecard should be translated to ensure alignment with any changes in direction.

- *Strategy.* Strategy represents the broad, overall priorities adopted by the organization in recognition of its operating environment and in pursuit of its mission. Obviously, your operating environment will change: It's probably changing as you read this. Any number of areas could affect your strategy going forward: changes in federal, state, or local laws; changes in the target population you serve; new members on your board; newly elected officials; or changes in funding levels. Each of these will entail a strategic response, and since the Scorecard framework is designed to translate your strategy into action, it would require modifications as well.

- *Strategy Map.* Should you experience a change in mission, values, vision, or strategy, your Map will inevitably require updating. Aside from those "structural" elements, you may deem other alterations desirable. For example, many agencies will change the wording of objectives to more accurately represent their core purpose or to clarify potentially confusing terminology. Additionally, you may revise the language employed in naming your perspectives to terms more in line with your unique culture.

- *Measures.* In addition to the preceding structural items, measures are subject to many changes over time. You may modify the method of calculation to better capture the true essence of the event under investigation, or the description may be enhanced to improve employee understanding of operational and strategic significance. Frequency of reporting could also be changed. For example, you may have attempted to track customer satisfaction monthly but the logistics of gathering the data simply proved too challenging.

In that case, you wouldn't abandon this important metric but would simply change the reporting period to something more amenable to measurement, perhaps examining it quarterly. Another important change is simply the raw number of measures appearing on the Scorecard. The majority of agencies, as they become more accomplished in the use of performance measurement, will decrease the number of indicators they track over time. As you saw in the preceding chapter chronicling the story of the City of Charlotte, as key business unit managers became more comfortable with the Scorecard system and its function and benefits, they reduced the number of measures they tracked.

- *Targets.* Targets will normally change on an annual basis as you review your Balanced Scorecard. Mid-year "course corrections" are also a possibility should you believe you've set the bar too high or too low.

- *Initiatives.* Like targets, initiatives will be updated annually, and should be reflected in your budgeting process as discussed in Chapter 10.

Updating your performance objectives, measures, and targets is yet another way to tap into the collective knowledge of your organization. Be sure to involve as many employees as possible to ensure that any changes reflect organization-wide interests. Surveying employees is an excellent method of gathering their feedback on Scorecard use and potential improvements. Exhibit 13.1 displays a ten-question survey that can be administered to employees at least annually to ensure the critical feedback and knowledge they possess is collected. Employees should answer the survey questions using a 1 (low) to 5 (high) scale, with their specific group or department in mind. The senior executive team would assess the high-level organizational Strategy Map and Scorecard. In addition to asking questions, the survey also includes a space for employee comments and recommendations for Scorecard improvements.

In this example, the surveyed employee gives her group's Scorecard 38 out of a possible 50 points. Any total over 35 would be considered positive, however, the composition of the scores provides as much insight as the aggregate. In this case, the Scorecard appears to be working very well in its intended capacity of informing employees about organizational strategy and providing a line of sight. It also appears this group reviews their results on a regular basis and uses the information to identify future improvement initiatives. However, it is also clear this employee is not happy with the reporting tool being used, the cause-and-effect linkages aren't clear, and as evidenced by her comments, Scorecard results are not stimulating organization-wide discussions. This input is invaluable as managers and employees look to develop future iterations of their Scorecard.[2]

Exhibit 13.1 Balanced Scorecard Employee Survey

Question	Score
Use of the Balanced Scorecard in my group has helped increase my knowledge of the organization's strategy.	5
Our group's Balanced Scorecard measures clearly demonstrate how we contribute to the achievement of overall organizational goals.	5
Our measures represent an appropriate balance among the four Balanced Scorecard perspectives.	4
Our measures are linked in a series of cause-and-effect relationships.	3
My input was sought during the development of our group's Balanced Scorecard.	4
In our group we review Balanced Scorecard results on a regular basis.	4
The reporting tool we use is efficient.	3
Managers and employees are held accountable for achieving Balance Scorecard results.	4
Analyzing Balanced Scorecard results allows our group to identify potential improvement initiatives.	4
Discussing Balanced Scorecard results with colleagues has increased my knowledge of their function(s).	2
Total Score	38

Additional Comments:

I would like to know more about the use of the Scorecard in other groups within the company. How are results reported, and can those results be shared with all employees?

Adapted from *Balanced Scorecard Step-by-Step: Maximizing Performance and Maintaining Results 2nd Edition*, by Paul R. Niven (John Wiley & Sons, 2006).

AN EMERGING DISCIPLINE: THE OFFICE OF STRATEGY MANAGEMENT

Throughout this book, I've discussed the importance of change: recognizing it, adapting to it, and modifying your strategy to benefit from it. Our survey of the change landscape has focused predominantly on factors external to the organization, including demographic and economic shifts, changing political climates, and altered economic states. But change occurs within the four walls of organizations as well. As the practice of commerce has evolved, particularly over the past 150 years or so, organizations have made several *internal* adaptations to meet the formidable challenges they faced.

Money has always been central to any organization, be it private, public, or nonprofit, but as the stewardship function has grown exponentially, we've seen the advent of the Chief Financial Officer (CFO) to track the complex web of debits and credits while complying with ever-changing statutes and regulations. Similarly, as technology has transformed the way in which we work and live, Chief Information Officers (CIOs) have become critical contributors at the strategy table of virtually all organizations. Cast your glance anywhere in the modern organization and you'll discover similar instances of specialization emerging: Chief Knowledge Officers, Chief Talent Officers, Chief Marketing Officers, and so on.

Most nonprofit and public sector organizations will employ many of the functional specialists outlined above and will also house a group known as "strategic planning." While the specific duties of a strategic planning function can vary tremendously given the enormous number of definitions spanning the strategy spectrum, as a common thread, most will concentrate on scanning the environment, seeking new information, and using their findings to help inform the organization's response to the changes it faces. The whole focus is on strategy formation. Strategy execution, however, is left to the entire agency: The responsibility for living the strategy, seeing it transformed into living, breathing reality each day is diffused among everyone occupying a cubicle, office, or suite within the organization. This is not surprising because strategy execution is everyone's job and requires cross-functional collaboration to occur. But as we all know, simply willing the silos to disperse and have people come together in a spirit of strategic harmony doesn't happen through slogans or speeches—the process must be managed as precisely and with as much rigor as every other specialty should organizations hope to achieve any benefit whatsoever from their strategic planning efforts.

Championed by Balanced Scorecard architects Kaplan and Norton, a new discipline is emerging within organizations seeking to bridge this strategy formation and execution chasm: the Office of Strategy Management (OSM). This novel approach applies the age-old wisdom of specialization to the challenge of executing strategy by resting in one group the dual responsibilities of facilitating the development of strategy and shepherding its execution, primarily through the Balanced Scorecard system. Let's take a closer look at this office and explore how you may use it within your organization.

As you will discover, the OSM could be considered an umbrella agency for many of the Balanced Scorecard tasks discussed throughout this book.

Functions of the Office of Strategy Management (OSM)[3]

Successful execution of strategy requires each person in the organization from every discipline to aggregate their efforts in a unified push towards a common cause. Coordinating that effort is the domain of the OSM. While in the past diffusion of efforts frequently transpired with no single group orchestrating the strategy execution process, the OSM takes responsibility for the complex and coordinated effort required to execute the organization's strategy. Collaboration and integration aren't left to chance, but are carefully managed under the auspices of the OSM. Although the art and science of the OSM are nascent fields, early research and practitioner experience has led to the following key functions falling under the umbrella of the office.[4]

Change Management In his classic work *The Prince*, Nicolo Machiavelli reminds us that "It ought to be remembered that there is nothing more difficult to take in hand, more perilous to conduct, or more uncertain in its success, than to take the lead in the introduction of a new order of things."[5] Decipher this quote and you realize it's synonymous with change. Strategy—the most critical enabler of organizational success—and change are inextricably linked because, at its core, strategy is about change: choosing a different set of activities than others to effectively serve your customers. Given the fact, and I believe we can all agree on this, that change is difficult for many people to accept, among the first responsibilities of the OSM is heralding the need for change—selling the burning platform for abandoning the status quo and embracing a new order. The OSM will outline the rationale for the change, discuss how it will be implemented, clarify expectations and, most vitally, clearly establish what benefits await employees willing to accept the change.

Strategy Formation and Planning The OSM doesn't have the responsibility for crafting the organization's strategy; that vital task is better left to leaders from across the organization's functions. However, the office facilitates the process through a number of potential responsibilities, including: gathering relevant strategy inputs such as environmental information, conducting scenario planning, facilitating strategic dialog and debate, and orchestrating the strategy timetable. To effectively execute this responsibility, it is critical that the OSM work closely with the senior executive team.

Balanced Scorecard Coordination The bulls-eye of OSM tasks is represented by their guardianship of the entire Scorecard process. The group will work closely with the executive team engineering the organization's Strategy Map and Balanced Scorecard, ensuring it acts as a faithful translation of their strategy. But Scorecard coordination spreads well beyond to providing education for all stakeholders, facilitating results meetings, and ensuring information systems are stocked with the appropriate data for decision making and analysis.

Strategic Communication Unfortunately, gold stars for communication are not in the immediate future for the vast majority of organizations. When it comes to sharing information, the rule of thumb for many appears to be "too little, too late, and top down." In the era of scientific management at the turn of the twentieth century, this oversight could be readily ignored: Employees of that epoch generally required little in the form of communication to perform their laborious and repetitive tasks. The knowledge economy of the twenty-first century, however, demands more from our leaders. Should they expect to win both the hearts and minds of their staff, they must engage in virtually constant communication of the building blocks of success: mission, vision, values, strategy, and the necessity of change. Working with other constituents across the organization (communications experts as an example), the OSM should coordinate communication activities centered on strategy. A key tenet of this work is the use of many and varied communication devices, including town hall meetings, presentations, and e-learning opportunities, all segmented by the audience.

Alignment As previously mentioned, the execution of strategy requires integration of many processes throughout the organization. The OSM acts as a connective tissue binding the processes together, ensuring their smooth functioning leads toward strategy execution and not redundancy and sup-optimization. Among the more important links is that between strategy and performance management, including personal development planning. Human capital is the real driver of the knowledge economy and every organization must ensure this scarce of resource is aligned to the strategy.

Initiative Management For many organizations, a high payback on their OSM investment is received when they actively manage the initiative process. The vast majority of truly "strategic" initiatives are cross-functional in nature, frequently requiring collaboration among business units, Information Technology (IT), and other entities, and thus must be managed in a cross-functional manner. While the OSM will not actively lead strategic initiatives, they supply the processes to ensure such initiatives are on track and making the strategic impact promised.

Governance Coordination Particularly in the private sector—given the spate of scandals we've witnessed over the past several years—boards require tools that provide an insightful view inside the organization's strategy and value-creating mechanisms. The OSM has the opportunity to break new organizational ground in this regard by working with the board and other external stakeholders to proactively determine their information needs and meet them in a timely and efficient fashion.

Performance Review Administration Strategy must constantly be monitored and tested in real-time to determine its efficacy, and the performance review meeting is the setting for this learning laboratory. The OSM coordinates the overall performance and strategy review process by determining the timetable, developing the agenda, facilitating the discussion, and ensuring follow-up actions are documented and completed.

Analysis of organizations gaining entrance into the Balanced Scorecard Hall of Fame has uncovered the increasing prominence of the OSM. As recently reported, "the 2006 winners rate themselves more highly in establishing an Office of Strategy Management (OSM). 53% believe they are best practice at this, as compared with the previous two classes (14% of the 2005 winners and 33% of the 2004 winners). Such improvement in a short period of time seems to reflect the priority that organizations place on establishing and investing in OSMs."[6]

The title of this chapter is "Sustaining Balanced Scorecard Success," and the only way that is possible is through the efforts of a group solely responsible for strategy execution and utilizing the Balanced Scorecard. Therefore, I am a strong advocate of the OSM notion and encourage you to develop such an office at the very outset of your implementation. In my consulting work, I've always warned clients from day one that without a person or group holding the responsibility to run the program when the consultant leaves, it's most likely destined to be about as stable as leaves blowing in an autumn wind. You don't have to call it an OSM, perhaps that's a bit too clinical for your liking. As with the Scorecard itself, the name runs a distant second to the practice itself. Establishing an OSM-like group—one that reports directly to your chief executive to ensure they have the power necessary to work effectively throughout the agency—is a giant leap towards making strategy execution a core competency within your organization.

AN OSM CASE STUDY: NEW BRUNSWICK (NB) POWER

New Brunswick Power is a publicly-owned electric utility operating in the eastern Canadian province of New Brunswick. The organization traces its roots to the early 1880s when the first power companies began to sell electricity in the province's major centers of Saint John, Moncton, and Fredericton. Today, in serving over 360,000 customers, the vibrant company operates one of North America's most diverse generating systems and interconnected transmission networks.

In the following sections, we'll trace the company's Balanced Scorecard path, culminating in their development of an OSM in 2006.

NB Power's Balanced Scorecard

As with many organizations implementing the Balanced Scorecard, success did not come immediately or easily for NB Power. The company's first exposure to the tool was in 2004. That year, CEO David Hay launched an aggressive program of Business Excellence, a collection of four programs aimed at supplementing the company's storied legacy of innovation and engineering excellence with twenty-first-century business practices. After considerable review, the Balanced Scorecard was chosen as the firm's performance management system.

The initial phases of the implementation took place during a time of significant upheaval at the company. A corporate restructuring that included job losses caused much unease among the company's long-tenured employee base, and the Scorecard, designed to bring clarity to the organization's vision and strategy, was reduced in many ways to an afterthought in management review meetings, as managers and employees alike struggled to understand their role in the new NB Power structure.

By 2006, with the pains of restructuring healing, the company committed to pursue its Balanced Scorecard agenda with renewed vigor and enthusiasm. CEO Hay, after conducting considerable research on the topic, determined that an OSM would greatly assist the organization's efforts in breathing new life into the Balanced Scorecard process. Within months, a new resource reporting directly to him was hired, and the nascent office was in place, ready to energize the company's strategy execution competence.

A little over a year later, the organization now has 75 cascaded Scorecards in place (on the way to 90), has created an innovative new process combining business planning, financial planning, and risk management, and have completely reengineered their management reporting and review process. It's time to learn how they did it.

NB Power's OSM

When including case studies in a book, it's customary (for me at least) to interview my subjects, compile notes, and draft pages that portray their story. That was my plan as I interviewed NB Power's OSM Director, Christian Richard. Emphasis on the words "*was my plan*." Very soon into the process, Christian's boundless energy and enthusiasm intervened and saw my best-laid plans jettisoned like a skydiver at 13,000 feet—voooomp, gone! Any time you're engaging with passionate people (see the City of Charlotte team for another great example), it's best to simply lay the tracks and get out of the way as they come steaming along. So, with apologies to case-study purists, here is the NB Power OSM story in Christian's words.

Paul Niven (PN): How was the OSM staffed?

Christian Richard (CR): The OSM was staffed based on operational experience and Balanced Scorecard experience. In addition to having a Director of the OSM reporting to the CEO, a Coordinator was appointed to the OSM team. To assist and accelerate the knowledge and expertise of the Balanced Scorecard, a support structure was established within the four operating companies (Generation, Nuclear, Transmission, Distribution and Customer Service) and Shared Services by way of Managers of Planning who are essentially an extension of the OSM in their own groups.

Each operating company has a Manager of Planning who reports to the Finance Director. Their main responsibility is to support the development and integration of the Balanced Scorecard in their respective organization. In addition to Scorecard-related activities such as cascading, ensuring alignment, strategic initiatives management, coaching, support, and facilitating senior management team reviews, they also facilitate risk assessment sessions. Essentially, the OSM establishes practices, guidelines, procedures at the executive level and then utilizes the Managers of Planning network to distribute this knowledge into the operating companies. This structure has allowed us to create many in-house experts on the Balanced Scorecard that has contributed to our success.

PN: What are the key roles and responsibilities of the OSM?

CR: The OSM was established to assist all NB Power groups in transforming their plans into reality using the methodology of the Balanced Scorecard, ensuring every employee's actions are aligned with, and focused on, the direction set by our Executive team. The OSM focuses on key elements of performance management including:

Implementing the Balanced Scorecard throughout the organization

Ensuring all Balanced Scorecards are aligned

Ensuring all employees understand our strategy and direction (strategic communications)

Managing the selection and execution of strategic initiatives

Administering performance review meetings

Facilitating the strategic planning process

PN: What were your priorities in the first year of introducing the OSM?

CR: We established four key priorities during our first year:

1. Implementing the Balanced Scorecard throughout the organization

2. Ensuring all Balanced Scorecards are aligned

3. Ensuring all employees understand our strategy and direction (strategic communications)

4. Managing the selection and execution of strategic initiatives

PN: What benefits have you seen from implementing an OSM at NB Power?

CR: The OSM has helped transform the Balanced Scorecard from something once viewed primarily as a Finance initiative to an active management tool that has become part of our day-to-day business. It has also brought focus and attention to the Balanced Scorecard and its associated processes. Additionally, it has also enabled the implementation to be accelerated significantly, not only because of the focus on cascading and alignment, but also because this is now seen as being directly supported by the CEO.

Another benefit of the OSM is evident from coaching that takes place at review meetings. It's clear that teams are now learning how to leverage the Balanced Scorecard by assigning accountability for measures, which is leading to better understanding of their businesses. The result is results! Teams are fostering commitment from employees, engagement, and relentless focus on the measures of their Balanced Scorecard.

The benefits of implementation are only the beginning. Time and time again, examples of breakthrough results are becoming apparent, with anecdotes of various groups enhancing their performance becoming more frequent. The real benefit is that—with the Balanced Scorecard—these groups can now demonstrate how they improved by simply pointing to their Balanced Scorecard results.

PN: What is your advice to other organizations developing an OSM?

CR: I believe that there are three key points that should be considered when creating an OSM:

1. *Establish your OSM early with the support of your CEO.* When beginning an implementation, visible support from your CEO is paramount. As you begin your Balanced Scorecard journey, the OSM should keep things as simple as possible, focussing on educating the most senior leaders of the organization first, identifying the early adopters, and working with them to cascade your first Balanced Scorecard. Then, use that implementation to promote the tool to other leaders. If this is done consistently, momentum will be created and you'll find that people will be asking for the Balanced Scorecard rather than the OSM imposing it on them.

2. *Allow for flexibility.* The OSM should provide procedures, processes, and guidelines, but never dictate; for example, insisting on the content of cascaded Balanced Scorecards would be a direct contravention of the spirit of the OSM. The group must position itself as an advisor, while leaving the cascaded Balanced Scorecards to be owned by the teams developing them. This is a key factor that will lead to teams applying this tool because it is theirs, not because they were told to use it. If it is not perfect the first time, that's okay;

work with the group as an advisor and coach them in the right direction.

3. *Never turn down an opportunity to do a presentation!* By following the advice in the first two points, you should generate a lot of interest within the organization around the Balanced Scorecard. This will, in turn, result in requests for more information. Never turn down an opportunity to address a group and promote the use and benefits of the Balanced Scorecard. This initial work will allow for a smoother implementation in the long run. A group's leader must be willing to wholeheartedly adopt and support a Balanced Scorecard implementation at whatever level they are in the organization. By educating and informing people early, you enhance the chances of exposing more early adopters to the Balanced Scorecard. This creates a virtual snowball effect: Identify early adopters, promote their success to expose more early adopters, promote their success and expose more, and on and on.

THE BALANCED SCORECARD IS ABOUT CHANGE

You're introducing far more than a new measurement system when you launch the Balanced Scorecard. A host of changes will accompany this powerful framework for gauging performance. You can anticipate a new language focusing on strategy and results emerging. Accountability will be enhanced as a result of the Scorecard's emphasis on gauging the effectiveness of your operations. Resource allocation is linked to results and strategy, not to last year's numbers. Alignment will be positively influenced as employees from across the agency are provided the opportunity, through cascading Scorecards, to demonstrate how their role contributes to long-term, sustainable success for the agency. The Balanced Scorecard combines all of these powerful elements to create the alchemy of positive results you need to thrive in today's challenging times.

Undoubtedly, some among your ranks will resist the changes discussed in this book. We all know resistance to change is natural. I believe the techniques presented throughout the book will equip you with the tools you need to disarm cynicism and resistance wherever it resides in your organization. The Balanced Scorecard holds tremendous promise when wielded with passion and commitment. For those dedicated to the constant pursuit of improvement and an unwavering desire to advance towards your mission, you will find a powerful ally in the Balanced Scorecard. As difficult as the road of change may appear, always recall the words of inventor and change advocate Charles F. Kettering who reminds us: "The world hates change, yet it is the only thing that has brought progress."

NOTES

1. Best Practices Benchmarking Report, *Developing the Balanced Scorecard* (Chapel Hill, NC: Best Practices, LLC, 1999).

2. Paul R. Niven, *Balanced Scorecard Step-by-Step: Maximizing Performance and Maintaining Results, 2nd Edition* (Hoboken, NJ: John Wiley & Sons, 2006), p. 288.

3. Paul R. Niven, *Balanced Scorecard Step-by-Step: Maximizing Performance and Maintaining Results, 2nd Edition* (Hoboken, NJ: John Wiley & Sons, 2006), pp. 294–296.

4. Robert S. Kaplan and David P. Norton, "Strategic Management: An Emerging Profession,"*Balanced Scorecard Report*, May–June 2004.

5. Niccolo Machiavelli, *The Prince*, W.K. Marriott, trans., Vol. 23, *The Great Books of the Western World* (Chicago: Encyclopedia Britannica, Inc., 1952), p. 9.

6. Linda H. Chow, "Emerging Best Practices of Hall of Fame Winners: Key Trends from 2004 to 2006," *Balanced Scorecard Report*, March–April 2007, pp. 6–8.

Appendix

The Importance of Terminology and a Balanced Scorecard Glossary

---

Roadmap for the Appendix   Each and every term relating to the Balanced Scorecard—from objective to measure to target to initiative—may connote different meanings to different people. For that reason, this chapter begins with a discussion of the power of words, those seemingly harmless things that Jean-Paul Sarte once termed "loaded pistols." We'll explore the potential danger of not reaching consensus on your Balanced Scorecard terms, and discuss an exercise designed to help you avoid this pitfall. I'll then provide a glossary of terms you can use to ensure a shared understanding among your team of Balanced Scorecard terminology.

A WORD OR TWO ABOUT WORDS

In his 1833 book, *On War*, Karl von Clausewitz declared that "the first task of any theory is to clarify terms and concepts that are confused . . . Only after agreement has been reached regarding terms and concepts can we hope to consider the issues easily and clearly, and expect others to share the same viewpoint . . ." I'm not a big fan of military metaphors in the business world since, unlike the results of war, I believe organizations should strive for an outcome in which everybody wins. However, I am particularly struck by the power of this German general's words. Reaching "agreement on terms and concepts" is not as easy as it sounds, especially when you consider there are over 14,000 meanings for the 500 most common words in the English language. It's amazing we're able to communicate at all!

Language can have a profound impact on an organization. Listen to what organizational learning expert Peter Senge has said on the topic: "Words do matter. Language is messy by nature, which is why we must be careful in how we use it. As leaders, after all, we have little else to work with. We typically don't use hammers and saws, heavy equipment, or even computers to do our real work. The essence of leadership—what we do with 98% of our time—is communication. To master any management practice, we must start by bringing discipline to the domain in which we spend most of our time, the domain of words."[1] This is particularly relevant in a world dominated by knowledge workers, one in which success is derived primarily from the transformation of intangible assets. Never has communication been so vital to the prospects of organizations, and of course, words are at the core of communication.

Consequences of Not Agreeing on Definitions

Confusing our words can lead to the transmission of mixed signals to employees and result in less than desirable outcomes for the organization. The two terms on the organizational landscape most prone to obfuscation are mission and vision. A few years ago, when working with a public sector client, I engaged the Balanced Scorecard team in a discussion of mission and vision. I provided my definitions for these terms—those that I shared with you in Chapter 5—and they appeared to resonate with everyone. Everyone, that is, with the exception of one person. To her, the vision was the core purpose of the organization and the mission was the desired future. We went back and forth on the issue several times, both of us articulating our best prose on the subject.

This is far more than a philosophical difference. Consider the ramifications when my client begins to communicate these terms to a broader audience. The vast majority will understand mission to be the core purpose of the organization, but one small pocket, those reached by the person holding a contrary opinion, will understand core purpose to mean vision. Undoubtedly, these employees will speak to one another, and of course we want people talking about these terms. But in this case, they'll be using different words to convey the meanings of two fundamental principles. I can hear the conversations now:

Kathy: "Hey Oliver, I hear we have a new mission statement."

Oliver: (with a light chuckle) "No, no Kathy, that's a vision, or at least that's what my manager calls it."

Kathy: "Well, I'm sure whatever it is they'll spend about a year figuring it out, so I guess it doesn't matter to us."

As the dialog demonstrates, confusion will surely reign. Equally discouraging, the leaders of the Scorecard initiative will undoubtedly lose credibility in the eyes of the employee base, the very group they must win over if they hope to achieve success on the initiative.

You won't be surprised to read that I recommend you use the definitions and connotations in this book. However, in the end it really doesn't matter what you call the concepts—remember Shakespeare's admonition: "What's in a name? That which we call a rose by any other name would smell as sweet." The key is using your chosen terms with unwavering consistency throughout the organization. If you've deliberated with your team on the concepts of vision and mission and as a group feel your *raison d'être* is best described as a vision, then so be it. Just ensure there is true consensus on the point and the term is communicated clearly to all stakeholders.

A Terminology Exercise

In the spirit of General von Clausewitz, I would like to introduce a terminology exercise. The task is designed to help you foster agreement on the key terms of your Balanced Scorecard implementation so that, as von Clausewitz aptly advises, we can hope to consider the issues easily and clearly, and expect others to share the same viewpoint.

The activity will be completed in two phases over the course of a week or two, depending on the current demands and pressures you face. Phase one is an individual exercise while phase two draws the entire team together. Begin by circulating to your Balanced Scorecard team a simple template that contains the Performance Management and Balanced Scorecard–related terms you use, or plan to use, in your organization. Advise the group they each have one week (or whatever timeframe you designate) to complete the template and return it to the Scorecard champion. Exhibit A.1 contains an excerpt from such a template. Once all templates have been returned, the Scorecard champion will prepare a document compiling all definitions supplied for each term.

In addition to the terms displayed in Exhibit A.1, I would suggest you consider including the following: Performance Management, Balanced Scorecard, Strategy Map, objective, measure, target, initiative, Budget, Stakeholder, Public Input, Performance Measurement, and Business Plan. Of course, you should add terms that are germane to your situation. For example, a local government organization will most likely include the term "General Plan." But, and this is a big but, don't overload the request with dozens of terms. It can prove to be a taxing exercise for those completing the templates and may take hours, if not days, to come to consensus on definitions in the group setting that follows. Focus on the key terms you will be using and attempt to keep it under 15.

To facilitate the discussion of terms at the Scorecard meeting that follows, I would suggest you use a combination of high-tech and low-tech devices. For example, capture the definitions for each term in either an

Exhibit A.1 Performance Management and Balanced Scorecard
Definition Template

Balanced Scorecard
Terminology Template

Before we develop a Balanced Scorecard and communicate it to our employees, it's important to ensure we're all in agreement on the many terms we will soon be sharing with the entire organization.

Please take a moment to provide a working definition for each of the terms contained in this package. The definition should convey your current understanding of the term, not a dictionary reference. Please support your definition with an example, or a sentence using the term in order to provide context.

We will discuss the terms at our next Balanced Scorecard meeting. Thank You.

Mission:_____

_____

Vision:_____

_____

Values:_____

_____

Strategy:_____

_____

MS Word or PowerPoint document, then display the document on a screen from a computer so that everyone can easily view what has been shared. Also distribute paper copies of the definitions, and have a flip chart and markers at your disposal.

The facilitator will begin the meeting by thanking everyone for their submissions and reiterating the importance of reaching consensus on Performance Management and Balanced Scorecard terms. He or she will then display the first term on the screen, read a portion of the definitions and examples provided, and invite comments. You can record any changes to your terms "live" using your computer, or on the flip charts you've stationed around the room. The range of discussion you can expect will depend almost entirely on the amount of consensus reflected in the definitions you've received from the participants. If everyone agrees in principle, it will simply be a matter of "wordsmithing" to concoct a formal definition with which all can concur. I can see the eye-rolling of readers everywhere as they read that last sentence. Yes, wordsmithing can prove to be an onerous chore of its own, I admit. To alleviate the pain it can bring, try instituting a time limit for each term. If you cannot develop an adequate definition that meets everyone's requirements within ten minutes, assign an individual or smaller group to work on it "offline," and move on to the next term.

As a consultant, I've had the opportunity to facilitate a number of these terminology sessions and I'm always pleasantly surprised at the amount of dialog and learning that results. The learning comes in a variety of forms. First and foremost, the team will have reached agreement on specifically what they mean by the terms that form their Performance Management and Balanced Scorecard lexicon. They've also constructed a solid foundation from which to launch both their Scorecard-building efforts and educational initiatives throughout the organization. Finally, and perhaps most importantly, this exercise gives team members an insight into the unique perspectives held by their colleagues. Exploring the perceptions of others, freely exchanging ideas, and being open to new points of view will all lead to a stronger team.

BALANCED SCORECARD AND PERFORMANCE MANAGEMENT GLOSSARY OF TERMS

When developing a Balanced Scorecard system, you'll quickly discover that even within your own organization, different individuals and groups will hold different meanings for commonly used terms. The glossary presented here will help you find some common ground by offering descriptions and definitions that have been used successfully in many Balanced Scorecard implementations. However, as noted earlier, while I recommend these definitions, what matters most in the end is not the definitions you use, but the *consistency* of their use. Everyone must be speaking the same language if you expect the Balanced Scorecard, or any change initiative, to be understood, accepted, and able to produce results.

Activity Measures   These measures typically track the actions or behaviors an organization performs using its inputs of staff time and financial resources.

Balanced Scorecard   An integrated framework for describing and translating strategy through the use of linked performance measures in four balanced perspectives: Customer, Internal Process, Employee Learning and Growth, and Financial. The Balanced Scorecard acts as a measurement system, strategic management system, and communication tool.

Benchmarking   The comparison of similar processes across organizations and industries to identify best practices, set improvement targets, and measure progress. Benchmarking results may serve as potential targets for Balanced Scorecard measures.

Cascading   The process of developing aligned Strategy Maps and Scorecards throughout an organization. Each level of the organization will develop Maps and Scorecards based on the objectives and measures they can influence from the group to whom they report. For example, a city's transportation department will develop objectives and measures based on how they influence overall city Strategy Map and Balanced Scorecard. Cascading allows every employee to demonstrate a contribution to overall organizational objectives.

Cause and Effect   The concept of cause and effect separates the Balanced Scorecard from other performance management systems. The objectives comprising the Strategy Map and the measures appearing on the Scorecard should link together in a series of cause and effect relationships to tell the organization's strategic story.

Customer Perspective   One of the four standard perspectives used with the Balanced Scorecard. The role of the Customer Perspective is often elevated to the top of the Balanced Scorecard model in public sector and nonprofit organizations.

Efficiency Measures   Evaluate the cost of each unit of service delivered. Typically begin with "cost per . . ."

Employee Learning and Growth Perspective   One of the four standard perspectives used with the Balanced Scorecard. Measures in this perspective are often considered "enablers" of measures appearing in the other three perspectives. Typically, three areas of "capital" are monitored here: human, information, and organizational.

Financial Perspective   One of the four standard perspectives used with the Balanced Scorecard. In public sector and nonprofit applications of the Balanced Scorecard, objectives and measures in the Financial Perspective are often viewed as constraints within which the organization must operate.

Government Performance and Results Act (GPRA)   Signed into law in 1993, the GPRA requires federally funded agencies to develop and implement an accountability system based on performance measurement, including setting goals and objectives and measuring progress toward achieving them. Places emphasis on what is being accomplished as opposed to what is being spent.

Human Capital   May be considered a metaphor for the transition in organizational value creation from physical assets to the capabilities of employees—knowledge, skills, and relationships, for example. Human capital is closely related to terms such as *intellectual capital* and *intangible assets*. Recent estimates suggest that as much as 75% of an organization's value is attributable to human capital.

Initiatives   The specific programs, activities, projects, or actions an organization will undertake in an effort to meet performance targets.

Input Measures   Track resources used to drive organizational results. Typical inputs include staff time and financial resources.

Internal Process Perspective   One of the four standard perspectives used with the Balanced Scorecard. Objectives and measures in this perspective are used to monitor the effectiveness of key processes the organization must excel at in order to continue adding value for customers, given the finite resources available.

Lagging Indicator   Performance measures that represent the consequences of actions previously taken are referred to as lag indicators. They frequently focus on results at the end of a time period and characterize historical performance. Employee satisfaction may be considered a lag indicator. A good Balanced Scorecard must contain a mix of lag and lead indicators.

Leading Indicator   These measures are considered the "drivers" of lagging indicators. There is an assumed relationship between the two that suggests that improved performance in a leading indicator will drive better performance in the lagging indicator. For example, lowering absenteeism (a leading indicator) is hypothesized to drive improvements in employee satisfaction (a lagging indicator).

Measure   A standard used to evaluate and communicate performance against expected results. Measures are normally quantitative in nature capturing numbers, dollars, percentages, and so on. Reporting and monitoring measures helps an organization gauge progress toward effective implementation of strategy.

Mission Statement   A mission statement defines the core purpose of the organization—why it exists. The mission examines the *raison d'être* for the organization, and reflects employees' motivations for engaging in the organization's work. Effective missions are inspiring, long-term in nature, and easily understood and communicated.

Objective   A concise statement describing the specific things an organization must do well in order to execute its strategy. Objectives often begin with an action verbs such as "increase," "reduce," "improve," "achieve," and so on. Strategy Maps are comprised entirely of objectives.

Outcome Measures   These measures track the benefit received by stake-holders as a result of the organization's operations. They may also be known as "impact measures." Outcome measures track the extent to which an organization has achieved its overall goals. Possible examples include "reduce incidence of HIV" and "increase perception of public safety."

Output Measures   These measures track the number of people served, services provided, or units produced by a program or service. Examples include number of inoculations provided and number of potholes filled.

Perspective   In Balanced Scorecard vernacular, perspective refers to a category of performance objectives or measures. Most organizations choose the standard four perspectives (Financial, Customer, Internal Process, and Employee Learning and Growth); however, the Balanced Scorecard represents a dynamic framework and additional perspectives may be added as necessary to adequately translate and describe an organization's strategy.

Stakeholder   Any person or group that has a "stake" in the success of the organization. Stakeholders for public and nonprofit organizations may include: employees, customers and clients, funders, elected officials, citizens, special interest groups, suppliers, media, financial community, and partners. All stakeholders must be considered when developing mission, values, vision, strategy; Strategy Map objectives; and Balanced Scorecard measures.

Strategic Management System   Describes the use of the Balanced Scorecard in aligning an organization's short-term actions with strategy. Often accomplished by cascading the Balanced Scorecard to all levels of the organization, aligning budgets and business plans to strategy, and using the Scorecard as a feedback and learning mechanism.

Strategic Resource Allocation   The process of aligning budgets with strategy by using the Balanced Scorecard to make resource allocation decisions. Using this method, budgets are based on the initiatives necessary to achieve Balanced Scorecard targets.

Strategy   Represents the broad priorities adopted by an organization in recognition of its operating environment and in pursuit of its mission. Situated at the center of the Balanced Scorecard system, all performance objectives and measures should align with the organization's strategy. Strategy remains one of the most widely discussed and debated topics in the world of modern organizations.

Strategy Map   A one-page graphical representation of what must be done well in order to execute strategy. Strategy Maps are composed of performance objectives spanning the four perspectives and linking together to tell the organization's strategic story.

Target   Represents the desired result of a performance measure. Targets make meaningful the results derived from measurement and provide organizations with feedback regarding performance.

Values   Represent the deeply-held beliefs within the organization and are demonstrated through the day-to-day behaviors of all employees. An organization's values make an open proclamation about how it expects everyone to behave. Values should endure over the long-term and provide a constant source of strength for an organization.

Value Proposition   Describes how an organization will differentiate itself to customers, and what particular set of values it will deliver. To develop a customer value proposition, many organizations will choose one of three "disciplines," articulated by Treacy and Wiersema in *The Discipline of Market Leaders*: operational excellence, product leadership, or customer intimacy.

Vision   A powerful vision provides everyone in the organization with a shared mental framework that helps give form to the often abstract future that lies ahead. Effective visions provide a word picture of what the organization intends ultimately to become—which may be five, ten, or 15 years in the future. This statement should not be abstract; it should contain as concrete a picture of the desired state as possible, and also provide the basis for formulating strategies and objectives.

NOTE

1. Peter M. Senge, "The Practice of Innovation," *Leader to Leader* 9 (Summer 1998): 16–22.

Index